Character Development and Storytelling for Games

This is the third edition of *Character Development and Storytelling for Games*, a standard work in the field that brings all of the teaching from the first two books up to date and tackles the new challenges of today. Professional game writer and designer Lee Sheldon combines his experience and expertise in this updated edition. New examples, new game types, and new challenges throughout the text highlight the fundamentals of character writing and storytelling.

But this book is not just a box of techniques for writers of video games. It is an exploration of the roots of character development and storytelling that readers can trace from Homer to Chaucer to Cervantes to Dickens and even Mozart. Many contemporary writers also contribute insights from books, plays, television, films, and, yes, games.

Sheldon and his contributors emphasize the importance of creative instinct and listening to the inner voice that guides successful game writers and designers. Join him on his quest to instruct, inform, and maybe even inspire your next great game.

Character Development and Storytelling for Games

Third Edition

Lee Sheldon

CRC Press
Taylor & Francis Group
Boca Raton London New York

CRC Press is an imprint of the
Taylor & Francis Group, an **informa** business

Third Edition published 2023
by CRC Press
6000 Broken Sound Parkway NW, Suite 300, Boca Raton, FL 33487-2742

and by CRC Press
4 Park Square, Milton Park, Abingdon, Oxon, OX14 4RN

CRC Press is an imprint of Taylor & Francis Group, LLC

© 2023 Taylor & Francis Group, LLC

First edition published by Cengage Learning 2004

Second Edition published by Cengage Learning 2014

Library of Congress Cataloging-in-Publication Data
Names: Sheldon, Lee, author.
Title: Character development and storytelling for games / Lee Sheldon.
Description: Third edition. | Boca Raton : CRC Press, 2023. | Includes bibliographical references and index.
Identifiers: LCCN 2022023874 (print) | LCCN 2022023875 (ebook) | ISBN 9780367248994 (hardback) | ISBN 9780367248987 (paperback) | ISBN 9780429284991 (ebook)
Subjects: LCSH: Video game characters. | Video games—Authorship. | Video games—Design.
Classification: LCC GV1469.34.A97 S54 2023 (print) | LCC GV1469.34.A97 (ebook) | DDC 794.8/3—dc23/eng/20220713
LC record available at https://lccn.loc.gov/2022023874
LC ebook record available at https://lccn.loc.gov/2022023875

ISBN: 978-0-367-24899-4 (hbk)
ISBN: 978-0-367-24898-7 (pbk)
ISBN: 978-0-429-28499-1 (ebk)

DOI: 10.1201/9780429284991

Typeset in Minion
by codeMantra

*First of all, I dedicate this book to all of my students
who patiently taught me how to teach.*

*Also, I dedicate it to all the game writers and designers
around the world and to those that teach the craft. It has
been a pleasure and a privilege to be one of you.*

Contents

PART II Creating Characters

Part III   Telling the Story

Preface to the Third Edition

A Third Edition? Why a Third Edition???
   What, you may wonder, was wrong with the first one, that I had to write two more? The answer is: things change. The video game industry has experienced multiple dramatic reinventions in the roller coaster ride that has marked its progress since birth.

In the early days of video games, the first personal computers like the Apple II and the IBM PC ruled. They were joined, and in a few short years eclipsed, by the first dedicated game platforms like the Atari 2600 and The Mattel Intellivision. When the bottom dropped out of the console market in 1983 and a whole bunch of copies of *E.T.: The Extraterrestrial* ended up in a landfill, personal computers enjoyed a resurgence.

Only 3 years later, the Nintendo Entertainment System was released. The first edition of this book was published in 2004, 2 years before the Wii, the "future" of game consoles, arrived. An MMO called *World of Warcraft* had just debuted. On June 29, 2007, Apple added a phone to its iPod music player. The resulting device's name, not entirely a surprise, was the iPhone, but who knew it could have soon earned the name iGame? The first prototype of the Oculus Rift was 5 years in the future.

The second edition of this book was published in 2014. The Wii was already just a memory, and the Xbox Kinect was about to follow it into obscurity. We just didn't know that when I was the writer on the Harmonix team developing the first iteration of *Fantasia: Music Evolved* for the Kinect. *Pokémon Go*, augmented reality's flag-carrying app, was still 2 years away. The Oculus Rift, after much fanfare, excitement, and dollars, was discontinued in 2021. Now, in 2022, imagine all the games, and the devices on which we play them, that have appeared in the past 8 years. How many have survived and how many have crashed and burned? VR continues to struggle to find a mass audience. But once everybody lives in the metaverse maybe it will finally find one.

Games today are played on multiple platforms. Windows and Apple personal computers are still in the thick of things. The Microsoft Xbox Series X and the Xbox Series S arrived together in 2020. Players can choose which one better fits their graphical needs. An upgrade of the Nintendo Switch was released in 2021. And Sony Play Station 5 was launched in 2022. There are now almost half a million games for cell phones. And games that tell stories remain incredibly popular because, well, because stories remain incredibly popular. Even *Fortnite* offers "event-driven storytelling."

A new edition of *Character Development and Storytelling for Games* is long overdue. But I warn you. In addition to all the new material, you will find in this book examples from video games, other media and eras in the distant past, a past before some of my readers were even born. Why? The new challenges writing for games present today to the stories told in the first two editions don't erase the lessons that have gone before. They make this book a living history and a reminder that as much as has changed there are still lessons to be learned whenever they first appeared.

So, if I found a good example in a game from the previous century like an Infocom text adventure or an MMO like *Everquest*, you will find them here. They often provided the inspiration for ideas in common use today. You will also find examples from passive media, mostly screenwriting, but playwriting, prose and poetry as well. Contributors range from ancient Greece to Hollywood to current writers and designers of games who have graciously agreed to share their knowledge with you.

This book will help you to tell meaningful stories with compelling characters no matter what the genre, type of game, or what platform it is played on. The rest is up to you.

Lee Sheldon
August 2022

Acknowledgments

Many people helped make this third edition of *Character Development and Storytelling for Games* possible.

I'd like to thank my contributing writers both official and unofficial: Mark Barrett, Hal Barwood, Bob Bates, Noah Falstein, Chris Foster, Nate Fox, Raph Koster, Steve Meretzky, Ken Rolston, and Mark Terrano.

Thanks are also due Alex Bradley; Jim Buchanan; Jurie Horneman; Chris Klug; Bill Link, Dorian Newcomb; Graham Sheldon; and the Game Design Workshop.

More general acknowledgments for all three editions of this book are owed Ron Austin, Eddie Bowen, Glen Dahlgren, Steve de Souza, Mike Dornbrook, Elonka Dunin, Phil Fehrle, Eric Goldberg, Brian Green, Hope Hickli, Jennifer Hicks, Geoff Howland, Scott Jennings, Jane Jensen, Amy Jo Kim, Peter Lefcourt, Niki Marvin, Brian Moriarty, Di Meredith, Andrew Nelson, Nick Nicholson, James Ohlen, Otto Penzler, Jeff Perkinson, François Robillard, Liz Robinson, Brenda Romero, Jeri Taylor, Jeff Tyeryar, John Valente, Doug Walker, Steve Wartofsky, Johnny Wilson, and Gary Winnick. Some of you will know why. The others will just have to take my word for it that you belong here.

And last but not least from CRC Press/Taylor & Francis Group I'd like to thank Sean Connelly and Danielle Zarfati.

I'm sure I've missed a few. My sincere apologies! To all named and unnamed go my deepest thanks.

About the Author

Lee Sheldon began his writing career in television as a writer-producer, eventually writing over 200 shows ranging from *Charlie's Angels* (writer) to *Edge of Night* (head writer) to *Star Trek: The Next Generation* (writer-producer). Having written and designed over 40 commercial and applied video games, Lee spearheaded the first full writing for games concentration in North America at Rensselaer Polytechnic Institute and the second writing concentration in North America at Worcester Polytechnic Institute.

The second edition of his book, *The Multiplayer Classroom: Designing Coursework as a Game*, was published by CRC Press in March 2020. The second edition continues the story of multiplayer classrooms from elementary schools to post-secondary classrooms, designed and taught by Lee and 16 other educators.

A companion book, *The Multiplayer Classroom: Game Plans*, was published by CRC Press in March 2021. Complete with design documents and associated production materials, the book covers in detail four multiplayer classroom projects, funded by grants or institutions and played in the real world in real time to teach and entertain. They were collaborations between Lee, as writer/designer, and subject matter experts in various fields. They are written to be accessible to anyone—designer, educator, student, or layperson—interested in game-based learning. The subjects are increasingly relevant in this day and age: physical fitness, Mandarin, cybersecurity, and especially an online class exploring culture and identity on the internet.

This third edition of Lee's book, *Character Development and Storytelling for Games*, is a standard text in the field. He is a regular lecturer and consultant on game design and writing in the U.S. and abroad. His most recent commercial game, the award-winning *The Lion's Song*, is currently on Steam. Recently he was a consultant on an "escape room in a box," funded by NASA, that gives visitors to hundreds of science museums and planetariums the opportunity to play colonizers on the moon. He is currently narrative designer on a new game for Microids in France.

Introduction

CHARACTER DEVELOPMENT AND STORYTELLING *for Games* is meant to be a resource for those teaching game development, students wanting to be writers or designers, as well as those who are already professional game writers and designers. The book will also be helpful to those who must work with us and who may want to talk intelligently with us at some point.

This is not a book of rules that, if slavishly followed, will guarantee success. You'll see that just about every time I try to lay down some canonical law to follow, I immediately think of exceptions. Don't be afraid to break any rules as you write, as long as you know exactly what they mean, why they're rules to begin with, and why you want to break them. Pablo Picasso knew this, as you'll soon see. It is one of the continuing themes running through this book.

Think of this as a book of ideas and of choices. Hopefully, it will help you to generate ideas of your own. And you will feel more comfortable when choices present themselves as you write. Knowing which choices to make is not teachable. It is part of that creative instinct we call *talent* whose secret voice guides us in our decisions every time we sit down at the keyboard. And anyway, those choices will be different for different people. Despite what writing gurus say, all stories are not identical. All stories are not Joseph Campbell's hero's journey. They are shaped by unique facets of the human beings who write them.

I have some strong opinions, and you will find them in here. Hopefully, if you disagree with them, you will still discover much that is helpful to you as a writer of games. Even better, your disagreement can lead to enlightenment for all of us. Debate is a necessary part of learning. Sometimes, as I wrote, I wished I could just stop and ask my own questions of you.

I warn you in advance that I'm going to drag in anecdotes and examples from all sorts of strange places (like the painter Pablo Picasso I mentioned above). This is how ideas blossom. I encourage you in your life, as well as in your writing, to be open to all of the arts and the world they seek to depict. Limiting oneself to a favorite genre or type of entertainment may be okay for our audience (although I wouldn't encourage it), but we owe it to our audience to draw from a much broader world of knowledge and experience.

This book is as much about game design as it is writing for games. The two are virtually inseparable. In fact, I'll seem to stray off course often into topics that appear to be only about design or examples from other media. These discussions are of value to our chief concerns, character and story, if only for background or context.

DOI: 10.1201/9780429284991-1

A lot of the challenges we face have been faced before, sometimes centuries ago, so I will throw many examples at you, such as references and images from other media. Ideas without context may be great for bumper stickers, but they are useless to us as creators. Game writing does not occur in a vacuum. It owes its allegiance to all media from Aristotle to Chaucer to those who write our games today.

When we look to other media to understand how to write for games, literature is not surprisingly a common first choice. We can learn much from literature, but games are mostly visual, a medium of action similar to drama and film. Game stories, like stories in film and television, need not (and should not) be convoluted, but as the mystery writer knows, it's all in the telling, and an apparently complex plot can actually be quite simple underneath.

Ignoring the progenitors of our craft is about as helpful as trying to study medicine by examining only your left big toe. All of the weapons of drama must be aimed at what we write. Story and gameplay should evolve simultaneously. Attempting to randomly tack one form of entertainment on to the other is to lessen the benefits of both. Even though they are very different, both can be woven together to create a single entertainment experience.

I am not a programmer. I am a professional writer. Through several careers, no matter what else I have been—story editor, producer, director, or game designer—I have always been a writer first.

You don't have to be a programmer to be a game designer, but you do need to know enough about programming to carry on meaningful conversations with programmers on your development team. You need to know enough to be able to at least suspect the difference between a firm commitment and wishful thinking. Contrary to popular belief, programmers aren't all liars, but they are the most optimistic crowd you'll ever meet. And you also need to know enough about how programming works so that player choices don't throw you. Don't be afraid to give the player agency, just learn how to accommodate it.

You don't have to be an artist, but you should know quite a bit about art. It saves time to be able to dismiss Jackson Pollock as a potential conceptual artist for your Disney treasure hunt game. His Mickey Mouse would make you unhappy.

You don't have to be a writer. But it helps to be able to recognize that you aren't. Just as you do have to be a programmer to program, you really should be a writer to write. Many people seem to think that because writing doesn't require manual dexterity the way art often does, or an ability to do math, that anyone can do it.

One problem we come across when attempting to discuss games is our lack of a common vocabulary. We have borrowed terms from other media, and then changed their definitions. We've made up our own words. A few gray areas of terminology should be mentioned here.

For the most part, I use *video game* and *computer game* interchangeably, particularly if the platform is irrelevant to the topic under discussion. At times I will just be sloppy and not modify the word *game* at all. Unless I specifically say so, assume I mean the same thing as video game or computer game. The distinction becomes important only when discussing hardware. Then computer games are played on personal computers, and video games are played on everything else from consoles to smart phones.

In game development, the word "genre" is often mistakenly used when talking about action, role-playing, adventure games, and so forth. In this book, I reserve the word "genre" for its more traditional definition of an artistic category. In painting, this could be expressionism or minimalism. In arts that tell stories, genres are mystery, romance, science fiction, and so on. Since we have these kinds of genres in games as well, I differentiate action, role-playing, simulation, and so on, as "types" of games.

Another tricky word is *script*. A script in my former life as a Hollywood writer was a teleplay or screenplay, which consisted of dialogue and descriptions of action. In games, we also use script to mean a simple sort of pseudo-programming language that can be translated into program code. I have often been called upon to write scripts in script, compounding the confusion when I meet with other developers to discuss a project. You'll find both types of script are discussed in the following pages, but the context should make which one I mean clear.

There is also the bewildering alphabet soup surrounding massively multiplayer games. Virtual worlds, persistent worlds, massive persistent worlds, and tongue-torturing acronyms such as MMORPG (Massively Multiplayer Online Role-Playing Game) and MMO (Massively Multiplayer Online) are only *sort of* synonymous. In the first edition of this book, I preferred the term *virtual worlds* used by Richard A. Bartle in his book *Designing Virtual Worlds*. But no one term adequately covers all of them today: persistent or non-persistent, massively multiplayer or the MUDs and MUSHes upon which they're based. So, you will be subjected to some of them at one time or another.

Today especially, the alphabet soup has thickened. We have casual games, social games, social network games, alternate reality games, augmented reality games, big games, pervasive games, serious games, applied games, crossmedia, transmedia, and dozens of other games. I'll do my best to differentiate between them. Wish me luck!

I try and provide the birth and, if appropriate, death dates for many of the real people you'll meet in these pages who have contributed to my understanding of, and love for, writing. I don't do this because of some textbook convention, but because I believe it is important to realize that we're not creating new paradigms here from scratch. We're building on concepts that in some cases date back to primitive men like Urk (790,067–790,025 BCE), that great mastodon hunter who became the "father of the campfire story." The dates will hopefully put into perspective how long people have been thinking about characters and story, and yes, writing *about* their creation, too.

In a book with the scope of this one, there are many details. Every human effort has been made to confirm historical references, quotes, and facts. Sometimes primary sources were available. Sometimes they weren't, but reliable secondary sources were. Often, I have had only anecdotal references to draw upon. In other cases, attempts to verify specific examples failed, and I've had to rely on my own powers of observation (good) or memory (fanciful). I'm going to make mistakes. This isn't a newspaper. I'm not a journalist.

If I get an example wrong, forgive me. Look at the substance of the argument instead. I guarantee that even if the example is inaccurate, it at least supports my thesis! Please send me corrections or additions. We corrected a bunch for the second printing of the first edition. This third edition you're reading is another great opportunity for me to make mistakes. If there is a fourth edition of the book, I'll be happy to rectify any goofs you find.

I've used the word *hopefully* more than once in this short introduction. This is a hopeful book. You hold in your hands most of what I know about writing for games and much of what I believe and practice, no matter what kind of writing I'm doing. It is meant to inform, to instruct, and maybe even to inspire. Use the ideas you can and discard the rest. Make your own choices. We are all on a journey toward a destination for which there is no single road.

PART I

Background

PRELUDE IN A FIRE-LIT CAVE

The body of one hunter was already cooling in the patch of low ferns where it had been thrown. A second hunter, gored twice in chest and shoulder, lay nearby, blinking at the sun filtered through the broad leaves of a towering tree. He would be abandoned, his bones picked clean by scavengers, bleaching memorials, and sacrifices to the hunt.

Men wielding stone knives were chopping meat into manageable slabs and scraping gristle from great swatches of hide. The work was done with little grace, speed the only importance. The meat must reach the tribe's current camp as soon as possible to be seared and consumed within a few short hours. Each lost minute tainted it and increased the chance of illness, possibly death, instead of nourishment.

Death was every bit as much a member of the tribe as the hunters, the gatherers of roots and berries, the cooks, and the artisans who fashioned the stone heads of spears and blades of knives. Death was a constant companion, sometimes cruel, at others merciful, inevitable as nightfall, a companion to be depended upon.

When all that could be carried had been harvested from the shaggy, long-tusked beast, the hunters began their weary trek back to the cave where they had taken refuge when autumn's first frost had touched the land only a few sunsets before. Their burden meant the traveling was slow. And they must always be on guard against some other predator that caught the scent of the easy meal they carried. At last, the mouth of the cave was spotted; other members of the tribe gathered about it, awaiting their return.

Once inside, among the women, children, and infirm—there were no old ones in this life—the meat was skewered on long stakes and placed in the central fire pit. Hide was distributed to the women to be fashioned into protection against the fast-approaching winter.

Lamentations were sung for the two hunters lost to the beast, the meal consumed, and the fire stoked against the encroaching darkness. All gathered round that fire now: hunters, women, children. Finally, the work-a-day chatter died, and all eyes turned to the chief of the hunters.

DOI: 10.1201/9780429284991-2

He was possessed of only one good eye, and his left hand had withered to a frozen claw after it had been savaged by the teeth of a great cat three winters gone. Yet he was the bravest of them all, the most cunning, and ablest of the hunters.

The chief hunter waited in the silence, biding his time, allowing the stillness to linger. He gazed into the fire as it sparked and spit from animal grease. At last, when the quiet was stretched taut as a tendon, he looked round at them and began to speak…

And with every word he knew, he told the story of the hunt.

CHAPTER 1

Equations

E VER SINCE TALES OF great hunts and hunters were told to awestruck listeners huddled around the protecting fire, consumers, from cave folk to moviegoers, have been drawn to the power of storytelling. The story is the single thread that is woven through the entire fabric of what entertains us. The appreciation of a good story is a gift not granted to any other species on this planet. It is reserved for Homo sapiens alone. Like other species, Homo sapiens also play games. From professional sports to the puns and word juxtapositions that pepper our conversations, games appeal to us on many levels.

We enjoy games. They have been a major source of our entertainment and a stimulus for our consciousness since we first focused our newly born eyes on a world of possibilities. Play was a way of dealing with the unknown. If our toes could be successfully played with, maybe they weren't something we needed to fear! We are the PCs of our own lives.

PC: an acronym for the player-character. In a game characters controlled by the player—and there could be more than one—are PCs.

Games and stories have much in common. Both deal with how we handle fear. Both can teach us about the world and ourselves. Both can challenge us, move us to laughter or tears. Both spring from the child inside, and both can keep us young. Each can exist separately from the other, and be consummately entertaining, yet there are also times when the two meet, support one another, and grow together into something greater than they were apart. One of the most interesting opportunities for games and stories to coincide is in the still *relatively* new form of entertainment, just a few years over sixty years old, called video games. And that is the focus of this book, a really old form of entertainment begun they say with the *Epic of Gilgamesh* hundreds upon hundreds of years ago.

Where to start? Let's ask some questions. Why do we make games? Is it a need to create? A need to express ourselves? A need to entertain? A need to illuminate the human condition? A need to make great wads of cash? Ask yourself why you want to make games as you read this book. You will never arrive at an answer that pleases everyone, but it's important to arrive at an answer that satisfies you. One goal you should be wary of: a desire to create Art with a capital "A."

DOI: 10.1201/9780429284991-3

Interactive entertainment has grown to be a significant source of pleasure and satisfaction for millions of people throughout the world. Opportunities are boundless for those who have the time and the patience to learn the skills necessary to build games and the talent to take advantage of those skills.

Today video games are a mass entertainment medium industry, and if you intend to write for that industry, you will need to know your audiences with an "s." Plural. More than one.

Art is not achieved by someone who sets out to make Art. The designation cannot be applied by the hopeful artist. Like it or not, whether it's a painting or symphony or book or play or film or video game, others will decide whether it's Art or not. Sorry, but you may never know that your work has become a classic, that others agree it "stands the test of time." What does this well-worn phrase mean? That the creator of that piece of Art has succeeded in enchanting generations unborn when the Art was created.

Antonio Salieri was the star composer of socially conscious Holy Roman Emperor Joseph II's court, but it is another composer of that time, Wolfgang Amadeus Mozart, we treasure. Salieri would have remained a footnote in music history were it not for Peter Shaffer's brilliant play, *Amadeus,* and the film adapted from it. But even with his newfound fame, Salieri's work does not get performed much today. Art endures. Popular opinion fades.

While Art isn't as out of reach as many might think, neither is it waiting around placidly for us to catch up with it. What is needed is a solid body of work we can learn from and a critical perspective with which we can study it. We can begin to *suspect* how a watch runs by watching the hands move or hearing the ticking sound it makes. But we learn how it works by taking it apart and putting it back together. We can see examples of how this happens in other youngish industries with aspirations to the capital "A."

My mentor at California Institute of the Arts was a screenwriter and director named Alexander MacKendrick. Sandy was an exemplar of the "golden age" of British film comedy, a period from the late 1940s to the early 1960s when motion picture studios (most famous of them Ealing Studios, where Sandy worked for nearly his entire early career) released what are considered by many to be classics of film comedy. The Ealing Studios' films such as *The Man in the White Suit, Kind Hearts and Coronets, The Lavender Hill Mob,* and *The Ladykillers* were notable for (among other things) their impeccable story structure, original characters, and their illumination of the humanity and truth in the goofiest of characters and situations.

In one course Sandy taught, we watched a handful of films over and over again: *North by Northwest, On the Waterfront,* and Sandy's own *The Ladykillers.* The purpose was to see beyond the entertainment value each film possessed, to see the seams, and to see how all the elements came together to create a unified entertainment experience. If you can get to the point where your favorite game no longer entertains you, you will have taken a crucial step toward understanding how it worked its magic. It can be a sad moment and an exhilarating one all at the same time.

Should games tell stories? They can, if we want. If we would like to involve emotions higher than an adrenaline rush, we need to reach the human spirit, not just endocrine glands. Characters and stories are time-honored ways to do just that.

Even *Minecraft*, the best-selling video game ever, ventured into storytelling in 2015 with *Minecraft: Story Mode* from Telltale Games. Telltale was notable for strong storytelling with games like *The Walking Dead*, *The Wolf Among Us*, and *Game of Thrones*, a property that happily already had game in its title! Unfortunately, Telltale Games closed its doors in 2018. End of that story, but not of stories in games.

Stories have gone from being the afterthought of early games like mission briefings or texts found in crumbling tombs, to today where they are considered to be of equal value to gameplay. Stories fit particularly well in many games. Why? Mystery provides one answer. Not mystery in a narrow whodunnit sense. But what do we call it when we figure out any mystery? We have *solved* it. And when we figure out a puzzle in a game? We have *solved* it. That isn't a coincidence!

Even though the debate whether stories and gameplay can ever be locked together in a single moment in time is over, they still often have a tendency to wrestle with each other like naughty siblings competing for parental attention.

Given some imagination, talent, and craft anything is possible in a game story. Imagination and talent cannot be taught, but they can be encouraged. Give a writer the tools they need to create, and both imagination and talent can blossom. Think of this book as a toolbox.

Stories are present in all other forms of crafted entertainment. In some, like live theater or daytime soap operas (now an endangered species thanks to the Internet), the story is often pre-eminent. It's not the puzzles that touch our hearts in *Gone Home*, it's the story that evolves across genres in a natural and moving way. I'm happy to report that today the writing of video games often commands the respect and professionalism equal to that we used to reserve for design and graphics and sound and programming.

Some of us who make games have a tendency to believe that our civilization came to interactive storytelling late in our dramatic development. In fact, interactivity was a part of storytelling from the very beginning. There is a scene in the film *The Wind and the Lion*, written and directed by John Milius, where the "last of the Barbary pirates," a desert chieftain portrayed by Sean Connery, is relating the story of his life at yet another campfire. As he spins his tale to his captive, played by Candice Bergen, his men, having heard it many times and knowing it almost as well as he does, prompt him to retell the most significant and impressive parts. They attempt to shape the story, and the storyteller, wise leader that he is, molds his yarn to suit their requests.

We can trust that as the chief hunter tells the story that opens this chapter, the men who were on the hunt with him will interject their recollections, and those members of the tribe who were not part of the experience will ask questions and respond with exclamations of amazement, satisfaction, or sorrow. Both the additional material added by the chief hunter's men and the response from the rest of the tribe will affect the narrative. How could it not?

Live dramatic performances have always taken into account that extra character, the audience, and adjusted accordingly. If the audience is responding with enthusiastic laughter to a comedy, the actors will draw on that energy to enliven their performances. If the audience is bored and restless, the actors may try harder to infuse their words with intensity, or they may just speed up their dialogue to minimize the experience for both them and the audience. William Shakespeare acknowledged the role his audience at the Globe Theatre, most notably those standing in the pit armed with vegetables, played in his productions.

Many years ago, I was at a performance of Paul Giovanni's Sherlock Holmes pastiche *The Crucifer of Blood* at a theater in London's West End. In the midst of the play, there was a sudden disturbance in the balcony which quickly became impossible for either the audience or the actors to ignore. A man actually shouted from the balcony those immortal words "Is there a doctor in the house?" Keith Michel, the actor portraying the famous detective in the play, repeated the question. There was indeed a doctor in the orchestra section of the audience, and a man who had suffered a heart attack was removed by ambulance to a hospital.

When the play resumed, the actors replayed the beginning of the scene that had been interrupted. Mr. Michel, to draw the audience back into the fun of the experience, sped through his lines, giving them deliberately comic overtones the text did not possess. Even though it broke "the fourth wall," a term we'll discuss in Chapter 8, the audience loved it, and was able to relax back into the play-going experience. His leading lady, Susan Hampshire, was not as taken with his efforts, and kept glaring at him, until he finally lapsed back into the rhythm of the play as directed and the reality of the performance.

Interactivity, that two-way street of storytelling, has always been with us, even if later media, such as film, radio, and television, have been largely insensate of the audience, at least during the actual performance. Happily, we still have live theater! If we were to express this relationship as an equation, it might look something like this:

Scripted / Rehearsed Story + Audience = Entertainment Experience

So, we have in video games a far more natural approach to storytelling than one might at first suppose, one that includes the participation of the audience, those individuals we call players.

Games and stories don't mix! This is often the first observation out of the mouth of someone who believes we shouldn't attempt to tell more than cursory stories in games, or that we need to throw out all the old "outdated" rules of storytelling and find some completely new paradigm like artificial intelligence to drive NPCs in games or force the players to do all the work and create any necessary story. Both actually have a place in games, but not as replacements to imaginatively drawn characters or carefully crafted stories.

> NPC: an acronym for non-player-character. In a game all of the characters not controlled by the player are NPCs.

Jerome Lawrence and Robert E. Lee's play *Inherit the Wind* was inspired by the Scopes Monkey Trial, held in 1925 where a teacher was prosecuted for teaching evolution. At the end of the film version, Henry Drummond (a fictionalized Clarence Darrow), played by Spencer Tracy, picks up a copy of the *Bible* and a copy of Charles Darwin's *Origin of the Species*, weighs each for a moment, then packs them away together in his briefcase (Figure 1.1). The symbolism is obvious. Biblical teaching and evolution can coexist. The same is true for stories and games.

FIGURE 1.1 The Bible and *Origin of the Species* side by side.

Games are a very different animal from stories. We all know that. While the word *game* is often taken to mean a competitive activity, the most general definition outside of academic circles is simply "a way of amusing oneself."

In fact, games that encourage active participation in storytelling are as old as games themselves. Children learn through playing games. They act out stories, play characters, and mold their stories and characters in reaction to their friends' actions. Adults role-playing *Dungeons and Dragons* at their kitchen tables enjoy the structure of a game that allows a fluid storytelling that adjusts to their play. Have a look at the following equation:

Game Rules + Scripted/Rehearsed Story + Players = Entertainment Experience

The secret to a satisfying entertainment experience is in the balance of its parts. Balance is a key concern in many areas of game design as well as writing. You'll discover it is one of the main themes we come back to again and again in this book.

If, in the equation above, the storyteller is unable to adjust to their audience, audience participation will diminish (or degenerate into heckling!), and the entertainment experience will be adversely affected. In the case of theatrical productions in Shakespeare's day, of course, the heckling was an acknowledged part of mass entertainment. Actors had to perform while sometimes being targets for spoiled vegetables lobbed from the "pit" and polite society was forced to endure this additional spectacle or sponsor private productions.

In our second equation above, if the game rules or the scripted story are too rigid to adjust to the improvisations of the players, the entertainment experience will suffer.

What games played on computers have altered in this mix is the replacement of human beings with algorithms on one side of the equation or the other. Instead of human storytellers responding to their audiences or actors adjusting their performances, we require the game's programming to adjust, a far trickier proposition, and one we will address often in the following pages.

Since we're messing around with equations, let's look at a common myth:

$$Life = Drama$$

Webster's Dictionary gives the following definitions of drama:

1. A play in prose or verse

2. Dramatic art of a particular kind or period

3. The art or practice of writing or producing plays

4. A real-life situation or succession of events having the dramatic progression or emotional content typical of a play

It is that last definition that is of most interest to us here. I remember a debate during a roundtable at the Game Developers Conference several years ago where a number of game designers insisted that if we witness a child struck by a car on the street we are seeing drama. But this position reflects a misunderstanding of the colloquial or common usage of the word, as in "Wasn't that a dramatic basketball game?"

What we really mean is "Wasn't that basketball game as exciting as the Disney movie about a basketball game we saw?" There is more to drama than real life. Drama only exists in real life when real-life events mirror dramatic structure and remind us of crafted drama we have witnessed. This is not to say that intense emotions cannot be aroused by an injured child or a close score in a sports contest. We may even call these examples "drama." But it is dangerous for creators of drama to assume that all we must do is follow Hamlet's famous advice to *his* players: "To hold, as 'twere, the mirror up to nature."

According to the definition, we must start with drama as a structure in which to wrap real life. Drama begets Real Life Drama. Therefore the progression looks like this:

$$Drama \rightarrow Real\ Life\ Drama$$

But wait! Which really came first? Wasn't it life? Shouldn't the cause and effect look more like this?

$$Real\ Life \rightarrow Drama$$

No, because even in the very beginning of storytelling and drama, back around that campfire after the woolly mammoth fell, there was an added step in the equation:

$$Real\ Life + Interpreter = Drama$$

Drama is built on the reflection human beings bring to the incidents and conflict of real life that is then communicated to other human beings. And drama is built from the human context that we wrap the realities of life within.

Just adding an interpreter to the equation doesn't guarantee drama of course.

$$\text{Life} + \text{Interpreter (Shakespeare)} = \text{Drama}$$

$$\text{Life} + \text{Interpreter}\left(\text{My Next} - \text{Door Neighbor Brad}\right) = \text{Trivialization}$$

Brad's a nice guy, but he's no bard.

When you add insight and perspective to life, it can become drama. It speaks to us as human beings and can enrich our lives. However, when you add imagery without meaning, life is not dramatized, it is cheapened. We will explore some of the building blocks of drama shortly and see how they relate to the craft of writing for games.

Okay, let's put all of the highfalutin' concepts we've just talked about aside and look at one final equation. Forget Art. Forget Drama. There is one primary equation that drives all entertainment industries:

$$\text{Entertainment} = \text{Fun}$$

Sounds obvious, doesn't it? Yet we are an industry awash in pet theories that disregard fun, new paradigms that ignore past and earth-shaking "discoveries" that only seem new to their discoverers because they are unaware of even the short history of our industry. A lot of these pet theories, new paradigms, and earth-shaking discoveries have been tried time and time again, and have failed miserably. To paraphrase George Santayana: "Those who are ignorant of the past are condemned to overlook it."

Finally, let's take some requests from our audience. We storytellers have a pretty good idea of what we want from our audiences. We want them to be entertained. But what do they want from us? If we listen closely, they will tell us:

- Take me to a place I have never been.

- Make me into someone I could never be.

- Let me do things I could never do.

Obviously, all entertainment media has the opportunity to take the audience to a place it's never been. But only a few mediums add the other two: theme park rides, masquerade balls, simulators, live-action role-playing, and, of course, video games.

If we can fulfill those three far-from-trivial requests, we will have succeeded. As authors, we may add more at our pleasure. We can share our philosophies of life; air our political views; teach; titillate; shock; comfort; challenge; empower; suborn. The choices are limitless. But it is those three requests from our audience that open the door for all else to follow. They are at the heart of certain mystical guarantors of entertainment like *willing suspension of disbelief* and *immersion*.

It will do us a lot of good if we keep these equations and requests in mind as we work.

CHAPTER 2

The Story Remains the Same

I N 2017, I WAS part of a panel at the Sweden Game Conference called *The Future of Storytelling*. Another panelist announced that learning all the old stuff you'll be learning in this book had no relevance to writing for video games. His opinion was that we should throw out the old rules and make new ones. Why bother with all this old stuff? I was rather grouchy when I responded that not understanding how stories have been constructed in older media gives us no platform from which to build writing for an interactive medium like video games. But games demand a new paradigm, don't they? You can't apply the techniques of linear, non-interactive media to games, can you?

Well… yes, you can.

An examination of art styles is far beyond the scope of this book but take a look at these two paintings by Pablo Picasso. Each is a portrait. The first is of Picasso's mother, painted in 1896 when the artist was 15 years old (Figure 2.1). The second is Picasso's daughter, painted in 1938 when the artist was 57 (Figure 2.2).

The point is not which subject Picasso was fonder of or which portrait you may like better. It's this: Picasso did not wake up one morning and, through sheer creativity and imagination, start painting in the cubist style that he and Georges Braque pioneered in the years before World War I, and that is today most associated with him.

He began by applying his considerable talents to far more traditional work. In short, he learned the rules he was later to break. He first learned composition, perspective, light, and anatomy—all the principles he needed to feed his vision. As he matured, his vision evolved, and his training enabled him to pursue it.

Now an argument can be made that these were at least both paintings. Games are very different from books or movies. One of the central themes of this book is—apologies to Marshall McLuhan—the medium is *not* the message. The principles of *storytelling*, as much as they may appear to change, in fact, remain the same. To tell stories, even in the relatively new medium of video games, we may extend those principles and even find new ones. To ignore the fundamentals of storytelling found in other media is to create work that fails to touch our audience, the players, yet we hear some people in our industry advocating to do

DOI: 10.1201/9780429284991-4

FIGURE 2.1   Portrait of Pablo Picasso's Mother, 1896.

FIGURE 2.2   Portrait of Pablo Picasso's Daughter, 1938.

exactly that. They argue that video games are an entirely new form of entertainment that must develop its own new models.

Yet other aspects of our medium that we embrace as ours alone are actually built upon principles borrowed from other media. Our interfaces imitate real-world control systems. Our graphics are grounded in art history and traditional animation. Pioneering work in artificial intelligence was done long before the first video game. If programmers can embrace research from non-game sources, if artists can apply rules of composition and use *chiaroscuro* lighting in our games, then it should be obvious that writers of games can also learn from those writers who came before us.

> Chiaroscuro: a painting technique that starkly contrasts light and shade.

George Santayana is oft quoted and just as often misquoted or paraphrased. Here, from *Reason in Common Sense*, is what the poor man actually wrote: "Progress, far from consisting in change, depends on retentiveness. Those who cannot remember the past are condemned to repeat it." Richard A. Bartle in *Designing Virtual Worlds* writes: "You have to *understand* a system before you can challenge it." Here then is an introduction at least to that linear, non-interactive stuff some are so eager to ignore.

ARISTOTLE AND THOSE OTHER GREEKS

We owe a lot to the Greeks for everything from democracy to Atlantis; and of course, writing as well. Aristotle wasn't the only Greek with useful information to impart, but we'll start with him. Let's turn back the pages of history and see who's who.

Aristotle

Aristotle (384–322 BCE) was a philosopher, writer, and teacher; student of Plato; and possibly a tutor to Alexander the Great. Although there is some question about whether this popular belief is actually true or not, it makes for a great story. His treatises, covering a variety of scientific and philosophical matters, from physics and natural history to politics, logic, ethics, and even dreams, are still published today. In fact, Aristotelian thought shaped Western culture for centuries, and it remains one of the pillars of our intellectual history.

It is through Aristotle that we are introduced to the *deus ex machina* ("God machine"), which is frequently trotted out to describe a fortuitous plot twist (at least for the author) that wraps up the final action in a story. We may frown on it, but in Aristotle's day, it was a perfectly respectable plot device, given that most stories were set in motion by those hands-on gods atop Mt. Olympus.

It was Aristotle who proposed the bedrock logical argument consisting of two premises and a conclusion:

- Every Greek is a person.
- Every person is mortal.
- Every Greek is mortal.

The work that most concerns us as writers is, of course, his *Poetics* written in 350 BCE. Like most of Aristotle's writing, there are not a lot of words in the *Poetics*. It's a short book. There's no reason not to read it. It is packed with ideas. Even though Aristotle chiefly concerned himself with tragedy and epic poetry (and, briefly, comedy), several ideas resonate even today in our drama, literature, film, and games. He was the first writer to talk about the dramatic reversal that in the past few years has enjoyed revived attention in books on screenwriting. This concept is important enough to have its own topic in Chapter 9, "Bringing the Story to Life," and we'll examine it then.

Expanding on Plato's observation that "art imitates life," Aristotle begins the *Poetics* with three elements of that imitation, or representation: the medium, or type, of art, such as music, poetry, and drama; the objects of imitation, who are defined as "men in action," the protagonists of today; and the manner in which the imitation is presented, either as narration or drama.

Aristotle notes that the ability to imitate is present with human beings from birth. It is how we learn. And he points out that we enjoy seeing others imitating. This pleasure gives rise to everything from earliest man mimicking the animals he hunted in ritual dances to one of the main reasons that people today watch plays, films, and television drama. Acting is pretending, make-believe, and imitation. The second element is of interest to us because this "man of action" is the player-character in games.

Aristotle categorizes the man of action in three ways. First are characters that are better than people in real life. These can be tragic heroes such as Oedipus, Hamlet, Citizen Kane, Anakin Skywalker, or even Dave Boyle, the character played by Tim Robbins in the film *Mystic River*.

In 1983, Michael Berlyn's text adventure *Infidel* gave gamers a tragically flawed character to play. The PC was obsessed with his work, arrogant, and driven, and this *Achilles' heel* ultimately killed him.

At the time some reviewers considered this a "twist" ending. It's not, of course, but rather the only logical conclusion for a classical tragic hero. It *was* a controversial ending, and players were understandably split on whether they liked playing a "loser" or not. Almost forty years later we have more playable tragic heroes. A couple come immediately to mind: Kratos in *God of War* and John Marsden in *Red Dead Redemption*. Still, we don't find *many* tragic heroes in games for two main reasons. First, they are uncomfortable figures, haunted, and often alone. Games are meant to be fun. Their creators have to work overtime to make these characters interesting to play, although not always "fun." Playable video game characters may be haunted, but they are rarely truly tragic. *The Last of Us* and *The Last of Us 2* are third-person action/adventure games that are not afraid to feature flawed characters and unflinching, abrupt tragedy. Usually, we see this type of character as an NPC. But the very fact that a game's interactivity can plunge the player into a story means that players really don't want to be a tragic hero who comes to a bad end. Non-Player Characters are a different story.

> Achilles' heel: refers to the one weak spot on the well-known Greek hero's body that literally brings about his fall. It is popularly used synonymously with tragic flaw.

Flawed non-player characters can add surprise and depth to the story of a game. Aribeth in *Neverwinter Nights* is an example of a woman who starts out in a typical heroic role, and even a quest-giver and mentor. But as the story develops, bitterness over the death of her sweetheart and a desire for revenge twist her thinking to the point where she has become one of the chief villain's most prized generals near the climax of the game story. We'll talk more about the various roles NPCs can play in games in Chapter 4, "Character Roles."

A way to have your heroic cake and eat it too is to have the player-character come to a bloody end by sacrificing themselves for a good purpose. The character can be a noble figure from the beginning or redeem themselves for past wrongs. We have plenty of examples of the former, but games shy away from the latter, again because the game element, the reason players buy the game, is to feel heroic in the more common definition we'll discuss next.

Heroes in games are more commonly archetypal heroes (see the "Campbell's the Hero's Journey" section). In the first *FPS* games like *Doom*, no attention was paid to the player-character at all. He was just a rough-looking face in the corner of the interface who got more battered and bruised as he took hits. Later games have fleshed out the look of the PC. Check out *Uncharted*'s Nathan Drake and player-characters from the *Assassin's Creed* games, Desmond Miles and Ezio Auditore.

FPS: first-person shooter, a popular type of action game.

Many characters today rarely change through the course of the game story, and they have little depth. This is one of the reasons that attempts at creating emotion in the *Transformer* films failed to resonate with audiences. The films were carried by the dwindling charms of CGI (computer-generated imagery) and spectacle, not character. When they were faced with characters about whom they knew nothing except a checklist of facts—characters with no capacity for growth—audiences should be forgiven if they didn't care what happened to them.

However, other characters are more complex, even given the restrictions on player-characters already mentioned earlier. *Silent Hill*'s player-characters are often revealed to have more going on inside them than standard heroes, where twists reveal elements of their pasts and the workings of fate. This can make them all the more interesting to play. In Chapter 3, "Respecting Characters," we'll explore the voyage of discovery that players can take to learn about the character they are guiding through the story.

There are also heroes in strategy games like *Heroes of Might and Magic* who function more as celebrity walk-ons, just special characters with unique powers at the disposal of the player. In the *Age of Empires*, *Company of Heroes*, and similar strategy games, the player becomes the hero, with god-like powers to manipulate soldiers, farmers, and entire civilizations.

The second type of character Aristotle discusses is one who is worse than most people. This is not the villain/antagonist for a protagonist to contend with, but the actual protagonist or central figure of a story. This type of character was, in Aristotle's day, confined to comedy. Comic figures like Moliere's hypocritical *Tartuffe* or Mavis Gary, Charlize Theron's acid-etched portrayal of an obliviously self-involved woman whose life peaked in high school in 2011's *Young Adult*, are deliberately written to seem worse than the rest of us. They are entertaining monsters that fascinate and appall simultaneously. Such characters often end as badly as *Oedipus* or *Hamlet*, if not outright dead, at least with all their high-blown pretensions and convoluted schemes in tatters. Of course, the audience takes delight in this: the difference between tragic and comedic characters. Bill Murray's character in *Groundhog Day* is redeemed in the end, a more common fate these days for these characters. However, Mavis will never grow to true adulthood. In each case, Aristotle's term "poetic justice" accurately describes their fates.

The third and last type of character Aristotle addresses is the one who is representative of the way people really are. By this, he is rounding out a dramatic class system and simply means those that are not worthier than ourselves or lower but somewhere in between. He is discussing drama, after all, and does not mean to suggest a character that may have its direct counterpart in real life.

Today, we often break down these three classifications, twist them and turn them, combine them, or subtract essential elements that define the classic models. It's important to remember that the drama and poetry Aristotle analyzed were very restricted and had been for centuries. While there is much to learn from him and his friends, we must also be aware of the ways in which our modern literature and drama have evolved.

For example, today we have the anti-hero, a popular character particularly in the late 1960s and early 1970s, when writers in all media created characters who struggled against the establishment: McMurphy, the rebellious patient at an Oregon state mental institution in *One Flew Over the Cuckoo's Nest*; and Luke, from ex-convict Donn Pearce's novel, *Cool Hand Luke*. The film version gave us the famous phrase, "What we have here is... failure to communicate." Paul Newman, the actor who played Luke in the film, had already carved out an anti-hero niche all his own a few years earlier in such films as *The Hustler* and *Hud*.

But what happens to anti-heroes? They often come to messy ends just like their tragic forebears. McMurphy is lobotomized. Luke is killed. Again, not necessarily characters who players might want to play. And since these types of characters are invariably extremely colorful, outrageous, and shocking, players wouldn't be too fond of the very real possibility of their characters being overshadowed if anti-heroes were NPCs.

Probably the most famous concept we take from Aristotle is that of the unities of time, place, and action. We first need to understand that Aristotle based this concept on the prevailing forms of drama and epic poetry that existed in his day. And there are many stories that do not observe them. *Gone with the Wind* and *Cold Mountain* cover huge tracts of territory, and Christopher Nolan movies like *Inception* and *Tenet* do the same, but the geography that is crossed is in the mind. Even so, the unities apply directly to all dramatic media today, and especially to video games.

Unity of Time

The story we are telling takes place in a limited and sequential time frame. This can be as little as an hour or two, as in films such as *Run Lola Run* or as long as weeks in a Netflix streaming TV series. The key points are that either way the time of the story is purposely limited to the time it takes to play out the action. There is no extraneous passage of time covered by a title reading "Later that Day," cuts to revved up clocks, or the pages fluttering off a calendar. And the tighter the time, the more tension can be created.

This is perfect for video games. From the intimate firefights of the *Modern Warfare* series to the real-time battles of the *Company of Heroes* games, the action plays sequentially. While the levels of these games, as well as first-person shooters and action games can be connected in a looser timeline, each level is an episodic story complete within itself. And because that story is confined to a limited and sequential "real time," it is all the more suspenseful.

Unity of Place

One of the jobs video games can do well is simulate an environment. We can create naturalistic or fanciful geography with consistent physical laws, and objects that can be manipulated. In single-player games, the environment must be extremely interactive. Players enjoy seeing the destruction their bullets and bombs make in the world of the game. They want to be able to open the drawers of a desk or run water from a tap.

In order to accomplish this level of physical interaction, these games limit the place where the action plays out. Each level or area is bounded either by logical physical barriers, barriers that fit within the fiction of the world such as NPC guards, or by less logical blockages in the landscape—impassable forests, un-swimmable rivers, and so on. If we didn't limit the geography *and* the number of interactions possible within the environment, the number of interactions would overwhelm an engine that must stay lean and mean to accommodate the game's action, and the number of locations would tax even the largest art staff. Even huge games like *The Legend of Zelda: Breath of the Wild* have boundaries the player cannot venture beyond.

The storyteller should gladly accept the limitations imposed in the same way that television is constrained to a limited number of locations and constructed sets. By confining the story in this way, less attention is paid to the environment. Each new setting is more information that a player or audience must absorb. Maintaining unity of place forces writers to pay attention to what is important: character and story and like unity of time, it helps create the necessary tension and suspense. The film *Attack the Block* stays within its social boundaries as much as the TV streaming series *Trapped* is confined by all that snow. Both benefit from an observation of the unities of time and place and the third one as well, which is action.

Unity of Action

This unity is interesting because it encompasses both stories limited in time and place and epics such as *Dune, War and Peace*, and *The Odyssey* by Homer. It eliminates all extraneous action that is not of central importance to the plot and theme. In each of the above cases, the scope of the story is immense, yet each scene is chosen with care.

Again, game authors limited by budget and time constraints can use this unity to help us decide what scenes and levels are necessary to the game story and which ones are a waste of resources. Any level may be a standout due to geography, effects, puzzles, uniqueness of enemies, and many other factors. But if that level does not advance the story, it is better saved for another game. As we explore the ways writers and designers can meld story with gameplay in Chapters 7, "Once Upon a Time," 8, "Respecting Story," and 9, "Bringing the

Story to Life," we'll see that we must take advantage of every opportunity presented to us, even more so than in other media. Superfluous material, however brilliantly conceived and executed, makes our job all the more difficult.

Keeping unity of action in mind while we write is also important because it focuses our attention where it belongs: on the story and the characters who drive it. It can rein in creative flights of fancy that may seem fun and exciting when they first grab us but become dead ends once they're fully explored. Experienced writers—particularly those used to tight deadlines and budget constraints—develop instincts as to what to include and what to discard as they write. This process of selection can pass almost unnoticed as the writer works, but it is as vital to a successful story as the impulse that gave it birth

Homer

It is Homer who has chiefly taught other poets the art of telling lies skillfully.

Aristotle

Homer (born circa 750 BCE) did not, as we may think, make up the stories of *The Odyssey* and *The Iliad*. Nor did he simply set down popular myths or historic events. The epic poetry of Greece was conveyed from generation to generation, mostly in oral form.

There is even evidence to suggest many hands were involved in the creation of these epic tales. Homer is certainly the best known of these, and the romantic notion of this blind man dictating stories to a faithful scribe is certainly in keeping with the bardic tradition he exemplifies. This shouldn't take away from our admiration of him. Shakespeare freely adapted others' stories, history, and mythology for his own purposes. That Homer was a skilled interpreter, natural storyteller, and inspired poet can be deduced from the fact that it is his name that is most revered by later Greek writers and philosophers when they discuss epic poetry.

Homer is important to us, the creators of games, because of the style in which his epic stories were told. Alfred Lord, in his book, *The Singer of Tales*, explicitly relates this type of storytelling to bardic tradition.

> Bardic tradition: bards were ancient Celtic poets, but their equivalent can be found in many cultures singing songs and telling tales passed down from generation to generation.

The origins of the bardic tradition are forever lost in the swampy miasma of preliterate history. Every story told by a hunter around a roaring fire, or a loving parent to a child just before the child drifts off to sleep, follows in the same grand tradition.

Two points are of most interest: the fluidity of this type of storytelling and its fundamentally episodic nature. The ever-changing story of bardic tradition that is influenced by teller, by audience, by region and culture closely reflects the interactive story. Interactive stories must react to the player just as bards and cavemen reacted to their audience; just as parents must adjust their bedtime stories to a child's question, "But Mommy, the prince wasn't really evil, was he?" "Um…no… he wasn't. He really had a good heart. Um… where was I?"

The episodic nature of the Homeric epics has even more potential for us as writers of video games. Here we see the first building blocks of a modular system that we will explore further in Chapter 13, "The Roots of a New Storytelling," and we'll revisit Homer, copying and refining oral tradition, then.

Sophocles

In Sophocles (circa 496–404 BCE), we have one of the great playwrights of Greece's golden age, an era that included such rock stars as Aeschylus and Euripides. The plotting of his *Oedipus Rex* feels as up to date today as it did centuries ago. In *Antigone* and *Electra*, his women characters are brilliantly etched, strong, and complex.

Like Shakespeare, Sophocles often acted in his plays, and was apparently something of an amazing juggler. One of his major accomplishments was adding a third character to plays. That's right, Greek drama up until that time was all duets. That's something to keep in mind the next time you're faced with cutting your cast of NPCs! He was also responsible for abandoning the practice of presenting a single story as a trilogy, preferring instead to tell a complete story in a single play.

These single plays were of the same basic length as the single part of a trilogy, yet they were based on the same stories and myths as their predecessors. And this is why he is of interest to the video game writer. What was the result of taking the action of a story spread out over three plays and reducing it to a single play? Pace was quickened. Drama was heightened.

Just as earlier I talked about the paradoxical benefits of the Aristotelian unities as they seem to limit time, place, and action, yet, in fact, serve to focus our writing, this condensing of Sophocles' stories made them that much more involving. Writers of video games start from the apparent disadvantage of having to find ways and means to tell their stories without interrupting the natural flow of the gameplay. Other media do not have this additional challenge.

As a result, we are also continually condensing our stories to fit within our own specialized restraints. What this process demands is clarity of vision. When Sophocles sped up the action to fit within the shorter performance time, he had to make sure that the action remained comprehensible to his audience, so he needed to simplify the stories.

Also, many of his audience knew the stories by heart before they entered the amphitheater. They would not have been receptive if their favorite parts were removed.

What a challenge! Yet he was able to pull it off with enough virtuosity that he won eighteen first prizes, and never finished worse than second in over 120 plays. In fact, in his first competition, he beat Aeschylus, the "Father of Tragedy" himself. Maybe it was because people were relieved by the shorter running times.

The point is that simply because we work under many restrictions not piled upon other forms of storytelling, this doesn't mean we need to settle for anything less. There is nothing more intrinsically difficult in writing a video game than in writing a play all those centuries ago. For every new challenge we face, there is a solution. There is no need for a badly written game and no excuse.

Aristophanes

There are other Greeks worth checking out, including Plato, Aeschylus, and Euripides, but the only other golden Greek I'm going to talk about here is Aristophanes (circa 448–380 BCE). Like Homer, his versions of popular stories are the only ones that survived, the only extant examples of Greek comedy.

There is much more comedy than tragedy in video games. Why? We've talked about players' reluctance to play heroes who end up face down in a pool of congealing dreams. The other major reason is that it is much easier to make people laugh than it is to make them cry. To write comedy, you only need to be able to take a certain impish outlook on life, combine it with a knack for timing and surprise, and you'll have them rolling in their cubicles. To write tragedy, you need to explore some darker sides of your character. While this doesn't seem to deter all those writers of the books that end up on Oprah's list, it's a voyage many writers of video games seem unwilling to take.

Video game writer Mark Barrett has suggested,

> The main reason that games have emphasized humor is that people who are laughing will forgive almost anything in exchange for those laughs. String enough laughs together, and you can even convince people that a game is a comedy—which is a specific narrative form—when, in fact, it is more closely related to a collection of jokes or gags. Humor in the form of jokes is also inherently self-contained, meaning you can slip it into the "holes" in gameplay, where other narrative forms require significant preparation and continuity over the course of the game.

Moreover, the humor in video games is generally confined within certain limits. It is, for the most part, doggedly mainstream, relying heavily on verbal wit that is, after all, easier to animate than pratfalls. Writers of video games are often fond of winking at the players, reminding them that the author is aware of them, however much that might harm their involvement in the story.

Video game humor isn't confined to subject matter as much as it is style, full of puns and put-downs, and it can be as deliberately gross as a visit from Borat. What's usually missing is Borat's socio-political edge. But please remember this: there is nothing edgy about fart jokes any longer, folks. They have successfully made the leap from the playground to Disney films.

Aristophanes wasn't above the occasional scatological moment himself. He wrote his comedies in an uncertain era of war and political upheaval. Greece was a nation in transition. All Greeks felt it, even if they didn't know where that transition was taking them. The comedy of Aristophanes was a comedy with a deep understanding of the foibles of human beings: bawdy, angry, unsparing in its disdain for dangerously narcissistic politicians, and shaded by melancholy and uncertainty about the future.

The Peloponnesian War was more than two decades old when one of his most famous plays, *Lysistrata*, told the story of wives who refused to have sex with their husbands until they brought the war to an end. It should not surprise anyone that it enjoyed a popular revival during the late 1960s for its sexual themes, as well as its explicit anti-war statement. *Chi-Raq*, a 2015 musical film from Spike Lee and Kevin Willmott, updated *Lysistrata* to gang violence on the south side of Chicago. In *The Wasps*, Aristophanes explored the decline of Athenian culture, particularly its legal system. In *The Knights*, he satirized the powerful, unloved, and unlovely politician, Cleon. He even went after respectable figures like Euripides and Socrates in other plays. Any of this sound familiar? In the previous edition of this book, I wrote "Today we may be shocked that a comedian might lose their late-night TV show over political comments. Aristophanes could have lost his life." I doubt if many people today would be shocked by the consequences those who, like Aristophanes, face when they stand up to power.

Aristophanes' comedy was comedy with a purpose, and that purpose was not only to make his audiences laugh. He also used comedy to challenge them and to make them think. It's important to remember his plays were not the theatrical equivalent of what some of us call applied games and others call (ick) serious games. Aristophanes' plays were mainstream entertainment. In games we have some delightful, hilarious mainstream comedies. Some of my favorite funny games are *The Secret of Monkey Island*, *Portal 2*, *The Stanley Parable*, and *Goat Simulator*. None of them take the personal risks that the plays of Aristophanes took. Mainstream video games simply haven't attempted much meaningful comedy at the level that other media routinely challenge their audiences. I'm not suggesting game writers and designers should take risks that may get them imprisoned or worse. But it's important to consider why comedy video games shy away from the attempt. We'll explore this question again when we return to comedy in Chapter 11, "Story Anatomy".

Jung's Collective Unconscious

If Sigmund Freud is the father of modern psychology, Carl Jung (1875–1961) is his free-spirited nephew. Whereas Freud's view of the unconscious mind was that of a dark and roiling mass of hidden secrets and dangerous passions, Jung saw it as a connection, a doorway between the individual mind and all of humanity.

Jung defined three parts of our psyche: the ego, or conscious mind; the personal unconscious, repository for memory both accessible and suppressed; and the collective unconscious, containing a memory shared in common with all humanity. Phenomena such as déjà vu and love at first sight, the similarities across different cultures of various symbols and myths, as well as parallels in everything from dreams to fairy tales, Jung wrote, are all examples of this collective unconscious, which can be studied only through its effects and never directly.

Jung's last book, *Man and His Symbols*, is a perfect synthesis of his ideas on the symbolism of dreams. It covers everything from the influences of ancient myths on modern man to symbolism in the visual arts. To understand Jung's theories, begin here at the end. It is great fuel to fire our creative thinking.

Jung is of primary interest to us for three reasons. First is his theory of the collective unconscious, this shared history of humankind we all carry within us. It can help us understand why others react in the ways that they do to what we create. If we can learn from it, we will be better able to reach our audience, the player.

The second reason is the importance of symbols, those atavistic signposts that show up unexpectedly in a phrase, a shape, a composition of light and color, and immediately imbue the moment with a greater significance than it might ordinarily have. We see symbols everywhere around us—in an expressionist painting, a church sermon, or a national flag. How those symbols can be used to invoke a particular reaction in the player will be explored in Chapter 8.

The third reason for taking a look at Jung is his cross-cultural studies of symbols and myths, spadework that directly influenced our last subject in this chapter: Joseph Campbell.

Campbell's Hero's Journey

> The latest incarnation of Oedipus, the continued romance of Beauty and the Beast, stand this afternoon on the corner of Forty-second Street and Fifth Avenue, waiting for the traffic light to change.
>
> *Joseph Campbell, The Hero with a Thousand Faces.*

I first stumbled across Joseph Campbell's *The Hero with a Thousand Faces* when I was a college student many years ago. First published in 1949, the book was enjoying a minor revival of interest in the turbulent late 1960s and early 1970s. It was a revelation to me. Here was the best book I'd ever read about my burgeoning vocation, writing, and it wasn't even about writing.

Campbell gives us the story of the hero's journey, a story that is remarkably and significantly the same in myths around the world. He uses this story to mirror nothing less than how we develop as human beings. We act out this journey in our lives, and to recognize it is to recognize ourselves.

The hero's journey is broken down into three major parts, almost like acts in a play. First there is a *Departure*. Here the hero is called to adventure. Someone is in need of aid, and the hero, an unimportant local character like Jack in *Jack, the Giant Killer*; someone with standing, but not perceived as a hero like Sir Thomas Moore in *A Man for All Seasons*; or a wanderer with no particularly notable deeds to the credit such as the gunslinger called *Shane*, is pressed to help. They may be confronted by a mentor figure or seek one out to assist them in their quest.

The next step Campbell calls *Initiation*, and this is the trek to reach the goal that will secure the needed aid. This journey may be physical or spiritual or both. As Campbell says, "Popular tales represent the heroic action as physical; the higher religions show the deed to be moral…" This second part is what we generally refer to as the *quest* or *mission* and plays a great part in the structure of computer games today, even though games often pay far greater attention to it at the expense of the *Departure*, which becomes little more than a briefing or assignment. One of the most important facets of this step is the necessity for the hero to change, and this directly ties in to character progression that we will look at in the next chapter.

The third step is *Return*, wherein the hero accomplishes their task, aid is rendered, and lives or reputations or souls are saved. In this part, the hero is rewarded with acclimation, riches, marriage, or most importantly, peace of mind. For the journey has been more than a voyage of discovery. It has effected a significant change in the hero's perceptions and beliefs that will continue to the end of their days.

George Lucas has acknowledged that Luke Skywalker's journey is heavily influenced by *The Hero with a Thousand Faces*, although he didn't need to, because the evidence is there in front of our eyes. More recently, the video game industry has rightfully rediscovered Campbell's work. And while it may be taken way too literally, this journey's importance cannot be overstressed. We'll return to it throughout the course of this book.

Primary Sources

One final note before we move on, and that concerns primary sources. Aristotle's *The Poetics*, *The Art of Dramatic Writing* by Lajos Egri, and *Play-Making* (1912) by theater critic William Archer have much to teach us as writers of video games. I will refer to all three in this book. Yet if I'd only read Egri, I might not have bothered with Aristotle, since Egri has little use for him, not to mention such accomplished playwrights as Eugene O'Neil and Noel Coward. Archer introduced Henrik Ibsen, one of the greatest modern playwrights, to the English-speaking world. But he was not kind to George Bernard Shaw or Anton Chekov. There is much we can learn from Aristotle, Egri, and Archer, but we must take anyone's opinions with a grain of our own insight.

There are many books that will gladly interpret the original plays and books we've been discussing here, as well as all the plays, films, books, and games I'll give as examples. I'm doing the same after all. But don't depend solely on them. None should be considered a substitute for experiencing the originals yourself. I fervently recommend that you seek out as many original works as you can, study them, and form your own conclusions. It is far more likely that you'll be able to absorb and synthesize the ideas in their original forms, and even come to disagree with others' interpretations, including mine!

From *The Great Train Robbery* to *Birth of a Nation*

People say our technology is changing so fast these days it's impossible to keep up with it. Janet Murray in *Hamlet on the Holodeck: The Future of Narrative in Cyberspace* suggests that in our industry we are still at the incunabula stage, using a technology still in its infancy. She points out that it took 150 years from Gutenberg's printing press to *Don Quixote*, a book we both find significant, but for different reasons. We will be examining *Don Quixote* in Chapter 13. For now, it is enough that it is regarded as the first true novel in Western culture. Maybe it's no coincidence that this novel gives us hints of how to handle interactive storytelling today in the infancy of *our* technology.

But I would argue that things move much faster now. Information and ideas spread like wildfire, or cyberattacks, threatening to overwhelm us. Innovation runs at a much faster pace.

Let's look at *The Great Train Robbery* (Figure 2.3). Produced at Thomas Edison's studio in 1903, it was written, directed, and edited by the head of production, Edwin S. Porter. The film ran about twelve minutes, chronicling the title robbery, the outlaws' escape, and their eventual comeuppance. It is credited as being the first narrative to use *parallel cutting* to create suspense and move the story forward. Reportedly, women fainted (I expect

Parallel cutting (aka parallel action): an editing technique where two related stories are intercut, jumping back and forth, as they move forward.

FIGURE 2.3   Yes, *The Great Train Robbery* is about robbing a train.

a few men did, too) when a villain pointed his gun directly at the camera and fired it. (Something network censors refused to let us do in the opening credits of *Blacke's Magic*, a TV show I wrote for in 1985.)

D.W. Griffith's controversial epic *Birth of a Nation* appeared in 1915. And to this day, it is an excruciating embarrassment to critics and scholars who rightfully honor its break-through filmmaking achievements while at the same time having to deal with the undeni-able fact that it is virulently racist, historically inaccurate, and politically naïve. It's as if Aristotle's *Poetics* extolled child molestation at the same time as they laid the foundations of drama. Despite this, film critic James Agee said of Griffith, "To watch his work is like being witness to the beginning of melody, or the first conscious use of the lever or the wheel; the emergence, coordination, and first eloquence of language; the birth of an art; and to realize that this is all the work of one man." *Birth of a Nation*: Seminal and repre-hensible all at the same time.

Twelve years separated the very first one-reel narrative film, *The Great Train Robbery* (1903), and D.W. Griffith's epic *Birth of a Nation* (1915).

Will Crowther's and Don Wood's *Colossal Cave*, the first adventure game, showed up on mainframe computers in its present form in 1976, a greatly expanded version of the original work Crowther began four years earlier. This game introduced interactive fiction to the world.

In twelve years over a century ago, the narrative film went from gurgling infancy to mass entertainment produced by a host of competitors. As we charge through this new century, now almost five decades after the debut of that game, let's look around. It took a lot longer. Games are only in the last few years finally evolving. Not just due to the addition of the latest technological trimmings like VR, augmented reality, and haptic sensors. But because of a growing appreciation for all that has gone before.

The Language of Drama and Film

The word "language" in this heading refers to terms that describe and techniques that utilize some basic concepts of dramatic writing and screenwriting. Much of the vocabulary of drama and film must be juggled before it can apply to video games, as we shall see. But there are several concepts that can be translated directly. We'll be returning to them again and again, but for now, here are some brief discussions to lay the groundwork.

Universal Themes

What is the story about? Good vs. Evil? Is that enough? You want an audience to willingly suspend their disbelief? Give them a theme they understand and are interested in. Whether it's the universal heroic quest tracked from culture to culture by Joseph Campbell, or the Greek-tragedy of families torn apart, give the story for your game, as any story, a reason for being told beyond the fact that it would be fun.

Don't give in to the mechanical repetition of cliché. Find new stories, or at least new meaning in old stories. Do RPGs really need another "There was a great conflict in the past between good and evil, now evil is coming back!" story that offers nothing more than a change of scenery and different names for weapons and spells? In contrast, look at games like *Never Alone*, *Life Is Strange*, *Thomas Was Alone*, *Valiant Hearts*, and *The Lion's Song*. Themes range from unconditional love and the need for friendship to the tragedy of war to the struggle to create.

In *The Art of Dramatic Writing*, Lajos Egri speaks of the word "premise." However, his definition of this word is closer to what we call today "theme." Premise is reserved for the idea or situation upon which a story is based. If we take premise to more closely resemble theme, though, his thoughts give us several important points to consider.

Every game story, as every play, should begin with a theme. This theme gives you your ending and all the steps leading up to it. Egri: "And it must be a premise worded so that anyone can understand it as the author intended it to be understood. An unclear premise is as bad as no premise at all."

The theme of Gary Ross's film version of *Seabiscuit* is there is worth to be found in every person. It was personified in this story of the little horse who could, and a generation of human beings squashed by the Great Depression, yet still managing to survive and to find hope in the future. Almost every scene was infused with this theme. It was the reason the film was made. It is easily understood and adds incredible depth to what could have been just another movie about a come-from-behind team winning the big game.

Egri again: "You… should not write anything you do not believe. The premise should be a conviction of your own, so that you may prove it wholeheartedly." If Gary Ross didn't believe that there was worth to be found in even apparently broken human beings, he could not have made his film with the passion he did. It's that simple.

Your theme does not have to be unique, but you must believe in it. That belief will not only convince your audience, but will give you better insight into the theme, suggest more ways to present it that rise naturally from your characters and story, and make it all the more powerful.

Egri even gives us hope when during the writing it seems we are losing touch with the theme that ignited us to begin with. He says, "If in the process you find your premise untenable *because you have changed your mind as to what you wished to say*, formulate a new premise and discard the old."

Everybody makes mistakes. The story you are telling may take a new direction away from the theme you started with. If it does, you have two choices: rein it back in until it is again on theme, or search for the theme you are illuminating at the expense of the original. Don't be afraid to throw anything away! As hard as it might feel at the time, you cannot fit square plot moves into round stories. It will be an exercise in frustration that, carried to its logical conclusion, will result in a bad story. And you can take heart in the fact that all that work is there waiting to be used again in support of another story or theme.

Egri:

> You can arrive at your premise in any one of a great many ways. You may start with an idea which you at once convert to a premise, or you may develop a situation first and see that it has potentialities which need only the right premise to give them meaning and suggest an end.

You can start with politics or war or jealousy, and build many different themes from each one, depending upon how you want to treat them. In 1964, two films with remarkably similar situations were released. One was *Fail Safe*. The second was *Dr. Strangelove, or How I Learned to Stop Worrying and Love the Bomb*. Both carried themes about the horrors of nuclear war. Both followed similar scenarios. Both were entirely different in treatment and how they chose to explicate their common theme. Take a look at *Platoon* and *The Green Berets*, two films about the Vietnam War that couldn't be farther apart in theme.

One last point from Egri: "No one premise is necessarily a universal truth. Poverty doesn't always lead to crime, but if you've chosen this premise, it does in your case. The same principle governs all premises."

This can save us a lot of grief. Writers who try to search for truths that are too universal often end up with the clichés I mentioned in the opening paragraph of this topic. Themes like "Doing bad stuff is bad" and "Evil must be fought" are obviously pretty universal, but instead of inspiring us to new interesting characters, settings, and stories, they often lock us into the same old themes of every other game out there. Want to make your game stand out from the crowd? Find a theme that is less lofty, but more personal. It will focus your writing and your game.

Drama

As we discussed before, life is not drama. A senseless death in real life is not drama until we human beings react to it and place it in a context that touches us and others. What then is drama? William Archer in *Play-Making* says "the essence of drama" is crisis. He quotes another writer, "No obstacle, no drama." Obstacles exist to be overcome by strength, intelligence, force of will. How do we apply this to the creation of games? We create a game structure that is built on conflict, that provides obstacles (including traditional puzzles, but not limited to them) to the player.

Obstacles can arise during action or conversation with other characters, and they are present everywhere in gameplay—traps, bosses, locked doors—think of them as obstacles, not just puzzles or targets. These obstacles can be the natural next step beyond those that still dominate so many games, replacing them with dramatic confrontations and suspense-filled predicaments that are the meat and potatoes of drama.

Conflict

Drama is not simply about conflict, but conflict certainly gives it momentum. Conflict provides the player with a need to continue. Too often, games fall into the trap of emulating Golden Age mysteries from the 1920s to the 1930s. Too many detective stories of that era confined all the action to the unraveling of the crime instead of a mystery that unfolds and deepens as we read.

In the video game *Myst*, the story is static, set in the past, and simply revealed bit by bit. In *Jak & Daxter*, on the other hand, we have the ongoing attempt by the Lurkers to release dark eco into the world, and the ongoing quest to help Daxter revert to his more natural form.

The conflict, of course, doesn't have to include danger except in the broadest sense: the danger of the breakup of a relationship can be just as compelling as the breakup of an alliance between two planets.

Egri has some things to say about conflict, too: "Conflict is the heartbeat of all writing. No conflict ever existed without first foreshadowing itself. Conflict is that titanic atomic energy whereby one explosion creates a chain of explosions."

His thesis is that drama is built in a series of ever-rising conflicts leading directly to the climax pre-ordained by the theme. Why are we so drawn to conflict in entertainment, even as we may try to avoid it in our own lives?

Egri:

> Since most of us… hide our true selves from the world, we are interested in witnessing the things happening to those who are forced to reveal their true characters under the stress of conflict…. In conflict we are *forced* to reveal ourselves. It seems that self-revelation of others or ourselves holds a fatal fascination for everyone.

Character

We'll have a lot to say about character in the following chapters. The important point here is that theme alone is not enough to get your story rolling; neither is conflict. Characters will drive the story, whether they are the player-character (solo games), many player-characters at once (multiplayer), or NPCs. All are important, and each presents its own special challenges as we shall see.

Cut Scenes

For years, cut scenes have been a standard means to tell story in all sorts of video games. Real-time strategy games would put the next campaign or level in context with a cut scene, as did squad-level games and single-character action games. In *Star Wars: The Old Republic*, a massively multiplayer game, cut scenes were used to further the story, provide eye candy rewards at the end of quests, or help hint at player goals. This is understandable. It was very simple to segregate gameplay from story. It meant that all the tricks of film were available to you, the writer. The player accepted that we were in story mode and took their hand off the mouse or game pad to passively watch.

However, we have learned over time that there are several problems inherent in stopping gameplay dead in its tracks to run a passive cut scene.

- You destroy any momentum built up in the previous gameplay section. The cut scene must re-establish momentum on its own.

- The shift in method of delivering the entertainment can be jarring and serves to accentuate the differences between gameplay and storytelling, harming immersion in the entire experience.

- Players play games to… well, play! They don't *want* to take their fingers off the buttons. They will impatiently stab at those buttons until the cut scene is done. It became a habit with many players. What was the normal solution to this? Allow players to escape out of the cut scene and advance directly to the next level of gameplay. This may not be much loss in a game that has given only perfunctory attention to the storytelling, but it enforces the habit, and makes it harder to use the cut scene effectively. And we should be trying to create story that is as entertaining as the game. We don't *want* players to click out of it.

Happily, today we are far more technically adept at integrating storytelling and action. We'll return to cut scenes in the chapters on storytelling that follow. They will always have a place in games. But used exclusively and indiscriminately they are the lazy writer's attempt at shoehorning story into games. We will explore better, less obtrusive, more organic ways of accomplishing the same thing.

PART II

Creating Characters

INTERLUDE WITH A MAN ON A STAIR

As I was going up the stair

I met a man who wasn't there

He wasn't there again today

I wish, I wish he'd stay away.

—William Hughes Mearns, *The Psycho-ed.*

The light on the landing above me was out, and the stairs climbed into deep shadow. It occurred to me, as it does to many people, I think, that the light bulb might have been shattered or removed; that someone might wait for me there under cover of darkness with harm in mind. But I continued up the stairs thinking, as many do, that my imagination was playing tricks on me, and I was being silly or, worse, paranoid.

He was standing there on the next flight of steps, silhouetted against the light from the top landing: a tall, athletic-looking man, features indistinct. My eyes grew more accustomed to the dim light, and I saw the automatic clutched in his hand. I stopped in mid-stride, glancing back over my shoulder down the stairs.

"Don't run," he said. His voice was low and very calm, almost a monotone. "Bullets travel faster than anyone can run."

"If this is a robbery," I replied, trying to keep my voice from shaking, "I don't have much money. I'm a writer."

"I know what you are," he said. "Better than you know me." He must have seen something in my eyes, because he went on. "You think I'm crazy, don't you? If it isn't a robbery, and you don't recognize me, then I must be a stray loose cannon rolled to a stop in your path."

"I wasn't thinking that. What do you want?"

DOI: 10.1201/9780429284991-5

"I want to kill you. Not because I'm crazy, but because I should be."

I shook my head. "I don't understand."

"Then let me explain. I know nothing about myself. Nothing up until the moment I woke up a fully grown man with a gun in my hand. My family was dead at my feet, and even though I never knew them, I was filled with the lust for revenge! Every moment now I must protect myself from madmen determined to kill me. So, *I* kill. Over and over again!"

"I'm not one of those madmen!" I protested.

"No, you're not. But let me go on. I have no family now. I never had any friends. I'm never hungry. I never sleep. I pop pills to keep myself going, different pills that I have to scrounge for in dirty corners and in garbage cans. I kill those hunting me in order not to be killed myself. That is my life. My *entire* life. Who would wish a never-ending nightmare like that on anyone?"

"I wouldn't."

His hand tightened on the automatic. "But you did!" he screamed. "You don't recognize my face, because you didn't give me one! I don't know my enemies any more than I knew my family! You think I must be crazy because I fight without real purpose, but you gave me none! What little reason I have to go on is nothing more than the clichéd revenge story you trapped me in!"

I stared at him, realization dawning. "You're Brutus Forss! The hero of the shooter I'm writing!"

He slowly brought his emotions under control, and his voice returned to the flat monotone with which he'd begun. "Yes, and you didn't respect me enough to give me a life. You killed my family for no reason, saddled me with a bad pun for a name, filled my mouth with hackneyed dialogue, and forced me into a violent, purposeless existence. Staying true to the unthinking, vengeful nature of my character, I've decided to take my revenge on *you*. And if you say 'Et tu, Brute!' I'll shoot you in the kneecaps first."

His finger tightened on the trigger.

CHAPTER 3

Respecting Characters

THERE'S A DOUBLE MEANING in the title of this chapter. The word "respecting" can mean "about." It can also mean "bestowing respect." It's not enough to populate a story with characters because you're supposed to. It's not enough to heedlessly scatter characters throughout a game like chicken feed in the barnyard mud because we need an adversary at this moment, a merchant here, or a puzzle-giver there. Characters have a right to their own lives in the game. And giving them that right—granting them purpose beyond the designer's convenience—in fact, makes it easier for us to tell our stories. There's no reason not to respect characters as much as we respect *collision detection*.

> Collision detection: algorithms monitoring the intersection of solid objects, as in a video game.

Not all characters need to be well-rounded because not all of them can be major characters. Minor characters can be brought to life with less detail, much the way an artist's sketch can still capture certain telling details, although perhaps not as explicit a likeness as a portrait in oil. We'll cover minor characters and even lowly "extras" later in this chapter.

THREE DIMENSIONS

William Archer in *Play-Making* notes that "the power to observe, to penetrate, and to reproduce character can neither be acquired nor regulated by theoretical recommendations." And despite what the current vogue in how-to-write books might want us to believe, Archer also reminds us that "...specific directions for character-drawing would be like rules for becoming six-feet-high." What we can do, however, is present some ideas to consider as we bring to life the inhabitants of our games.

We call well-rounded characters *three-dimensional*. The same term is applied to the physical world around us and to digital art that is represented by height, width, and depth. That description of characters is often used as is, but it actually does have a definition. The three dimensions of a character are physical, sociological, and psychological. And they apply to all major characters in a game, whether they are the player-character or significant non-player-characters.

DOI: 10.1201/9780429284991-6

The Physical Character

The easiest dimension to reveal to your audience is the physical character, particularly in visual media. What does Robert Langdon look like in *The Da Vinci Code*? Tom Hanks with a questionable haircut. What does Walt Disney look like in *Saving Mr. Banks*? Tom Hanks with a mustache. What does Mr. Rogers look like in *A Beautiful Day in the Neighborhood*? Tom Hanks in a sweater. *News of the World*? Full white beard and a really big hat. So too we draw (both in words and pictures) our characters to fit their roles in our games the same way Mr. Hanks is groomed and dressed to fit his.

And most often, they're drawn to reflect the character's personality or function in the game. But often we stop there, simply layering on a toolbox of skills, mannerisms, and catchphrases as we need them in the game. To create a well-rounded character, we need a bit more.

In the game *Ico*, a boy is born with horns, a physical deformity that recurs in his small village, and is viewed by the villagers as a bad omen (Figure 3.1). Their attempts to kill him lead directly to the adventures that make up the story. Here, the physical character is notable both for the unique entry point it provides into the story and the fact that at the beginning of the game it is more important than either of the boy's other two dimensions.

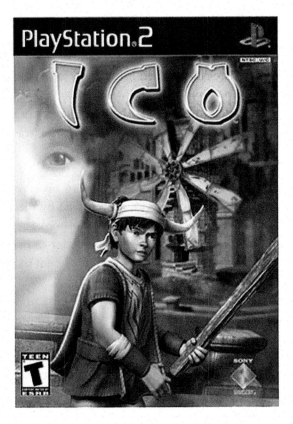

FIGURE 3.1   That's not a Viking hat. Ico's horns are real.

The Sociological Character

The sociological character includes the character's past, their upbringing, and their environment, both local and cultural. By giving a character a past, we put their actions in perspective. They are no longer simply authorial conveniences, but they add weight and interest to the character. In the Sly Cooper series of video games developed by Sucker Punch and Sanzaru, Sly's character is drawn and animated as a wily raccoon. But add family tradition, and in the first game the recovery of the Thievius Raccoonus becomes more than just the final goal of that game. It becomes an essential character-driven goal, and it underlines the game's theme.

Environment in this context is not only where the character grew up, but also where the character is *now*. One of the most interesting parts of *The Elder Scrolls: Blades* is the damaged town you can rebuild. In a sandbox game like *The Legend of Zelda: Breath of the Wild* you can choose to buy and furnish your own home. *Breath of the Wild* features many environments, and the player doesn't necessarily have to finish one before exploring another.

> Sandbox game: a game that allows players to freely explore an open world.

Or the sociological character can be unveiled by circumstance in the more structured levels of an action game like the *Super Monkey Ball* series. The characters may need to draw on different skills or knowledge dependent on their environment, but they cannot be dragged out the first time they are needed. Even the James Bond film franchise (not heavily into three-dimensional characters) reinvented Bond in *Casino Royale*'s prologue flashback where we see the new, rough-edged Bond earning his 007 status for the first time with a grueling battle in a men's lavatory. In 2021's *No Time to Die*, a major surprise in the iconic character's past is revealed.

A word of caution: it is far too easy to go overboard on a character's background. It is easy to confuse lists of details of a character's past with pertinent information that helps mold the character. Just as drama is selective of incident where life gives us every moment, so too a character's past should be filtered by necessity. If you know where you want your character to go, it is only necessary to provide a route, not a map of the world.

The Psychological Character

We build a relationship with the characters we write, just as we do with people we meet in our lives. If we want that relationship to grow stronger, we need to know the person as well as we can. The difference is that we theoretically know *everything* about a character we write, every treasure buried on the lost islands of their souls. But as we can spend too much time on their past, we can also spend too much time on what that past has made them, if we're not careful.

Instead, we look at the actions of the character, their attitudes, their opinions, their view of the world. And we do it without letting the character in on the fact that we know as much as we do. Characters who explain themselves are not only boring, but they are not true-to-life. We writers know a secret. Even the most self-centered of human beings knows less about themselves than they may think (case in point: Mavis Gray in the film *Young Adults*). If the characters are too self-aware—"I know I'm a self-made man, Pamela, and am rough around the edges. But gosh darn it, honey, underneath it all I have a warm heart and a pretty decent brain to boot."—it's a sure way to spot a hack writer.

Sometimes the most unaware of characters can be the most interesting. There is a sweet delight for an audience that is ahead of a character whose own actions or words condemn them. "But how did you know the killer had carved a star into the lieutenant's left palm?" "Well, I read about it in the newspaper account of his death." "That fact was never published! Take him away!"

The Coen brother's first film, *Blood Simple*, takes this delicious moment to a relentless, hilarious, and ghastly extreme: *none* of the characters knows who is doing what to whom. They all think they have a grasp on the situation, but they're all totally wrong. Only the audience knows what they're missing.

We reveal the character, particularly the psychological dimension, through action. We don't stop the story dead to do it, anymore than we should stop the action for exposition, a topic we'll get to in Chapter 9, "Bringing the Story to Life."

"By His works ye shall know Him." A well-written character doesn't have to explain themselves. They may not even know how. They are revealed by what they choose to do.

When is the best time to reveal the psychological dimension of a character? In a moment of crisis. It's easy to wear a mask when everything is going smoothly in drama as well as in life. But watch the mask get stripped away when the character is faced with a crisis.

In *The Art of Dramatic Writing* Lajos Egri created a chart of questions for writers to ask themselves when they attempt to create 3D characters. I have adapted that guide, reproduced here (Figure 3.2), for use in writing for games classes. Keep your answers concise, no more than a line or two. Do not write full biographies, but instead jot down ideas that will gradually come to shape a character. These do not have to be created for every character in a game, but they will help to flesh out main characters. Expect these lists to grow and morph as your understanding grows of who the characters are and where they fit in your world.

CHARACTER PROGRESSION

As Lajos Egri reminds us, "There is only one realm in which characters defy natural laws and remain the same—the realm of bad writing. And it is the fixed nature of the characters which makes the writing bad. If a character in a short story, novel, or play [or game!—ed.] occupies the same position at the end as the one he did at the beginning, that story, novel, or play is bad."

Minor characters may not need to change. They may only be present for a single moment in time, and not every one of the moments can or should be a satori for every single character. But major characters, whether PC or NPC, must, like sharks, keep swimming or they will die. This change takes two forms: growth and development. They are often thought to mean the same thing. They don't.

Growth

Character growth describes the changes that occur to the character as they progress through the story.

3D Character Guide

(From *The Art of Dramatic Writing* by Lajos Egri)

Physical (What we see)

1. Sex, age
2. Height and weight
3. Color of hair, eyes, skin
4. Posture
5. Appearance: good-looking, over- or underweight, clean, neat, pleasant, untidy. Shape of head, face, limbs.
6. Defects: deformities, handicaps, birthmarks. Diseases.
7. Heredity

Sociological (Background, present environment)

1. Class: lower, middle, upper
2. Occupation: type of work, hours of work, income, condition of work, union or nonunion, attitude toward organization, suitability for work.
3. Education: amount, kind of schools, grades, favorite subjects, poorest subjects, aptitudes
4. Home life: parents living, earning power, orphan, parents separated or divorced, parents' habits, parents' mental development, parents' vices, neglect, abuse. Character's marital status.
5. Religion, race, nationality
6. Place in community: leader among friends, clubs, sports
7. Political affiliations
8. Amusements, hobbies: books, newspapers, magazines

Psychological (How the character thinks and feels)

1. Sex life. Moral standards
2. Personal premise, ambition
3. Frustrations, chief disappointments
4. Temperament: choleric, easygoing, pessimistic, optimistic.
5. Attitude toward life: resigned, militant, defeatist
6. Complexes: obsessions, inhibitions, superstitions, phobias
7. Extrovert, introvert, ambivert
8. Abilities: languages, talents
9. Qualities: imagination, judgment, taste, poise
10. I.Q.

FIGURE 3.2 3D character guide.

In *Dark Side of the Moon*, written by Mark Barrett and me, the player-character, Jake Wright, moves from a shy, lackadaisical young man to a relentless seeker of the truth, then on to the determined protector of an entire alien race. The growth would have been artificial and unbelievable if we had not planted the seeds for this transition early in the story. The first clue that there is more to Jake than meets the eye is the fact that he has embarked on this trip to a distant moon in the first place, instead of shrugging it off, as he had most other things in his life. It is the love for his uncle that gives him the initial impetus that simple curiosity alone could not have. And in his search, he finds the strength to stand up against corporate slavers and the soulless creature who murdered his uncle.

Jake is the player-character, and as such, his growth brings us other issues to deal with that we will explore later in this chapter.

Beyond helping to portray a fully realized character, growth assists us in our storytelling. Growth implies forward momentum. Character growth helps to propel us through the story of the game. Matching moments of character growth to moments of conflict in the story is surprisingly easy once you know the character and have mapped out the conflicts they must face.

We need character growth. For that reason, we must know where, psychologically, the character is when the story begins. If the character begins triumphant, we'll have to tear them down. If they start in the gutter, it will be a lot easier to enjoy the road they take to the throne.

Development

Character development is, as William Archer says, "… not change, but rather unveiling, disclosure." He compares it to the developing of film. A drama ought to bring out character as the "photographer's chemicals 'bring out' the forms latent in the negative." He uses Ibsen's Nora in *A Doll's House* as a prime example: "… we cannot but feel that the poet has compressed into a week an evolution which, in fact, would have demanded many months." At the end of a play, Archer insists, "We should… know more of the protagonist's character than he himself, or his most intimate friend, could know at the beginning…."

Terry Mallory, Marlon Brando's character in *On the Waterfront* both grows and develops. As he moves through the film toward his ultimate bloody confrontation and triumph on the docks, his character grows from a man who has always played by the rules of the corrupt union to a man driven by the developing realization of where his life has brought him. "I coulda been a contenda, Charlie!" he cries in the famous taxicab scene.

So, in *Dark Side of the Moon*, if Jake Wright grows, how does he develop in the game? He learns along with the player a truth about his past, and the player at last sees what Jake himself may never know: the source of his strength and courage. It was in the genes all along.

THE PIVOTAL CHARACTER

The pivotal character is the character who sets the story in motion. It can be the protagonist Hamlet who begins his course of revenge after the visitation by his father's ghost, or "honest, honest" Iago, apparently dedicated to the interests of his lord, Othello, until his promotion is turned down. *The Mandalorian* is the title character, but not the pivotal character in the Disney+ TV series. It's Grogu, affectionately known as Baby Yoda, who launches the adventure.

Egri tells us, "Without a pivotal character, there is no play. The pivotal character is the one who creates conflict and makes the play move forward. The pivotal character knows what he wants. Without him the story flounders… in fact there is no story."

The protagonist can be the pivotal character. Sly Cooper is an example of a player-character protagonist who is also a pivotal character. In many games, the pivotal character is

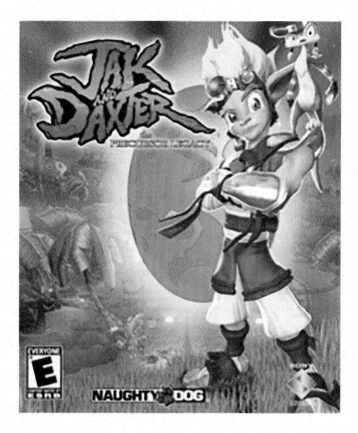

FIGURE 3.3   Jak is not the pivotal character. It's that rat on his shoulder.

the antagonist, who, with *Pinky and the Brain* determination, is bent on world domination in one form or another. Most RPGs begin with an evil force already at work. The player-character reacts to the resulting crisis.

If neither the hero nor the villain is the pivotal character, you still need one. In *Jak & Daxter: The Precursor Legacy*, it is the sidekick character, Daxter (see Figure 3.3), who sets the story in motion. His transformation into a rodent by falling into a vat of dark eco sends Jak, the player-character, on the search that is the spine of the game's action to help Daxter regain his original physical form. As for sidekicks, we'll have more to say about them in the next chapter.

There's a twist that games bring to the concept of a pivotal character. In games, it could be the character who sends the player on missions or quests who is a pivotal character in *gameplay*, and yet another character may be pivotal to the *story* of the game. Oh brave new world that has such people in it!

"A good pivotal character *must have something very vital at stake.*" Egri emphasizes. He "is necessarily aggressive, uncompromising, even ruthless." Here we can see why both villains and anti-heroes make particularly strong pivotal characters.

Is it necessary to have a pivotal character in every game that tells a story? It's hard to avoid it. And why should we? It works as well in games as it does in other storytelling media. It personalizes what's at stake by giving it a recognizable face. It creates the initial crisis that drives the action. And it's a good reason why at least one of our characters is in the game to begin with beyond a simple gameplay function. Just avoid killing off or otherwise endangering a PCs family member. It's a cheap cliché. And Brutus Forss is out there somewhere on those dark stairs snarling at you.

THE PLAYER-CHARACTER

First, a moment of silence for heroes everywhere. Villains are fun to write. Sidekicks can be wild and crazy. Even mentors with their air of mystery can seem deep and interesting. But what have heroes got going for them? Writers (and audiences) are forever complaining how hard it is to keep them as entertaining as all of the other characters in a story, yet they are arguably the most important character in that story.

Take heart, heroes. You are only bland and uninteresting if you're written that way. You are actually the most complex character in the story. The player will learn more about you than any other character, and through you, may even learn something about themselves.

It's a heavy responsibility. Don't get pompous or bombastic. Keep your goals simple and your dreams infinite. The player must embrace you and want to share your life in a bond that may seem like marriage, however fleeting. And remember this: the game can't exist without you.

Identified by several names such as player-character, PC, player-controlled character, or avatar, this is the most important character in the game. The PC is the direct link between player and game. How they interact with the game world reveals much about their nature and the nature of the game. These are design choices as much as writing choices, but the two must go hand-in-hand. For just as the player-character has a function in the game, they are also the *protagonist* in the game's story.

> Protagonist: the principal character in a work of fiction.

Whether human being, furry animal, alien creature, faceless general, or smiley yellow bag that eats dots and has reason to fear ghosts, the character controlled by the player is the most complicated and challenging character to write.

And we must answer several questions writers of other media don't face before the PC can be written.

IS THE PC MEANT ONLY TO BE CONTROLLED BY THE PLAYER, OR IS IT MEANT TO BE THE PLAYER?

In most games, no matter what type, the PC is distinct from the player, a puppet to be manipulated to carry out actions in the game world that the player desires. This is true whether the PC is original or borrowed from another medium. However, you will occasionally see one where the player becomes the lead character in the game. Most often, the point of view (POV) for these games is first person, where you do not see your character but are looking through your character's eyes. In a first-person shooter, as we'll see later, the POV may be first person, but you are still playing a character in the game fiction.

> POV: the Point of View of a player within a video game.

One good example where the player-character and you are one and the same is the original adventure game, *Colossal Cave*. This tradition continued with text adventures from Infocom, such as *Zork*. *The Stanley Parable* talks directly to you, the player. And Virtual Reality is so immersive because the camera is the player's POV and not peeking over your avatar's shoulder. Although most VR games still give you a character to play rather than yourself.

The theory behind allowing players to play themselves in a game is that it facilitates a greater level of immersion. Certainly in the earlier text adventures, it helped the reality of the worlds to preface player actions with "you" as in "You find yourself in a maze of twisty passages, all alike." This is actually second person, a POV rarely found in media outside of video games. And it continues in use in many games today, even when, in the bulk of these, you control a player-character with its own personality. We'll go into POV in greater detail later on. Despite the use of second-person text, most games today feature player-characters distinct from players. There are three reasons for this:

- Computer games are happiest as a visual medium, and text is usually suffered only as a necessity.

- We have a tradition of *empathizing* with characters in other visual media, such as film, television, and live drama.

- Games today are attempting to have more sophisticated storytelling. We see this even in the development of the *Myst* games where the first game was nothing more than the unraveling of a backstory, and the later sequels feature ongoing story in which the player-character becomes actively involved.

> Empathy: the ability of human beings to understand the feelings of others, even fictional characters, to such a degree that they adopt those feelings and experience them almost as if they were their own.

Because we can empathize with well-drawn fictional characters; because players recognize, if only unconsciously, the significance these made-up protagonists play in a story; and because with them it is far easier to involve a player in the fictional narrative, it is now accepted that a greater immersion is possible if the player-character is *not* a representation of the player. All the following questions here assume the player-character is only controlled by the player and is *not* meant to actually be the player.

IS THE PC ORIGINAL, OR BASED ON A CHARACTER FROM ANOTHER MEDIUM?

On the face of it, when we are adapting a character from another medium, it would appear that a lot of our work has already been done for us. And while it's true some of it has been done, new work is also created. (See Chapter 7, "Once Upon a Time," for related differences between original material and adaptations.)

Obviously, we don't have to create the character from scratch, either in its behavior or its physical appearance. In fact, to vary from these is to court disaster by ignoring audience expectations. But we must translate actions in response to game challenges that are true to the adapted characters in terms of both personality and abilities. If in an adaptation the player is faced with a challenge that requires the player-character to act in a way inconsistent with the way they are portrayed in the source film or book, or to possess a skill that character didn't have, it immediately feels false to the player.

So the gameplay must be constructed with that character in mind. This may seem obvious but consider this conundrum: many designers want as open-ended a world as possible, meaning the number of actions a player can choose for their character should feel as broad and as natural as possible. Games like *Duke Nukem* and *Grand Theft Auto* infamously allowed players to shoot or run over just about anything that moved. Imagine, though, Superman or Dr. Who wantonly killing innocent citizens. Even Dexter (Dexter Morgan, our favorite serial killer, not Jak's sidekick Daxter) has his scruples.

Another challenge is imitating how the adapted character expressed themselves in the original material. Being able to emulate the style of another author is an essential skill for writers adapting that author's work. As I write this book, I'm adapting a novel, updating the story, originally set in the 1930s, to the present day, incorporating the original structure, but adding entirely new elements as well. The one rule I can share with you, should you find yourself in this complicated position is to know the material you're adapting inside and out! Parenthetically, if you have any interest in writing for a television series, the same rule applies. Learn the series, know it, mirror it, then confidently, but quietly, show the producers you speak their language, the language of the characters and storylines. Anything less won't do.

Good screenplays are written lean and mean without a lot of extraneous detail. That's fine for a medium that can fill in additional detail thanks to directors, costumers, set designers, and so forth. It's not so good for adapters. Not only must you stay true to what you know from the previous work, you must often provide additional detail to flesh out the game. The television adaptors of recent versions of the Hardy Boys and Nancy Drew books have added science fiction and supernatural elements to their storylines, a decision that some might find suspiciously more like *Stranger Things* than the original books. But let's say you want to add an element that is not quite as radical.

For example, if you want to provide an exciting action sequence on motorcycles, but there is no moment in the original material showing the PC riding a motorcycle, you can include a single line of dialogue or a shot of the motorcycle in the PC's garage sometime *before* the sequence (and not right before!) to add that skill to those previously known. If you reveal that the PC can pilot a helicopter *right before* they are forced to escape from a high-rise rooftop by piloting a helicopter, it looks like the *deus ex machina* it is. It will annoy the player. Whereas, if you plant your mention of the skill a few levels before, the player will accept it. This brings up another general point about skills and immersion that we'll take a look at in a moment.

Is there one solution? No. In *The Riddle of Master Lu*, I was faced with writing, not a known fictional character from another medium, but a character based on a real person: Robert Ripley of Ripley's Believe It or Not! fame (Figure 3.4). My choice was not to exactly re-create the man. This could have proved difficult. His unconventional private life, particularly his relationships with numerous women, was some cause for scandal and not

FIGURE 3.4   The player-character in *The Riddle of Master Lu* was truly a "man of the world."

something the grantors of the license to his character would have appreciated in a family video game. I concentrated instead on his spirit, his boyish enthusiasm, his fascination for the bizarre, and his real-life love for adventure that reportedly made him one of the models for Indiana Jones. All were qualities that served the character well in the game.

Once the decision has been made to make the PC a character distinct from the player, the writer must next decide the relationship between the two.

HOW MUCH DOES THE PLAYER KNOW ABOUT THE CHARACTER?

Early on, the writer/designer must make choices about what we call the player-character's ego. This refers to the PC's innermost thoughts. Does the character share them with the player or withhold them? This question and the next cover this two-way street.

Even after deciding the player-character is not the player, the writer/designer must decide how fleshed out the character should be. As I said earlier, protagonists are usually not nearly as much fun to write as villains. Compare Leonardo di Caprio's character Amsterdam Vallon to Daniel Day Lewis's character Bill "Butcher" Cutting in *Gangs of New York*. The characters have many similarities: colorful names, distinct wardrobes, important missions, and more. Yet Cutting is written with such an obvious joy in his horrendous villainy, and Amsterdam, even with a revenge plot of Shakespearean dimensions, is written as more wishy-washy (at least in the central part of the film) than Hamlet.

Why? Because the filmmakers want us to identify with Amsterdam, not with Bill. And just like them, the game writer is faced with the possibility that providing a player-character who is too fully drawn, and who may have so many differences in speech, attitude, ethics, favorite sports, whatever, from players, they may have difficulty seeing themselves as the character.

Next, the writer/designer must grapple with keeping knowledge between player and player-character balanced. The audience knowing more about what is really happening than the protagonists in the film *Blood Simple* may be wildly entertaining. But a player knowing more than the character they control can harm the illusion of the player-character's life within the fiction of the world, just as the PC knowing more than the player can cause problems as well. This dilemma would seem to be unique to games, but luckily there are parallels in other media to help guide us.

First, here's a plea from the heart: never, ever, ever consider amnesia as a means to keep the knowledge shared by the player-character and the player consistent. It's such a cliché that to call it a cliché is a cliché. You may quote me. There are plenty of other ways to tackle sharing the knowledge between player and PC.

One way to keep player and player-character knowledge balanced is to make sure the surprises in the story they share are surprises to both of them. This is the technique of first-person mystery novels and the films that mimic them with voice-over narration, the detective in every scene, and so on. These rely heavily on Aristotle's unity of action. If you *must* cut away to a scene the PC is not observing, don't reveal a slew of information that puts the player ahead of the PC in the knowledge race. The only reason for doing this is if you are creating suspense, as when we discussed parallel cutting in Chapter 2, "The Story Remains the Same."

Better still, avoid it even in that case. Instead of seeing mysterious hands wiring a door with explosives, force a zoom in when the PC approaches the door to focus on the tripwire barely seen through the crack between door and jamb. Yes, you've taken control (very briefly) from the player, but it is a technique we are all familiar with from TV and film. If you intend to use this device, just set it up early on, maybe a couple of times, in situations where it isn't so critical, to prepare the player for its use later on.

In *Dark Side of the Moon*, there is a secret about the player-character Jake's parentage that we needed to withhold from the player until late in the game, even though we learned quite a bit about his past through flashbacks and other clues. To preserve the surprise, we made sure that Jake himself did not know the secret by establishing his bickering relationship with the woman he thought was his sister. It's psychologically valid. Players take it to be sibling rivalry, or even just two people who don't get along. Yet not only does it set up the surprise, it also prepares the player for the revelation that they aren't so closely related after all.

Another approach is to put the PC in locations with which the character would be unfamiliar. If the player-character is assigned to investigate the disappearance of all the inhabitants of a space station, create a character who may be the 23rd century's equivalent of Sherlock Holmes, but confine their actual experience to earthbound mysteries. Now you can simultaneously reveal new information to both player and PC in the mission briefings.

Puzzles can be concocted from simple operations. Give the player the challenge of adapting the PC's earthly skills to the new environment.

If you want to maintain the fictional reality of the character, try to avoid the mistake of setting up a PC who by their knowledge and training *should* know how to do something and then making it a puzzle how to do it. I'm reminded of the LucasArts game *The Dig*, with Steven Spielberg's name on the box, and written by Orson Scott Card, author of the wonderful science-fiction novel *Ender's Game*.

Here is the opening situation in *The Dig*: you are part of a crack team of experts headed for an asteroid on a collision course with earth. Your mission is to plant charges beneath the surface of the asteroid and knock it off its course. Upon arriving near the asteroid, the player discovers that the first puzzle is how to guide the explosives to the asteroid's surface in an abbreviated version of the earlier game *Lunar Lander*. The PC, supposedly a top expert, meticulously trained, has no idea how the controls work because you the player were never taught how to use them.

This first challenge in the game completely trashes the fiction of the game world because you, the supposedly well briefed, thoroughly prepped expert, must learn by trial and error how to place the charges just so the game can have a puzzle at that point.

HOW MUCH DOES THE CHARACTER KNOW ABOUT THE PLAYER?

This is not as odd a question as it might first sound. Basically, it is a reference to the "fourth wall."

We'll return to this concept in Chapter 8, "Respecting Story." For now, it's important to note that the PC can be written with various stages of awareness of the player. If you clicked once on one of your player-controlled minions in 1994's real-time strategy game *Warcraft: Orcs & Humans*, you would get an attentive response. Do it too many times in a row without issuing a command, and the character would complain, "Quit poking me!" Here the fourth wall is only broken if the player repeatedly tries an essentially useless action. Its function, in addition to eliciting a smile, is to help the player get back on track.

> The fourth wall: a theatrical term alluding to the fact that traditional theater sets have three walls: upstage and one on either side. The audience views the play through the invisible fourth wall while the actors perform as if it is as solid as the other three.

Save your game and Floyd, the irrepressible sidekick in *Planetfall*, will respond, "Oh boy! Are we gonna try something dangerous now?" Here we have a more overt wink at the player. Floyd is not only aware he's being manipulated by the player, he is even aware of the player's actions outside of the game world.

Breaking the fourth wall is nothing new. Even before there were actual characters in Greek drama, the chorus would address the audience directly. Shakespeare and his own interactive audience standing in the pit both loved the soliloquy. Actors were lucky if all the pit population did was yell back at them and not lob the dregs of their dinners as well. Characters in Eugene O'Neill's play, *Strange Interlude*, voiced their inner thoughts to the audience. The play was parodied by Groucho Marx's Captain Spaulding in *Animal Crackers* (Figure 3.5).

FIGURE 3.5   Groucho Marx takes on Eugene O'Neil in *Animal Crackers*.

> Pardon me while I have a strange interlude.... Here I am talking of parties. I came down here for a party. What happens? Nothing. Not even ice cream. The gods looked down and laughed. This would be a better world for children if the parents had to eat the spinach.

It's no accident the richest cracks in the fourth wall are usually found in comic games, often in response to a player attempting to do something the game engine can't handle such as in *Full Throttle*: "I ain't puttin' my lips on that!" It's far easier in comedy games to accept these asides directly aimed at the player than in more serious games where they can undermine immersion. Yet it was often a staple form of humor in early computer games and still crops up today. In *The Stanley Parable* the fourth wall isn't just giddily breached, it's demolished.

Our struggle creating immersion in a game and empathy in its characters is already difficult enough without additional pitfalls. Outside of a humorous world fiction, it is unnecessarily jarring. It's a gamer's choice, not a storyteller's choice, to remind the player they are playing a game and not inhabiting a realistic world, a world where the willing suspension of disbelief is crucial to believing in it. If a writer feels the need to do so in a normally inappropriate setting, they should have a damn good reason to break the rules and enough skill as a writer to pull it off. Otherwise, it can come across as sophomoric and amateurish.

IF THE PLAYER-CHARACTER NEEDS CERTAIN SKILLS, MUST THE PLAYER HAVE THEM, TOO?

Many types of gameplay can coexist inside a single game. Shooters feature adventure-game-like puzzles. Role-playing games can require the hand-eye coordination of a first-person sooter. Yet one type doesn't travel as well: simulations. Much of the fun and challenge of a simulation is in learning to operate the intricate controls of a jet plane, a tank, a train, a spaceship, or any number of exotic vehicles we may never get our hands on in real life. Simulations pride themselves on getting the controls, physics, and feel as accurate as possible. Nothing breaks a player's willing suspension of disbelief more than when they are required to be a master marksman but must work like crazy to hit the broad side of a barn.

A similar dilemma occurs when a role-playing game aimed at a large audience requires a certain level of FPS skill to be successful in combat. Lots of people who love RPGs don't have the reflexes to be skilled swordsmen or to "chain" a number of keystrokes triggering special combat moves.

IF THE PLAYER CAN CONTROL MORE THAN ONE CHARACTER, HOW DOES THIS AFFECT THE NPCs AND STORYTELLING?

Now we return to non-player-characters, or as they are commonly known, NPCs. They populate the world of a game. They shoulder a large portion of the burden of moving the story of the game forward, and they come in many shapes and sizes. They also provide a focus for the player's emotions. The only emotion a player may feel on the death of a player-character who can be resurrected at the beginning of a level or back at a bind point might be frustration. The deaths of thousands of soldiers in a strategy game might mean defeat, but the player will not be attending each individual funeral as commander-in-chief. However, the death of a companion the player-character has adventured with, come to know, even relied upon, can be a potent source of much deeper emotion. We'll explore this next as we look at major non-player-characters.

Major Characters

Presenting and developing the story of your game through static game-world elements like books, journals, scrolls, historic markers, or any other kind of voluminous text is all very well and good, but there are several drawbacks. For one, no matter what game designers may want you to believe nobody, *NOBODY* wants to stop their gameplay to read pages of prose, or chapters of books, or long paragraphs, or listen to lengthy speeches however beautifully performed.

For another, the more a player is reading or passively listening, the more they aren't playing, and players don't like this. Forcing players to wade through great swatches of text or dialogue only makes them impatient and irritable. Yes, Bioware and Bethesda, I'm glancing in your direction. So, designers are forced to allow them to skip through the text by continually pressing a designated key or button. Now, it's true that the players with the itchiest trigger fingers miss essential exposition that might have drawn them into the story, brought them greater insight into characters, or given them clues to help them solve puzzles. When that happens, designers must find other ways to provide this information.

One solution is of course to provide NPC characters. I only played 2002's *Asheron's Call 2* for a couple of months. Far less popular than Turbine's original *Asheron's Call 2*'s vision of the world of Dereth was a cold land of empty cities and vast landscapes populated only by creatures to be slaughtered. It made me think of a brightly colored amusement park where there were no barkers or ticket-takers or ride operators and all the attractions were closed.

Turbine did redeem itself with the delightfully populated *Lord of the Rings: Shadows of Angmar* MMO, released five years later. And think of 2017's *The Legend of Zelda: Breath of the Wild* with its huge cast of NPCs. The more NPCs you have, the more digestible pieces you can break your story into. We'll be talking a lot about all the ways in which NPCs populate game worlds and facilitate storytelling in the chapters that follow.

Finally, as stated previously, not only can major non-player-characters help move the plot along, but they also help to generate emotion. Floyd, the robot in *Planetfall*, whom I mentioned in the opening paragraph of this chapter, is a prime example. Steve Meretzky, Floyd's proud papa, has been designing games, in a variety of genres and for a variety of platforms, for over forty years.

> In games up to that point, there had been lots of very minor characters (the thief/troll/cyclops in *Zork I*, the wizard/demon/dragon/princess in *Zork II*, various suspects in *Deadline)*, but because there were so many, none of them was very fleshed out. I wanted to "put all my eggs in one basket" and have one really good character instead of many half-baked ones. After that, deciding that Floyd would die was just about my second major decision. Certainly well before I decided to give the game a humorous streak, perhaps even before I decided on the game's setting. I just thought that if I put all that effort into creating a character the player would care about, that character's death would be the best possible payoff; the most bang for the buck.
>
> While I assumed it would be an impactful scene, I certainly never imagined it would have the reception that it did, either right away, or decades later!

Minor Characters and Extras

Populating the game world with only major characters essential to story and gameplay works fine if the scene is the isolated house in the film *Ex Machina* or the islands of the adventure games *And Then There Were None* and *Myst*. And game designs cognizant of budget restraints often keep character animation to a minimum. Even major characters are often modeled upon identical skeletons.

We don't have to paint minor characters with the detail we lavish on major characters—we rarely have the time—but they can do more than simply add to the verisimilitude of the setting. No matter what the type of game, genre, or platform, if it is the city streets of the *Grand Theft Auto* series, the bustling towns of *The Elder Scrolls: Skyrim* or the island of *Fortnite*, minor characters often have crucial, if brief, roles to play in the game, and in the story. They can sell the player useful items, share gossip, reveal quests, even fight at the player's side, even without the more extensive biographies we create for major characters.

Here, we can shorthand the character creation process. Charles Dickens was a master at capturing his characters great or small in a single paragraph. Here is his description of a major character, that old reprobate, protagonist, *and* pivotal character Ebenezer Scrooge:

> Oh! But he was a tight-fisted hand at the grindstone, Scrooge! A squeezing, wrenching, grasping, scraping, clutching, covetous old sinner! Hard and sharp as flint, from which no steel had ever struck out generous fire; secret, and self-contained; and solitary as an oyster. The cold within him froze his old features, nipped his pointed nose, shriveled his cheek, stiffened his gait; made his eyes red, his thin lips blue; and spoke out shrewdly in his grating voice. A frosty rime was on his head, and on his eyebrows, and his wiry chin. He carried his own low temperature always about with him; he iced his office in the dog-days; and didn't thaw it one degree at Christmas.

It passes as a description of the physical dimension of Scrooge's character, but also ties the physical so tightly to the psychological we don't just see him, we *know* him, and we don't like him much either! Now meet a relatively minor character in Dickens' *Bleak House*. Inspector Bucket:

> Mr. Snagsby is dismayed to see, standing with an attentive face between himself and the lawyer at a little distance from the table, a person with a hat and a stick in his hand who was not there when he himself came in and has not since entered by the door or by either of the windows. There is a press in the room, but its hinges have not creaked, nor has a step been audible upon the floor. Yet this third person stands there with his attentive face, and his hat and his stick in his hands, and his hands behind him, a composed and quiet listener. He is a stoutly built, steady-looking, sharp-eyed man in black, of about middle-age. Except that he looks at Mr. Snagsby as if he were going to take his portrait, there is nothing remarkable about him at first sight but his ghostly manner of appearing.

Dickens gives Inspector Bucket the same size of an introduction to the reader, despite his much smaller role than Scrooge. Using Bucket's almost magical entrance, Dickens is able to describe his character through the eyes of another; not just his physical appearance, but his intelligence, his stealthiness, his own ability to study character, all traits that add up to a very special, and possibly dangerous man. Bucket is, by the way, one of the first detectives in English literature.

We may not have the luxury of longish descriptive paragraphs in games where we want to move the action along, but we can certainly sketch our characters equally vividly. The tools at our disposable include:

- **Recognizable character types or personalities.** Some examples include the garrulous salesman, the flirty serving wench, the hard-as-nails assassin, and so on. These serve as shorthand readable by the player. "Ah!" the player exclaims. "I know what's up with him!" These can easily become stereotypes if we're not careful, though. The trick is to give the character some attitude that will rescue them from the clutches of stereotype: the serving wench is actually very prim and proper. The assassin is dictating his memoirs into a cassette recorder as he focuses the sights of his rifle on his next victim.

- **Professions.** This attribute can quickly tell our player, who has played many other games, what role they are expected to play: the librarian, the policeman, the ticket clerk.

- **Physical mannerisms.** Does the character twitch? Do they shy away when the PC approaches? Do they reach for a weapon?

- **Turns of phrase or accents.** Do you trust a character who insists you can trust them? Probably not. Is someone with a Scots accent a native of the fishing village in the Hebrides where you find yourself? Probably.

- **Clothes.** Will that beggar in rags be a good sort to hit up for a loan? Will you want to take the young lovely sitting at the bar in bustier and garters home to mom? Probably not.

- **Distinct attitudes and opinions.** A few short phrases sprinkled throughout the conversation. "Yup, the mayor has a mule for sale, but count yer change. He's a politician." "I'd like ta hep ya out stranger, but I been watchin' the sky. It just ain't a good day fer it, no sireee, not a good day at all." "Well, as my dear mother used to say…" *Puzzle Quest*'s overly talkative dwarf, Khalkus, is a good example, despite the fact he speaks with a clichéd Scots accent.

Extras are NPCs who don't even get to talk, but we notice them even when they're not around. The lack of extras in a haunted house at midnight is easy to justify. The lack of extras on a city street at noon is more difficult. It's one of the reasons we have so many games set in artificially closed environments or with justifications, like a post-apocalyptic theme or an alternate universe: "Where the race who had built the towering structures of steel and concrete had gone remained a mystery…."

Maybe they all ended up in Robert Culp's palm in the *Outer Limits* episode "Demon with a Glass Hand." (Set incidentally in one closed environment: The Bradbury Building in downtown Los Angeles.)

It is refreshing to see populations going about their business peripheral to the forward thrust of a game. It allows for *Matrix*-like irony: "Little did they know the truth about what was going on!" It also creates opportunities for suspense, as we shall see in a moment (Figure 3.6).

I confess I'm using the term "extras" a bit loosely here. In other dramatic media such as TV and film, the word refers to non-speaking parts, also known as *background*. If extras are given a single line of dialogue or a special bit of "business," they immediately are elevated into bit players who are paid more and might even get an on-screen credit. In video games, extras are often given at least one line of dialogue along the lines of "I have no time to talk now," or "I'm late, I'm late! For a very important date!" to politely or impolitely brush off the player-controlled character within the fiction of the game, and to inform the player that they have nothing to offer that will further the story or enhance gameplay.

FIGURE 3.6 Robert Culp is the "Demon with a Glass Hand."

Try to avoid giving extras a particularly notable single line or two that they spout every time you click on them. Particularly try to avoid giving multiple characters the *same* single line as Skyrim's infamous, "I used to be an adventurer like you. Then I took an arrow in the knee." The line has become a meme, but at the expense of immersion in the game. Skip ahead to the topic Entrances and Exits in Chapter 6 to see easy ways of avoiding the needless repetition of NPC dialogue.

True non-speaking extras can be used to good account if they add something to a scene or level, especially in games where the player cannot talk to every NPC. For example, to their credit, numerous first-person shooters, particularly those in contemporary real-world settings, will include "civilians" as well as hostile targets, and often penalize players for killing non-hostiles, much the way such targets are added to police academy firing ranges. It can instill a sense of caution in the player if it's clear that blasting everything in sight will result in losing the level or losing crucial points necessary to achieving the highest score.

Another use for extras is as true background. Fiction-enhancing choke points, like locked gates or guards, can prevent players from entering a certain location, at least part of the time, and at least from that entry point. But it can be obvious to players if this is not done skillfully.

Here are a couple of ways that non-speaking, or at least non-interactive, extras can add drama to the game. First, we have a shooter level where the player is being pursued by enemies through sewers beneath the city streets. It's a nice, contained, easy-to-model setting for a level, but the designers also want to indicate the irony that just above the player-character's head the regular world goes on oblivious to the dire happenings below, and also create some additional suspense in the bargain. So, the game's artists devise a section of the sewer tunnel with rungs set in the concrete wall. The player climbs the rungs to a grate where simple passing shadows and the sound effects of shoes on pavement, car horns, and so forth tell us a city street lies just beyond. But the grate is immobile. As the shadows flick across the PC's face or the screen in first person, the player realizes that no escape lies that way. Perhaps the PC in this game has voice commands like "Yell." But the yell, when produced by the game in this locale, comes across as muffled. There's no way those above will hear it.

More adventurous designers with a little more time and art budget on their hands could enhance the scene by an omniscient cut of the street above. This could be a low angle, tilted down at the sewer grate. We see only passing feet: polished men's shoes, sneakers, high heels, and maybe unseen by pedestrians, the PC's fingers wiggling through the holes in the grate à la Harry Lime in *The Third Man*. This quick shot, lasting no more than two or three seconds, is the least obtrusive, and often most dramatic, use of cut scenes.

Players may be able to see into the courtyard of a high-level NPC's home, but are blocked from entry by the locked gate or guards. They could then take note of a brief cut scene of security precautions; glimpse a kidnapped prince; overhear a brief exchange of NPC dialogue between nameless minions indicating a breach in trust between enemy commanders; or so much more. How players are allowed to react to what they see is, of course, up to the designers. Is this the only information to be learned? Does it imply a possible quest? Will physical force provide entry, or is there another way into the apparently inaccessible area?

The other consideration is how the moment is treated: it could be simply a pantomime repeated endlessly for the PC who pauses while passing by. Or with some thought, it could be constructed as a variable experience with multiple permutations.

Separating true extras in a game world from the NPC quest givers or merchants we will cover soon can be a chore sometimes. One design decision distinguishes the notable NPCs in some way. A very gamey solution is to float explicit markers like question marks above the heads of important NPCs. This solution certainly serves its purpose, but it comes at the expense of immersion and the fiction of the world. Another solution is to establish that certain *types* of NPCs can be useful, such as town criers and bartenders.

Another decision is to just ignore the problem, letting players discover which NPCs may be of importance. This school of thought maintains the fiction of the world. People in real life rarely have signboards floating above their heads. The problem is that it can become an artificial obstacle to a player's progression through the game. It is frustrating to players if they don't have any idea who they should speak to, and it's frustrating for designers if they build intricate substories that players rarely stumble across.

In 2006 I began a project with my students at Indiana University to create a multiplayer world called *Londontown* set in Victorian London. One of the annoying design solutions I wanted to address was these visual markers over the heads of NPCs signaling that they had quests to offer the player. This had been a standard trope for years and it drove me crazy. Here we were trying to immerse players, convince them that their PC inhabited a real world however fantastic, but NPCs had big question marks over their heads to indicate they had information or quests to deliver. The unlucky NPCs who had nothing important to offer could be avoided.

I wanted to find a more unobtrusive way to indicate an NPC's importance without such an obvious device. A colleague of mine, Norbert Herber, was an expert on generative music, a term coined by Brian Eno, a member of Norbert's degree committee.

> Generative music: music that is created systemically to be changing and always different.

We worked together—Norbert did most of the work—to create a system of music, a musical score that played like a movie soundtrack that followed the PC and responded to whatever choices the player might make. One major benefit was that a change in the game's soundtrack would give the player an idea if an NPC was worth talking to. Although we started with the idea to replace those big, obtrusive question marks, the concept soon expanded to indicate an NPC's emotional state and their environment. Were they happy? Fearful? And finally, we wanted the music to dramatically underscore where the PC might find themselves: in a dark alley? How about a questionable pub? Or what if a beautiful garden triggered ominous music instead of the expected bird-like piccolos? This idea echoed what I called modular storytelling, a concept we'll examine in Chapter 14.

Unfortunately, *Londontown* never became a reality, but I never gave up on the idea. As recently as 2019 while teaching at Worcester Polytechnical Institute I tried to find some students who might be interested in a much smaller game called *Song Street* focusing on these ideas as their Major Qualifying Project, but without success.

Of course, most NPCs that are important to story or gameplay are usually easy to distinguish. They are the major characters.

AVOIDING STEREOTYPES

Square-jawed heroes, hook-nosed villains, gravity-defying big-breasted women, wisecracking cowardly sidekicks, wily thieves, scheming clerics, wise bearded magicians, old crone-like witches, stubborn dwarves, grass-chewing rustics... the list is a long one. Take a profession or race or physical trait and, thanks to centuries of character creation, almost immediately a personality trait pops into your mind. These are *stereotypes*.

> Stereotype: a generalized, non-contextual portrait of an individual that does not take into account unique qualities all individuals possess.

Relying on stereotypes in narrative fiction is not as bad as in real life where failing to see the real person behind a stereotype can harm a relationship, prevent communication with strangers, or be a life-threatening danger that threatens millions of people. There may be cases where deliberate stereotyping to make a point is advantageous in fiction. But for the most part, stereotypes work against the veracity of the narrative. Since they are so common, we don't notice them or take them for granted, particularly because they appear to be staples of most genre fiction, and stories in games are, without exception, genre fiction.

We might understand how many human beings can fall into the trap of stereotyping through parental indoctrination, peer influences, and a parochial view of the world they inhabit. But what excuses might a writer, someone hopefully a bit more worldly and openminded, have? There are several.

- **No realization they *are* stereotypes.**
  As writers, we owe it to ourselves to observe and absorb as much of the world as is humanly possible: its art, its people, its geography. There is simply no telling when a random bit of information or a serendipitous insight might be useful. I'm still waiting for my childhood hobby of paleontology to become useful in the construction and history of a video game. However, there are many writers who have grown up not consuming media outside of their favorite genres, or taking the time to explore, however briefly, what other people are doing and thinking in the world.

- **Stereotypes are easy to write.**
  All the work has been done for us. The characters almost write themselves. We know how the dark-eyed vixen is going to act before she can get a word out. Other similar characters have worked in other games or other media. We want to repeat their successes. Why not borrow their characters?

- **We may justify their inclusion by citing time constraints.**
  We've all been faced with impossible deadlines and seemingly unmeetable milestones. There is such a temptation to just pencil in stereotypical characters and tell ourselves that we can always go back and flesh them out later. But there never is a

later. Characters are due some proper respect and their fair share of our consideration. Take a break from the cool action scenes and take the time to give the characters their due.

- **Stereotypes are often confused with archetypes.**
  Archetypes are universally recognized. Some of our gamers may want the chance to interact with goddesses in leather. Others want to team up with dashing, romantic men who will sweep them off their feet or succumb to their charms. We want everyone, regardless of sexual orientation, to play our games, to live out their fantasies, sure, but unless we turn those fantasies into living, breathing individuals, the experience will be hollow.

- **Some types of games, like RPGs, rely on them for player-character creation.**
  Players want to play the stealthy rogue, the benevolent cleric, the elven archer. Since these characters are developed very mechanically *on purpose*, they should occupy a special exception to the rule. The largest problem with your game in this case may not lie with stereotyped characters at all, but the stereotypical setting you want them to live in. We'll look at setting in Chapter 8, "Respecting Story."

Falling back on stereotypes is certainly easier than finding new characters either in life or in our imaginations. Certainly some of the appeal in RPGs is allowing the players to assume roles more glamorous and enviable than we might play in life. But stereotypes diminish the overall gaming experience. They limit the sophistication of our stories. And as a result, limit our audience. Try to catch yourself doing it. Take the extra time and struggle to avoid stereotypes.

To recognize when you are writing stereotypes, ask yourself questions: Does the character look, talk, and act exactly as you'd expect them to? If there are no surprises, you've got a stereotype. Do the concept sketches the artists are making from your description look a lot like the concept sketches from other games? Stereotype.

To write characters the player will want to know and play with, we first must respect them. We must take the time to know them even better than they know themselves. We must give them a life within the game, not just a gameplay reason for being there. We need to choose how they will grow, and how much they will learn about themselves. If they are stereotypes, they are stillborn. There is no possibility for growth or development and players will quickly tire of them. Characters drive the story. If they are boring or derivative, the story will be the same.

CHAPTER 4

Character Roles

CHAPTER 3, "Respecting Characters," introduced some concepts from drama and film that can be useful to us as we write characters in games: the three dimensions of character; character progression through growth and development; and pivotal characters. We then moved to the *types* of characters we find in games such as PCs and NPCs; a breakdown of NPCs into major and minor characters and extras; and finished with stereotypes and how to avoid them.

Using that as a foundation, let's look at the various roles that characters play in our games. There's no better place to start than story.

THE CHARACTER'S ROLE IN STORY

Story structure can spring from many sources: a situation, a relationship, an ideal, a need to educate, whatever. But it is borne on the backs of the characters that inhabit that structure. We can be touched by the death of an "old yaller dog," but we are most often and easily touched by the plight of our fellow human beings. Our stories should be populated by characters who compel us to watch them or interact with them. These are characters that we want to spend time with, maybe because we like them (Floyd, the Robot from *Planetfall*, is a classic example), or perhaps because we are mesmerized by their evil as we are mesmerized by the swaying cobra (Hannibal Lector).

If we want players to care what happens to characters in our games, it isn't enough for them to be three-dimensional. Static characters don't freeze gameplay, but they confine it to the purely mechanical act of making the correct moves. If reviews of a game say it's just more of the same, no matter what genre, you can bet the mechanics of its genre have been copied, maybe a few new cool moves have been added, but not much attention has been paid to character or story or both. Even a great story is not enough. It must be inhabited and driven by great characters.

Much can be made of Lajos Egri and others decrying Aristotle's insistence that *action* (*muthos* in the original Greek) is the essential element in drama and not character (*êthos*). As William Archer points out, it is a waste of ink. Of course, action is the most important element. Stories can exist without character (many action films and action games do), but

DOI: 10.1201/9780429284991-7

none can exist without action. The word "drama" means doing, not simply saying or existing.

However, accepting action as the fundamental element in drama doesn't mean it is the noblest. When talking about action preordained by the gods, maybe it is. That is the model Aristotle was working from after all. As Egri says, "Fate was supposed to play the chief role in the drama. The gods

> Action: It can often be thought to be synonymous with activity as in an "action" film. Its more correct definition for our purposes is "something done, as opposed to something said."

spoke, and men lived or died in accordance with what they said." But William Archer puts the debate in perspective when he writes:

> The skeleton is, in a sense, the fundamental element in the human organism. It can exist, and, with a little assistance, retain its form, when stripped of muscle and blood and nerve: whereas a boneless man would be an amorphous heap, more helpless than a jellyfish. But do we therefore account the skeleton man's noblest part? Scarcely. It is by his blood and nerves that he lives, not by his bones; and it is because his bones are, comparatively speaking, dead matter that they continue to exist when the flesh has fallen away from them.
>
> *William Archer*, Play-Making: A Manual of Craftsmanship

Action equals bones. Character equals all that other messy stuff. As Archer concludes, "Action ought to exist for the sake of character: when the relation is reversed, the play may be an ingenious toy, but scarcely a vital work of art." We're going to discuss that tricky word "art" in Chapter 20, "The Responsible Writer."

Characters drive the story. They create the conflicts. The only emotion in a game experience without good characters is the emotion derived by the player from the gameplay: frustration, anger, exhilaration, triumph... the thrill of victory, the agony of defeat.... To create emotion through story, we must start with character.

In video games, the protagonist is almost invariably either the primary character controlled by a player or the player themself. I say "primary" character because players can alternate control of two or more characters in succession, as in the adventure game *The Beast Within: A Gabriel Knight Mystery* or, as previously mentioned, in the *Call of Duty: Modern Warfare* games. Players can also concurrently control to a greater or lesser extent an additional character such as a sidekick or companion in *The Elder Scrolls: Skyrim, James Bond 007: Bloodstone*, or *Star Wars: The Old Republic*; or parties of several characters in squad-based tactical games such as *Tom Clancy's Ghost Recon* games. Some games provide a single group of fellow adventurers either in the beginning or acquired throughout a game. Others allow players to recruit and drop party members at will. We'll get to the benefits and drawbacks of each approach shortly.

In war games or strategy games like *Company of Heroes: Tales of Valor* and *Civilization VI*, the player may control armies or populations of entire cities or kingdoms. In these games, discussed in more detail in Chapter 15, "Game Types," the player is very much the protagonist with little or no emotional attachment to their minions, treating each NPC or unit as nothing more than a piece on a game board. In the other examples, however, a very real emotional attachment is possible and can be exploited by the author.

POPULATING THE WORLD

The original *Myst* is set in an empty world where the player is the only living, breathing character in it. *Asheron's Call 2* was, as already noted, its massively multiplayer equivalent. In an effort to simplify massively multiplayer games and make them more accessible to a wider range of players, one supposes, *AC2* presented us with a world almost entirely empty of NPCs. There were sentient *mobs*, but they were cannon fodder, nothing more.

> Mob: short for *mobiles*, a term coined by Richard Bartle to describe creatures in a game moving in a controlled but unpredictable way.

Sequels to *Myst* have added characters, and as different designers tried their hands at *AC2*, more NPCs appeared. They were only thinly drawn functionaries, handing out quests, and when I stopped playing the game, they did little to dispel the feeling of an empty, essentially lifeless world. Yet obviously the designers of these games came to realize that populating these worlds even with minor characters gave them a much-needed touch of life.

In Chapter 2, "The Story Remains the Same," Aristotle helped us as writers of games by insisting on unities that, while heightening drama, allow us to create games with fewer characters and locations. Some games lend themselves to this far better than others. The designers of *Star Wars: The Old Republic* by necessity needed to populate their universe. Players would expect at least an approximation of the teeming streets and skyways of Coruscant and Nar Shaddaa. So, as many NPCs as possible were added as window dressing, as well as droids beeping past and taxis roaring overhead. All of these add tremendously to the atmosphere of the game.

NPCs can function as more than local color, too, as we'll explore in this chapter. To confine NPCs to the background is to miss opportunities of character development and storytelling, not to mention the gameplay functionality they can provide.

COMMENTARY AND GOSSIP

We rely on characters in stories to help us understand how we feel about the events that are unfolding. We can share a character's POV. In *Full Throttle*, the player-character is Ben, a Harley-riding, hard-hitting biker with a rough-and-tumble sense of humor. We see the game story through his eyes and can experience the world in character. One of the standard menu items is "kick." The same game without Ben would be an entirely different experience and not nearly as much fun.

In a more general way, NPC characters can provide commentary on a game's action, filling in gaps in the exposition, putting the action in perspective, and clarifying the murky parts. Players need not identify with minor character commentators to benefit from their knowledge. And we as writers can use such characters in all sorts of interesting ways.

The song "Master of the House" from the musical *Les Miserables* describes in melody and *recitative* the character of the landlord, Monsieur Thenardier:

> Mine host Thenardier
> He was there so they say,
> At the field of Waterloo
> Got there, it's true
> When the fight was all through
> But he knew just what to do
> Crawling through the mud
> So I've heard it said
> Picking through the pockets
> Of the English dead
> He made a tidy score
> From the spoils of war

"Master of the House" Lyrics © Herbert Kretzmer,
From Les Miserables

I mentioned in Chapter 3 how Dickens could sketch a character in a paragraph. Here's one in song. The point here is not to bemoan the lack of musical games with NPCs breaking into song, but to give them another purpose as commentators or gossips.

> Recitative: lyrics that are spoken rhythmically with slight melodic variations rather than sung.

We find NPC town criers, bards, and bartenders in many games to be handy sources of information. They are usually always passive, unfortunately, waiting without lives or thoughts of their own until a player clicks on them, and they can offer tidbits of general information on monthly events, locations of quest givers (see the last section in this chapter), hints of where good hunting may be found, and so on. Other minor characters and extras wander the streets as nothing more than local color, as we saw in the preceding section.

Yet, here is a perfect opportunity for illuminating characters. These NPCs shouldn't explain who they are, or what they're about, but who their neighbors are, particularly if their neighbors are major characters.

In any game, single-player or multiplayer, NPCs can gossip about other characters to avoid the amateur writer's characters who overexplain themselves. Even better, the character being gossiped about can have an entirely different story like Monsieur Thenardier, who also sings in "Master of the House."

> Welcome, M'sieur
> Sit yourself down
> And meet the best
> Innkeeper in town
> As for the rest
> All of 'em crooks

Rooking their guests
And cooking the books
Seldom do you see
Honest men like me
A gent of good intent
Who's content to be
Master of the house

"Master of the House" Lyrics © Herbert Kretzmer,
From Les Miserables

Let's go down this road even farther. There can be disagreement among the NPCs about another's character. In fact, depending upon to whom players are speaking, different players could have entirely different views of a character, something our games offer that other media do not. We can then mold player opinion by turning off negative comments about a certain character if the player speaks to three NPCs with positive gossip first. We then can replace the more accurate gossip with noncommittal comments to lead the player down any garden path we choose. Player impressions may get them into trouble with NPCs if players act on one set of information. Noncommittal comments might then switch to a third state: "That'll teach you to listen to the wrong kind of people! Too bad you didn't come to me first!"

One of the things all multiplayer games concentrate on is building the community of players. The more friends a player makes in the game, the more likely that player is to hang around. Having NPCs give conflicting information is a good way to do this. Comparing stories from different NPCs can seed player discussions as they try to determine who is telling the truth.

The first massively multiplayer game I worked on was *The Gryphon Tapestry*, a game that unfortunately didn't make it past a limited closed beta in 2000 before its financing dried up. I'll go into the relationship matrix we set up to track players' relationships with non-player-characters in Chapter 6, "Character Encounters," but I mention it here because it affected the gossip function that was built into all our NPCs. If a player's relationship wasn't very good with a particular NPC, that NPC would be less forthcoming with gossip and might even lie. In addition, different NPCs were inherently better sources of gossip than others and not just along stereotypical lines. The cook at the manor house in one village wanted to be thought of as someone "in the know," yet her gossip was usually quite worthless. There was one exception to this. She had helped raise the daughter of the house, who was devoted to her and often let her in on secrets the daughter might be expected to know (Figure 4.1).

We are respecting the characters enough in this example to make them more than functional props in the game. By giving them vivid personalities and lives of their own, we enrich the world they inhabit. By giving them their own opinions and prejudices, we can weave sophisticated relationships between them. The result is not just towns that are little more than theatrical sets with parrots squawking the same phrases over and over again in front of them, but communities of living, breathing characters who are far more interesting to interact with as they fulfill the functions the design requires.

FIGURE 4.1   Character sketches from *The Gryphon Tapestry* by artist Alex Bradley.

In *The Gryphon Tapestry*, commentary and gossip added to the community feeling of the game. In beta we would watch as players met at the local pub to share their day's adventures, only to discover that the view of a particular NPC might have been contrary to the impression another had. The debates about which one to believe and what the truth might be were extremely entertaining.

Mark Terrano, the Design Director and a Founder of Mountaintop Studios—is currently working on a new competitive team game. Here he shares a procedural approach to what he calls the propagation of conversation, a system giving NPCs the ability to react to the events around them.

> In a world where the NPC inhabitants notice and remark on changes, "leveling up" isn't just a marker on your character page, but everyone in town seems to notice something is different about you and mention it. Buying a new set of armor gets appreciative nods, cheers, and shouts of praise when you walk down the street. When your team returns from slaying the Evil Dragon, everyone in town seems to be already talking about it. In a big city, they might not have all the details, but they'd all heard of one being killed nearby. Merchants seem to remember you and greet you by name. Rumors (developer foreshadowing) would be talked about in town, whispered in alleys, and, of course, everyone still commented on the weather.
>
> Each snippet of conversation, when created, is given a scope (how far it travels/age), an impact (economic, social, health, and safety), and how someone would normally react hearing it (good, bad, indifferent, trivial). NPCs can then have general behaviors that are triggered by information that is moving around in the world, conversationally connected in a great social web.
>
> Players will feel a sense of integration into a larger whole, a real community—and intimately be part of your world as they see their own experiences woven into its history.

LIVING USEFUL LIVES

Many games treat minor characters as functionaries only, assigning them a single role to play and shoving a line or two of "character" dialogue—or simple dialect—into their mouths. This method does not respect the characters. It ignores all the ways that characters can support the story and the overall game experience. We'll explore some typical roles that characters play in games in a moment. But as we look at each one, remember these need not be in isolation. Any NPC can be a gossip. Any NPC can be part of a faction or team that has attitudes toward other factions in the game as in *X-COM: Enemy Unknown*. Any NPC can have needs, stated by soliciting players' aid in the form of errands or quests. *Undertale* tracks relationships between the PC and the enemies they face.

There is a definite benefit to both writers and their stories when we give NPCs multiple reasons for being in the game. It gives us multiple facets to their characters. Before we know it, even the lowliest minor character can blossom without much effort on our part. An NPC that functions as a merchant/gossip/quest giver instead of just a merchant *must* have more going for them before we even start to apply those functions.

The downside is that multiple roles can mean additional user interface (UI) issues. The last thing we want to do is create more well-rounded characters only to have them buried beneath menus. This is one reason (and there are many) why all the elements of the game experience—gameplay, story, character, graphic style, soundscape—should ideally be developed together. Too many times I've been stuck with the task of "adding" story to gameplay and an engine already in place, or adding gameplay to some linear story, sometimes original but most often derived from linear media.

My biggest challenge ever was a full-motion-video (FMV) game called *Temüjin* I worked on in 1996 where I was handed completed video scenes with real actors on real sets and tasked with altering the story until it made sense, which required changing characters already committed to film *and* adding gameplay. I wouldn't wish that on my worst enemy!

If we start with the idea of our minor characters being multifunctional, we have at least a fighting chance that the engine and its interfaces will not become bloated or complicated in the same way they might if we tried to add functionality to the characters after the work on engine and interfaces had already been done. Just as story grows out of characters and gameplay can emerge from story, story and character can emerge from gameplay. It is a two-way street, and we should be traveling both directions as we build our games.

Adding multiple functions to our characters does not, of course, guarantee that they will become three-dimensional all on their own, and if they're minor characters, there's no special reason they need to. But to literally bring the world of a game to life, it must be inhabited by creatures who truly live in it. Giving them multiple functions can be as useful a tool to the writer as it is to gameplay, but we still need to think about *who* each NPC is, not just what functions they can perform.

THE PLAYER-CHARACTER REVISITED (PROTAGONIST)

When talking about the character's role in the story, I usually identified the protagonist as either the player-controlled character or the player themselves. This is true of all games whether there is a single player-character or multiple characters the player can control. And here is one way in which games depart from other media. In drama, the protagonist is, according to Egri, always the pivotal character. This definition is not that clear-cut today. As I pointed out in Chapter 3, Iago is not the protagonist of *Othello*, even though he is the pivotal character.

Confining the protagonist to the player-character is not much of a limitation because look at what we gain in the process. We give the audience, our player, active involvement in the progress of the story. Because of that, the player-character should be Egri's "main character… the person at the center of the action." But this does bring up an interesting dilemma, a variation of which writers face every week in series television: character death.

Death of a Player-Character

> I'm gonna show you and everybody else that Willy Loman did not die in vain. He had a good dream. It's the only dream you can have—to come out number-one man. He fought it out here, and this is where I'm gonna win it for him.

> Arthur Miller, Death of a Salesman

I took over as head writer of the daytime soap opera *Edge of Night* in 1983. (The "The" was dropped as the first word of the title during my tenure, I believe, to toughen it up. "Edge" is a stronger word without the article.). Almost immediately I was informed by the producers that the actress playing one of the show's longest-running characters did not want to renew her contract. She wanted to try her luck in Hollywood. Television, including daytime, is often a good rung of the career ladder for actors to climb on their way to movies.

The character, Nicole, had already been recast several times throughout her long life on the show. We discussed recasting yet again, but those who had been with the show longer than I pointed out that the usefulness of the character may have run its course. The once-popular character of Miles had not had much to do since marrying her, and if she were out of the picture, it would liberate him. So, we decided to kill her.

This was possible because soap operas have huge casts of characters, all of them protagonists to a point, although not always pivotal. Each character's life depended most on popularity with viewers, a fact an actor will quite rightly use to their advantage in contract negotiations when their popularity is high and mention less if their character has fallen from grace with the audience. As it was, there was quite an uproar when we offed Nicole in a wonderfully nasty way. I received a letter from one stricken fan who had named her daughter after Nicole. Tear stains had smeared the ink.

Producers of serial stories routinely hire actors to play characters that apparently will live forever. At least until their contract demands grow higher than their perceived value to the show. Then they become all too mortal. It's a tricky decision. Shows remain on the air because of their characters more than their stories.

In the fourth season of *Star Trek: Next Generation*, we were faced with the Wesley Crusher problem. Here was the only young character in the series, well-acted by Will Wheaton. Wesley had been allowed to develop into a sort of Superboy. It was the writers' fault, no one else, and we had to deal with it. We finally decided to send him off to Starfleet Academy (the place, not the game!) instead of killing him, to give us the option of bringing him back at some point, particularly since his mother was still aboard the Enterprise.

We could have killed Wesley. It would have been much harder to kill one of *Charlie's Angels* or any member of the casts of so many shows. Yet in computer games, we kill the player-character over and over again. Why? And why would anyone want to play a character so inept at survival?

It's no coincidence that so many games deal in death, just as it is no coincidence that many popular TV shows are set in arenas like crime and law and medicine where life and death struggles can be played out week after week.

> Arena: A physical location or background where a story takes place such as a circus, tennis or an *Afterparty*.

Game developers recognize, as do producers of television and motion pictures and publishers of books, that the stakes don't get much higher in a story than when there is a life in the balance.

But a challenge unique to our medium of expression is not just the potential of the player-character dying, but of that character dying more times than Christopher Lee got staked by Peter Cushing in all those Hammer Dracula movies combined. It is a primary game mechanic in many shooter and squad-based games to kill the player-character. There are two major reasons often cited for this: (1) It provides a penalty when the player fails, and (2) as in other media, it hopefully raises the stakes.

Can we kill off the player-character permanently? We can in an arcade game where players must start from scratch each time they step up to the machine. To do so is to erase the investment the player has made in the PC—all that advancement in levels, skills, and quarters. There is occasionally a minority movement in virtual worlds in favor of permanent death. Unlike single-player games, the investment of time and effort makes it an extreme penalty and I strongly recommend avoiding it. Though to make certain that players don't heedlessly ignore their safety and to create some tension and a sense of consequences and loss, massive persistent worlds do impose less drastic penalties such as damage to the player's equipment, loss of items, or some kind of progress in the game.

Player-characters are routinely resurrected. In multiplayer games players can resurrect their companions who have "died." They pop right back up, raring to fight again. There's usually no indication in the game or its universe of how exactly this can happen. Obi-Wan Kenobi didn't jump to his feet after he died. His robe lay there empty, and only his otherworldly presence remained to guide Luke to use the force. Unless the context is very carefully established, these solutions can only become obvious placebos for the player to swallow as the character, in which they've invested three years of their life, sails out to sea like the fiery funeral ship of the Vikings. I've explored a generational game structure, but it is compelling to me for different reasons than softening the blow of player-character death. It can present a continuing history of characters, playable or not.

We've seen how TV series and movies in particular wrestle with this problem. What do they do? They kill off with reckless regularity characters the immortal protagonist supposedly cares about.

Brutus Forss' anger at the beginning of Chapter 3 is righteous. Writers of games have fastened on "kill an NPC the player-character cares about" because we are apparently stuck between a rock and a hard place. Even in games that are *not* part of a series, we don't want to kill our player-character, as we discussed in Chapter 2. Yet we want the player to care about the character that is their avatar in the game. In a game where there is no death, it's not a problem. But if there are villainous opponents, and the opponents *can* die, it can upset the balance and negate the "raised stakes" of a life and death struggle.

There is no universal solution to this dilemma, and I doubt we'll find one—any more than the Holy Grail will turn up or a chemical process will be found to alter the atomic structure of Pb into Au. The important point is whatever solution we come up with must be in context. In *Assassin's Creed: Origins* and *Assassin's Creed: Odyssey* the player-character "desynchronizes" instead of dying because, as the games' lore explains, they didn't die right then in the character's historical timeline. A science fiction solution won't work in a real-world setting. A comedic solution would jar the player in a realistic combat simulation.

Some possible ways to avoid player-character death are listed in Table 4.1.

An easy solution not listed above is to allow the player to control several characters throughout the story of a game. In *Call of Duty: Modern Warfare 2*, the player-character, Joseph Allen, dies early on. In *Dark Souls*, one of the most difficult video games ever developed, the player-character is a cursed undead, who resurrects after death, but not without consequences.

And yes, I can think of a very prominent and controversial example of a major game released in 2020 where the player-character died. That decision and other controversies still surround the game. The questions raised about video games and the diversity of those who play them guarantee we'll be discussing them for quite a while to come.

Do we really need an alternative to player-character death? If we want to tone down the violence, it's better to start with theme, rather than player-character death, and create a game where other stakes are made as high as life and death. This is not to say you cannot have a story with relatively little on-screen violence and still kill off your protagonist. Dickens' *A Tale of Two Cities* keeps violence and gore "off-screen," and even manages to achieve an upbeat ending while Sidney Carton is being trundled off to the guillotine:

> It is a far, far better thing I do, than I have ever done; it is a far, far better rest that
> I go to, than I have ever known.

Here is a character at peace and triumphant—not a tragic character even at the moment of his death.

But game writers have a couple of things going for them that other media don't have. Death of the player-character is a game mechanic. It is one of those elements of gameplay that is accepted by players, just as power pills and being able to carry an entire armory of weapons in the PC's pockets are accepted. If the context is preserved (the weapons are appropriate to the arena), it need not break immersion any more than the fact the player is holding a controller in their hands instead of a samurai sword.

In *Stars Wars: The Old Republic*, still a force with multiple updates since its release in 2008, you, the player, simply get a choice: a medical probe can be dispatched to resurrect you (with longer wait times, the more times your avatar bit the dust). Or you could simply get revived at the nearest med center. These are helpful solutions missing from films. Obi-Wan Kenobi sort of returns, but his lightsaber swinging days are definitely over.

TABLE 4.1   Alternatives to Player-Character Death

Genre	Method	Notes
Sci-Fi	Clone/desyncronize the PC	The new PC will have a shared memory of the game up until now. (Thanks, Carl Jung!)
Sci-Fi	Artificial human/android	Brain circuits undamaged. The PC can be repaired.
Sci-Fi/Fantasy	Regenerating tissue	Whether through futuristic medicine or the nature of the nonhuman the player manipulates. (Dwarves are supposed to be good at this.)
Sci-Fi	Auto-teleportation	The PC automatically snapped back to command post when health reaches a critical level.
Sci-Fi	Time travel	The time travel device has a timer that resets automatically to moments before the fatal confrontation. This, of course, *is* a death, but without death's sting.
Modern combat	Unconsciousness	Evac'ed to field hospital.
Modern combat	Squad-based	NPC squad member drags PC to safety.
Police action	Unconsciousness	GPS locates PC, and PC is rescued by paramedics.
Police action	Squad-based	Different arena, same method as modern combat example above.
Any	Capture	PC must escape. Different prison/detention method/guards each level.
Any	Simulator	As real as the others, but PC is actually in a simulator with an instructor overseeing.
Any	Plot-based	PC has something villains need. This is used over and over in film and TV to justify why bad guys don't kill heroes when they get the drop on them.
Any	Plot-based	Chief villain is related to/in love with PC. This can be happily combined with death of an NPC close to hero for a double dose of emotion!
Horror	Undeath	Hero is an attractive zombie who can be incapacitated for a time, but eventually lurches back to his feet.
Any	*The Game*	Film with Michael Douglas and Sean Penn. PC appears to die and be resurrected, but it's all a hoax.
Fantasy	*Highlander*	Player *is* immortal except for one thing: (decapitation/stake through the heart). Just keep those swords and stakes away from the villains till the final level!

Companion death is also not an issue in *Star Wars: The Old Republic*, since you can resurrect them yourself, so there is no chance for a *Planetfall* emotional moment of loss.

And the other thing we have going for us as gamers is that *because* player-character death is a game mechanic, we can still find ways to empathize with the player-character even if they don't die. And herein lies a clue why we need not concentrate on creating all our emotion in the game only through an NPC. Players care about their PCs even before they boot the game simply because they *are* the player-characters.

We can give them any number of gut-wrenching and heart-tugging dramatic moments without killing the PC off. And we don't need to create a single NPC the player-character (or player!) cares about to do it. As human beings, we can care about all sorts of issues, values, and ideas. Let's take just one: personal freedoms such as speech, liberty, equality, worship, privacy, and so many others. As in *Oddworld*, you can create forces depriving the player-character of any of these freedoms or any combination thereof, and you're going to rouse empathy in that character, even if life is not one of the freedoms you deny them. From totalitarian military states to mad wizards, any number of villains can be out to get the player-character through many different means. Any of them could strike to the heart of what makes us humans. That alone makes it possible and worthwhile to find ways to avoid player-character death, so that we can break the monotony of story that it by itself imposes.

VILLAINS (ANTAGONISTS)

Villains can do all sorts of nasty things to player-characters. That's why we love them and hate them all at the same time. Villains also seem to have more fun than heroes, which is why we writers love to write them!

> Antagonist: the opponent or adversary of the protagonist.

I try not to state out-and-out rules in this book, but here's one where I can't help myself: the *antagonist* must be every bit as intelligent and powerful as the protagonist. A weak adversary creates a weak hero. Never ever *ever* make the mistake of giving the villain an *obvious* weakness in the same way we lame a tragic hero with an Achilles heel.

This rule is so important that Egri repeats it twice on the same page:

> The antagonist in any play is necessarily as strong and, in time, as ruthless as the pivotal character. A fight is interesting only if the fighters are evenly matched.

And:

> Let me now repeat it again: the antagonist must be as strong as the protagonist. The wills of conflicting personalities must clash.

We will talk about reversals and surprise in Chapter 9, "Bringing the Story to Life." But it is the strong antagonist who forces such surprises and reversals to occur, those heart-stopping moments that can make us cry out loud at the screen.

It would seem as if we have a dilemma here. How do we design the game so that the player can win, if the player's NPC opponent is their equal? Let's look at sports. No matter how evenly matched opponents may be, one team always wins in the end. There may be a tie in a soccer match, but by the end of the season the tie will be broken or rendered meaningless. The most exciting athletic competitions are those where the outcome is unknown up until the final seconds, and so should it be in our games.

How does the player manage to advance if the force they apply is met with an equal and opposite force? There are a number of ways to do so.

- Saddle the antagonist with minions who *are* minions because they are not as powerful as he is. Take a look at a Jackie Chan film to see how very strict the hierarchy of bad guys is, as they line up like suicidal ducks to be flying-kicked out of their feathers. We've adopted this hierarchy literally in games.

- Provide the player-character with increasingly better weapons (not necessarily the kind that kills—information can be a powerful weapon in any game) to barely overcome the forces the villain throws at them.

- Create a *McGuffin* that both player and villain must constantly be striving and sacrificing for to obtain. The McGuffin can be as powerful or as inconsequential as those in the films of the man who invented the term:

- Give the villain a tragic flaw, but don't make it obvious, or don't make how to take advantage of it obvious. Just make sure that it's set up early enough, so it won't feel like a *deus ex machina* dropped on the player like an anvil from our old friends the Greek gods.

- Subject both the player-character and the villain to the ironies of fate. This is tricky to do in the final confrontation, but to both help and hinder the player early on it can introduce an apparent random element that heightens suspense.

McGuffin: a plot-enabling device. A term coined by master director Alfred Hitchcock to describe the reason all the intrigue and running around is happening in his movies. It is ultimately unimportant. The chase is all. Examples include the microfilm in the sculpture in *North by Northwest* (who remembers that?); Mister Memory's memorized international treaty in *The Thirty-nine Steps* (The title is actually a reference to the parts of the treaty, but who remembers that?); the wine bottle stuffed with uranium salts in *Notorious,* and many others.

In the previous section on player-character death, I mentioned the very interesting dramatic situation where the protagonist and antagonist actually have an emotional bond. The ultimate version of this would be identical twins, or the many alternate Jet Li's in the film *The One*. An interesting variation on allowing one equal to defeat another in that film was that as Yulaw the antagonist (and pivotal character) killed his counterparts in other alternate universes, he gained their strength. He killed the first few easily because they were unaware they were being stalked. But by killing them off, he also increased the strength of the protagonist, Gabe.

It stands to reason that to create an antagonist worthy of our protagonist, we need to develop them as fully as our central character with their physical character, sociological character, and psychological character all in play. This can be difficult because while the player-character is always on-screen, the antagonist may not be on-screen very much until the end. This is especially true in boss mob story structures where we may see the villain being villainous only in cut scenes removed from the action. This is a device borrowed from genre fiction in other media.

* * *

CUT TO:
INT. BLOFELD'S LAIR-DAY
Ernst Stavro Blofeld, face in shadow, strokes his ice-eyed white Persian cat.
BLOFELD
Find Bond and kill him!

* * *

We'll discuss this point-of-view, called the *omniscient POV*, more in Chapter 6. A better way to reveal the villain's character is through their moves and countermoves as play progresses. You don't need to know anything about a chess opponent you meet on the Internet. You'll learn all you need to know soon enough by their game.

And in video games, we can introduce the antagonist to the player by the nature of the McGuffin the antagonist relentlessly pursues; those they recruit to serve them; how they treat civilians; the wording of a ransom note; the architecture of their lair. As many dimensions as you need to fill out a character can be found by how they touch all aspects of the world around them. There is no need to rely on that dossier from Central Exposition. In fact, it's far more fun if a couple of those reversals we want to introduce are surprises because the mission briefing was flat-out wrong.

An even trickier situation arises in a mystery. How do we develop the character of the villain if we don't know who they are? We call upon all those gossipy NPCs. How does Christopher McQuarrie, the writer of *The Usual Suspects*, pull it off? Through witness accounts, rumors, and a list of crimes, we learn something of the psychological, sociological, and even physical dimensions of Keyser Soze's character. We know him by his works. And after all, realizing the rabbit McQuarrie has waiting in the hat, how else *could* he have built a complete portrait of his chilling, amoral, criminal mastermind?

We need to respect all our NPCs, our villains more so than most. They must appear to be every bit as capable of winning the game as the player. Have I said that enough? Think the player-character might need even more help? Let's talk about another character who can help tip the scales in their favor.

MENTORS

Joseph Campbell speaks of the mentor characters found in the mythology of many cultures in *The Hero with a Thousand Faces*:

> For those who have not refused the call [to adventure], the first encounter of the hero-journey is with a protective figure (often a little old crone or old man) who provides the adventurer with amulets against the dragon forces he is about to pass.

Where would Cinderella be without her fairy godmother? Still at home scrubbing the floors. Where would Luke be without Obi-Wan Kenobi? (Figure 4.2) Still on Tatooine raising crops. "Protective and dangerous, motherly and fatherly at the same time," writes Campbell

> this supernatural principle of guardianship and direction unites in itself all the ambiguities of the unconscious—thus signifying the support of our conscious personality by that other, larger system, but also the inscrutability of the guide that we are following, to the peril of all our rational ends.

The mentor is a far more complex figure than popular entertainment usually dishes out. The mentor can be supernatural, or have unusual powers, but it is not a requirement. For our purposes in games, it is a useful character for a number of reasons. Mentors can provide the following information:

FIGURE 4.2   A classic mentor character: Alec Guinness as Obi-Wan Kenobi.

- **Backstory**: What has happened in the world of the game before actual gameplay begins. It can be both generalized and personalized for the protagonist.

- **Story hints**: Like setting up a new level; pointing to where the next step in the story might be located; potentially helping characters; and spotting dangers to avoid.

- **Gameplay hints**: On everything from special powers the player can draw upon to how to use your Switch, an interesting breaking of the fourth wall to help ease the player back behind it once again.

- **Memory Jogger**: Remind the player what they have completed and what their immediate and long-term goals should be.

- **Training**: Teaching new abilities or revealing arcane knowledge.

- **Quests**: In the form of jobs the player must accomplish.

- **Support for the player's efforts**: "Good work! Only four more wizards to defeat!"

- **Rewards**: Interim rewards for players, as well as possibly bestowing the final crown.

Unlike other characters who may not know the protagonist, the mentor is often already a part of the player-character's life, if even in a minor role. They either expand their mentor role to face the new crisis or move into it from a seemingly innocuous former role. A wandering beggar could turn out to be a disgraced swordsman capable of training the player-character in new skills. In either case, the mentor knows the protagonist and has some idea of what the player-character is capable of and what their background may be. Or the mentor can use supernatural means to bone up on the protagonist via devices such as a crystal ball or those fat dossiers that litter mentor's desks that can only have been provided by Central Exposition.

Story and puzzle hint systems have grown in sophistication over the years—from printed documents found in the box that contained the game to in-game Help menus to objects within the game world, such as books and computers player-characters can access to NPC characters ready to impart wisdom as needed. In my mind, it is the NPCs who provide the most help and who damage the player's immersion the least. Story or puzzle hints can be built, depending upon how difficult the designer wants the game to be, in many layers of dialogue from the NPC. I would avoid treating the acquisition of these hints as a problem for players to solve the way we used gossip earlier. Hints are an often necessary intrusion. It's best to get them over as quickly and as seamlessly as possible, and not frustrate players and remind them they're playing a game. That is the opposite of what we're trying to achieve.

Gameplay hints, as stated in the list, are problematic at best as far as immersion goes. But since it appears that few gamers bother to read the documentation, we provide them either outside the game or online, an in-game solution must be found. One of the benefits that console games have over games on a personal computer is that the controls are dedicated for the most part to gaming and are very standardized across many games on a platform. If you play one game on an Xbox, you can get the hang of many more quite quickly, even a PlayStation or a Switch. So, in this case, designers can at least keep world-breaking contact with the players to a minimum.

Mentors are excellent memory joggers. Obi-Wan kept Luke (and the audience) from getting too sidetracked and forgetting what his ultimate goal was. In video games, mentors work even better. We may play games over a period of days, even months (hello *Breath of the Wild*!), and not steadily. It may be fairly easy to remember exposition over the two-hour running time of a movie, but next to impossible to call it instantly to mind if we haven't picked up that Switch in a couple of weeks.

I know this is a painful reality for some designers to face. We may want our games to be so compelling that players *can't* put them down for more than meals or a nap. But the reality is they will. It's far better to worry about keeping them compelled when they *are* playing. If the game is fun, they'll come back like the prodigal son in Luke 15.11-32, forgetful perhaps, but ready to re-engage.

Mentors save us an interface, and we can keep the text in the game to a minimum. Dialogue by necessity should be terser than the written word even if both are presented to the player as text. Mentors can respond in character, say, with irritation when a player-character returns to them before the completion of a mission or quest, and, in character, remind them of what they've accomplished or still must do. Mentors have a stake in the story and in the PC, and this can add drama where in a journal there may be only lists.

Mentors can cross dress as trainers. These are NPCs who teach new abilities to the player-character—or player-characters—in a virtual world. Yoda, Luke's second mentor, was also his trainer. Obi-Wan sent Luke to him to learn the more practical aspects of the force, like levitation and swinging that light saber. We can use the mentor as the sole trainer, or save only the special skills for him, if there are other trainers in the game. We'll take a deeper look at trainers in a moment.

Mentors can function as quest givers, although they should probably be confined to the main quest of the story. It's a good thing to give an NPC multiple functions, but bad to burden a single NPC with too many. To keep the through line of the game clear, don't rely too heavily on the mentor for minor assignments and side trips.

Players need constant pats on the back and reassurance, just as they do in noncomputer games and sports. Good coaches often become surrogate parents for players. The only equivalent we have in games is the game master in multiplayer worlds. *Horizons: Empire of Istaria* was a promising MMO released in 2003 (and still around after passing through the hands of several owners). In the game, players were able to unlock new content as part of any ongoing story line. The "World Master" for the server I played on showed up now and then to offer encouragement or dire threats. But in most multiplayer games and all single-player games, we don't have coaches or game masters. Mentors are the perfect choice to fill that role, providing carrots of praise and the occasional stick of warning to help keep players engaged.

Finally, of course, the mentor can reward players with new skills, items, cash, and any number of things to improve their chances in the game. Interim rewards are tremendously important to players. Of course, they can be handled by system messages like "Congratulations! You've just found a Horn of Creature Calling that will summon creatures to fight at your side!" But how much more immersive and dramatic it is to have our mentor reach up and pull that same horn from the shelf where we've seen it sitting from the beginning. "Here is a horn my father gave me. He was a simple shepherd who once saved a great magician's flock from wolves...."

And if the mentor should survive (no reason not to kill them off as a nice reversal near the end), and be present at the end of a story, then if they don't bestow the ultimate reward to the player, you can expect to find them winking nearby, or shuffling off into the distance with a slight wave of the hand, their mission accomplished.

We will talk about conflict in Chapter 5, "Character Traits." Here, I want to mention that conflict between hero and mentor can be a good thing. The best part of the film *Remo Williams: The Adventure Begins* is the relationship between Remo and his mentor played by Joel Grey. They can barely tolerate each other, and each gives as good as he gets. This tension provides opportunities for great conflict and humor, particularly in the first act of the movie when Remo is learning his new trade.

SIDEKICKS

Cortana in *Halo* is a shipboard AI harkening back to Arthur from *Journeyman Project II: Buried in Time*, a helpful but at times annoying AI personality on a chip you install in your time suit. Sidekicks don't have to be other physical beings, but most of the time they are. And whereas mentors are in many ways greater than their protégés (at least until the climactic action when all they can do is stand by and cheer, "Use the force, Luke!"), sidekicks are a step down the food chain.

Sidekicks provide comic relief, the occasional helping hand, sometimes useful exposition, or are just a foil to bounce ideas off. Sometimes they're just there to make the hero look good. Robin isn't all that wonderful if all he does is ask questions so Batman can patiently explain what his Boy Wonder brain is unable to grasp.

But sidekicks can be much more. Daxter, as we've seen, is a pivotal character, as well as a sidekick. Even Gabby Hayes (Figure 4.3) could occasionally rescue Roy Rogers from calamity.

FIGURE 4.3   Roy Rogers and his classic sidekick, Gabby Hayes.

The sidekick is the perfect NPC to generate emotion, if it is he who is in danger. Yorda in *Ico* is a good example of this. She is pretty much helpless without Ico's aid. He can't even communicate with her. Yet with charming animations, as when they run hand-in-hand, or through clever game mechanics such as making the safe places in the castle benches where she lays her head on Ico's shoulder when they rest, a tender relationship is built. And the final scene, much debated, provides, at least to me, a fitting conclusion.

We can go so far as to kill off sidekicks as in *Planetfall*, but in many games we run the risk of alienating the player. The death of a sidekick can make it look like the player has failed. Jak may fail to change Daxter back at the end *of Jak & Daxter: The Precursor Legacy*, but Jak has succeeded in a far greater purpose, and Daxter doesn't die, he is just still a rodent.

Another useful role for sidekicks is as a surprise villain. Okay, not much of a surprise in *Othello* when Iago turns, and it happens right in the beginning. A much more famous example is one of Agatha Christie's first novels. Her audience was raised, as she was, on stories where detectives like Sherlock Holmes patiently pointed out clues to their befuddled Watsons while never really explaining anything at all until the very end. She cleverly played on her fellow mystery authors' habit of writing their detectives and sidekicks as these recognizable personalities (see the "Avoiding Stereotypes" section in Chapter 3), then dropped her brilliant bombshell. Her Watson character is the murderer. It's been done since, but never so well, or at the exact point in time where it worked the best. And, yes, I'm deliberately not giving you the title of the book.

As far as game mechanics go, sidekicks can be the hint system come alive or the pipeline to Central Exposition. The best use of a sidekick in storytelling terms, though, is somebody to whom the player-character can talk at any point in the game. Yes, occasionally the sidekick can get sidetracked, lost, kidnapped, or distracted by a mission of their own, but for the most part, the player-character and sidekick go through the game as Siamese twins.

For this reason, because the sidekick can be a huge resource for the writer to reveal character exposition and backstory, the sidekick needs to be as vividly drawn as the hero with a distinct personality that complements the protagonist's character. Like mentors, sidekicks need not see eye-to-eye with their heroes. They are often sidekicks precisely because they don't worship the ground their heroes walk on. It helps the character of the protagonist if they can tolerate an edgy relationship with their sidekick.

Do all player-characters need sidekicks? Not at all. Don't cram a sidekick into an action/stealth game story like *Tom Clancy's Splinter Cell*. They'd just be in the way. If such a relationship fits the game story though, it can be incredibly useful to the writer.

Companions can be found in RPGs like *The Elder Scrolls V: Skyrim* and *Star Wars: The Old Republic*. In fact, in both games, the relationship can grow beyond sidekick. In *Skyrim*, you can marry your companion (opposite or same sex) *after* fulfilling their heart's desire. In *Star Wars: The Old Republic*, you can advance your relationship beyond friendship, too (opposite sex only). However, how do you do that? Give them presents. Buying affection? Again, a one-dimensional idea of a relationship.

These may be simple relationship systems to develop, but both leave a lot to be desired in games that give you so many options for slaughter. In the Facebook game *Indiana Jones Adventure World*—originally called simply *Adventure World*—I explored the possibilities of maintaining a long-distance relationship that leads to a "messy" breakup in a few very short bits of text. I'll provide more detail in Chapter 18.

SERVANTS AND PETS

We are now segueing from the roles of major characters to the roles of minor characters, and while there can be some traffic back and forth—a servant can be a sidekick like Sancho Panza to Don Quixote—we are now mostly dealing with characters who are almost defined by their roles. Servants and pets certainly fall into this category.

Servants are NPCs whose basic function in the game is to assist the player-character. Servant may not be a particularly politically correct word, but it adequately describes them. Sometimes they're friends, sometimes superior officers, but basically they're here to serve. Unlike sidekicks, they often do not follow the protagonist around. We'll find them back at headquarters researching leads or following up clues the player-character uncovers or offering additional exposition or gameplay tips like Bentley and Murray in *Sly Cooper and the Thievius Raccoonus*.

Another example is Lambert, the Third Echelon teammate of Sam Fisher in *Tom Clancy's Splinter Cell* games. Bentley and Murray are delightful characters in their own right. In the beginning, there is little more to laconic Lambert than the world-weary attitudes he shares with Fisher. He's there as a servant, nothing more. In subsequent games and the novels based on them, however, he is developed more fully until his death. How he dies depends on what console you played the game on: much more elaborate than a simple branched ending in a game on all systems.

Hopefully, you can already see where I'm going with this. There is no reason not to flesh out a servant character. Bentley and Murray aren't three-dimensional, but they don't need to be. They are essentially minor characters, removed for the most part from the developing storyline of the game, although they show up in connective tissue cut scenes, and Murray does get into the act at one point. In Chapter 3, I suggested how to bring minor characters to life without complete psychological and sociological workups. In comedy, we can sometimes get by with less effort on characterizations, relying on distinct variations on established personality types, as long as we're careful not to leave them as simple stereotypes. On the other hand, the *Splinter Cell* games developed Lambert as the series progressed to a place where his death mattered. Good news, Lambert. You've been upped in status from servant to mentor. Bad news is you're dead.

Pets are yet another link down the food chain. Don't worry—it's not a long chain. We're almost done. We run across them mostly in virtual worlds. Pets could be summoned by enchanters as in *Dark Age of Camelot*, tamed by Creature Handlers in *Star Wars Galaxies (SWG)* or wild horses you capture and tame in *The Legend of Zelda: Breath of the Wild*. In *SWG*, players could assign dialogue to them. One idea to consider is increasing their functionality by allowing them to carry a portion of the player-character's inventory. Another is to train them to loot mobs killed by the player-character. Both are sensible ideas. Every time you add to an NPC's functionality you are expanding their character. A horse becomes very important in a major boss battle near the end of *Breath of the Wild* although I admit I kept falling off. Please don't tell anyone.

But let's look at how Disney handles pets: Aladdin's monkey, Abu, or Jafar's parrot Iago (he turns up in the strangest places!) in *Aladdin*; or Flounder and Sebastian, Ariel's companions in *The Little Mermaid*. Children are delighted when pets talk back; seem to be smarter than their owners; get into trouble and must be rescued; or rescue their masters and mistresses in return. Most importantly, they are characterized.

In an article on the website Ranker, Ariel Kana named "The 13 Greatest Pets in Video Game History":

1. Yoshi, Mario's domesticated dinosaur

2. Argo, your faithful horse in Shadow of the Colossus, who matches Planetfall's legendary Floyd by making the ultimate sacrifice for the player

3. Rush, the robot dog from Megaman

4. Lamarr, the Head Crab from the Half-Life series

5. Epona, Link's song-loving horse introduced in Ocarina of Time

6. Rammy, the Animal Orb from Castle Crashers

7. Zombie Dogs from Resident Evil 3

8. Shadow, the Husky from Dead to Rights

9. Blob from A Boy and His Blob

10. Dog from the Half-Life series

11. Mr. Bigglesworth from World of Warcraft, loyal companion of Kel'Thuzad

12. The Chocobo from the Final Fantasy series

13. Dog, who stays with you whether you choose good or evil in *Fable 2*

Now that's loyalty and that's a pretty eccentric list in general. But it illustrates a variety of "pets" with strikingly different personalities, even if their actions are limited.

The bottom line for this section is no matter how minor the character, it deserves the respect of the writer. Any way we can help lift even servants and pets out of stereotypes or mindless automatons, the better.

MERCHANTS

We see them in one form or another in many types of games including most RPGs and almost all virtual worlds. In an early *Ultima* RPG, merchants were portrayed as having lives and loyalties of their own. For the most part, we have lost that today. They are often little more than a menu of items to buy or sell. Occasionally they have evolved a bit more. Today they can be part of a game's quest system, sending players on both minor and major quests. They can be the giver of a "FedEx item," or the receiver, as well as buying and selling as we will see later.

In 2004, I wrote: *The Gryphon Tapestry* merchants were inhabitants of the world, not just functionaries. In addition to buying and selling items, they handed out quests, gossiped, and sometimes trained players in new skills. This alone increased their worth as characters, but we tried to go farther and individualize each one, so that a tavern keeper in one village had a distinct personality from his counterpart in another village. In that same game a merchant vanishes, launching a full quest line. This made the world seem all the more real, and the characters in it more like living individuals than cardboard cutouts scattered across the map.

In *The Elder Scrolls: Skyrim*, released in 2011, however, merchants were much more individual, many doling out quests based on their characters, and many were marriageable as well. It may take more time, but even if a character's only function is that of a merchant, there is no reason whatsoever not to respect that character enough to give them a life of their own.

TRAINERS

As I've shown, NPCs can and should wear many hats. It's an easy aid to fleshing them out into fully realized characters. As stated earlier, mentors might be trainers. So can merchants. So can NPCs who teach their own profession like assassins, musicians, healers, and cooks.

In many single-player games, trainers are usually fairly limited in number, if they exist at all. If a player can choose the type of role they are going to play, only that type of training need be necessary, but again they can serve multiple functions.

In a virtual world, there can be many paths to greatness, and many trainers may be needed as a result. Individual players may choose from a smorgasbord of classes and professions. In some, players may be able to train in many different disciplines, adding to skills as necessary, or even shedding those they no longer need.

Often, players just receive new skills automatically at the completion of a level or a quest. In Chapter 5, we'll explore alternatives to this bare-bones approach. But it's worthwhile to point out here that dispensing with trainers robs us of the opportunity to create interesting characters and relationships to bring our stories to life.

QUEST GIVERS

There are many functions that NPCs can have. But none of them need exist only as stereotypes or as mannequins cut and pasted from town to town in a game. Writers! Don't let programmers convince your producers that cutting and pasting is a great way to save time! It allows the seams to show. It harms immersion. It limits storytelling and rich characters. Don't give in! *Dungeon Siege*, a very typical RPG that was famously not all that interested in depth of character or story, at least personalized characters across its large, if linear, world. If they can do it, anybody can.

Even though this topic is called "Quest Givers," I include mission assigners as well. Missions are simply the more modern version of the quest. Quests and missions are very important to us as storytellers, and I'll discuss them in detail in Chapter 10, "Charting New Territory."

Since quests are one of the most important tools at the storyteller's disposal, it should follow that quest givers are some of the most important characters we can write. This is true because quest givers provide us with an opportunity for consistency. And consistency helps make our worlds more believable to our players.

Whether single-player or multiplayer, our worlds must make some sort of logical sense, or our players will be lost. If we have real pirates suddenly showing up at a high school prom, we'd better have a damn good explanation for how they got there.

We must remember to keep the quests *consistent* with the character giving them and hopefully with the player-character as well. *Dark Age of Camelot* was set in a basic medieval/fantasy universe. Yet, in a single quest, I encountered two NPCs who used the decidedly non-medieval/fantasy phrase "do a number on." This comes to us from modern organized crime, not medieval fantasy.

Tolkien never wrote dialogue for Saruman like, "I'll gather up my orc armies and do a number on the Riders of Rohan." If it's inconceivable to the man who single-handedly codified the mythology that is the basis for *Dungeons & Dragons* to write a line of dialogue like this, it should have been inconceivable to the writers of *Dark Age of Camelot*. They didn't have to be as good of a writer as he was, but the lead writer at least should have caught this. So, even though quest givers or mission assigners may be minor characters, they are due their author's respect. Give them some life of their own and keep the quests they hand out consistent with their characters. Don't allow warriors to hand out mage quests or quartermasters to hand out search and destroy missions.

Time now to move on to character traits, those that can be shared by all characters, and those specific to certain types.

CHAPTER 5

Character Traits

T HE PLAYER-CHARACTER AND THE NPCs who inhabit the game world have common traits as well as qualities that are distinct. When we discuss mobility in this chapter, we will be primarily talking about the mobility of non-player-characters. When we discuss character emotion and memory, only NPCs are covered. Player emotions will be examined in Chapter 11, "Story Anatomy." The remaining topics are shared equally. Skills and professions can be available to both, and both are revealed through action. In the "Characters in Opposition" section, we begin to explore relationships between characters: relationships NPCs have with each other, and between player-characters and NPCs. Here we'll confine ourselves to the reasons behind establishing relationships for dramatic purposes. In Chapter 6, "Character Encounters," we'll look at ways to bring these relationships to life within the game.

MOBILITY

Static NPCs, those that stand in one place throughout the entire game, are convenient for both players and programmers. Players like to know that their favorite auto mechanic and weaponsmith will always be available when they're needed. It's nice to be able to return to where you obtained a mission to collect your reward. Some NPCs may not even inhabit the interactive space of the game's world, appearing only as images on communication devices within the world, or on the game's interface, although even then some contextual explanation for their presence on the interface is usually desirable—for example, if the part of the interface where the character appears represents a communication device.

Hybrid NPCs might also show up as static characters in the game world and only become truly mobile in cut scenes. While this helps bring motion (and possibly emotion) into the world, it does so at the expense of making the player even more aware of how different cut scenes are from the rest of the game, a problem we will tackle later.

As we saw in Chapter 4, "Character Roles," populating the world brings it alive, and while static NPCs—particularly articulate ones—can help, even those whose rightful place may be behind a store counter can feel mechanical to the player and detrimental to immersion. Part of the solution to this is to write them as distinct characters. Another part of the

DOI: 10.1201/9780429284991-8

solution is to also add NPCs who can move about, whether in a localized space or throughout the world of the game.

CONTROLLING THE SPACE

On the surface, the two-character play *Oleanna* by David Mamet is about a charge of sexual harassment against a college professor by a female student. Actually, it is about a struggle for power. The play is set in the professor's office. As directed in the beginning, he is seated behind his desk, and the student is perched uncomfortably on a utilitarian chair (Figure 5.1).

As the play progresses, the ebb and flow of the power struggle finally begins to tip decisively toward the student until at the end she is comfortably ensconced in his chair, and he is shifting uneasily in the other chair.

Direction in theater is all about positioning the characters within the space bounded by the set. The most rudimentary task facing the director is establishing sightlines so the entire audience can follow the action.

Allowing the audience to follow the natural course of the action is important in film as well. Orson Welles, concerned about producer Al Zugsmith's penchant for re-editing his directors' work, staged many scenes in *Touch of Evil* in single master shots or establishing shots that showed the entire scene at once. He supplied virtually no coverage, that is, additional shots like close-ups, or two-shots; instead, he orchestrated his actors to step in close to the camera for those angles (Figure 5.2).

If the producer had tried to cut out pieces of these scenes, the result would be jarring jump cuts that disrupted the continuity of the scene.

Jump cut: when two separate pieces of a film are edited together with the expected transition or connection between them missing.

Next, the director must be aware of the aesthetics of composition to add visual interest to what the audience is watching. There are a lot of characters onstage when Brutus and his fellow conspirators assassinate *Julius Caesar* in Shakespeare's play and when Marc Antony delivers his famous funeral speech:

FIGURE 5.1 *Oleanna*, a struggle for control of turf. (Source: www.haroldpinter.org.)

FIGURE 5.2   Orson Welles arranges his actors with far more precision than his tie.

FIGURE 5.3   Marlon Brando takes the high ground in *Julius Caesar*.

Friends, Romans, countrymen, lend me your ears;
I come to bury Caesar, not to praise him.
The evil that men do lives after them;
The good is oft interred with their bones.

William Shakespeare, Julius Caesar

The director must carefully arrange a composition that, unlike a painting, is fluid, changing from one moment to the next. Without this care, the crowd becomes a featureless rabble and detracts rather than adds to the drama. Director Joseph Mankiewicz used the height of his set as well as the depth to compose the scene in his film version of *Julius Caesar*, placing Marc Antony on stairs high above the other characters, emphasizing the power and moral superiority of his words (Figure 5.3).

We don't like stairs very much in video games. They can either add the necessity for additional character animation or make our characters look funky going up and down if we avoid extra animations. Ramps are an improvement and are sometimes disguised as stair graphics. The opportunities for more interesting compositions make the effort to include height as well as depth of scene worthwhile. The balcony scene from *Romeo and Juliet* and the fire escape scene from *West Side Story* directed by Stephen Spielberg (deliberately mirroring Shakespeare's original), would be drastically changed if Juliet happened to live on the ground floor, not to mention that the physical side of their relationship might have progressed much faster! (Spoiler Alert: Maria's fire escape went all the way up to her floor…).

And, as in the example from *Oleanna*, directors must also be aware of the shifting balances of emotion and relationships between characters that can be expressed through staging. A character who stands when another sits is in a dominant position. A character who moves uncomfortably close to another is being aggressive. (Something I enjoyed demonstrating in my classes to some hapless student sitting in the front row.) A character who doesn't look at those sharing the same stage is considered aloof (or may just be preparing for a soliloquy, of course!). We recognize these actions on an instinctive level. We see them often enough in real life. And there is a more primitive instinct at work buried in our unconscious. We know what it means when the defeated wolf exposes its neck for the killing bite.

We can use this instinctive awareness of the significance of certain spatial relationships between characters in games to add emotion and dramatic tension to our scenes. It is particularly important because our characters—even today with now routine sophisticated motion capture performances—are not always as expressive as live human beings. And resorting to cutting in for close-ups can disrupt the flow of the action. Instead of relying on cut scenes to establish relationships, we can use these techniques borrowed from theater and film to suggest relationships even as the player remains in control of the player-character.

For example, an NPC who cowers away from us doesn't have to tell the player they are fearful. We can see that they are. (See "Exposition in Action" in Chapter 9 for other ways to show players things they need to know without burdening them with lengthy text passages.)

An irritating NPC can attach themselves to us like the talkative bore, Noober, in the village of Nashkel in *Baldur's Gate*. Granted, the name is an immersion-damaging play on the word *n00b*, but the idea is still a good one.

> N00b: derived from the word newbie, meaning a newcomer to video games. Newbie became noob, and then it evolved into n00b with the replacement of the o's with zeros in *l33t*. It has now evolved in real life to mean a sort of general fecklessness.

An aggressive NPC in a first-person shooter might step in close to the player-character, even trying to back us into a corner, instead of simply opening fire when he spots us.

Imagine the player is Alice, and she desperately needs information from a white rabbit who is constantly disappearing around corners and down dark holes. Here the NPC's mobility becomes a puzzle.

…before her was another long passage, and the White Rabbit was still in sight, hurrying down it. There was not a moment to be lost: away went Alice like the wind, and was just in time to hear it say, as it turned a corner, 'Oh my ears and whiskers, how late it's getting!' She was close behind it when she turned the corner, but the rabbit was no longer to be seen…

Lewis Carroll, Alice's Adventures in Wonderland

l33t (aka d00dspeak): a pseudo-language that developed on bulletin board systems in the 1980s and became widely adapted in multiplayer gaming and elsewhere on the Internet. Now in general usage among a certain segment of the Internet population, it was originally intended to get around language filters. It is characterized by deliberate misspellings like "teh" instead of "the" and the use of numbers in place of letters as in "phat l00t" which means "spoils of combat that are of exceptional quality."

The mobility of the player-character is taken for granted. This is the character we move through the game after all. We may give them all sorts of transportation options, which, if consistent with the game world, enforce the reality of that world and the stories we mean to tell there. We can also alter their natural mobility in interesting ways.

In addition, we can give insight into the character or increase suspense by removing that mobility to a greater or lesser degree. One of the most famous examples of this in films is LB Jeffries, James Stewart's character in Hitchcock's *Rear Window*, a globe-trotting photographer suddenly confined to a wheelchair by a broken leg. It is due to this temporary physical disability that his restlessness, his insatiable curiosity, and his high-tech lenses turn him into a peeping tom and a witness to a possible murder (Figure 5.4). In an interesting twist of fate, Raymond Burr, the actor who played the suspected villain in *Rear Window*, ended up playing a detective also confined to a wheelchair in the TV series *Ironside*.

FIGURE 5.4   A cast on Jimmy Stewart's leg leads to the arrest of a killer.

FIGURE 5.5 *The Flower Collectors* is a videogame homage to *Rear Window*.

Rear Window was also an inspiration for 2020's *The Flower Collectors* from Mi'Pu'Mi Games (Figure 5.5).

Just as we saw *Ico*'s horns as a catalyst for the game's action, Princess Yorda's *lack* of mobility makes her dependent on the player-character and offers the player a unique set of challenges. In terms of story, it places her life in Ico's hands. In terms of gameplay, it offers a unique variation on physical puzzles. The player must ensure that *both* Ico and Yorda surmount each hazard.

The player-character can have their mobility affected in any number of ways. It can slow them down or speed them up. They may be able to swim or not. *Brothers: A Tale of Two Sons* includes a particularly poignant example dealing with the ability to swim. The PC may be blind or corpulent or incredibly thin. Not only do these kinds of choices suggest gameplay, but they obviously are also a part of the physical dimension of a character.

In *Dark Age of Camelot*, NPCs called Filidhs (the name in ancient Irish law for the professional bardic class who were more schooled than ordinary bards) strolled from town to town in Hibernia, informing players who asked about various quests they had heard of in the vicinity. The game did a check on the player's list of completed quests so that the Filidh only mentioned quests new to the player. NPCs who do not remain stationary bring otherwise static areas to life; help characterize and separate game locales.

In the early days of *Everquest*, one of the best items in the game was a pair of boots called *Journeyman Boots* that granted their wearer increased speed and were very handy for getting across vast continents or escaping from dangerous creatures, especially for characters who had no ability to cast speed spells. The key to the quest for obtaining the Journeyman Boots was to talk to a gnome NPC named Hasten Bootstrutter who was said to frequent the Rathe Mountains. Two problems made the quest difficult. The first was that Hasten, like many *Everquest* quest NPCs did not put in an appearance very often. And when he did, he did so swiftly, speeding from place to place, stopping only briefly, and then speeding on.

Astute readers may question why I often use apparently older examples to illustrate points in this book. I have three responses: first, they are still valid. And second, it's because the MMOs I cite in particular are often still running somewhere. Loyal fans have refused to allow them to die. For example, *Everquest*, first released in 1999, and the first

MMO I played with regularity, is still in development. A staggering 18th expansion, *Veil of Alaris*, was released on November 15, 2011. In addition, a limited free-to-play version and a reduced-cost version both became available in March 2012. True to their nature, persistent worlds have a tendency to persist. And third, our industry has the unfortunate habit of reinventing the wheel. Before you proclaim your new discovery of game design, do some research. Even if no one corrects you, save yourself the embarrassment. Other game designers *know*.

Back to Hasten. His second problem was ingenious because it not only increased the difficulty of the quest, but it was also in keeping with Hasten's character, as obviously was his name. So here an NPC's mobility becomes part of a puzzle. And this can be found in other puzzles and quests where an NPC will only appear at a designated place at a certain hour or moves through the game world from location to location. We'll catch up with Hasten again in Chapter 19, "Enabling Story in Virtual Worlds," by the way.

Homer wrote epic poems, as we know, not sonnets or haiku. One of the important features of the epic style is the reappearance of characters throughout the telling of the story. *Star Wars: The Old Republic* relies on this device often in the continuing story of each player-character, stories that are woven throughout the entire game.

This structure is unique. In most RPGs, including *Baldur's Gate 3*, the PC experiences a lengthy character creation process. Then the PC moves into a more generalized story. In SWTOR, a PC's story runs throughout all 50 levels of the initial release. A huge amount of time and resources was expended to make each character's experience remain personal.

Epic structure suits games beautifully. As we move from level to level or location to location, the reappearance of a character gives us the following information:

- **A sense of mobility, even if the characters are essentially static.** This character could still be, for the most part, static, moving only in the sense that they appear at different places in the game world at different times in the story. Here's an art-cheap solution to NPC mobility!

- **An opportunity to advance the NPC's character.** The more times a character appears, the more subtle the growth or the development of the character can be.

- **An opportunity to advance or alter their relationship to the player-character.** NPCs can show up from level to level, their relationship to the player-character altering as the player progresses. A lowly informer from level one may have their life saved by the player-character in level four, and then be driven to help the player-character for free in level seven.

- **An opportunity for foreshadowing.** The NPC can appear Cassandra-like to warn of dark perils ahead.

- **An opportunity for recap as the NPC congratulates the player on past deeds.** It's the comforting presence of a familiar face in alien surroundings. Game space can be extremely literal in small areas but disorienting across levels or far-flung locations. The familiar NPC can help anchor or orient the player to a new setting.

- **A feeling of fateful inevitability that can add to pace.** In the odd pseudo-spaghetti western *Hannie Calder*, starring Raquel Welch, actor Stephen Boyd plays an enigmatic character known only as "The Man in Black" who appears at key dramatic moments. The audience knows he must be significant but must wait until the very end of the movie to learn what that significance is. (No, he's not a film critic.) This takes us into Carl Jung symbolic territory, that shadowy realm we'll look at again briefly in Chapter 8, "Respecting Story."

- **A way to cut down on the number of characters in the game that must be drawn.** A reoccurring character can provide the exposition and services that might have been rendered by several characters before the game started to strain the perimeter of the project budget.

In some games, NPCs can be truly mobile. This is often unavoidable in the literal space of the game world. If an NPC needs to get somewhere, and the player-character is standing there watching, the NPC may make at least the pretext of a graceful exit before teleporting to their next appearance. In *The Elder Scrolls V: Skyrim*, a character who will accompany the player-character on a quest usually "runs on ahead" and meets the PC at the location where the quest will commence. This gives the player a chance to attend to other business before going off to meet them. Not to worry, they are always patiently waiting. In SWTOR, the character may exit in a cut scene and be gone when gameplay resumes. Others, such as freed prisoners, run a short distance and then fade from view. Practical if not elegant.

If we as designers don't want that character followed, yet we still want to maintain the verisimilitude of our world, we have to find some obstacle to place in front of stalker player-characters: a door slammed in the player-character's face; NPC speed greater than the PC's, so they just out-distance them; or allowing the NPC to jump into the only cab in sight are examples of obstacles that help maintain the fiction of the game world.

So, we can use the mobility of characters in any number of ways. A static world is a dead world. Mobile characters bring it to life. The type of mobility can add to both character dimension and story. What other traits add to gameplay, contribute to story, and illuminate character?

PHYSICAL SKILLS

In simulations with story added, we get "you are a crack helicopter pilot" and then you must learn from scratch, crashing often. The same is true in many types of games, as we saw in the *Lunar Lander* example from *The Dig*. It is one of the most fiction-destroying conflicts between character and gameplay we come across. Players of simulations are much more forgiving of this paradox than players of action games who expect to be proficient with all sorts of exotic firepower as soon as they find a new weapon. We'll address the special case of simulations later, but in all other types of games we must make allowances for players' true skills, and simplify for them, or all those crashes will stop the story dead and could make them come to hate their avatar.

Once we make the choice to simplify real-world mechanics in favor of gameplay mechanics, we're faced with another challenge. The skills must be in character and in the context of the game world. Most games handle this well in terms of gameplay but often at the expense of character and immersion.

Skills are the bedrock of the development of the player-character in games, whether the PC is a super spy or a sous chef. The PC can learn special new moves, as well as find new tools and weapons. Often, these moves are generic, for example, an elaborate circling kick common to martial arts. Hopefully, they are in character for the PC, such as a thief's special moves like sidling along a narrow ledge. They serve a double function: a reward for completing a level and almost certainly, they will be needed to overcome an obstacle later in the game.

In role-playing games, there are complicated trees of skills. At first glance, these skills are vastly different from one another, depending on the type of character the player has chosen to play, their profession, and racial characteristics.

Without doubt, some skills can be unique. A warrior in most RPGs lacks the ability to heal, and most mages cannot wear the heavy armor of warriors. Still, many skills have counterparts in all characters. This is done for play balance, so that while players may appear to select a vast array of races, professions, and skills, in fact, they are often selecting little more than different names and character graphics.

One way to enhance character is often overlooked in most games when special skills are applied. Story and gameplay are very different. Game designers have a natural tendency (being gamers more often than writers) to introduce skills only as part of gameplay. The player can be told at the end of a level—often in a line of text ending in an exclamation mark—that they have learned "Critical Strike III!" or "a new language: Grislik! Now you can speak to Grisls!" This is an easy (and cheap!) way of informing the player, and while it might make sense in terms of gameplay, it destroys the illusion that the player-character is gaining proficiency in a real world.

It's like one of those TV commercials where a disembodied announcer suddenly speaks to a character alone in their own home. This has been a convention of commercials since advertisements first started appearing in print and the pictured character spoke directly to the reader. It works fine in commercials—although these days the convention is often mocked even as it's being used—but has no place when we're trying to preserve the fiction of the world, and it passes up a golden opportunity for character growth or development.

Without much additional effort, the special move or skill can be tied to the player-character more closely. It can be magically granted or taught by a mentor or other character who has a relationship with the player-character. It can be an undiscovered, or even better, an *underdeveloped* talent that the player-character becomes more proficient in as it is used.

Now couple this with a delivery system that doesn't harm the fiction of the game world. Many games use NPCs as trainers already. But who wants to stop their progress in the game and go off to train someplace for even a few minutes? They shouldn't have to. A simple change of the game text from "Congratulations! You've just learned a new skill: Crêpe Making!" to "A Cordon Bleu chef has consented to teach you how to properly prepare crêpes!" might work fine. In Chapter 6, "Character Encounters," we'll see how to develop this specific relationship between player-characters and "trainer" NPCs, as well as other relationships.

Skills can be added to NPCs and player-characters. We see this all the time in many games where NPCs, who either join the player-character or are controlled by the player, gain skills and power as long as they survive in the game. Sometimes it is left to the player to choose new skills for party members or companions, and sometimes those skills are added automatically.

In action games, mobs get increasingly more difficult. Why? Because the challenges must be increased. But why introduce bigger monsters every level? Why can't the surviving monsters from a previous level go running to *their* mentors and demand to be taught skills to counter the player's own?

Dungeon Keeper gave an entirely new perspective to action and strategy games. It was a wicked role-reversal game where players controlled all those mobs they were usually mowing down. We don't need to go that far every time. But giving mobs who have already been defeated by the PC the opportunity for revenge is far more interesting and respectful of world fiction than just respawning them. Allowing them to come back for more, armed with new skills, also gives us the chance to grow and develop them as characters. This personalizes the battle and increases the tension in the same way the *Halloween* series' Michael Meyers had the ability to bounce back from axe blows, fire, hanging, and all sorts of other grisly attacks that usually would have finished many a good monster. It's a wonder that there's still anyone left alive in Haddonfield. Those residents still ambulant should really consider moving before Michael returns yet again.

New skills can be applied to any NPC: sidekick, mentor, major or minor character. Both the application of a skill and the character's reaction to it are easy ways to add dimension to characters.

PROFESSIONS

For NPCs, roles and professions are really one and the same. Quest Giver is a role but not a profession. Trainers can be both. The teacher of a skill may do it for a living, having never actually been required to practice what they preach. An interesting facet of LT Bonham, Tommy Lee Jones' character in the film *The Hunted*, is that while he was an exceptional trainer of killers, he had never killed anyone. We have enough examples of people who weren't talented enough to be successful at a skill that they teach instead to inspire the derogatory comment: "Those who can, do. Those who can't, teach." This is attributed to that caustic observer of humankind, George Bernard Shaw, a friend of William Archer. The actual quote from *Man and Superman* reads: "He who can, does. He who cannot, teaches."

Ironically, William Archer was himself a failed playwright. Archer puts it a bit kindlier: "Assuredly, if I had the power, I should write plays instead of writing about them; but one may have a great love for an art, and some insight into its principles and methods, without the innate faculty required for actual production."

Some trainers can be both teacher and practitioner. Other NPCs have professions to serve their characters or the story but have no specific role in gameplay terms. Traditionally, these characters were confined to cut scenes. However, to segregate characters in cut scenes, or other nonfunctional parts of the game, often makes little sense. One of the things that sets our characters apart from those in other media is that ours can serve story *and* gameplay. Writing characters who only perform one function doesn't respect them. They are being wasted.

As I said in the introduction, creating a game with story in it is an adventure in balance. Both gameplay and story deserve equal attention. If one doesn't get its due, that component will feel weak. It's a vicious circle. Create enough games with weak story and people will begin to think stories in games *must be* weak. Stories need the support of characters. And since those characters can be used to support gameplay, it is a shame to squander them.

RACE

Race in fantasy RPGs does not mean Asian, Black, Caucasian, or Hispanic, but is used to differentiate between human and nonhuman sentient beings such as elves, dwarves, lizards, and ants. Each race is usually given certain unique characteristics: both strengths and weaknesses. Traditionally, some are better suited to certain professions; for instance, elves are presumed to be better archers, thanks to J.R.R. Tolkien; and ant-like creatures can be super productive like the Klackons in the *Master of Orion* series of strategy games.

That is not to say that players cannot choose to play humanoid characters with skin color and other features to duplicate the appearance of human races. This is offered in many genres of games. Some players choose to mimic how they look in real life. A detailed character selection process allows for a huge range of looks. Changing your character's dress can be a reward in games like *Sea of Thieves*.

Relationships between races in games are often carefully distanced from life here in our real world. Racial differences, even animosities, are easier to deal with when we're talking about lizards and cat people. One exception to this could be found in the MMO *Earth & Beyond*, which ran from 2002 to 2003. In *Earth & Beyond*, racial animosities, even if among aliens, bore more than a passing resemblance to our own troubled planet.

For most games, the argument goes that we're creating games here that are fun to play. And in multiplayer games there are very real risks of tension between players. I remember when *World War II Online* was in beta in 2001 that there was publicity and concern over the fact that some players wanted to know if they could play Nazis and if there would be concentration camps.

Pussyfooting around race in single-player games, though, only cuts writers and players off from the grand diversity that racial and cultural differences can provide us. Games often disguise the ethnic and cultural aspects of their characters, particularly when they are villains, much in the way we were censored in the 1970s in television when we attempted to portray organized crime. So, we ended up with a lot of characters with New York and New Jersey accents with last names like Smith, Graham, or Robinson. I wrote an episode of *Charlie's Angel* where I satirized this censorship. I made the criminal organization a men's club. Unfortunately, it was changed by that episode's producer back to the typical white bread crime syndicate of the era.

In 2002 Rockstar, a company known for controversy for such titles as the *Grand Theft Auto* series and *Bully*, created an uproar with *Grand Theft Auto: Vice City*. The game was the subject of protests from Haitian-American groups for their portrayal of Haitian gangsters. Rockstar responded that the protest was focusing on remarks made by fictional characters from a rival Cuban gang, and it was taken out of context. Both the protest and the defense are borderline for me. Both are based on stereotypes.

We shouldn't create games that overtly lecture our audience. They are meant to entertain. But we can influence that audience in innumerable ways. Writers who think about these things must answer this question: "Do we portray society as it is, or as we might like it to be?" Each of us must answer that question in our own way. Whatever the answer, we do owe it to our characters, our audiences, and ourselves to approach the issue with the concern it deserves. And the same concern for race also occupies us when we discuss sex.

SEX

No, I'm not going to discuss how to write sex scenes in your game, or how to hide them from the general public and then pretend you didn't put them there like Rockstar's debacle with the notorious Hot Coffee sequence in 2004's *Grand Theft Auto: San Andreas*. I believe in free speech. If you want to put a sex scene in your game, and it is dramatically valid, don't hide it away like some adolescent who gets caught on a porn site by their parents.

The industry doesn't need to give more excuses to crusaders and politicians to promote censorship laws. Some common sense and adult handling of adult material would have been far more preferable. A situation like that, so easily avoided, harms all of us who make video games. Okay, back to the real topic.

Time to mention stereotypes again. Don't write them! Even if they are drawn that way! A big step toward respecting characters is to respect the human beings they are modeled on. We have plenty of examples of NPCs in computer games who are less than gorgeous, although they usually are mentors, sidekicks, villains, and the like. What do we do with the player-character?

When the first edition of this book was published in 2004 game players identified either as either men or women. For the second edition in 2014, I wrote:

> While the demographic is changing, the primary market for video games in most game types remains young and male. Young heterosexual males like to look at sexy women. So, whenever we see female characters, they are scantily clad and abundantly endowed in every ad and on every box. There are a variety of body types for the male characters in *Star Wars: The Old Republic*. But all the female characters, even the aliens, seemed to have had enhancement surgery from the same doctor on Nar Shaddaa.

As I write this in 2022 binary gender identification is a thing of the past. Yet I have not seen a survey of who plays games that address this reality. Happily, my response to those who continue to present gamers with stereotypical characters remains pretty much the same. Regardless of sexual orientation players like to identify with preternaturally fit and attractive characters in movies, and in games they like to play them. But body types do not have to fall into a narrowly defined "gorgeous" category. To see how developers tackled one character whose appearance changed again and again over the years, have a look at Lara Croft from *Tomb Raider* in 1996 to *Shadow of the Tomb Raider* in 2018.

Visual appearance isn't the only trait we have to be careful about when designing our player-characters. We took some criticism in *Dark Side of the Moon* for our PC Jake Wright, even though it was a first-person game and Jake was never seen. Some reviewers, and players too, thought he was voiced too "wimpily." We wanted him to start out at least as an uncertain young man to give him room to grow, but never got him to the point where his voice matched his later heroic actions. This would not have been as much of a problem, I think, but because you can't see the character in a first-person game, you are forced to rely solely on voice performance.

Any game that gives players the choice to create a non-binary gendered character gives us an additional thing to think about. The mix of versions of a PC may be graphically different in body language, voice, or other characteristics, but today they are almost always functionally identical. An exception was Jill Valentine in the first *Resident Evil* game. While physically weaker than her male counterpart, Chris Redfield, she possessed skills and weapons to compensate, proving that single-player games could be designed so that gender differences could be used to differentiate how each sex attacks the obstacles in the game. The important point to remember is that with any choices we make, the danger of stereotyping is always present. It is essential that we know our characters at their core and portray them honestly and without bias.

Other media gives us a whole range of lead characters who are strong. Let's stay away from art and literature and focus on genre fiction since that is what most popular entertainment is all about. Genre fiction requires strong protagonists, even if their strength is at first hard to find.

Films have their sword-wielders like Miranda Otto, Éowen in *Return of the King*, and their gun-toters like Jodie Foster's Clarice Starling in *Silence of the Lambs*, Angelina Jolie's *Salt*, and others. But these women have a lot more going for them than their abilities with weapons. Some of them also manage time for the romance often required of them, although Clarice is really just in love with her job, and Evelyn Salt's husband is killed in front of her.

Salt was actually written for Tom Cruise in the then male title role. So was the tough-as-nails character of Ripley, played by Sigourney Weaver in the *Alien* film series. But the same actress, Sigourney Weaver, was also the agoraphobic psychologist in *Copycat*, Dian Fossey in *Gorillas in the Mist*, and a strong first lady in *Dave*. *Speaking again of Halloween*, look how Jamie Lee Curtis's spunky Laurie Strode, who is basically only fighting for her life in *Halloween*, becomes the tormented woman who finally takes the fight to Michael Meyers in *Halloween H20* (1998), and Halloween (2018). Although she's basically on the sidelines in 2021's *Halloween Kills*.

Games should be able to give us player-characters who are skilled and fun to play, no matter what their gender orientation. Any can be a superhero or a villain or just a peripheral character who adds a special dimension to your game. The physical dimension is the easy one. That also means it's easy to rely on it too heavily. Once we make the effort to reveal their psychological and sociological dimensions, the physical dimension regains its proper stature equal to the others.

Here's one last example. Éowen's stand against the Nazgul is even more thrilling because we've seen what she is capable of beyond swordplay in her helping the people she will one day lead: her unquestioning defense of her sometimes less than kingly father and her obvious love for Aragorn. Because we have been allowed to see these other facets of her character, there is more at stake, and the climactic battle becomes emotionally charged on all sorts of levels beyond the visceral.

Today the wide range possible in sexual identity can pave the way to fuller, richer characters. Just avoid stereotypes. Instead create characters who feel real. If you are making a point about sexuality, fine. If you are not, fine. In either case write *interesting* people! Commit yourself to your characters. Make them come alive and give them a story worthy of them.

CHARACTER EMOTION

We writers deal with two types of emotions. There is the emotion we hopefully generate in our audience. We'll talk about what our audience, the player, is feeling in Chapter 11. Here we are going to look at the emotions of our characters.

In *Earth & Beyond* (2002), there was a Jenquai quest from an NPC you'd previously gone on a quest for. This time you're informed that a Progen shipment of weapons needs to be intercepted. Jenquais and Progens have a long history of conflict, and there is little love lost on either side. You go to the coordinates given, and sure enough, there is a ship there, but its captain claims it is not carrying weapons but children. Is he telling the truth? If he is, then do you withdraw or blow him out of the sky anyway? I chose to let him go and returned to the NPC who was furious with me, calling the children of our enemies "weapons." It is a beautiful example of an NPC revealing character through emotion in response to a player's actions.

Emotion doesn't just happen in our characters. We can't pick and choose from a shopping list of emotions and expect them to feel real. This leads to stereotypes and clichés. Emotion must be prepared for in a character's creation and invoke the actions that character takes.

Sometimes the *lack* of emotion can be equally compelling. We have the extreme of the heartless, soulless killer in dead teenager movies because relentless evil is, on the surface at least, more dramatic than the petty evil of an embezzler. Yet when such evil is combined with the mundane character, the result is even more gripping. In *Devil in the White City*, Erik Larson's bestselling book of the 1893 Chicago World's Fair, we meet H.H. Holmes, one of the most prolific serial killers of all time. Larson contrasts the remarkable architectural and construction effort that went into creating this wonder of the age with Holmes' methodical building of his hotel complete with private gas chamber and crematorium. Holmes was no flamboyant Hannibal the Cannibal. He was a pharmacist, fussy, quiet, and reserved; and he went about his business with a deliberate precision that matched the fair's builders.

When more emotion is called for, it cannot be dragged out of the bleachers just because the game demands it. The characters, if three-dimensional, have the seeds of emotion planted within them. The emotion is inevitable because of who they are. The film *Mystic*

River proceeds with the inevitability of a Greek tragedy that is overtly on display for most characters, and for the most part, they work beautifully, with the possible exception of Annabeth Marcus, played by Laura Linney. She has a chilling turn at the end of the film that while it may explain why she stays with her husband (Sean Penn), still feels like little more than a shocking surprise.

Emotion is prepared for not only with character growth but with its development, too. A character can hold the emotion inside longer and longer, letting it build until it must erupt like lava from a dormant volcano. I wrote earlier about a character on *Edge of Night* who I killed off. Her name was Nicole Cavanaugh. Her husband Miles did not allow himself to grieve for her, keeping his emotions locked inside for a week's worth of shows at least. He fends off his friends who offer various shoulders to cry upon. The audience was thrown by this usually compassionate doctor who could get very emotional about helping his patients, but who seemingly refused to mourn his dead wife. He remains as unmoved as a head on Mount Rushmore until one night, alone on his apartment's balcony, his emotion bursts forth as *anger* at Nicole's leaving him. Once he could deal with his anger, and all the conflicting emotions it produced in him, he could begin the process of mourning and healing.

With the proper background, growth, and development, a character is finally ready to experience the emotions that draw an audience, our players, into the story of our game. They can't then just occur. There is still another step, and that is we must choose the correct moment for their release. Mistimed emotion can be as ugly as unprepared-for emotion.

CHARACTERS IN OPPOSITION

A monologue can be a wonderful thing. Characters can experience a range of emotions in solitude. But there is more to drama than introspection. As we'll see drama is most often achieved when characters collide.

Conflict

Conflict has several definitions, all of them relevant.

That third definition is interesting. Conflict can occur *within* characters as well as *between* them. For the most part, we'll be considering conflict between characters, but it is good to be aware of the potential for interior conflict, as *Hamlet* has shown us.

Lajos Egri states, "Conflict is the heartbeat of all writing." And "Since most of us... hide our true selves from the world, we are interested in witness-

> Conflict: (1) A state of open, prolonged fighting: warfare. (2) A state of disharmony: clash. (3) The opposition or simultaneous functioning of mutually exclusive impulses, desires or tendencies. (4) A collision.

ing the things happening to those who are forced to reveal their true characters under the stress of conflict."

William Archer is blunter: "... we need go no further than the simple psychological observation that human nature loves a fight, whether it be with clubs or with swords, with tongues or with brains." (Games have the first two down anyway!)

It is not enough to set up a single conflict and let the player-character bang up against it over and over again. Conflict is seeded throughout a story in much the same way that clouds are seeded to provide rain. As the characters progress, the stakes of each conflict should rise like floodwaters. This can't be done artificially. "Oh! Almost at the end of the fourth level! Time for another conflict!" Egri calls unmotivated conflicts like these "jumps." Conflict jumps are as distracting to an audience as jump cuts are in a film. Rising conflict grows naturally as strong characters grow in the intensity of their opposition toward one another.

Egri: "In a play, each conflict causes the one after it. Each is more intense than the one before. The play moves, propelled by the conflict created by the characters in their desire to reach their goal."

Here is another solid reason to develop characters and story along with the gameplay. Now narrative and gameplay are not at war with one another but working in concert. If they are created together, puzzles don't appear out of thin air; NPCs won't arbitrarily show up as obstacles, and boss mobs won't just attack because it is the end of a level.

Again, we see story and gameplay complementing each other. This is great for a game design, but we don't want all our characters getting along so well! How do we prevent that and ensure that there will be plenty of opportunity for conflict?

Orchestration

Egri uses this term to describe the selection of characters that writers make to ensure conflict in their story. He says,

> When you are ready to select characters for your play, be careful to orchestrate them right. If all the characters are the same type—for instance, if all of them are bullies—it will be like an orchestra of nothing but drums.

That we should populate the world of a game with a range of characters is self-evident. Without diversity, they would all get very monotonous. But simple diversity is not enough. The characters should not only be different but orchestrated as well.

Characters can be of similar professions, religions, political persuasions, races, sexes, anything; but they shouldn't be the same *type* of people. One could be dedicated to their job, another indifferent. One could be a Mother Teresa, another a hate-filled fanatic. Both could be priests. One might be moderate, another a right-wing ideologue. Both could be Asian. One teenager might be very traditional, another might be indistinguishable from teenagers of other races. One businesswoman might be Estée Lauder, another might be Martha Stewart.

Once we've established potential conflict, we should remember to keep the characters equally strong, as we've discussed. Strong in mind, strong in purpose. Worthy adversaries create drama in games as on the playing field. A soccer game with a winning score of 1 to 0 is much more exciting than a game with a score of 14 to 1. In the end, one side may win, or it may even be a draw. It is the getting to that inevitable conclusion that gives us our drama.

"Orchestration," Egri says, "demands well-defined and uncompromising characters in opposition, moving from one pole toward another through conflict." Those poles are character growth. As our player-character battles the villain, the player must adapt because the villain changes. I'm not talking about artificial intelligence, but scripted adjustments that alter the playing field as the game progresses. In such a dynamic environment, the possibilities for tension and surprise are infinite. And these are qualities the best stories share with the best games.

Memory

> There's rosemary, that's for remembrance.
>
> *William Shakespeare*

> It doesn't matter who my father was; it matters who I remember he was.
>
> *Anne Sexton*

Each writer has their own favorite theme. We come back to it as inevitably as the tide returns to shore. "Favorite" may be the wrong word. We are compelled toward these themes by all that makes us who we are. We have no choice in the matter. My theme is memory. The past and my characters' recollections of it haunts them throughout my stories.

I call such moments of memory in my writing "echoes." They can be the verbal reminiscences of characters: flashbacks, symbols, flashes of déjà vu. When Tim Robbins climbs into the wrong car for the second time in his life in *Mystic River* and turns to look out the rear window, it is a powerful echo that the audience hears on a Jungian level.

It shouldn't be surprising that I'm most generally regarded as a mystery writer since mysteries often concern themselves with buried secrets, some literally. A play I wrote, *The Man Who Came to Murder,* concerns a decades-old automobile resurrected by workers digging a pool in the backyard of a modern Hollywood Hills home. There is a corpse inside. My personal favorite of the episodes I wrote for *Charlie's Angels* is called "Rosemary for Remembrance." It begins in a cemetery where the above Shakespearean quote is carved on a tombstone, and that story also features the literal unearthing of an important object from the past. Fifteen years later I wrote an episode of *Star Trek: Next Generation* called "Remember Me." An epidemic of disappearances strikes the Enterprise, and only one character can remember those gone, including some characters' closest friends and most of the regular cast members.

In the computer game *The Riddle of Master Lu*, the player-character Robert Ripley visits lost civilizations and must solve their many secrets of the past to survive. I've already mentioned how the mystery of Jake's past in *Dark Side of the Moon* drives him. In Gameforge's *Star Trek: Infinite Space*, a casual MMO I wrote for in 2010, there was ample opportunity for many different characters to be haunted by their pasts. In the first Agatha Christie novel I adapted as a game, *And Then There Were None*, all the characters must face their past transgressions. Even in media as collaborative as TV and computer games, writers and designers can explore those themes closest to our souls.

I don't mean to suggest that everybody—or anybody—should adapt memory as their own. But memory is an excellent way to expose backstory, reveal character, and create emotion.

I was designing a new adventure game called *Sideshow* when we decided *The Riddle of Master Lu* deserved a sequel. *Sideshow* was set aside, and financial difficulties of the company resulted in neither game being completed.

The story of *Sideshow* concerned a player-character who suffered horrific nightmare flashbacks about a childhood friend who fell to his death from a roller coaster ride. After an opening nightmare, the PC, now an adult, arrived back in his hometown, which he had not visited in many years, to try and come to terms with the original incident, and to figure out why the nightmares had returned after so long a time.

The amusement park that made the town a tourist attraction closed soon after that accident, and the town was now struggling to stay alive. So here I had an opportunity to contrast the town of the past with the town of the present. For this purpose, I designed a button on the interface that I called a Memory Key. At any location in the game that the player-character knew, the button would glow. When the player clicked on the button, they heard a voice-over memory of what the location used to look like.

* * *

A1. LOOK AT DOOR OR BUILDING

DAVID (V.O.)

Willow Falls Public Library. Growing up in a small town like this, the only ticket we had to the rest of the world was through that door.

* * *

This device gave me several opportunities for character, story, and gameplay:

- The memories were useful in creating the contrast of the two towns, past and present.

- They provided needed exposition.

- They provoked an emotional response in both PC and player that grew over time as the player became more invested in the character.

- I could contrast the boy character with his dreams and the adult character with his nightmares, revealing character growth and development in the perspective he brought to these memories.

- Other characters would have a different recollection of past events. The player, armed with knowledge from the Memory Key, could recognize those differences.

- I was also able to include clues and items from the town's past to solve various present-day puzzles. For example, the hidden cache beneath the hideaway the boys used to play in (based on a similar hideaway I played in as a boy—write what you know!) provided the player-character with several useful tools.

In 1999, one single-player design that I later adapted for a possible virtual world included generations. In essence, the player played not one, but multiple characters, three in the single-player version. In the multiplayer version, it allowed for true player death, something I have otherwise avoided like the plague. The player really could live through their children.

This idea of being able to play succeeding generations in the same family fascinated me. The rites of passage… the memories…. In both designs, the game engine took screenshots of the significant moments of a player-character's life, such as the battle with a spectacular opponent or the completion of an epic quest. Then in the next generation, a family album could be accessed to relive those moments and, in the multiplayer version, share them with friends.

Memories evoke powerful emotions. Whether or not your theme has anything at all to do with memory or the past—though many do, it seems—memory can be an invaluable tool for writers of games.

REVEALING CHARACTER THROUGH ACTION

As I said in the introduction, games are an action medium. Every time we stop to make players read text or listen to long speeches; we are essentially hitting the pause button for them. Sometimes pauses are a good thing. We want to design natural breakpoints into the game in the same way that chapters break up a book or commercials divide network television into acts. Breaks between levels or rewards like the cut scenes that appear when players complete special quests in *Final Fantasy XI*, even the pause key itself, can provide a needed break in the action for those other needs gamers occasionally have like food and rest and real life.

Mostly though, a gamer whose gameplay is interrupted is an impatient gamer, and impatient gamers are unhappy gamers. A lot of writers in all media wrestle with this issue. And it's important enough that I'm focusing on it twice: once here with characters, and again in Chapter 10, "Charting New Territory," when we're examining story. It may not be possible to reveal character solely in action, but every chance we can, we should do so.

Noah Falstein is an advisor and consultant on games for health and was formerly Google's Chief Game Designer. Here he takes a look at revealing characters through the action of gameplay:

> Every freshman writing class reiterates the admonition, "Show, don't tell." This is solid advice; it is much more engrossing to read an account that shows a character doing something interesting than to have a character or narrator simply tell the reader what happened. This applies to stories in the interactive realm as well. But with interactive storytelling, there's a transcendent principle: *do, don't show.* Build the relationships into the actions the player takes and the direct relationships that the player experiences through the game, not in the backstory.

In the first segment of *Starcraft*'s single-player campaign the player-character reports to a General. The General is clearly not to be trusted, but there's no choice as the player must follow his orders. Then he abandons you at a critical moment—not in a cut scene, but in the midst of a tough battle—and you are left to fend for yourself against what seems like impossible odds. The creators of *Starcraft* could simply have told you that the General was a bad guy, or shown him strangling underlings in classic Darth Vader fashion, but it was much more effective to have him betray your proxy in the midst of gameplay and let you suffer the effects directly by having to fight your way out of the situation. Then later in the game when the General returns to the field of battle and you're given the chance to get your revenge, it is a ruthlessly satisfying resolution. By building the story arc into the game-play itself and having the repercussions of the General's actions affect the PC, the Blizzard designers and writers achieved a powerful impact.

Let's make sure we understand what we mean when we say *action*. It is not synonymous with physical activity, which is its common definition. Physical activities such as sports, fighting a fire, chases, and combat are action, but they are not the only type of action. We also call making a decisive decision "taking action." A commentator can describe a chess match as filled with action: two minds battling it out with move and countermove. A sharp exchange of dialogue in a courtroom drama is action.

Any one of these is an opportunity to reveal character. Let's start with physical activity since that's what action consists most of in games. In sports, we see character, or the lack of it, in every contest: the gracious victor or the player who throws their racket against a wall; the linebacker who helps up the quarterback he's just sacked or the tackler who deliberately tries to injure an opponent to take them out of the game; the boxer who waits for their opponent to climb to their feet or the one who hits below the belt; the enforcer in hockey; the cheat; the team player; the braggart; the encouraging teammate; the taunter. The list is long.

How characters face danger reveals much about them. In 2004, a firefighter in Wyoming was sentenced to ten years in prison for setting fires to create work. Contrast this with the heroism of firefighters heroically combating an epidemic of fires in the western United States who do their jobs in the face of destruction of forests and wildlife on an unimageable scale.

We don't need monologues, voice-overs, or comments from other characters. "Hey, Jim Bob! Lookit that dude drive! He really knows what he's doin'!" We can *see* they know what they're doing. Or not. Walter Hill, writer and/or director of action movies like *48 Hours*, *Streets of Fire*, and *The Warriors* is reputed to have answered a reporter's question on character like this: "How do I write character? I have somebody stick a gun in his face and see how long it takes him to blink." Whether you agree with him or not, that's revealing character in action!

There is no need to waste a physical action scene with just action. Look at *Die Hard*, and then Google "die hard copies." The good ones figured out how John McClane (Bruce Willis) reveals character in almost every scene whether he is crawling through one of those ubiquitous air ducts or pounding a terrorist to a pulp.

What about the other cases? The Cuban missile crisis reveals character in *Thirteen Days* in scene after scene of anger, fear, conflict, and decisive decisions, many of which take place in rooms with paneled walls. The chess games in *The Queen's Gambit* reveal character with every movement of a piece on a board. We want to keep our character revelation short and sweet. Remember our impatient gamer? Remember too the moment at the very beginning of the movie *Air Force One* when Harrison Ford gives his speech, and the reactions of his Chief of Staff and Secretary of Defense when he diverges from his prepared remarks. A startled look and two lines of dialogue establish that something very important is happening, and these two characters don't like it very much.

The battling of two minds can be full of action, little of it physical. Long before *L.A. Confidential*, Curtis Hanson wrote *The Silent Partner*, a nifty little thriller set at Christmas time in a bank at the Eaton Centre in Toronto. It so captivated me that I sat through it twice in a row. The story concerns a bank teller (Elliot Gould) who realizes that a Santa Claus (Christopher Plummer) ringing a bell for charitable donations is actually casing the bank. Gould decides to rob the bank *before* Plummer can so that Plummer will get away with only a small portion of the swag and Gould can pocket the rest.

This happens quite early in the movie. The rest of the film is devoted to a battle of wits between the two with remarkably little physical action. Although there are a couple of shockingly violent scenes, most of the physical action deals with sticking fingers into marmalade jars and running after garbage trucks. The true action of the film concentrates on the increasingly ingenious mind games the two play on one another once Plummer realizes what has happened. The film uses those games to reveal more layers to each character as the film progresses, especially in Gould's seemingly deferential bank teller.

We don't need to eliminate physical action. Far from it. But we can certainly intersperse other types of action amidst the mayhem, and *all* action gives us a chance to reveal character.

I conclude this examination of character in the next chapter where we will discuss ways to handle the encounters between player-characters and NPCs.

CHAPTER 6

Character Encounters

I**T'S EASIER TO WRITE** dialogue for a *Frozen 2* Elsa talking doll than a highly mobile three-dimensional character of purpose and service like, well like the actual Disney character. We need to do it though. We need to respect our characters enough and give them the attention they deserve so that they are as entertaining as any other feature of our games.

In the previous chapters, I've tried to suggest some ways to bring these characters to life. Let's say we've succeeded, and our game world is now populated with interesting NPCs instead of dolls, NPCs with the potential to touch our hearts as much as characters in any other entertainment medium. Our players will want to interact with them!

PERCEPTION

There is no truth. There is only perception.

Gustave Flaubert

Let's start with perception. It will help the discussion if we look at a third psychiatrist, not as well known as Freud or Jung, but one who spent a lot of time studying perception and communication. His name was R.D. Laing (1927–1989). His views on mental illness were shaped by existential philosophy and were often very different from mainstream psychiatry. His best-known book, published in 1960, is *The Divided Self*, an effort to make the inner world of the mentally ill—in particular schizophrenics—comprehensible to the rest of us.

The contributing factors of this complex disease have been debated since the mid-19th century. It manifests itself in so many different ways, there is no objective test. In fact, the debate now includes whether schizophrenia is a single disorder or many. Causes may be found in some or all our three dimensions of character, although neurobiology is the current focus of researchers.

A lesser-known book Lang wrote in collaboration with H. Phillipson and A.R. Lee, was *Interpersonal Perception* published in 1966. Laing was not only interested in individuals, but the interactions between people. I'm not going to try and explain all the complex concepts in the book but want to share with you a synthesis I made of one central point.

DOI: 10.1201/9780429284991-9

When two people talk to one another, miscommunications happen even when both are paying attention. Our perceptions of a single conversation are affected by any number of factors from momentary distractions to outright psychosis. Basically, what the speaker thinks they said and what the listener thinks they heard can be radically different. The truth floats somewhere in mid-air between them. Perception is fluid and transitory. We can use that.

There was an interesting scrap of text that showed up on the Internet late in 2003. Its attribution is doubtful, but it gives us another look at perception.

> Aoccdrnig to a rscheearch at Cmabrigde Uinervtisy, it deosn't mttaer in waht oredr the ltteers in a wrod are, the olny iprmoetnt tihng is taht the frist and lsat ltteer be at the rghit pclae. The rset can be a toatl mses and you can sitll raed it wouthit porbelm. Tihs is bcuseae the huamn mnid deos not raed ervey lteter by istlef, but the wrod as awlohe.

Notice that the thesis of the paragraph is proven by the way the material is presented. Very cool! What is really going on when we read the paragraph? The brain is making connections for us. We can use that, too.

Our last example of perception is well known to most of us who have directed or edited film. It's called the Kuleshov effect, named for pioneer Russian filmmaker Lev Kuleshov (1899–1970). In 1919, at age 20, Kuleshov intercut a rather lengthy shot of an actor named Ivan Mozhukhin with the shots of a bowl of soup, a corpse, and a woman in the bed you see here in Figure 6.1.

Mozhukhin's expression is carefully neutral. Yet when intercut with the soup, an audience sees a hungry man. When intercut with the corpse, the audience sees remorse or maybe satisfaction at a job well done. When intercut with the woman, the audience sees lust; or a man pleased he has satisfied his lover; or a man dealing with rejection. Kuleshov's purpose was to illustrate the power of *montage*.

> Montage: the film technique of conveying ideas or emotions by juxtaposing different images.

The lesson was not lost on his more famous colleague, Sergei Eisenstein, whose seminal montage sequence on the Odessa harbor steps in the 1925 film *Battleship Potemkin* inspired Brian DePalma's homage in *The Untouchables* in 1987. Those who remember the past are destined to repeat it.

To understand how to communicate with computer-driven characters, it helps to understand how human beings communicate with each other. If we don't hear part of a comment, our brain attempts to fill in the missing bits. If we don't understand something, our brain searches for possible paths to that understanding. We make connections even where there are none. Our conversations are a series of attempts to communicate. Schizophrenics are an extreme example, according to Laing, of people attempting to communicate, however inappropriately, filling in square blanks with round ideas. It is important to differentiate between what a schizophrenic thinks they are saying and what they are really saying and parse the difference.

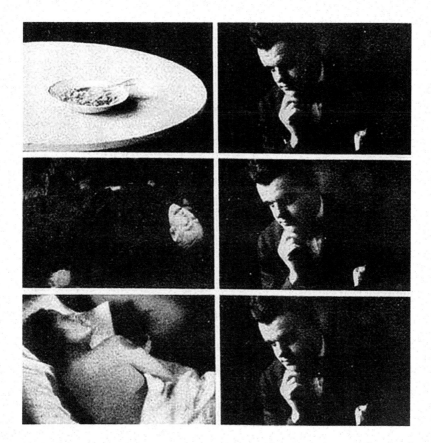

FIGURE 6.1 Kuleshov effect images.

Drama is not reality, remember? Writers don't have the knowledge or perception to duplicate reality, nor should we try. Reality isn't very dramatic most of the time. Luckily, we don't have to duplicate it. What we *can* do when writing characters is to approximate human behavior and stop there, just as an animator takes it as far as they can, then stops.

Just knowing that the player is going to fill in the blanks is key to how they will respond to our characters and interact with them. We can take shortcuts and choose which characteristics (traits or qualities) to highlight. If our choices are good enough, the character will be three-dimensional even with surprisingly few characteristics. A rich character is not an overly explained character. You don't create a Scarlet O'Hara with three physical characteristics (raven hair, sparkling eyes, 18-inch waist), two sociological characteristics (southern belle, spoiled rotten), and four psychological characteristics (haughty, flirtatious, determined, brave). Making the 3D Character Guide lets you look at your character from different perspectives. It's which ones you as a writer choose to emphasize that are important.

Laing's studies of perception and Kuleshov's experiments with montage are two good places to start to learn *how* the player will fill in the blanks. We want our characters to interact, not realistically, but as naturally as is possible.

PERSPECTIVE (FIRST PERSON VERSUS THIRD PERSON)

From perception, it is a natural transition to *point of view*, or POV. When writing a screenplay POV is used to indicate that the camera is seeing a scene through a character's eyes. This perspective is also called *first person* in literature, one of three major perspectives from which a story is told. The other two perspectives are second person and third person. There are even sub variations of these, such as first-person narrator, first-person reporter, limited omniscient, and objective, but these are not applicable in visual media.

Most camera angles in movies are in third person with only occasional POV shots to draw attention to a particular feature of a scene or to heighten suspense. One of the rare exceptions to this is *The Lady in the Lake*, a 1947 film adaptation of Raymond Chandler's mystery novel directed by and starring Robert Montgomery as Phillip Marlowe (Figure 6.2). Except for brief glimpses in mirrors, and hands that appear at the bottom of the frame as in first-person games, the camera is firmly in Marlowe's POV.

The effect is gimmicky and off-putting, yet it has shown up in several "interactive movies" and live-action video games over the years.

The conceit is more successful when it is only one aspect of a computer game where the game action is in first person as well. When the POV is split, the effect can be jarring, as in the adventure game *Under a Killing Moon* where the game action is in first person. But when it's time for dialogue, the detective, Tex Murphy, steps into the frame.

Unlike film, where the POV is changed very deliberately to create certain effects, splitting POV arbitrarily was one of those classic mistakes like

> Axis: an imaginary line drawn between the subjects of two inter-cut shots. Both should normally be photographed by a camera on the same side of that line, or the actors will appear to be looking in the same direction and not at each other.

FIGURE 6.2   Marlowe's face puts in a rare appearance in *The Lady in the Lake*.

crossing the axis. The player may not notice that anything is "wrong," but that part of the brain raised on the language of film is momentarily distracted.

Live theater is always third person, whether the play is seen through the traditional proscenium arch; in the round (where the audience surrounds the stage); or where the actors move among the audience as in *Sleep No More*, an adaptation of *Macbeth* that premiered in Lower Manhattan in 2011. *Tamara*, a play from the 1980s, written by John Krizanc, attempted branching storylines in live theater. It was first produced in the many rooms of an American Legion Hall (transformed into an Italian villa) in Hollywood. This style of production is now sometimes referred to as promenade theater. I'll return to this topic in Chapter 10 when we look at audience participation again.

Novels are generally third person, also known as *omniscient view*, although there are large bodies of work in first person. Many detective novels are written in first person so that the reader can follow the unraveling of the crime along with the detective or the perpetrator. This is one of the reasons Montgomery chose a Phillip Marlowe novel by Chandler for his first-person experiment. The books are written in first person.

I haven't done any actual counting, but perspective in games today seems to be split about the same way as novels. More are designed as third person, but first person is a healthy minority. Virtual Reality is the notable exception. VR pretty much demands a first-person perspective. Some games routinely offer both perspectives, and they allow the player to switch perspective by pressing a button on the controller.

Second-person perspective games, as mentioned earlier, are easily identifiable by use of the pronoun "you." This perspective was dominant from the very beginning of text adventures. A well-known example from *Zork* is: "You are in an open field west of a big white house with a boarded front door." As graphics became more and more sophisticated, second-person usage declined. One major exception is those games that use scrolling text to tell the player what is happening: "You pick up a red power pill!" "You've earned 45 Legacy points!" "You hit the dragon for 34 points of damage!"

These types of messages use more than their quota of exclamation points. They're not very immersive but certainly informative.

How do we make the choice between first and third person? Or should we even worry about it when we try to bring our characters to life? Sometimes the game engine or the type of game makes the decision for us. Real-time strategy games often require an omniscient third-person POV to see as much of the game action as possible at any one time. First-person shooters, of course, can place the player inside the player-character with only a weapon visible. Players experience the game world as if we were seeing it with our own eyes. This gives the world an almost tangible sense of place. And, theoretically at least, when NPCs turn to look directly at the player, it heightens the immersion, as long as we don't break the spell by jumping back and forth between the PC and the NPC.

Immersion is not a new word, nor is our usage of it new. In addition to meaning "sinking within a fluid," it turns up in the 1913 edition of Webster's Unabridged Dictionary as "The state of being overwhelmed or deeply absorbed; deep engagedness."

Third person, since we're comfortable with its place in our collective film language unconscious, would seem to be a comfortable choice, if we want to create empathy. It means that when we interact with NPCs or other player-characters, the interaction will appear on the screen much as it would in a movie. We see the PC in the visual frame of the game, usually either as an over-the-shoulder shot or moving throughout the game's landscape with the fluidity of a movie character.

Empathy, as Webster tells us, is an identification with or understanding of *another's* feelings or situation or motives. This is a good thing. Luckily for us empathy isn't dependent upon perspective.

If the first narrative movies had not emulated live theater's necessary third-person point of view, but to distinguish themselves from stage plays had decided to tell their stories in first-person POV, empathy would be just as natural for us today in first-person films. And first person has its place. Remember the gun firing at the camera in *The Great Train Robbery* and how effective it was? Here's the shot of the shot seen round the world (Figure 6.3).

So, if empathy is not dependent on perspective, is immersion? It is caused by a whole range of factors from fascinating characters (our goal of course) to size of images, and many more in between. I'd argue that all of them can create immersion regardless of perspective. We can become immersed in a book as fully as a game or a hot bath. We become unconscious of the turning of the pages. Each chapter ending gives us a moment to catch our breath. Time stops for us. Later we must catch back up to the rest of the world that went on its merry way while we were lost to it.

I'll suggest that it isn't the perspective—however much we seem to debate it—that matters at all in the end; it's the craft with which we make use of it. Non-player-characters can be written the same for either first person or third.

There is one more character we need to look at before we move on. Empathy is identification with another. What about our identification with the player-character? Perspective would seem to play a big role in that. In first person, we can't see our avatar, or maybe only

FIGURE 6.3 The first first-person shooter in *The Great Train Robbery.*

its hands. In third person, we see our representation right there on the screen. Is there a difference in how we write the player-character?

Only one of the three dimensions of character would seem to be primarily affected: the physical. In third-person point of view, graphics can give us a lot of the details. In first person we need to rely on the opinions of NPCs and voice acting. These can illuminate all three dimensions. Remembering to steer clear of stereotypes in the character themselves, a deeper voice can convey size and authority; vocabulary or a public-school British accent can suggest education; vocal quality can suggest timidity, sexiness, and so on. Writers, of course, are most concerned with the NPC dialogue—word choices of the player-character, for example, vocabulary and the rhythms of accents.

DIALOGUE

You guide your PC along the street. You come to a large Victorian house with a sign out front. You click on the sign and learn the house is not only a residence but a doctor's office. You go in. Standing inside a small waiting room is an elderly man: Dr. Adams. You click on Dr. Adams.

ADAMS

I love watching all the children I brought into this world smoking or drinking or cholesterolling themselves into early graves. Piling into trees at 90 miles an hour. Ingesting chemicals that turn brain cells to jelly. Fascinating profession: medicine. We learn far too much! And the thing we learn that cuts the deepest is that we'll never know enough to stop them. Or ourselves. We're all on the same ride...to oblivion...and we're all determined to make that ride as short as possible!

Does this game mechanic sound familiar? The player-character comes upon an NPC, clicks on the NPC to "activate" it, and the NPC obligingly spits out exposition, its life story, its function in the game, or some other important information. It does this without thought to any passing stranger. This is not respecting the character. This is reducing it to a game convenience, no more. It is ignoring all sorts of possible opportunities to create a real character with a life of their own within the game. However well written the actual speech may be, the writer/designer has already limited themselves as well as the character.

People don't respond on command. They have reasons for talking to us, and they choose what they want to say. If we remember Laing, we'll see that there are more layers to any conversation than one, just as there are more dimensions than just one to a character. How can we begin to bring that character to life? We might walk in on a conversation between two NPCs. We don't need to click on anybody. The conversation is triggered by the PC's entrance and is written to indicate we've interrupted it. It doesn't have to start at the beginning. We will fill in the blanks.

Now let's add the doctor's daughter, Nancy, to the encounter. Adams, a retired doctor, is bitter that he's brought too many babies into the world only to sign their death certificates long before their time. Nancy is also a doctor. She has taken over his practice. She still possesses an idealism all doctors must hold on to, if they are to minister to the ill and not just apply treatment.

* * *

NANCY

Dad, you love this town, and you know it!

ADAMS

That's right, my dear. I love watching all the children I brought into this world smoking or drinking or cholesterolling themselves into early graves. Piling into trees at 90 miles an hour. Ingesting chemicals that turn brain cells to jelly. Fascinating profession: medicine. We learn far too much! And the thing we learn that cuts the deepest is that we'll never know enough to stop them. Or ourselves. We're all on the same ride…to oblivion…and we're all determined to make that ride as short as possible!

* * *

The two might break off now as they realize they aren't alone. Note that this isn't a cut scene, but a moment of interaction between two NPCs while the player-character, let's call him David, looks on. If the writer is uncomfortable about the chore of having two NPCs to talk to, Adams might exit angrily. If not, Nancy can be embarrassed at being overheard, and Adams can be aggressive, demanding to know what the PC is doing there. Or Adams might be unhappy about hearing his private opinions aired to a stranger, and Nancy might step into the breach with a word of welcome or inquiry.

But let's stay with the small piece of an encounter we started with. How has it improved? To begin with, of course, by giving him someone to talk to, someone he may actually love and respect, Adams has motivation to voice his frustrations. He's no longer a *Frozen 2* Elsa doll. Next, we're plunged into the middle of a real scene. We didn't cut away from the action for it, even if for a moment we snuck control away from the player to ensure they witness the exchange. If the moment is short enough, compelling enough, *entertaining* enough, equal to such scenes in other media, the player shouldn't mind.

But there's still a problem. Thanks to the human ego, we all think the stories we have to tell others are fascinating, and we will ramble on. But drama is not reality. Drama reserves its speeches for special moments and gives them special names like *monologue* or *soliloquy*. Drama is much more at home, particularly these days, with the give-and-take of two characters in conversation. Our shortened attention spans—created in part by the fact that with only 23 or 47 minutes to tell stories, both network and streaming television must pare dialogue to the bone—are significantly different from more leisurely times when speeches were in general longer. Audiences used to have more patience!

In the two decades I wrote television and movie scripts—from 1974 to 1994—the average length of a scene in scripts shrank from five pages to two and a half. We don't just cut out the beginnings and ends of scenes these days. Those have been gone from the very beginning of drama. See the "Point of Attack" section in Chapter 9, "Bringing the Story to Life." We fillet scenes until there is nothing left but meat. And with rare, important exceptions, the dialogue is an exchange, not a single speech. The limited TV series *Midnight Mass* is a notable exception. Characters exchange soul-searching monologues with a regularity rarely seen in television.

Dialogue in games is much more like film than it is in plays or books. Or it should be. Games share with film the ability to pitch the action at a very fast pace. Leaner dialogue, delivered in spurts punctuating the action, is far more effective in not interrupting the action than long-winded passages. Yet here we are in games, writing these lengthy speeches. If we try to emulate the exchange of dialogue in movies or TV shows, we ghettoize it in a cut scene. Why?

One reason may be technical. Give-and-take dialogue in an in-game encounter are often chopped into separate files, whereas a single long speech would only need to be in one file. But in the various games I've written and designed, I've never seen a game engine that balked at multiple files.

Another reason might be that it's easier. As soon as you add an extra character to an encounter, you jump from one possibility to three: the PC and one NPC can interact. The PC and the other NPC can interact. The two NPCs can interact. But if those interactions bring the encounter and its characters to life, we're shortchanging that interaction not to allow them. No wonder players get so tired of the dialogue and characters and storytelling in games that we're forced to reserve a button on the controller or a key on the keyboard to allow them to jump through it or ignore it altogether. No wonder players and developers alike may conclude that fully realized characters and rich stories aren't worth the effort in games.

Here is the encounter as it was written for the game *Sideshow* in 1995:

* * *

NANCY

Dad, you love this town, and you know it!

ADAMS

That's right, my dear. I love watching all the children I brought into this world smoking or drinking or cholesterolling themselves into early graves.

NANCY
(to Player-Character)
This is an ongoing debate . . .

ADAMS

Piling into trees at 90 miles an hour. Ingesting chemicals that turn brain cells to jelly. Fascinating profession: medicine.

NANCY

We save lives.

ADAMS

We learn far too much! And the thing we learn that cuts the deepest is that we'll never know enough to stop them. Or ourselves. We're all on the same ride... to oblivion... and we're all determined to make that ride as short as possible!

* * *

One more point: it may look like I've just doubled the length of the scene, and it does take up more space on paper. In fact, the time it plays out in the three versions I've shared is identical. We haven't interrupted gameplay any longer just to create an exchange instead of a monologue. The reason is the same reason TV and movies prefer short exchanges to long speeches: they move faster. *The Old Man* is a notable exception. Whether the player reads the text or listens to an actor speak it, the words pick up pace when they're broken into smaller speeches. Plus, with the addition of a *character in opposition* to Adams, we've also increased the drama, and that increases pace.

Try it. Get a stopwatch. Act the first monologue aloud. Don't just read it, act it. Notice how you must not only pause for breaths, but to make the moments happen. By this, we mean taking the time to separate all the individual thoughts in a long speech so that each one is comprehensible to the listener. Remember my anecdote in Chapter 1, "Myths and Equations," about Keith Michel in *Crucifer of Blood*? When he sped up his delivery of his lines, he deliberately stopped making the moments.

Watch any of Kenneth Branagh's film adaptations of Shakespearean plays to see how the director and his other actors find the meaning in each Elizabethan line and especially the long speeches. They don't just recite them.

We'll get to cut scenes later, but with more attention to encounters within the gameplay, fewer cut scenes will be needed.

What else can we do with dialogue? We can be self-conscious about how we as writers talk. Do all the characters sound like us? Usually, that's a bad thing if we're writing a variety of characters from different cultures or walks of life. If they all share a similar background, they can share similarities, but differences in word choices, favorite expressions, and so on, should be found. And this shouldn't be a mechanical process. Instead of lists of accents or slang expressions or stock phrases in foreign tongues, if we start with three-dimensional characters, those characters inform us how they will talk.

Let's look at accents for a second. Writers and designers, to make their characters sound different when they're voiced, often give them accents. When actors, whether professional voice actors or those used to being in front of the camera, are asked to voice characters, the demands on their performances change.

First, professional voice actors have a repertoire of different-sounding voices with a variety of accents. This is necessary because often a single *voice actor* can voice many characters just as they do in animated TV shows and films. But one way they can differentiate between character voices is with accents. And if you're not careful, you can get a variety of immersion-breaking accents in your game. How many times have we heard dwarves voiced as Scottish and rogues with distinct New York accents?

Some developers will justify such choices by saying they're adding comedy. The player is aware they are hearing a jokey accent. Well, as we'll see

> Voice actors: Retain a naturalistic quality that stresses character.
> Voice-over announcers: Train themselves to talk in over-modulated speech patterns so that their message is clear.
> Make sure you know which one you're getting for your game. Some actors can do both, but unless you want your scenes to sound like CNN, hire voice actors, not voice-over announcers.

in Chapter 10, "Charting New Territory," there is comedy that enhances immersion, and comedy that fights it.

How about writing accents in text speech that players must read? Ever notice the difficulties role-players online get into when trying to do a character in text? It was fun to add an accent to your character at the kitchen table playing *Dungeons & Dragons*. It's a lot harder to duplicate that accent in a text chat window and make it comprehensible. If the other players can't read it, you're breaking their *immersion*.

Writers face the same dilemma. We do need to know accents and regional slang. But we shouldn't try to precisely replicate them on the page. Remember, people fill in the blanks. Writing an accent is catching its rhythm and inflections, not its spelling. Use spelling of accented words sparingly, as no more than the occasional garnish on a salad, or you will lose your reader.

Before we get into various ways to handle interactive game dialogue, I want to look at the most important thing you can do to bring your dialogue to life. Get beyond "how people talk," in what we call colloquial speech. We're doing drama, not reality!

Don't even stop with writing characters in different voices with their own rhythms and inflections. Take colloquial speech and add an edge to it. Twist it. David Mametize it.

The dialogue of writer David Mamet (1947–) is so distinctive, it has its own word to describe it: Mametspeak. It is anything but colloquial. Listen to the characters in movies Mamet has written and directed such as *House of Games*, *Oleanna*, *The Spanish Prisoner*, and *State and Main*, as well as those he's just written, such as *The Untouchables*, *Ronin*, and, of course, the film adaptation of his Pulitzer Prize-winning play, *Glengarry Glen Ross*, where salesmen, desperate to do anything to close a deal are treated to a little motivational speech. Alan Arkin is Moss. Alec Baldwin is Blake.

* * *

"Moss: What's your name?

Blake: *F**k you!* That's my name!

[Moss laughs.]

Blake: You know why, mister? 'Cause you drove a Hyundai to get here tonight, I drove an eighty thousand dollar BMW. *That's* my name. You see this watch. This watch cost more than your car. I made $970,000 dollars last year; how much did you make? You see pal, that's who I am and you're nothing. Nice guy? I don't give a s**t. Good father? F**k you. Go home and play with your kids. You wanna work here-close."

* * *

"Close" means "close the deal." That's a tiny portion of a long speech. Mamet isn't afraid of long speeches, but he knows when to use them.

I am by no means suggesting we try to emulate Mamet's dialogue. It is extremely stylized, sort of an amalgamation of street colloquial and the staccato delivery of early Harold Pinter in *The Birthday Party* or *The Caretaker*. *Filmmakers Magazine* called it "a poetic impression of streetwise jargon." There is a reason Mamet reuses actors in the films he directs. Some, like William H. Macy, can bring the dialogue to life. Others make it sound arch and mechanical.

The key to Mamet's dialogue is it is impossible *not* to listen to it. It's close enough to the way we've heard people speak, we can buy into it, yet we are startled by its cadences, and that forces us to listen even closer. Read—and listen to—the language of Studs Turkel's Chicago, Flannery O'Conner's South, and the prose poetry of Ray Bradbury and John Le Carré.

In 1984 I was writer-producer of a TV series called *Blacke's Magic*, a mystery show starring Hal Linden and Harry Morgan. One of the episodes took magician Alexander Blacke (Linden) and his con-artist father (Morgan) to a small town whose entire population vanishes during the night. They were visiting the town for sentimental reasons. It was at the fairgrounds here where Morgan had wooed and won Alex's mother, now dead for many years. Morgan finds a tree where he carved "Lenny Loves Lizbeth" decades before and traces the heart surrounding the words with his finger.

* * *

LEONARD

Her eyes sparkled…catchin' the light from the Ferris wheel…I close my eyes, an' I can see her so clear…

And faintly, soft as memory, CALLIOPE MUSIC sneaks in beneath the scene, and the echoes of delighted children SCREAMING in make-believe fright.

LEONARD

She'd joined up with us in Fresno, dancin' as parta Big Ed Twiliger's troupe. But she was no hootchie-kootch. She moved like a brightly colored curtain brushed by the wind along an open window…or like the long slow curl of an emerald wave…. She was gonna dance on the Great White Way, and I…

The memories and music FADE.

ALEX

What, Pop?

LEONARD

For the first time in my life, I had no ambitions, 'cept one. To love her, cherish her, grow old in her arms…Never made it to Broadway…I always regretted…

ALEX

No, Pop. No regrets. It was a wonderful life, and she loved you for it. We both did.

* * *

Harry Morgan's wife of many years had died recently. I wrote the scene for him, and he played it beautifully. I broke up the speech with sound cues and Alex's one interjection when Leonard arranges what he's trying to say. It was television after all. But its rhythms are deliberately the rhythms of poetry. We both knew it wasn't colloquial. Neither of us cared.

We should not be afraid of the poetic richness of our language. We hear colloquial speech all around us. We tune it out. To write it is to invite our player, whether they be listener or reader, to tune it out. Take the time to transform it into something the player is compelled to listen to, and they won't mind taking their hand off the controller for a short while.

DIALOGUE SYSTEMS

There have been a lot of different systems developed to facilitate conversation between the player-character and NPCs in games. All are compromises. While an NPC can "speak" either in voice or text, players are, for the most part, forced to talk with the same devices they use for all game mechanics: the keyboard or control pad. There are exceptions. 2003's PlayStation 2 game *Lifeline* from Konami allowed the player to issue vocal commands to the player-character. The results were mixed, as they are whenever parsers or voice recognition systems are employed.

The range of these systems is great: from the non-existent—in *Riven* you watch other characters, you don't interact—to elaborate AI-based systems like Chris Crawford's StoryTron. We'll spend most of our time between these two extremes. Some of the systems listed here may have only a historical value since we seem to have settled into a few favorite ones, but even the most arcane seem to reappear from time to time.

NPC dialogue can be text or spoken aloud. AAA games are voiced unless there's a stylistic reason for not voicing them. They're obviously more naturalistic. Social games use mostly text. It's a storage issue as well as a cost issue. Sound files are larger than text files. Actors must be paid.

Early virtual worlds used to employ text almost exclusively. There were usually a *lot* of NPCs and voicing them all could be prohibitively expensive. There was also the issue of communication between server and client. Large sound files take longer than long text files to travel between the two, and not all can reside on the client where computer-savvy players can peek at them before they should. Finally, text was a more private medium of communication. It allowed multiple players to interact with NPCs simultaneously without disturbing one another. Today, if we have huge budgets, every voice can be heard. In a talk at the 2012 Game Developers Conference, Richard Vogel, executive producer of *Star Wars: The Old Republic*, told a stunned audience of developers that there were over 240,000 lines of spoken dialogue in the game, voiced by hundreds of actors. That was good enough for a Guinness World Record. 2018's *Red Dead Redemption 2* reportedly contains 500,000 lines of dialogue. As of 2020, *TIL Las Vegas* holds the Guinness World Record at only 65,000 lines of dialogue. I'm not going to try and figure out how those three things can all be true.

The following dialogue systems are listed in order of increasing sophistication. The more sophisticated the system, the more natural it can be, whether voiced or text, and the more opportunity for character revelation and storytelling we have, but it can also be more difficult to pull off. The following are not all the variations designers have attempted when introducing dialogue into their video games, but they're a good cross section.

Canned Speeches

Canned speeches are the first logical step beyond not interacting at all, and they are without a doubt the easiest conversation system we have.

Half-Life, Legend of Zelda, Goldeneye, Diablo: many games have used this system where the player-character doesn't speak. *Bioshock* used this approach. It was still popular in social network games such as *Indiana Jones Adventure World*, that I wrote for in 2011. I'll come back to this game later.

A canned speech can be forced on a player. An NPC pops up out of nowhere exhorting you to invite your friends or comment on gameplay. Or it can be triggered by clicking on an NPC, communication device or a door or a gopher hole or….

The NPC may begin to speak, or a menu may appear if the NPC performs multiple functions. The NPC then spouts a predetermined response. This response can be a single speech repeated each time the player chooses to speak with the character, a series of repetitive responses, or a long speech.

If the speech is in text, it can open in a chat bubble or on the UI (User Interface), or appear in its own window, masking the action and forcing the player to pay attention. If the speech is long, its window may have scroll bars, or it may be cut into pieces accessed in sequence by pressing the X button or clicking the mouse. The speech may be broken up like this to provide more easily digestible chunks, so the text will fit comfortably on the screen; or to not-so-cleverly hide the fact it's one of those long text passages again.

Many console games fall back on canned speeches for a good reason. No one in their right mind is going to attempt a parser-driven text conversation system on a console. Even beyond the limited nature of parsers, attempting to enter words with a game controller is like trying to build a flagpole by gluing dimes together in a stack. Eventually, you'll get there, but it's much better to just buy the flagpole and fly your flag.

Some designers, more comfortable with gameplay than writing, may choose canned speeches as the simplest method to get all that nasty talking out of the way. If parsers are mentioned by some enthusiastic programmer, the designer can also argue that even typing on a keyboard is immersion-breaking. The reason we have experiments in voice communication and control from time to time is to get away from the cumbersome keyboard. Choosing menu items may be too much work, and while they are a convention we often accept, they need not be so overt as pop-up windows.

If an NPC has multiple possible interactions, we can create a less jarring way of choosing among them than a pop-up window. For example, if the NPC is static, we can use the environment they inhabit. If they're a merchant who's also a quest giver, gossip, and trainer, we can place hotspots on various objects in their shop. If we want to buy something, we select the merchandise counter or a display of garden tools. If we want a quest, we might select a Help Wanted notice board that could display errands the player can do, or could trigger them to ask the player-character if they're looking for a job. Selecting an NPC directly would give us a greeting and exposition determined by our relationship to them, if any. We'll examine relationships shortly. Selecting the prized golden hoe they have prominently displayed on the wall behind them might prompt them to ask if we'd like to learn gardening.

Canned speeches need all the help they can get to keep the player in the world. Removing other immersion-harming reminders like basic menus can only help them.

Story is usually preserved by canned speeches, allowing little variation. It needn't be. If the underlying philosophy of the storytelling is nonlinear, then even canned speeches can be adapted to it. But I'm getting ahead of myself. We'll get to story. There's often no mechanism for handling the reality of a repeat visit with canned speeches. Once that single file is in place, everybody is happy and moves on. We'll look at an alternative in the following "Entrances and Exits" section.

Canned Conversations

The player-character carries on a single preordained conversation, but this time the player gets to witness the PC's side of it. Instead of just pressing the X button to hear the next part of the canned speech, the player-character interjects questions or comments in the way I added Alex's "What, Pop?" to the scene from *Blacke's Magic*. This system was all but dead on the PC, replaced by canned speeches, probably for the sake of simplicity, until the late 1990s when virtual worlds like *Everquest* and *Asheron's Call* resurrected it. Many game platforms still must be concerned with storage space. We're adding files after all. But again, text files are tiny, and we see canned conversations making a comeback in mobile phones and handhelds like the Nintendo Switch. The Switch also has games with built-in voice chat between players, if you'd also like to talk with other humans.

The reason canned conversations are superior to canned speeches is obvious. It feels more natural to respond to an NPC than to just poke them to continue talking. Sure, the player-character's speeches are just as canned as the NPC responses, but it is a step toward more natural conversation. The player may now have menu choices that go beyond TALK TO, BUY, SELL, REQUEST TRAINING, and ATTACK. There may be an indication of subject matter for discussion that the player can select from.

The NPC usually inhabits the game world. Although they can appear on the interface for convenience, they are not really at home there. It removes them from the world they are supposed to populate. That's why we try to find in-game mechanisms to prompt them. There is an exception. Players can have a foot in both the world of the game and the real world. Once the player starts directing the speech of the player-character, interface mechanisms can be used more easily. Players use them to direct the PC in how to manipulate the in-game environment. In this case it seems less immersion-breaking to allow the player to choose interface-based replies to the NPC. We've seen several of these.

Mood Meter

Games like *Return to Zork* and *Necropolis* gave players choices on how to respond in conversations. In a conversation, the player could choose from an array of emotions, graphically represented, and then the player-character spoke dialogue based on the choice. I've seen this used since then as well, but it is not very common.

This was obviously an attempt to streamline conversations by avoiding the need to read and then select dialogue choices from menus. It had the added "advantage" that the player wouldn't know what the player-character was about to say, only whether they would respond belligerently, diplomatically, or whatever. My feeling is this solved a problem that didn't really exist. Players were used to selecting choices from menus (we'll get to this system shortly), and surprising them with dialogue is not always a good thing, as we'll see in this next example.

Attitude Chart

A variation on the mood meter was the attitude chart from the Tex Murphy games. The player chose from a series of player-character attitude descriptions like Play It Cool; Get Tough; Pour on the Charm; Dazzle with your Wit; and so forth.

The danger here, of course, was the player's idea of pouring on the charm or being witty might not correspond to the game writer's idea. The player's surprise at hearing the line of dialogue might include annoyance. You really don't want your players angry at you: "That's the developers' idea of funny, huh? I'm wittier than that!" The same game also toyed with the player's expectations by deliberately giving the player-character lines the *character* thought were charming and witty, but obviously weren't. This added humor—the Tex Murphy games were tongue-in-cheek—but really amounted to playing a meta game with the player, reminding them that they were not really Murphy or a part of the game world.

Although seen occasionally over the years, neither the attitude chart nor the mood meter enjoyed much popularity. The interest the player might have had in seeing what dialogue their selection triggered was at the expense of the integrity of the game world. They are offered here as interesting experiments in communication. They may give designers ideas for variations on the systems or, at the very least, save designers before they stray too far down a dead-end path.

Iconic Choices

This is an attempt at a short-handed topic list that keeps the choices visual. 1996's *Circle of Blood* (UK: *Broken Sword: The Shadows of the Templars*) used icons to represent topic choices and NPCs available to talk to. Instead of the topics being listed as "Tell me about George." Or "Do you, Henri?" the icons replaced the words with faces of the individuals in question.

This method removed the pitfalls of the attitude chart and some of the immersion-breaking game aspects of both it and the mood meter. However, it is still vague, where vagueness is unnecessary. Icons in general are frustrating challenges we face every time we design the UI. How do we make sure an icon's function is recognized and not misinterpreted? Do we use the same old icons, or at least variations on them, much in the way international symbols are used? Icon design is an art all its own and outside the scope of this book. This system is dependent on mastering it.

A sloppy icon system will disconnect the player from the game world, the exact opposite of what it is trying to achieve. It's an interesting system, however, and I expect while we may not see any mood meters or attitude charts again anytime soon, iconic conversation systems may be worth re-examination.

Topic List

The player picks from a list of topics: this list can include generic topics, as well as specific topics added as the game progresses. *Legend of Zelda* has a rare and rudimentary form of this: the fishing shack, racecourse, and so forth. *Syberia* moves the list halfway into the world by presenting it off to one side as if their protagonist were glancing at notepads.

Topic lists do show up in more recent games, having survived the previous attempts to do away with them. At their best, they're simple and straightforward, cut down on verbiage, and, when integrated even partially into the game world, are not as immersion-breaking as they could be.

There are a couple of ways to handle the topic list. The topics can disappear after they've been chosen. If the information gleaned from the NPC's response is important, it can be automatically added to some memory-jogging device like a player journal or in game recorder.

The topics may remain on this list, perhaps grayed out, but still selectable. This allows the player to go back over topics to immediately refresh their memory, but at the expense of immersion when the NPC responses are rote.

Whereas icons, mood meters, or attitude charts rarely led to anything more than a single reply or brief exchange, true topic lists can be the interface into a simple branching dialogue structure, or even a web-like structure. These will be studied in more detail in Chapter 14, "Modular Storytelling."

Some topic lists try to be a puzzle unto themselves. The list of topics must be gone through in its entirety. Clues or puzzle elements may be hidden in the foliage. This can be problematic, particularly if the game is awarding the player points for achievements, forcing the player to scroll through more dialogue than necessary to find obscure bits of dialogue that are scored.

All four of the previous conversation systems had merit, and I should add that I enjoyed playing all the games. The fewer words the player had to read, the better. They were clever attempts to avoid, or at least truncate, menus that displayed actual dialogue, therefore limiting the amount of reading necessary. To achieve this, however, they gave up clarity.

We're removed one step from the natural flow of the conversation. And they can interject an immersion-harming game played between designer and player—What is my player-character going to say next?—for immersion in the actual conversation. The next group allows for even more sophisticated interaction between player-character and NPC, but at the risk of adding more words to read.

Highlighted Text

This is a conversation system that is popular, especially in virtual worlds. It's basically a topic list embedded within a paragraph of NPC text dialogue. Both *Dark Age of Camelot* and *Horizons* used it. The player clicks on highlighted text, and this leads to another response. This can be used in NPC quest dialogue or if NPCs offer more than one service. Highlighted text can be **bolded**, a different color, [in brackets], and so on.

This variation allows for the topic list choices to be within the context of the conversation. The examples I've seen have used it only to select canned speeches. Like them, it requires no dialogue from the player-character, although in *Dark Age of Camelot* the NPCs sometimes attempted to voice the player-character's thoughts: "Now, I know what you're thinking, enchanter…." An awkward conceit.

Highlighted text works quite well in gameplay, which explains its popularity, at least on PC monitors. Until high-definition TVs came along, selecting choices embedded in the text was not much fun. Highlighted text doesn't avoid any of the limitations of canned speeches in general, but also doesn't have to be used only to access them either. While there is no give-and-take between characters, it could be used, as other topics lists can be, as a transition to a simple branching or Web dialogue structure.

Dialogue Menu

The dialogue menu can be found in a number of single-player games and MMOs and has been around a long time. It rises and falls in popularity. Bethesda and Bioware have both relied on it in their RPGs. While it gives the writer even more opportunity for character revelation, especially of the player-character, it adds more text to read—one reason it only occasionally shows up in handheld games or smartphones, and why designers are forever trying to find ways to shorthand it.

It seems to take three forms, either in text or when voiced. The first is a logical descendant of the attitude chart. The player chooses from a list of choices to direct at an NPC, but then the dialogue, while akin to the choice, is different. In *Star Wars: The Old Republic*, this is a gameplay mechanism. You can earn Light or Dark side of the Force points, depending upon whether your choice is compassionate or severe. You can also earn Affection points from your current companion. The Force points allow access to various levels of special items. The Affection points open up lucrative side quests that your companions would like to see accomplished.

The second form of the dialogue menu is more common. You select a choice from the menu, and your character voices that choice, barring any recording glitches, exactly as written.

In the third form of dialogue menu, only the first or second line of a longer speech is displayed. You hear your character voice what you can see, but they may then launch into an extended speech.

As in topic lists, dialogue choices may disappear after being selected. They can also remain to be selected again. An even more sophisticated approach to the dialogue menu is making groups of choices disappear after the player has chosen just one. This design obviously does not belong on an in-game topic list object like a notepad, but it is the most naturalistic approach.

It flows much more like a real conversation where one topic veers off on to another, and then to another, and so on. "But!" cries the astute reader, "How do we plant exposition in the conversation, if the player does not choose the correct dialogue? Isn't that choice lost to them?"

Not really. I'm going to save most of this for Chapter 14. But let's take a worst-case scenario. Let's say in any given conversation between PC and an NPC named Abbott, I, the writer, have three pieces of exposition I want to get out. I also have two important character beats I'd like to establish. Now let's say I've planted one of these five "important things" in each of NPC Abbott's responses to my five dialogue choices A–E. The player selects A. B–E vanish so that a new group, F–J, can appear based on that choice. I've created variations of F–J. Once the game knows the player has chosen A, the variations of F and G include the necessary exposition from B and D. And for an encounter with Costello, a different NPC, the game will know that A, B, and D have been covered, and will therefore incorporate variations that include C and E.

Our next step, of course, is to match nonlinear gameplay with nonlinear story advancement and allow the player to visit either Abbott or Costello first. We include checks, so that we know who's on first, and the appropriate variations fire as needed. Again, more of this in Chapter 14.

"But!" the super astute reader retorts, "That's wasteful! If there are five dialogue choices and four of them vanish when we choose one, the effort that went into the NPC responses—including paying the voice actor—is wasted! All those variations? More waste!" It takes longer to write, no question. More thought and logic testing are needed. If you're looking for the *Lazy Writers Guide to Writing*, this book isn't it. Write the extra variations. You'll find the effort isn't that much greater. You'll be surprised how similar the variations can be. Cut and paste, change a couple of words, and move on.

As for those pesky voice actors who get paid by the hour? I've directed quite a few voice sessions. For the second Agatha Christie adventure game, *Murder on the Orient Express*, in 2006, I directed Vanessa Marshall, the voice actress for the player-character. Once the character voice was found, since the variations were remarkably similar, we tore through them. I have usually matched or beaten the time and expense budgeted for games whose authors didn't bother to seed their important exposition throughout a naturally flowing conversation. I wasn't able to direct actor David Suchet, who voiced his most famous character, Hercule Poirot, for the game, but he knew the character so well, only an introductory conversation between us was really needed.

Another advantage of dialogue menus is the opportunity to share the dialogue choices with the player. The player can now intelligently choose not only topics (topic list) but also ways to approach those topics (attitude chart) and how hard to hit them (mood meter). Further, one of the reasons we like characters we empathize with in other media is that they do things we can never do. They can also—through our talent—be far more witty, articulate, and wise (or boring, tongue-tied, and stupid!) than the player themselves.

Here's a chance to share that with the player. We give them the chance to stand up in a conversation with Albert Einstein or Dorothy Parker or Socrates and hold their own. Make the player into someone they could never be. Allow them to do things they could never do. Remember?

In some of my games, from the early *The Riddle of Master Lu* (1994) to all three of the Agatha Christie games through *Evil Under the Sun* in 2007, I used full sentences. In *Star Trek: Infinite Space* in 2010, I fashioned elaborate stories almost entirely in dialogue in lieu of fully interactive away team missions, a budgetary sacrifice. But it was an intriguing challenge that paved the way for my work in social games: telling involving stories in tweet-sized snippets of dialogue.

Natural Language/AI-Based Conversations

At the far end of the spectrum from no conversation, we have natural language/AI-based conversations like those found in 2012's independent game *Prom Week* from UC Santa Cruz's Expressive Intelligence Studio. They are outside the scope of this book but are fascinating. Like most AI, research developers wisely limit the scope of possible interactions with their Intelligent Virtual Agents. We're nowhere near ready to turn over dramatic conversations with major characters to AI in commercial games, but one interesting line of investigation is to create more natural-feeling minor characters. I invite you to explore their many possibilities.

From the preceding, you might assume the only system I like is the dialogue menu. You would be wrong. In my mind, some form of the dialogue menu works best, *if* rich dialogue is a choice for the game. I think all developers working with dialogue are hoping something better comes along!

I have also used canned speeches, canned conversations, topic lists, and highlighted text too—sometimes more than one type within a single product. A topic list might suffice for a merchant who has no other function. Highlighted text might work fine for a quest NPC. A canned speech or conversation might be perfect for an encounter with a minor character. We should keep our interfaces consistent, but we can't possibly put in the effort with our minor conversations that we do with our major conflicts, any more than we have the time to treat all characters, great and small, equally.

Some game designs require little character interaction, and canned conversations may suffice. Just as some movies emphasize action over character, so do many games. We don't want to overwhelm the rest of the game with our conversation system any more than we want to overwhelm the story with gameplay All the elements of the entertainment experience must work in harmony. Save the conflict for the characters themselves.

Oh, and a final word about conversations in virtual reality. Until we work out natural language processing, VR will be just as bound to the same dialogue systems mentioned above as the two-dimensional worlds we play in.

ENTRANCES AND EXITS

Whatever conversation system we choose, a few variations will help enormously to preserve the fiction of the world and the naturalism of the conversations. It is easy to introduce some variation into the moments we first encounter NPCs and when we leave them. It is the first opportunity we have to begin to establish a relationship between player-character and NPC, and it should be embraced for that, not avoided.

Let's look again at Aristotle's unities: time, place, and action, and how they can affect entrances and exits.

Time

In real life, conversations don't necessarily begin at the beginning, progress through to the end, and then stop. We come in on the middle of them, pick them up later, decide we want to talk about something other than what the person we're talking to does, and so on. To replicate these possibilities in game conversation, we identify natural entrance and exit points, paying close attention to the passage of time, as the PC experiences it in the game. Again, compromises must be considered, particularly concerning the art necessary to cover more than a few possibilities, but we can strive to address at least three variations:

1. If the player concludes the conversation, then immediately reopens it without doing anything else.

2. If the player remains in the area, but does other things, or briefly leaves the area and returns.

3. If the player is gone for some time before returning.

The player-character can handle these. Or the NPC. It doesn't matter.

Place

Whether the NPC is static or mobile, the locale affects our arrival and departure. If the NPC can see the player approach, they might want to comment on the sword the PC is carrying in their hand. The player-character might interrupt them if they can't see the NPC arrive. The NPC can be coded to turn to face the player-character when the PC comes within range, not just when the player pokes them with a mouse click.

Action

If the meeting between PC and NPC is cordial, the PC may earn a friendly farewell. If the meeting goes poorly, a hail of bullets might chase the PC out the door.

These are simply examples of writing and programming NPCs who are *aware* of their surroundings, the player-character, and how they feel about them. Entrances and exits in real life are extremely important, often accompanied by elaborate, centuries-old rituals. For example, the handshake evolved from an approaching person holding out their hands to show they weren't carrying a weapon. Nuances like these are easy to do, and the rewards can be great: more actions to draw upon to illuminate our characters. As I write this during the COVID-19 pandemic the handshake may be an endangered greeting, replaced by bumped elbows, waves, open arms, and touching rackets, the way boxers greet one another at the start of a fight. Games won't look much different. We rarely see many PCs and NPCs shaking hands.

Return Visits

Many games succumb to what some designers consider a necessary evil: the repetition of repeat visits. Players don't always know they have exhausted an NPC of whatever primary use it had in the game, and that revisiting the NPC will not further the plot or provide additional gameplay. Most writers will be asked to provide a single generic line an NPC can say in response to a return visit. One thing that destroys the illusion that the game is anything other than a game is when NPCs repeat the same old stock phrases over and over when you return to them. Simply because their utility is over doesn't mean we can abandon them, acknowledge they were simply tools, and move on. Their responses during return visits should make as much sense as possible within the fiction of the game.

In most cases, we get simple repetition. In some situations, there is a little variety built into a few characters, but only of canned speeches. A few basic variations wouldn't add all that much coding or art production.

Another trick is to choose a generic series of remarks, hopefully related to the character or situation, but that don't require specific game-affecting responses. Then choose a generic series of responses to the *type* of remarks chosen. You can then mix and match these in any number of ways, creating the illusion of continuing small talk. We successfully applied this system that we dubbed CHAOS Intelligent Conversation Modules to create hundreds of different "small-talk" combinations in *The Riddle of Master Lu* back in 1994. We were expanding it to player-character voice-overs in the uncompleted sequel *The Siberian Cipher*.

In the location Sikkim, whenever Ripley (the player-character), having exhausted all of a certain temple guard's pertinent information, returns to talk to the guard, he can still do so (Figure 6.4).

And the guard will not answer him with a single repeated phrase typical to many games such as, "I have no more time to waste on you, begone!" When the player clicked on the guard, the engine "shuffled" (more on this in a moment) a "deck" of five possibilities, and then pulled one of the following lines of dialogue for Ripley to speak:

"Can you tell me more about the temple?"
"I'd like to hear what those of the temple believe."
"If an outsider were interested in the sect, what would you tell him?"
"Can you tell me some of the key doctrines of the Temple of the Hidden Way?"
"Numerous Westerners are fascinated by the Eastern religion. What would you tell them about your beliefs?"

The following lines of dialogue were *not simply* shuffled. They could be called as single lines; two lines could be given together, or three, or four, all the way up to all eight. And *any* of the lines could be said by the guard *in any order*.

These lines, like Ripley's, were voiced by an actor. I directed the actor to deliver them so that they could be combined in any of the previously mentioned ways. I directed actors to begin each piece of a reply in a neutral manner and likewise end each piece in a neutral tone.

FIGURE 6.4 Ripley questions the philosophical guard.

The actor only recorded each line once. The combinations were then built by the game engine on the fly. Here were the separate lines:

"We believe in the testing of the faithful."

"We believe only through questioning can we find answers to that which puzzles us."

"We believe that to learn one must study."

"We believe one may not reach true enlightenment until one has found the Hidden Way."

"We do not believe in trial and error."

"We believe in method and reason."

"We believe anyone who proves himself worthy, by throwing off the trappings of the outer world, may join us."

"We welcome questors from all lands."

We shuffled the stacks of remarks and responses and discarded each as it was used. We did not randomize them. Shuffling guarantees two things. One, while the player will begin to hear at least partial repetitions, they won't be in the same order. Two, they'll hear *all* the possible combinations before there will be any exact duplicates. How many unique combinations are there in the above example?

One colleague has pointed out to me that the methodology behind CHAOS is the same used when character animations are drawn to begin and end at neutral positions so they can be seamlessly connected to one another. Another noted the similarity to "tiling" in graphics where the geography of an area is built up using terrain tiles with edges drawn to connect to other tiles in what is called a tile set.

It's not a full conversation. It will never compete with a fully scripted conversation. But it makes reasonable sense no matter how it is constructed by the game engine. It's not much harder to write than "Take a hike, Mike," repeated over and over. And the additional database and recording costs are negligible.

We must also consider several other variables. If we solve a problem for an NPC that gains us a necessary clue or item, gameplay may be satisfied, but narrative often isn't. In *Return to Zork* (1993), one of two games that were frustrating enough for me as a player to be a catalyst for me becoming a designer, there was a puzzle that involved the reuniting of two lovers: a ferryman and a witch. Another puzzle involved finding the lost child of a club owner. In both cases, once the puzzles were solved, there was no acknowledgment by the NPCs that the player-character had affected them in any way. The reunited lovers treated the player-character as a stranger. The only state that had changed was the puzzle was no longer available. At the very least, there should have been a simple recognition of the player's actions. We must respect the characters!

RELATIONSHIPS

Creating characters in isolation only takes us so far. As we populate our worlds, we place NPCs near one another, and give them similar professions and different opinions. It's only natural that these NPCs begin to develop relationships with one another and with the player-character.

First, we'll look at large groups whose structure and relationships with each other can resemble religions, political parties, and racial and cultural groups in the real world. When we want to orchestrate how these groups interact, we can lump all of them under the heading of Factions.

Factions

> When you're a Jet,
>> You're a Jet all the way
>> From your first cigarette
>> To your last dyin' day"

West Side Story

When you're a Jet, you're a Jet all the way. Unless you're in a virtual world, of course. If they made a virtual world based on *West Side Story*, the Jets and the Sharks would be two factions the player could choose from (Figure 6.5).

Asking the player to choose between two or more groups early on in a single-player game can alter the entire experience. The most basic factions we can construct are the broadest like good and evil. If the player chooses the dark side of the force, the challenges they face in the game, and the tools they have at their disposal to overcome them, will be different than if they'd chosen the good side. The areas of the game where the player-character is safe or at risk can be reversed. And the NPCs they encounter, if they know of that choice, should respond accordingly.

The player-character's faction may be visible for all to see, or secret. Whether the player-character's faction is in the majority or minority; ruling class or oppressed slaves; respected or suspect; in effect, which passport the player-character carries can shift story, relationships, and gameplay as a result. In *The Elder Scrolls IV: Morrowind* and *The Elder Scrolls V: Skyrim*, an NPC's attitude toward the player can change, depending upon a player's faction and reputation.

In MMOs, factions play an equally strong role. In factions in *World of Warcraft*, players from the Alliance and Horde learn to attack the opposing faction at an early age. If you're

FIGURE 6.5 Tony and Maria are members of opposite factions in 2021's *West Side Story* remake.

an overt rebel in *Star Wars Galaxies*, you will be attacked by Imperial stormtroopers. If you keep your rebel affiliation secret, they will not suspect you.

Whether we're creating a single-player game or a multiplayer game, major factions can be extremely helpful, and allowing the player to change their allegiances adds another dimension. In the strategy game *Heroes of Might and Magic III* (1999), there is a moment in a scenario where players were given the opportunity to switch sides in the conflict that had overtaken the world. If a player chose to go over to the opposition, that scenario was much easier to complete. But then the player discovered that later scenarios were more difficult. Switching sides wasn't as easy as trotting across a battlefield to shake hands (or elbow bump?) with your enemy, and it could be equally challenging in games. A traitor once, a traitor twice? Suspicion often followed such a choice. An interesting, if dangerous, game might be built around a character perched precariously between two opposing factions. We could call the game *Double Agent*.

Factions don't need to be huge groups either. As in *West Side Story* or *Grand Theft Auto: Vice City*, factions may be gangs fighting for control of their turf, either a physical neighborhood or a source of income. The important thing to remember is to orchestrate factions just like characters. If the factions aren't in opposition, opportunities for conflict and drama are limited.

One final interesting thing to note is that factions, unlike individual characters, don't necessarily have to be balanced in power. Whereas the best games in sports come from two strong opponents, there are also fans of the game, without a real stake in either side, who will root for the underdog. And there is, of course, the grand delight that audiences or readers take when their heroes start out on what appears to be an obvious losing side and then instead triumph.

The film *Independence Day*, or the arrival of the Borg in *Star Trek: Next Generation*, forces the characters we empathize with to confront a seemingly undefeatable enemy, and the triumph is all the sweeter when that enemy is finally vanquished. The second part of "Best of Both Worlds," the two-part episode that introduced the Borg, was the first episode I worked on. Interestingly, Mike Pillar's script featured a forcible shift in allegiances from the Federation to the Borg when Captain of the Enterprise, Jean-Luc Picard, was "assimilated" by the Borg. After his rescue, he still retained a certain residue of his time as a Borg, and there was the suspicion, among his closest shipmates and even himself, that he might revert.

The Player-Character and NPCs

In addition to group relationships, we have relationships between the player-character and the NPCs who share their world. In single-player games, these can be closely scripted, or constructed with choice built into the gameplay. In either case, relationships should grow and develop just as individual characters do. Remember our decision on *Edge of Night* to kill Nicole? Her relationship with her husband Miles had become static. Most of the possible relationship changes between them had been played out over the years. To repeat them was to be redundant, a trap soap operas that have been on for years often fall into. Every "bad girl" will eventually seduce every "good man." Every character will be accused of a crime they didn't commit. Everybody will fall in love with their best friend's sweetheart.

A game world populated with interesting NPCs is only the first step. Whether the player-character is in opposition to an NPC or in love with them, relationships are an opportunity to reveal both characters and to carry the story forward. The player-character's relationships with those NPCs make the player feel that their avatar inhabits that world and is not simply playing a game set there. The distinction is vital. It is the difference between a game that relies solely on its gameplay for success, and a game that has all the elements of popular entertainment in other media.

While we can construct every step in the ebb and flow of multiple relationships between a player-character and NPCs in single-player games quite easily, it's harder to track them in virtual worlds. Like soap operas, virtual worlds have no true end. They run until they die. Thousands of player-characters can inhabit them. One solution is to create a few factions and leave it at that. Very simple, and if only a few major interactions are possible, we can set flags to keep track.

If a Jet wants to buy a candy bar on the Shark's turf, it may cost him more, and the storekeeper may be fearful or hostile. If a Shark strolls down a dark alley on the Jet's turf, he may find himself under attack simply because of his gang affiliation. But what about Tony and Maria? Or all the thousands of Tonys and Marias who inhabit the *West Side Story* MMO? What if the Tonys are player-characters and the Marias are NPCs or vice versa?

Writers can and should fall back on programming to help them manage the infinite numbers of variables that occur when all those player-characters interact with all those NPCs. You don't have to be a programmer. I'm not a programmer. But you do have to think like one. Programmers love simple, elegant solutions where only a small chunk of code with a few variables to pop in can drive an entire system in a game. The dark side of this thinking is a quest system that is only fast-food menu-type errands with no opportunity for character revelation or story. The bright side is reflected in the relationship system that follows.

One of our primary goals for NPCs in *The Gryphon Tapestry* (1999) was to make NPCs as real as possible, granting them multiple functions—reasons for being in the world besides just having roles as merchants, trainers, and so on. We wanted them to have lives and relationships of their own. It was relatively easy to construct a web of relationships connecting the NPC inhabitants of a town, as well as creating other relationships to reflect faction differences between towns. But we wanted a system that would allow player-characters to have ever-changing relationships with NPCs as well.

The visible result of the system could mean an NPC would trust a player-character enough to gossip with them. A tidbit an NPC confided to one player-character might be the truth if the NPC were well disposed toward them, but another tidbit could just as easily be a lie if they didn't much like how the player decided the player-character should behave. An NPC merchant might be grateful to a PC and give them a discount on their next sword. A trainer might refuse to help a player-character who had wronged the trainer's friend. This wrong should be subjective, of course. The trainer and the PC could be on opposite sides of a disagreement. In this last example, we see NPC relationships and player-character and NPC relationships working in concert. Once scripted but changeable relationships among NPCs were in place, we needed a player-character/NPC relationship system to keep track of how NPCs would react to the way players chose to live their lives in the world.

Here is what we came up with. The TGT Full System that follows was my first pass at it. Dorion Newcomb, artist and co-designer on *TGT*, took my version, broke it down, and decided it was more complex than it needed to be, particularly given the time we had to implement it. Instead, he came up with a much more simplified system that we ultimately decided to adopt. Our feeling was that players would be so amazed by the changing relationships with NPCs that even the simplified system provided, they wouldn't miss the full system, and we could always revisit that system when the game had been live for a while and the concept had been stress tested. This was in 1999.

TGT Full System

The NPC Base Score is determined by assigning a rough score to the NPC in six areas: Like, Respect, Loyalty, Trust, Admiration, and Love. The rough score in each of the three categories is added up, and an average is determined. This then becomes the NPC's Base Score. Table 6.1 comprises the suggested range of values that could be assigned to any NPC for a specific interaction.

Table 6.2 represents the base personality that an NPC could be assigned. This would represent an NPC who had a general dislike of other characters.

Table 6.3 represents the maximum values that can be assigned for each category according to each player. Each player has a default of null in each category, and it is only through interactions with the NPC that these values are modified. For example, if a player

TABLE 6.1   NPC Personality Chart

Positive Descriptor						Scale							Negative Descriptor
Love	6	5	4	3	2	1	0...−1	−2	−3	−4	−5	−6	Hate
Admiration	6	5	4	3	2	1	0...−1	−2	−3	−4	−5	−6	Contempt
Trust	6	5	4	3	2	1	0...−1	−2	−3	−4	−5	−6	Mistrust
Loyalty	6	5	4	3	2	1	0...−1	−2	−3	−4	−5	−6	Disloyal
Respect	6	5	4	3	2	1	0...−1	−2	−3	−4	−5	−6	Disrespect
Like	6	5	4	3	2		0...−1	−2	−3	−4	−5	−6	Dislike

TABLE 6.2   Calculating the NPC Personality Values

Positive Descriptor	Value	Negative Descriptor
Love	−2	Hate
Admiration	−1	Contempt
Trust	1	Mistrust
Loyalty	2	Disloyal
Respect	−2	Disrespect
Like	−2	Dislike
Generalized Value	−4	

TABLE 6.3   Player Relationship Modifier

Positive Descriptor						Scale							Negative Descriptor
Love	6	5	4	3	2	1	0...−1	−2	−3	−4	−5	−6	Hate
Admiration	6	5	4	3	2	1	0...−1	−2	−3	−4	−5	−6	Contempt
Trust	6	5	4	3	2	1	0...-1	−2	−3	−4	−5	−6	Mistrust
Loyalty	6	5	4	3	2	1	0...−1	−2	−3	−4	−5	−6	Disloyal
Respect	6	5	4	3	2	1	0...−1	−2	-3	−4	−5	−6	Disrespect
Like	6	5	4	3	2		0...−1	−2	−3	−4	−5	−6	Dislike

successfully completes a difficult task for the NPC, their character may receive an additional positive point in both the Like and the Trust categories.

Table 6.4 shows an example of how the PC to NPC relationship value is generated, and how these specific categories are added together to generate a generalized relationship value.

Table 6.5 shows the values and their meanings behind the generalized NPC to Player Relationship Value. These categories are guidelines for understanding the relationship, and these values can be tested instead of more specific category tests.

TGT Simplified System

Table 6.6 is Dorion's version. It allows for easier implementation and quicker customization. Some depth is lost, but the variety of possible relationships remains fairly high. The rough score in each of the three categories is added up, and an average is determined. This then becomes the NPC's Base Score.

This category represents the emotional feelings that an NPC has toward the player. An NPC may increase their like (dislike) value for the following reasons: the player listens and provides good counsel; the player does favors for the NPC; the player compliments the NPC; the player helps others in times of need, and so forth. An NPC may decrease their

TABLE 6.4 Calculating the Player to NPC Relationship Value

Category	NPC Personality	Player Relationship Modifier	Player to NPC Relationship Value
Love (Hate)	−2	+3	1
Admiration (Contempt)	−1	+2	1
Trust (Distrust)	1	−2	−1
Loyalty (Disloyalty)	2	0	2
Respect (Disrespect)	−2	−1	−3
Like (Dislike)	−2	−4	−6
Generalized NPC to Player Relationship Value			**−6**

TABLE 6.5 Generalized NPC to Player Relationship Value

Score Range	Descriptor
25 to 36	Adores
10 to 24	Amiable
9 to −9	Neutral
−10 to −24	Strained
−25 to −36	Despises

TABLE 6.6 NPC Personality

Positive Descriptor											Scale											Negative Descriptor
Like	10	9	8	7	6	5	4	3	2	1	0	−1	−2	−3	−4	−5	−6	−7	−8	−9	−10	Dislike
Trust	10	9	8	7	6	5	4	3	2	1	0	−1	−2	−3	−4	−5	−6	−7	−8	−9	−10	Distrust
Respect	10	9	8	7	6	5	4	3	2	1	0	−1	−2	−3	−4	−5	−6	−7	−8	−9	−10	Disrespect

like (dislike) value for the following reasons: the player lies to the NPC; the player refuses to help the NPC; the player displays cruelty to the NPC; or the player performs selfish actions which hurt others.

TRUST (DISTRUST)

This category represents the amount of responsibility that the NPC will place on the player. An NPC may increase their trust (distrust) value for the following reasons: the player successfully completes a task that the NPC assigned to them; the player keeps their word and does not reveal private information to other NPCs; the player demonstrates honesty in their relationship to the NPC. An NPC may decrease their trust (distrust) value for the following reasons: the player receives a task for the NPC but does not complete it; the player breaks a confidence or reveals private information about the NPC; the player lies to the NPC.

RESPECT (DISRESPECT)

This category represents the amount of admiration the NPC has for the player's abilities. An NPC may increase their respect (disrespect) value for the following reasons: the player has developed a high skill level in a skill that the NPC values; the player provides meaningful help or services to other NPCs that this NPC knows; when the player must make a decision, it is one that is harmonious with the NPC's world view. An NPC may decrease their respect (disrespect) value for the following reasons: the player has no skills that an NPC values; the player has avoided helping other NPCs that this NPC knows; the player makes decisions that are discordant with the NPCs world view.

Table 6.7 represents the base personality that an NPC could be assigned. This would represent an NPC who has a general dislike of other people.

Table 6.8 represents the maximum values that can be assigned for each category according to each player. Each player has a default of null in each category, and it is only through interactions with the NPC that these values are modified. For example, if a player

TABLE 6.7   Calculating the NPC Personality Values

Positive Descriptor	Value	Negative Descriptor
Like	−2	Dislike
Trust	1	Mistrust
Respect	−2	Disrespect
Generalized Value	**−3**	

TABLE 6.8   Player Relationship Modifier

Positive Descriptor											Scale											Negative Descriptor
Like	10	9	8	7	6	5	4	3	2	1	0	−1	−2	−3	−4	−5	−6	−7	−8	−9…−10		Dislike
Trust	10	9	8	7	6	5	4	3	2	1	0	−1	−2	−3	−4	−5	−6	−7	−8	−9…−10		Distrust
Respect	10	9	8	7	6	5	4	3	2	1	0	−1	−2	−3	−4	−5	−6	−7	−8	−9…−10		Disrespect

TABLE 6.9 Calculating the Player to NPC Relationship Value

Category	NPC Personality	Player Relationship Modifier	Player to NPC Relationship Value
Like (Dislike)	−2	−2	−4
Trust (Distrust)	1	2	3
Respect (Disrespect)	−2	−1	−3
Generalized NPC to	Player Relationship Value		−4

TABLE 6.10 Generalized NPC to Player Relationship Value

Score Range	Descriptor
19 to 30	Adores
6 to 18	Amiable
5 to 5	Neutral
−6 to−18	Strained
−19 to −30	Despises

successfully completes a difficult task for the NPC, they may receive an additional positive point in both the Like and the Trust categories.

Table 6.9 shows an example of how the player to NPC relationship value is generated, and how these specific categories are added together to generate a generalized relationship value, as shown in Table 6.10.

Table 6.10 shows the values and their meanings behind the generalized NPC to Player Relationship Value. These categories are guidelines behind understanding the relationship, and these values can be tested instead of more specific category tests.

These are by no means all the issues involved when we write character encounters. For example, game writer/designer Hal Barwood notes that a variation on simply repeating canned conversations is having three variations of the same material for return visits: "First encounter with the specialized NPC, hear (or read) the long version. Second encounter, get a quick summary. Third encounter, get an even quicker brusque summary to enforce the idea that possibilities have been exhausted." This is a simple and reasonable compromise between story and gameplay that can also add a couple of relationship beats in how the NPC reacts to each return visit.

The important thing to realize here is that we have not exhausted all the ways of handling encounters. There is no reason to keep repeating the few approaches we're most familiar with. Before the design document turns to iron, take the time to experiment with your own.

PART III

Telling the Story

INTERLUDE ON THE WAY TO SAN FRANCISCO

(With apologies to Geoffrey Chaucer)

It happened that, on a rainy day in March, as I lay
In Chicago, at O'Hare, grounded by a long delay,
Ready to resume my pilgrimage and start
To San Jose, fervent gamer at heart,
There came at night's core to that airport
Some nine and twenty of a motley sort
Of sundry folk who had failed to reach
Connecting flights, stranded pilgrims were they each
That toward San Francisco town would fly.
The benches were narrow, but at least they were dry.
And fairly well we there were eased, every one
Full of Starbucks, pizza, or a sweet Cinnabon.
And shortly, when midnight had gone to rest,
So had I spoken with them, each companion guest.
A fellow pilgrim in me perceived,
I was of their fellowship received.
We made agreement that we'd early rise
To catch the first available flight, as I will to you apprise.
But none the less, while I have time and space,
Before yet further in this tale I pace,
If it may be in accord with you
To describe the shape of this accidental crew.
Whether short and stout or lean and tall,
Of the fairer sex, or not fair at all.
In truth how their characters appeared to me

DOI: 10.1201/9780429284991-10

Whence they came and their psychology,
And even what clothes they were dressed in.
And with a writer thus will I begin.
Gray-haired and without apparent means,
Unshaven in sweatshirt and worn blue jeans.
After his description, and you know him full well,
We'll hear what tale he perchance can tell.
In hope that it will speed the night,
Distracting us from our communal plight.
For as we know stories hath ways
To pass such nights and ease our days.

CHAPTER 7

Once Upon a Time

I N THE LAST FOUR chapters, we have discussed the writing of characters. Characters came first in this book and were also represented in its title because we can't begin to tell our stories without them. Our themes grow from character. The most brilliantly written story will not move us unless characters we empathize with are a part of it. We're not going to abandon our characters as we turn to stories, the topic of Part III. Rather, we're going to add story to the mix. Character and story should be developed together, and as we're about to see, so should stories and games.

BUILDING A HOME FOR CHARACTERS

Geoffrey Chaucer (1342–1400) was a minor diplomat, once held for ransom by the French, as well as a poet. His years spent traveling about Europe on various errands for King Edward III gave him much background for his most famous work, *The Canterbury Tales*. The tales are the first selection of short stories in English and have earned him the title of "Father of English Literature." As I began this book with characters before moving to stories, so, too, did Chaucer.

His original plan was for a total of 124 stories, but in 13 years of writing, he completed only 24, about a group of middle-class pilgrims who had stopped at an inn in Southwark while on their way to Canterbury. The Middle English in which the tales were composed was a patchwork of the Anglo-Saxon's Old English and Norman French, courtesy of William the Conqueror. Don't feel bad if you find it difficult to piece together the recognizable words that have survived to this day. Old English was already on the way out when Chaucer was writing. My pastiche of the tale's prologue that begins this section is modernized pseudo–Middle English that owes more to *The Adventures of Robin Hood* with Errol Flynn (Yay, Warner Brothers!) than any actual version of the language.

There are plenty of scholars who have done interlinear and side-by-side translations of *The Canterbury Tales* and to them we owe a debt of gratitude, because they deserve to be read. Things don't become classics by accident. The characters, everybody from church officials to con artists, are vividly and realistically drawn. The stories deal with themes as contemporary today as they were in Chaucer's time: marriage, sex, infidelity, greed, church corruption, and more.

DOI: 10.1201/9780429284991-11

The tales are a perfect transition from our study of characters in games to stories. Chaucer was intensely interested in his characters as individuals, more than just "types." His stories were built on characters.

There is another reason to take a fresh look at the tales. They are written in a format that will seem familiar to writers of games. There is a frame to the tales: the pilgrimage, a traditional structure Chaucer was familiar with from *The Arabian Nights* and *The Decameron*. A structure that we can recognize today in television. TV drama has been with us ever since 1930 and *The Man with a Flower in His Mouth* from Great Britain. A multitude of books have been written describing how television progressed over the years since then.

Today we have seen the passive media landscape change from TV series where stories began and were completed in a single episode or an occasional special event like the miniseries. We still have series (often comedies) with a "season" presenting a single mini drama resolved in each episode. But thanks to Netflix, Amazon Prime, Hulu, BritBox, and many others we also have multiple "limited" series that ignore "seasons" and offer series that run for only six to ten episodes, presenting a single story through line that can include multiple smaller stories. The same can be said for *The Odyssey*. Homer would have been right at home with this structure.

In the previous edition of this book, I noted the transition to this new structure in TV shows like *Breaking Bad*, *Dexter*, and *Sex and the City*. Today's limited series are also delivered in new ways. Many will still dump all six, eight, ten episodes at once, but the newest trend we're beginning to see are series that are ready to air now, withholding episodes, releasing only one or two every week. Welcome back to the 1950s! However it is delivered, Chaucer would have loved episodic TV.

The story in many games is broken down exactly the same way. We call them levels or quests, separate episodes within an overarching story. For this reason, *The Canterbury Tales* holds an honored place in the evolution of episodic storytelling that began with Homer, and that is a brick in the foundation of the new storytelling I'll explore in Chapter 13, "The Roots of a New Storytelling," and Chapter 14, "Modular Storytelling."

Chaucer recognized that characters alone are not enough. They must inhabit stories. He also realized that stories without due attention paid to characters were unlikely to touch the reader. It seems obvious today, but this was a revolutionary concept back then. Before Chaucer, storytelling in England was confined to romances of high-born men and women whose entire characters could usually be described in one word: either "handsome" or "beautiful." Oh, and possibly "brave" for the men. Women were done at "beautiful."

STORY OR GAME: WHICH COMES FIRST?

All those three-dimensional characters you're now inspired to create for your games need stories to live and breathe in. At what point in the development process do you need to concern yourself with story? There are three possible scenarios.

While showering one morning, I may be struck with a great, original, never-done-before idea for a game. Instead of the typical console treasure hunt action game where the player searches for pieces to a larger puzzle, or batteries to power a machine that will defeat evil, what if we reverse it? The player must deposit something in receptacles guarded by fearsome beasts. And… and… these somethings must be built by all these other creatures whom the player must convince to do the job by performing tasks for them, or maybe bribing or blackmailing them, but that isn't important. What is important is to flesh out that game mechanic as quickly as possible into a design, start to think about levels, get a prototype up and running—oh, and we'll call the land where this all takes place Grayarea, and the player-character will be called Murk, and he'll be handsome… and brave!

Those of you who ply your trade writing for games already know where I'm headed with this. How many times have you been hired on a project after the design is well under way? It sometimes seems to be the norm. The scenario usually runs something like the following.

The developers have been sitting around in conference rooms for weeks coming up with one great, original, never-done-before idea for gameplay after another. Suddenly one of them realizes, "Hey, we haven't spent a lot of time on the story…." All eyes turn to Norm who's been building complicated structures out of paperclips down there at the end of the table. "Norm, didn't you once take a writing class in high school?"

Norm immediately brightens, knocks over his paperclips, and admits it's true, and he didn't take just any old writing class in high school, it was called *creative* writing. Norm has a new action item to take away from the meeting, and everybody gets back to the real work: designing the game. Cut to four months later in that same conference room. The first two levels are marginally playable, and Norm's first six-page draft of the story has been read and is now being discussed. The producer glances at the game development Gantt chart, exchanges a look with the lead designer, and says, "Norm, this is great, but I think we need to bring in an outside writer…."

Another variation on this theme is the lead designer who decides they will write as well. Four months later in that same conference room, the designer's first six-page draft of the story has been read, and everybody in the conference room is either squirmy or slunk down in a chair. Nobody wants to say to their boss, "Norma, this is great, but I think we need to bring in an outside writer…."

Sometimes the realization never hits. Sometimes months into the design process, a freelance writer is brought in to add story to the game. The characters are already drawn, so they don't need any more help with that character stuff.

The second scenario goes something like this. A writer comes into a meeting with the developers. They hand them a story, usually by Phillip K. Dick. "This guy's written a lot of stories that have become great movies. We can't afford to option any, but we want you to write us a story that will feel like a Phillip K. Dick story that we can build a great game around." The freelance writer packs up their laptop, heads off to catch a plane, and returns four weeks later with a story that reads as if it were written by Dick himself. They're thanked, promised that the check is in the mail, and leave to catch another plane.

Freelance game writers know I'm not making these two examples up. How many times have you been hired on a project after the design is well under way? How many times have you been hired at the very beginning and then sent packing with a "Thanks a lot! We'll take it from here!" Both don't just happen; they happen all the time, even if the writer is on staff. *Both* scenarios happened to different projects at a certain company where I once worked.

In one case, I had to pick up the pieces. In the other, after a huge amount of wasted money, the game was never released.

Gameplay and story work best together when developed together. Trying to tack a story onto an already existing game design or attempting to cram gameplay into a solid story structure, are recipes for mediocrity, if not outright disaster. If each element in a game is to share equal importance in the entertainment experience, it needs to be constantly balanced with the others. We need to develop the story and gameplay together so that each creative process can feed off the other.

Characterization and concept art collaborate in this way. How many times has an artist been inspired by the first lines of prose describing a character? How many times has a writer been inspired by seeing a sketch of the character? It is a two-way street that results in a synergy of two separate but equal crafts creating something that is greater than both of them.

One of the first questions we face before sitting down to write the story of a game is its origin. It should come as no surprise that games based on original ideas are the most attractive to designers—we get to use our own ideas. Developers and publishers like sequels because engines and assets may be reused; teams start with a leg up on the material; and if the first game attracted a following, the sequel's future is rosier. Publishers like adaptations from other media for the same reason they like sequels. The franchise is established in the public eye. Of course, in all cases, a great game must follow!

If the developer is lucky enough to have all three options available, what issues should writers and designers be aware of as they begin? Let's start with the story that springs from imagination alone.

ORIGINAL MATERIAL

In the almost thirty years I've been writing, designing, and producing games, I've rarely been given the opportunity to work on my original ideas. The games have been based on other media, franchises, sequels, designs already in progress, or someone else's sketchy concept.

The only game designs I ever worked on which were my idea from the beginning were *Sideshow*, and that was shelved so I could work on the Ripley's sequel, and the alternate reality games I wrote to teach everything from Mandarin to cybersecurity. Some of these have been collected in *The Multiplayer Classroom: Game Plans*, published in 2021. The three Agatha Christie games were based on novels by … um… Agatha Christie. *Star Trek: Infinite Space* was, believe it or not, based on material from another medium as well. I'm currently working on yet another game based on another medium. Even those games where I had much freedom like *The Riddle of Master Lu* and *Dark Side of the Moon*, the initial concept was not my own (Figure 7.1).

I think every writer must want to do original work, or why be a writer at all? Of course, even in twenty years of writing series television, I rarely had that chance either. Even pilots I wrote were sequels or based on other media, with a single exception. So, what is the writer to do? I try to approach each project with an open mind. I find within it elements that hook me and that I can make my own: a character, an aspect of the arena, the theme, a twist, a

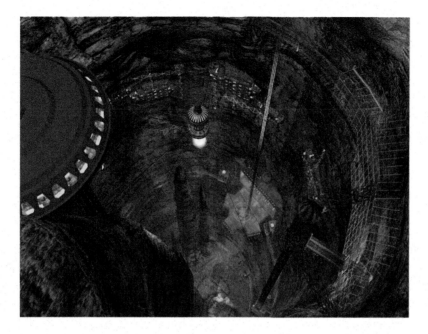

FIGURE 7.1 *Dark Side of the Moon* (apologies to Pink Floyd!).

surprise or two. And I find original ideas that work within whatever parameters are laid out for me. I'll discuss this more in the next section, "Adaptations from Other Media."

Being able to realize your own dreams by writing something that is your vision from start to publication is a holy grail in collaborative media. And if you get the opportunity, don't squander it. Books are different, of course. My books have all been entirely my own vision from start to finish. Yes, I have nobody else I can blame!

Where does the writer begin? It can be almost anywhere: an engaging character, a one-line story hook, or an exciting gameplay element. If you don't start with a theme from the outset, then one had better present itself very early on. But not all ideas, even great ones, are meant to be games.

Every story can't work identically well in all media. When the idea for a story starts to percolate in my brain, it doesn't take long for me to see what form of expression it wants to take: novel, game, play, film, TV pilot, and so on. I've written all of them. Each has its own distinct needs. Some ideas, of course, do cross media, as we'll see in the next section.

Another key point, which I bring up throughout the book, is that games don't do complex stories well. But as I've already mentioned, mystery writers know the best approach is to offer a simple story disguised as a complex story. It isn't necessary that the game story be like this, but it makes it easier to come by story twists and turns that add to the story and give it the weight to balance it with the gameplay. A simple story without surprise or twists can be excruciatingly dull, no matter how well crafted. The *only* exception to this is tragedy, where fate's hand is clearly shown, and events march inexorably toward doom. As we've seen, games don't do tragedy much, so that simple type of story is mostly lost to us.

The trick is to make sure that, even with twists and turns, the story remains clear to the player without vast amounts of exposition. That is why the underlying McGuffin is simple, even if the chasing after it appears complex. Less is more. Creating a simple story is a big help. Creating an action-filled story is a big help. We must make certain, however, that both elements are conducive to gameplay.

One way we can surprise players isn't available to passive media. In 2008, I designed a fourth Agatha Christie game, *The ABC Murders*, where the player was allowed to play Hercule Poirot, as well as several other characters who assisted him, in distinct geographical locations. They were playable only when Poirot was not around until the very end. One of the playable characters was the murderer. And in the climax, as Poirot pointed his finger at the murderer, the POV suddenly switched to the killer. As the killer, the player made a last, fateful decision in the story. I was curious to see what players' reactions would be. Sadly, the game was never made. Ah well, we'll visit the first three games in the series in the next section.

A major component a game idea needs is the opportunity for interactivity: the important design question is What will the player do? Remember the quote from Noah Falstein. "Do, don't Show." An arena should, by its nature, provide the player with gadgets, weapons, locks, characters, vehicles, and all sorts of other elements the player can interact with or manipulate.

The idea must make sense, not only for games but the type of game, too. If we want to portray World War II in a game, and want the player to see the big picture, it would be better to make a strategy game or a virtual world like *World War II Online*. A squad-based combat game could move from engagement to engagement through the course of the war, but some of the big picture would be lost except in the background briefings between missions. If we want to drill down farther, a single-character shooter like the *Medal of Honor* series gives us lots to do as a soldier, but the major developments of the war are usually lost to us, much like they would be to a soldier in actual combat. First-person shooter gameplay does not focus on the big picture. It shouldn't have to.

In the opening cinematic prologue of *Call of Duty: Modern Warfare 3*, your player-character—or at least the character through whose eyes you're looking—is hustled into a car by armed men. As the car moves through war-torn city streets, the camera focuses here and there to capture brief moments of violence, heightening the disorientation and suspense. The point is: choose the style of game to match the scope of your storytelling.

Another choice to make is genre. You may be an ardent bug collector and have found an exciting game mechanic for creating a virtual killing jar, and great cursor control for piercing those frail little bodies with big pins. But you do have to know something about the marketplace before you expend the next year or more of your life, and a few million dollars, to base a game on your passion. (Force the player to collect those same bugs in a vast swamp full of alligators, poisonous reptiles, piranhas, and poachers, though, and you may have something.)

I'm so tired of seeing the same old genres made into games over and over again: fantasy, science-fiction, survival horror, post-apocalyptic futures: many of them inhabited by zombies. In 2021 alone over a dozen zombie games were released. Even *Red Dead Redemption* added a zombie expansion pack a while ago. Can *Animal Crossing: Raising the Dead* be far behind? (I will confess I had a great time with Plants and Zombies, although the game had little to do with horticulture.) The fact is that the genres listed above are so popular because players already know what will be expected of them and they lend themselves to high body count gameplay. Still, to me a worse offense than a hackneyed genre is a me-too product, which essentially duplicates games already on the market.

We're in a Catch-22 situation here. Until developers spend the time and energy to bring exciting products in other genres to market, we seem stuck in the same old ruts. Yet the same old ruts are hard to get out of because best-selling products can still be found in them. If we're going to do a familiar genre in a familiar way, we start with two strikes against us in the originality department. Two strikes also in the marketing department, since we'll need something better than cooler explosions to reach the radars of gamers.

We need to assume latest-generation graphics and animation and smooth gameplay. What can set our product apart, therefore, is context, and context is story and character. If we can make these compelling enough, we can be noticed in the mass of other games with the same beefy male or busty female with an automatic pistol in the ads. And yes, even if you avoid stereotypes in the writing, the marketing department hasn't read this book, and it will still slap them on your game.

If we're going to try a new genre, or one rarely explored like romance, or bug collecting, it's all in the execution. The player will accept just about anything if the experience is entertaining. *Roller Coaster Tycoon* had a good chance. *Garment Sweatshop Tycoon?* Not so much.

Unfortunately, we cannot create original games in a vacuum. We must be aware of the market. If we're lucky, there's somebody a few cubicles over whose job it is to gather that research. If we're even luckier, the research will support attempting a genre and type of game that we enjoy. Writing or designing a pet project without taking externals like demographics into account is irresponsible, and a waste of time and money.

These are all issues the writer/designer should consider when creating original material. And there are more. The abilities of the team can affect the decision. Before you embark on that huge world game, it might be a good idea to see who on the team has made one before or even played one.

Knowing the type of game you want to make is essential. Don't be afraid that your baby may get infected by knowledge. If you don't want to create a game like all the others, at least play those others; study them and learn how they were built.

This is how we learn—from others' mistakes as well as their successes and from our own mistakes and successes. I worked for a previously successful company that was making a type of game, an MMO, with which they were unfamiliar. It was a brave attempt. But the design lead was very leery of having his ideas influenced by the game establishment. He knew what his vision was and was determined to see it through no matter what might be happening at other game companies; an understanding of the new player base he wanted to reach; or what the market realities were. That game was in development for years, cost millions of dollars, and ultimately was first released as the type the developer was most comfortable with: a solo game. Later, a version of the MMO was released on GameTap, but was canceled. The developers announced a free MMO version and… the saga continues through several more permutations, but we, my faithful reader, will thankfully move on.

The new game that was going to revolutionize its type never saw more than a glimmer of the light of day because of the designer's fear of being overly influenced. If you believe strongly enough in your original vision, have the courage to confront and learn from the visions of others, however much you may disagree with them, and be willing to seek a win-win situation by adapting some elements while discarding others. To hide from the game establishment will end in your game remaining hidden as well. A continuing theme of this book is to learn the rules before you turn your back on them.

ADAPTATIONS FROM OTHER MEDIA

The major reason we do a video game adaptation of material from other media is the success it has already enjoyed that will hopefully result in more sales of our game. Of course, this doesn't always work. Take films, for example.

Due to the lengthy development cycle of games, the video game versions are best started as soon in the production cycle of a film as possible. Unfortunately, the best cast or most talented director cannot guarantee a hit movie.

I faced exactly this predicament when I was working on *Wild Wild West: The Steel Assassin*. Even with our game slated to be released at the same time as the video version of the film starring Will Smith, Kevin Kline, Salma Hayek, and Kenneth Branagh and directed by Barry Sonnenfeld (*The Addams Family, Get Shorty*, the *Men in Black* films), we had no choice but to press on (Figure 7.2) even after the film opened to terrible reviews, mediocre business and Golden Raspberry Awards for both the film and the direction. Money had been spent and contracts signed.

Even when a movie is good and does good business, it is painfully obvious that that doesn't guarantee a game's success. Maybe the film's subject matter is simply not suited to another medium, and the gameplay suffers. Or maybe the game developers just drop the ball. As I said previously: not all ideas, even great ones, are meant to be games.

Sometimes there is simply no crossover interest between the audiences that loved a movie and gamers who might want to play in the same fictional setting. This is why we

FIGURE 7.2 *Wild Wild West*, a game with the characters from the film but the spirit of the TV series.

see that most adaptations are genres like fantasy or science fiction. The crossover audience has been well demonstrated. This is also one of the reasons why, despite numerous efforts over a number of years, a romance-themed massively multiplayer game, whether based on a property in another medium or not, still remains unproduced.

The audience of a soap opera, I was told by an advertising executive as I was about to become head writer on *Edge of Night*, consisted in the main of traditional, stay-at-home housewives, college students, law enforcement professionals, and incarcerated felons. Obviously, some of these had access to computers and an interest in computer games, but the largest group, housewives, did not, at least in 1983. Today, many more do, but most of them are no longer watching the few remaining soap operas.

The next issue we face when adapting is staying true to the material. First, the very crossover audience we're trying to reach has definite expectations about how the subject matter will be handled. It would be dangerous to take a werewolf and plunk it into a story about starting a shelter for homeless dogs.

Yes, it's dangerous… but not impossible! Look at Charlie Kaufman's wildly different take on the bestselling nonfiction book *The Orchid Thief* by Susan Orleans when he adapted it as a motion picture. The result, *Adaptation*, is a free-wheeling fantasy about the nature of the job he undertook, hence the title. He put himself at the center of the story and invented a brother, Donald, who also shared screenplay credit (both Charlie and Donald are played by Nicholas Cage).

The fictional Donald is actually the commercial side of Charlie's ego, and a critical scene in a hotel room sets up the bizarre shift in tone of the film that baffled many moviegoers.

Staying true to the material does not mean a literal adaptation. It can't. Even with three motion pictures to adapt the *Lord of the Rings* trilogy it is not a literal adaptation. Peter Jackson and his team faithfully preserved the major incidents of the books, rightly concentrating on the most significant and visually arresting moments, but more importantly, they captured the spirit of the novels.

Adaptation: The film also skewers screenwriting guru Robert McKee (acidly portrayed by Brian Cox) and all the other cult leaders of writing who profess to have templates to writing success. If you're reading this book to find such a template, you're doomed to disappointment. There's no such thing.

Otherwise, the films would have been impossibly long, impossibly expensive and unwieldy. Jackson was forced to make some cuts (like Tom Bombadil) that annoyed purists but were forgiven by the general audience because the spirit of the books had been so ably captured. Of course, we have more latitude in TV series and movie series these days. Amazon Prime spent a fortune on *The Lord of the Rings: Rings of Power. The Wheel of Time* has announced a second season. *The Witcher* has promised a third season. Even with over a two-and-a-half hour running time the 2021 film adaptation of *Dune* only covers half of the book with a wink at the end to the audience that "It's only beginning…" The ten episodes of the Apple TV+ adaptation of Isaac Asimov's *Foundation* trilogy are said to be just one quarter of the books. Three more seasons are planned. All these adaptations take liberties with the source material. The HBO Max adaptation of *Station 11* diverges quite a bit from the book it's based upon.

In *Runaway Jury*, the film based on John Grisham's bestseller, the industry targeted by the trial was changed from tobacco to firearms since tobacco was already on its knees and gasping for breath, and the firearms industry has yet to be successfully brought to task even to this day. Also, of course, it isn't cynical to point out that firearms made for a much more visual opening to the picture. The story moves remained similar, and the twist on the two characters who promised to "deliver" the jury remained the same in spirit, even with the change of culprit.

So, trying to capture the spirit of work from another medium rather than copy it literally, is the safest route. But again, there are exceptions. A classic bit of Hollywood folklore tells us that John Huston handed his secretary Dashiell Hammett's novel *The Maltese Falcon* and told her to take out all the description and type up the dialogue in screenplay format. That was the first draft of his adaptation. Of course, it may have helped that Hammett's style was lean enough and his page count low enough to make the exercise possible. I doubt if the secretary would have had the same success with James Joyce's *Ulysses*.

I'll also point out that there are video game versions of most of the examples above with the following exceptions. The video game *Foundation*, released in 2019, is not related to the books. Interesting comparisons have been drawn between *Station 11* and *The Last of Us*, but there is currently no game version of the series. And while the spirit of the hard-boiled detective style has been borrowed from *The Maltese Falcon* multiple times in games like *L.A. Noire*, *Heavy Rain*, *Hotel Dusk: Room 215* (one of my favorite DS games), and *The Wolf Among Us*, the original itself has not been adapted as a game.

In addition to capturing the spirit of material from another medium we need to decide whether to tell the same story—borrowing characters and set pieces but altering the action to suit gameplay—or start from scratch with the same characters in the same world, but with an entirely new storyline.

Telling the exact same story is difficult for several reasons. Action that works well in a film may not translate to gameplay. The story moves, when analyzed, may turn out to be unaffected by the central character's action, or happen in scenes where the protagonist is not present. To adapt them literally, we'd need to use cut scenes without the player-character to advance the story. It can be done, but it removes the player from the game action.

Another reason that literal adaptations are tricky is that games are puzzles, and players advance through them by solving those puzzles, whether they're mind-benders like François Robillard's laboratory puzzle from *The Riddle of Master Lu* or simple actions like gunning down a Nazi soldier. Adapting the exact plot of a movie, particularly the resolution, also means that the player knows the ending already. This isn't such a problem when adapting a book to film or a movie to the stage. The audience goes to see it to relive memories, as well as seeing a favorite story in a new form. Even then, adapters often make changes, again to endings, to retain a surprise or two.

For the video game of Agatha Christie's *And Then There Were None*, I changed the identity of the killer in the most famous detective story ever written, because it *is* the most famous detective story ever written, and too many people know whodunnit. The scariest pitch I've ever made of an idea was in a boardroom in the Chorion offices in London. At that time, they were the owners of the rights to the Agatha Christie stories. But even more challenging was the fact that I would be pitching this new killer and motive to Mathew Pritchard, the grand dame of mystery's grandson. Whew!

For *Murder on the Orient Express*, I thought to change the identity of whodunnit would have been sacrilege: that identity has become a classic all on its own. But I did add an addition to the story that occurs after the player helps Hercule Poirot explain his *two* solutions.

I am always concerned when the player's avatar is a famous detective. Whether Sherlock Holmes, Phillip Marlowe, or Hercule Poirot, much of the pleasure the reader or filmgoer derives, is watching how the brilliant sleuth sculpts all the clues into a big finger pointing directly at the culprit. How much less fun it is to know exactly what the detective knows as soon as he or she knows it. This is why, forced to use Poirot in *The ABC Murders*, I also allowed players to play supporting investigative characters.

For *Murder on the Orient Express*, I created a new character for the player to direct, a young woman named Antoinette Marceau who was a composite of two characters from the original story. In this way, the player seeks out clues under the direction of an incapacitated Hercule Poirot (confined to his cabin by a leg injury caused when the train hits the snowbank that strands it in the mountains); yet the player can still be amazed when Poirot puts the final pieces of the puzzle together with the player's help.

In the third Agatha Christie game, *Evil under the Sun*, I preserved the identity of whodunnit, but changed the storytelling in a couple of significant ways. First, again to avoid Poirot giving away all his secrets too soon, I tried a more radical departure from the book, placing the story in a flashback told by Poirot to his friend Captain Hastings, so that the player could still be surprised by the fruits of Poirot's "little grey cells." Poirot tells the story in such a way that Hastings is the player-character, not the world's greatest detective. So, the player, as Hastings, controls Poirot's actions in the flashback story, but is constantly critiqued in voice-overs by the real Poirot in his mind. It's really not as complicated as it sounds! Remember all those sidekicks heard only in voice-overs like Wheatley in *Portal*? Or the player vs. narrator dynamic in *The Stanley Parable*? The experience is similar. Here are some example snippets of dialogue:

HASTINGS (V.O.): I say, old man… Are we looking for anything in particular?
POIROT (V.O.): We are indeed, Hastings. We look for that which is not here…
HASTINGS (V.O.): Oh that's a big help…

And another:

HASTINGS (V.O.): Dash it all, Poirot! Your little idiosyncrasies are infuriating!
POIROT (V.O.): Nonsense! They are part of my charm!

Exercise is not a passion Poirot pursues:

POIROT (V.O.): Non, merci, Hastings. The rowing is not for Poirot. I exercise the little grey cells.
HASTINGS (V.O.): I know there's no use asking if you'd have a quick swim out there to have a look.

POIROT (V.O.): I am happy you realize that, my friend.

If the player wants Hastings to test a theory, Hastings has Poirot say:

POIROT: Would you mind asking one of the ladies at the hotel to open the jar?
GLADYS: Why a lady? Surely any of the sturdier gents could do it?
POIROT (V.O.): Well, Hastings. This is your plan. What do you say to that?
HASTINGS (V.O.): Tell her... tell her you have a phobia about other men opening jars for you.
POIROT (V.O.): What?! That is absurd! She will think Poirot is a lunatic!

When necessary, Poirot could also function as the game's hint system:

POIROT (V.O.): Hastings, unless the cat is encased in the ice, do not poke the ice pick at her!

It is a tricky balancing act. You must decide for yourself if it is more fun to witness Poirot in action and to be amazed at his genius, or to be Poirot exercising his little gray cells to the amazement of the NPCs. Just remember player failure does occur in games!

When Dame Agatha wrote during the World War II years, she wrote to take her readers' minds off the horrors of war, such as bombs dropping out of the sky on their very houses, substituting the far more genteel horrors of murder at a sun-drenched resort, an actual hotel on Burgh Island off the South Devon coast. From the safe distance of several decades, I brought the war into the story, adding a German U-Boat to the finale.

And the night that Poirot allows Hastings to walk in his shoes, it is to keep both of their minds off the fact that this is the eve of the first bombing raid that became the London Blitz (Figure 7.3). By adding perspective gained by the decades since that night, I was able to write a coda that was a summation of not only a more innocent time but also a more innocent kind of detective fiction, now known as the Golden Age.

FIGURE 7.3 The war strikes home in the video game version of *Evil Under the Sun.*

Epilogue

INT. HERCULE POIROT'S FLAT – NIGHT

Poirot and Hastings.

POIROT: The case it is now complete, my friend. You have walked in Poirot's shoes.
HASTINGS: Poirot, I'll be honest with you. Now that I've given it a try, your job is not as
      easy as I thought! But thank you for the experience.
        (quieter)
      I am proud to be your friend.
POIROT: (bows)
        And I am honored to have you as mine, Hastings. We have passed the hours
      most agreeably!
HASTINGS: Yes. I thank you for that, too.

Air raid sirens begin to go off outside. Poirot looks up. CAMERA TILTS to the ceiling.

EXT. LONDON – SKYLINE – NIGHT

Air raid sirens blare near and far as searchlights come on in rapid succession, scanning the sky.

INT. POIROT'S FLAT

CAMERA TILTS DOWN. Poirot lowers his gaze to CAMERA again. The SIRENS are
MUCH FAINTER to underscore the scene.

HASTINGS: I'm sorry, old chap. I should trot on over to the War Office, I'm afraid.
POIROT: (nods)
  And so it begins.
HASTINGS: Don't you worry. No more holidays at the beach for a time maybe, but we'll
      pull through, you'll see.
POIROT: I pray you are right, my friend…

EXT. LONDON – SKYLINE – NIGHT

The searchlights scan the skies, reflecting off the occasional clouds. The SIRENS slowly
FADE OUT entirely. Until all we hear is Poirot's voice.
POIROT'S VOICE
    I feel like the dinosaur, Hastings… Gone is my world where good always triumphs
    over evil… where the clues they all add up to the satisfactory solution… where the
    murderer never escapes… This will be war as we have never seen it… Whatever the
    outcome, the cost it will be high… and I fear the world… it will never be the same…
                                     FADE OUT.

The fourth Agatha Christie novel I adapted, *The ABC Murders*, as I mentioned, was never produced. In that game, the murderer was the same, but I felt that even though players may remember the gimmick of a killer who disguises his true motive and real target as one of a series of serial killings, the actual murderer's identity was a bit more obscure.

Hal Barwood is currently working on his 10th novel. You can find out all about him @ finitearts.com. Here he shares some of the challenges in adapting the character Indiana Jones to video games.

"I've built three Jones games. Successfully adapting Indy's character to interactivity meant paying attention to four key ideas:

First of all, in a game there is no Harrison Ford to admire, and it wouldn't matter if there were—the player is the star, and Jones is merely his avatar. Instead of basking in reflected glory, the player is asked to roll up his sleeves and go to work; to understand and solve exactly the kinds of problems that movie heroes solve for us. This means that a lot of the fun is to be found in the world around Indy. Special care must be taken to make it a rich and varied experience, and to explain his situation in it.

Second, the twists and turns of a good story can easily seem like rococo decoration in an environment where action speaks much louder than words. Plots must be lean. Games are ten times longer than movies, however, so there's still time and space for a lot to happen.

Third, character means one thing in a movie and something else in a game. On the silver screen, the hero's most important attributes are his dramatic characteristics—for example, Indy's burning desire to investigate the mysteries of antiquity, his eye for women, his greed. In a game, his most important attributes are his fists, his whip, and his revolver. Players care little about who Indy is and a lot about what he can do. In designing *Fate of Atlantis*, a puzzle game, I was careful to include action elements. On his way to the fabled city, the player had to evade Indy's enemies while riding a camel, winning a car chase, operating a balloon and a submarine, and using his fists."

Finally, games are good at creating a different emotional experience than movies. Conventional feelings like love, hate, and sorrow—the emotions of literature and drama—give way to frustration, determination, and fiero—the emotions of sport. Accordingly, in designing *The Infernal Machine*, I included a lot of dangerous stunts, some pretty fierce combat, and a series of exotic boss monsters. After each challenge, the game offered substantial rewards in the form of cool power-ups and wild new territory to explore.

> Fiero: a word from the Italian that means "pride." In this context, we take it to mean the thrill of victory or triumph denoting achievement as well as pride.

As evidenced by his games, Hal chooses to adapt the franchise and its characters, and not the literal plots of specific films. This did not prevent him from respecting both the characters and the spirit of the franchise, even as he put them into original stories. In my first adaptation, *Once upon a Forest*, based on a Twentieth Century-Fox animated film, I stayed close to the original, condensing it and altering it for gameplay, but staying true to the characters and the ecological theme of the film.

Later, when I adapted *Wild Wild West*, I created an entirely new story. I was not enamored of the screenplay. It took a winking, smug, ultra-hip approach to the original. How do you spoof a show that was already a spoof? The same arch treatment of my favorite television series, *The Avengers*, also ruined that movie for me. (Boo, Warner Brothers, for both remakes!)

The screenplay was all I had to go on when I began writing. I retained the updated train of the film because it made a great base of operations with plenty of cool gadgets for players to use, and we based our design of the train on photographs of the film's sets. But I decided to remain true to the spirit of the original television series even though my James West and Artemus Gordon were obviously based on Will Smith and Kevin Kline.

Both approaches have their challenges. Unless you are told how to adapt, you must ask yourself what is the best way to bring the source material to life? The important thing to remember is that when the gameplay and story are developed in concert, the balance between the two can be more easily maintained.

SEQUELS

Congratulations! The first game was a hit! Now what? There is no fixed rule that sequels will be worse than the originals. Several movie sequels to the TV version of *Charlie's Angels* ranged from pretty good to pretty not so good. *Lara Croft: Tomb Raider* reboots, *Tomb Raider* in 2013, and *Rise of the Tomb Raider* in 2015 revitalized the franchise with better writing, gameplay, and Camilla Luddington. *Godfather II* and *Aliens* were at least equal to, and in my mind anyway, superior to the originals.

Why do some sequels work, and others don't? Games have a built-in bonus for sequels: improved graphics. More pixels, more polygons, and better lighting effects all help sequels to look "better" than the originals.

There are several different ways to approach sequels. The most obvious one is the worst: rehash the original. It took the Lara Croft franchise until 2013 to add to the mix, deciding to stop playing it safe and go beyond what had worked before. *Godfather II* built on its predecessor, creating an epic story that cut between a prologue to the first film: Vito Corleone's (Robert de Niro) rise to power, and the assimilation of Michael Corleone (Al Pacino) into the family business after the deaths of his father Vito and brother Sonny in the first film. *Aliens* took a single character, Ripley (Sigourney Weaver), and the acid-blooded antagonist from the original film, yanked them out of the haunted house subgenre of *Alien* and successfully dropped them into another subgenre: the squad-level combat movie.

Some ideas, whether games or movies, are better off not spawning sequels, but that won't stop studios from making them. "We blew up a chicken coop in our first game. Let's blow up a barn in this one!" *Bigger* does not necessarily translate into *better*. That's a second danger to be wary of in sequels. Recognizing that an identical rehash may appeal to hardcore fans, but not bring in any new customers, we can try for the Roman approach. "Fights between bears and lions sold tickets at the Coliseum last season, but I'm seeing some empty seats out there now, any suggestions? Yes, Flailius?" "How about we toss a few Christians in there, boss?"

Motion pictures and games go down this same rocky path every time there is a new technical achievement. CGI creatures were pretty cool the first fifty times we saw them, but each successive iteration must be even better than the last. The ogre in *The Fellowship of the Ring* was impressive when it attacked in the Mines of Moria. There are more ogres in *Return of the King*, and they are given a larger role to play. Nevertheless, they are easily eclipsed by Gollum. The irony is that Gollum's success owes as much to Andy Serkis, the motion capture actor, as to advances in CGI.

A successful sequel, like *Portal 2*, needs its own identity. The *Aliens* carried on the way the alien did in the first film, and there were more of them, but the context in which they were placed would have made a good film, *even if it had not been a sequel.* Unfortunately, the same cannot be said for the *Alien vs. Predator* films. The sequel must stand on its own merits as a complete entertainment product. And that's how it is best to approach it.

We can be grateful that some of the work has already been done for us. If we can add some more polygons to our characters and smooth out some rough spots in the animations, it's much easier than starting from scratch. The player expects similar gameplay, and hopefully we don't need to rebuild the engine from scratch. If we already have a successful game mechanic, all we need to do is find ways to tweak it or find different situations where it can be used in new, spectacular ways. We begin as writers knowing any returning characters, and we can welcome the opportunity that the sequel gives us to explore them in even more depth. And while we don't want to repeat the same plot, it should balance similar elements with new opportunities to stretch our characters in interesting ways.

It becomes clear what players are enjoying in a game. The important thing is to give them more, plus making sure the game can stand on its own and be entertaining, without thought to how the original was. Again, it's a matter of finding the balance between characters we already like and new characters that are equally compelling; story and style (see the next section) that is reminiscent of the previous success, but not just a copy of it; and gameplay that adds new features the same way the first game did that set it apart from the crowd.

FINDING A STYLE THAT FITS

Finding the correct style for the story we want to tell seems like a no-brainer. A squad-level counter-terrorist game like those in the *Rainbow Six* series requires a hard-edged style to action and dialogue that would be as wildly out of place in the wacky side-scroller *Super Mario Bros.* series, as the Marx Brothers would have been playing the leads in *The Hurt Locker*. But it isn't as cut and dried as that. In every tragedy Shakespeare ever wrote, there was humor, for example, the drunken porter in *Macbeth*.

Or Hamlet's flirtatious teasing of Ophelia.

"Lady, shall I lie in your lap?" (A double-entendre meaning to have sexual intercourse.)

"No, my lord.'

"I mean, my head upon your lap." (Surprisingly, not a similar double-entendre.)

"Ay, my lord."

As we learned in high school English class, the humor was used to give the audience some relief from all the carnage and angst. Any game can benefit from not taking serious subject matter *always* seriously. One of the things we haven't done enough in games is comedy-drama. Our genres may not appear to lend themselves to such subtleties, but *Star Trek* always featured the sparring between the cantankerous McCoy and unflappable Spock, even at the direst moments. And comedies have been built around otherwise tragic situations. The doomed bride Shelby in *Steel Magnolias* (Julia Roberts's star-making role) was the center around which the other very human but very comic characters swirled.

Poor old poisoned Nicole from *Edge of Night!* I need to resurrect her again. I deliberately intercut the shocking scenes of her death during a live broadcast at the fictional TV station—Nicole was a newscaster—with comedy scenes of always frazzled Mitzi at her restaurant trying to enlist the aid of the thuggish chauffeur Gunther after her cook had walked out during the dinner rush. So as Nicole died, and the broadcast was disrupted, Gunther was busily burning hamburgers and barking at customers. This was *not done* to give the audience any relief at all. I wrote it that way to keep them off-balance, to make the death even more shocking when played off against the humor of the restaurant scenes.

We'll talk about comedy more in Chapter 11, but here are some other points about style to consider. Comedy should be:

- **True to the material.** Every so often, people will try to upgrade a Shakespearean play. Kenneth Brannagh's *Hamlet* was set in the early 1900s. *West Side Story* and *Romeo + Juliet* update *Romeo and Juliet* to New York and L.A. street gangs. But all remain essentially true to the material. However, in the 1960s, that breeding ground for experimentation in all walks of life, there was an off-Broadway production of *Hamlet* performed on roller-skates. Hmmm.

- **The best style to tell the story.** *Pork Chop Hill* and *M.A.S.H* were both films set during the Korean war, but whereas the first film was grimly realistic in its depiction of war, *M.A.S.H* was irreverent and hilarious, even as gouts of blood were hitting the roof of the surgical tent. It's not the setting or arena that suggests the style, but the story told within it.

- **A style that makes sense for our medium.** I'd love to do a narrative musical game. It's one of my favorite genres. The second play I had produced was a musical. But it would have to make sense as a game as well. The musical genre alone shouldn't prohibit it from being a game, but unless it was *PrettyBelle*, it might not work as a first-person shooter. (Don't worry if you've never heard of *PrettyBelle*. It was a stage play I saw starring Angela Lansbury that closed in Boston, never making it to Broadway.) Remember the bug collector idea? It's all in the execution. This is not to dissuade anyone from making a musical game, but to caution you to be true to both the source material and genuine gameplay.

- **A style that remains consistent throughout the game (no matter what style we settle on).** If we interject drama into a comedy game, it should still be a legitimate part of the story and the world, and it should spring naturally from our characters. Remember Laing told us that even schizophrenics are not just crazy. They have an interior reality which may be at odds with the rest of the world, but it isn't a box of isolated tics. It is a consistent reality.

LINEAR VERSUS NONLINEAR

One of the great misconceptions many writers and designers have when they sit down to write a story for a game is that they think the story must be linear. I hear this time and time again from writers who should really know better. I can understand it if the person holding this view is a writer newly arrived to our industry from other media. I can understand if it's another member of the development team that knows little about how storytelling is developed. It makes no sense to me when someone who understands that games can be nonlinear, but still doesn't see how to make a story game that way.

This misconception is used all the time as an excuse for seemingly intelligent people and well-known designers to say things like, "Story must be linear. That's why story and games don't really go well together." Or "Story forces the game to be linear, but I want the player to be able to do whatever they like in any order, so I won't have story, just backstory or context."

In one sense, progression through all games is linear. Every time a player moves from level to level in an action game, they are following a linear path. In fact, in the strictest sense, each game experience is linear because the player makes only one set of choices about what to do. Let's say a player reaches an obstacle they can't get past, so they backtrack in the level to find something that will help them: a hint, an item, or another obstacle that must be overcome first.

Even if the player returns again and again to the first obstacle, then goes off in multiple directions until they figure out how to get past it, they are following a linear path of their own making. That path can end up looking like 100 feet of tangled string tossed in a drawer, but as long as you recognize that the player is always moving forward through the game, even if the player retraces some of their steps, they will find signposts pointing the way to success like clues, necessary objects like keys, etc. And their final path will be linear (Figure 7.4).

The gameplay, however, can be as nonlinear as we want (Figure 7.5). This is obvious in a treasure hunt game where players can access many discrete areas and may move from one to another and back again as they learn where to dig.

Both examples may seem to make any coherent storytelling impossible. Yet, in fact, it's perfectly possible, even desirable, because it is storytelling that doesn't get in the way of the player experiencing the game in whatever order they choose.

The main areas of gameplay, for example, different parts of the world in *The Riddle of Master Lu*, were nonlinear. They could be played in any order. But many reviewers didn't notice because they thought they'd cleverly discovered the *golden path* to victory. There wasn't one.

Golden path: This refers to the optimum path a player may take through a game to experience the game design to its fullest.

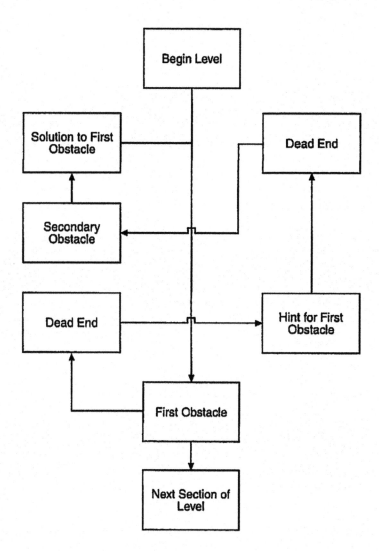

FIGURE 7.4   Linear experience in nonlinear space.

We game designers sure are an eclectic bunch when it comes to describing game elements. We use the word *mana* to describe a measurable amount of energy that powers our magic spells in RPGs. The word *mana* means a supernatural or spiritual power and comes to us from various Melanesian and Polynesian religions. In New Zealand today, highly regarded individuals are said to possess mana.

The word *avatar* was used to describe the player-character in the *Ultima* series of RPGs. It was popularized in Neal Stephenson's science fiction novel *Snow Crash*, where it referred to a representation of someone in a virtual reality where that person could interact with their surroundings. It actually comes from Hindu mythology, where it meant the temporary body or incarnation a God adopted when visiting earth.

Golden path comes from Zen Buddhism and refers to the Buddha's eight-fold path to nirvana or enlightenment. Unfortunately, the idea of a "golden path" in game design forces

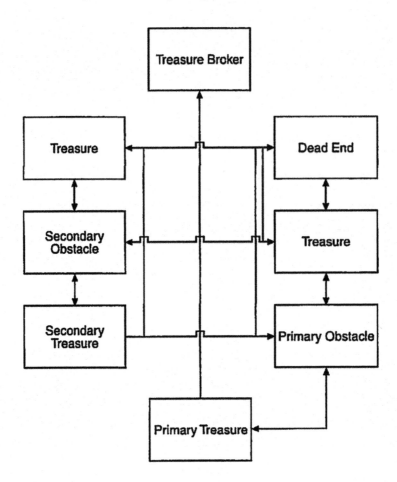

FIGURE 7.5 Nonlinear gameplay.

linear thinking on game designers as much as any story might. Thinking in terms of paths at all is misleading. Nonlinear doesn't mean many paths. It means *no* paths. There are not two, but three, possibilities open to us.

We can place the player in a long, narrow tunnel. A side-scroller action game is essentially a long tunnel viewed in sections from the side. The player-character can move forward or back, maybe even up and down, but side-to-side movement is limited by two-dimensional space pretending to be three-dimensional. When action games first moved into 3D space, designers would still try and keep players on tracks or "rails" so they couldn't stray too far.

We can place the player in a twisty maze of passageways where there may be many side passages and dead ends. Some of those side passages may eventually find their way to our destination, but a golden path is the "best" choice, even if without a map it isn't clear what the exact steps along that golden path may be. Games like *The Elder Scrolls V: Skyrim* and *Red Dead Redemption* cleverly disguise their fairly linear storylines with open-world "sandbox" play. The player can choose to wander at will, crossing paths with the story as rarely or as often as desired.

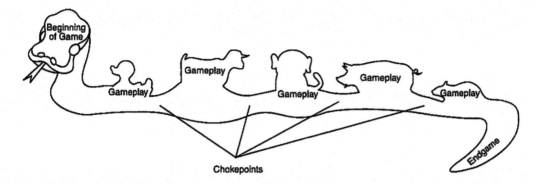

FIGURE 7.6   Linear structure with big bites of nonlinear gameplay.

Or we can place the player in an open space dotted here and there with interactions: mobs to kill, merchants to trade with, treasures to locate, and quests to undertake. This is the truest nonlinear game space. It can also be the most difficult to manage.

Some games use all three possibilities. They narrow the world to literal paths in the mountains; give players many passages to explore in sewers beneath a city; and even provide open spaces like a grassland or swamp. Yet the storytelling is strictly linear. Such a game's levels can only be played in one order, despite the lesser or greater degrees of freedom of movement in each level.

This is the popular "python" approach to providing the player with freedom of movement, yet still forcing them through a linear storyline. Think of the game's structure as that of a python who has swallowed several animals. He might look like this (Figure 7.6).

The narrow sections are called *chokepoints*. They can be levels, but they don't have to be extracurricular to the game world. They can be locked doors, bridges that collapse behind the player-character, palace guards, a boat that has run out of fuel, and so on. In his book, *Game Design: The Art and Business of Creating Games*, Bob Bates defines them as "points beyond which the player can't go back, other than by restoring a saved game." There can be a practical technical reason for this that has nothing to do with storytelling. Bob points out that "If you design a multiple-disc game with a huge world and allow the player complete access to the entire world at any time, you are designing in the problem of annoying disc swaps for the player."

Happily, although disc swaps are a thing of the past, this was certainly true for me in *Dark Side of the Moon* back in 1998. The nonlinear structure of both game and story led to way too much disc swapping. We tried to break the discs up by "levels" of the huge mining colony, but anytime the player hopped on an elevator, or took the mystical shortcut of a "river of light," they swapped discs. These days, *Breath of the Wild* (not a small game!) is a digital download to my Switch. *Sea of Thieves* and the perennial "early release" of *Baldur's Gate 3* and a bunch of other games co-exist happily on the Windows side of my MacBook Pro thanks to Boot Camp.

The python structure creates the illusion of nonlinearity for a game, while only needing it at certain spots. It can be very comforting to writers who think game stories must be linear.

But there is no need for writers and designers to try and wrestle the game structure into a linear form just because they want stories in their games. Any of the three forms (tunnel, maze, or open space) lend themselves to storytelling as much as they do gameplay. The first happily accommodates linear story. The second requires some branching or Web structure. The third requires a modular approach to storytelling. We've certainly seen our share of the first structure and even some of the second. The third we will explore in detail in Chapters 13 and 14 when we look at game stories that have no need to be linear at all.

AVOIDING CLICHÉS

We've talked about avoiding stereotypes when writing characters. Now it's time to look at the similar damage that clichés can do to our stories. Just as our shared unconscious understanding of film language sends up a warning flare when the camera axis is crossed, the game player's antennae begin to twitch if either story or gameplay is stale and derivative.

Clichés are a recipe for boredom. Yet so many game stories are dependent upon cliché! Genre writing can be a crockpot of cliché. Some inexperienced writers just dive in headfirst, assuming genre writing must be clichéd. Others decide to cop an attitude toward the genre. The clichés remain, but now there's a lot of winking and chuckling behind the scenes as if to say, "Yeah, we know this stuff is pretty bad, but that's what we're stuck with when we do film noir."

Here is another reason people think stories in games don't work. How unfair it is to assume that because some writers cannot get beyond clichés that game writing can only be clichéd and therefore boring! How many times have we heard a reviewer say about the story in a game, "It's about what you'd expect from a game." I don't care if the reviewers are willing to shrug it off. Writers can't. Game stories deserve as much respect as character.

How do we avoid clichés? By learning to recognize them when we see them. How do we do that? There are three ways.

The first should be obvious. Stories are built on characters. Build a story on stereotypes, and you will most likely end up with clichés. Stereotypes tend to speak in clichés, make clichéd decisions, and act in clichéd ways.

The second is to make the story our own. Our truest characters are part ourselves and part observed behavior. Sometimes they can be the same. Sometimes we can't tell if they are or not. Our truest stories are combinations of our life experience; observed bits of reality that are "dramatic" even if they are not truly drama; and stories that are drama because they are translations of life seen through the eyes of our fellow writers.

The third is to know how the story we're writing relates to all those other stories people have already told. We *can* learn from studying and analyzing the work of other writers. We will see how they successfully handled a love scene or an action sequence. But if we start to break their methods down into their component parts, we run the risk of discovering lists. You know the ones I mean; those lists that writing gurus are so fond of making up: ten Potent Conflicts to Ensure Dramatic Stories, twenty-five Plot Moves Gamers Love, and fifty Emotions that Will Bring Your Characters to Life.

You can find such lists in *Cosmopolitan* ("10 Things Men Don't Want to Say, but Want You to Do!" "15 Erogenous Zones Men Need to Know about Now!"). Those lists won't actually make anyone a better lover. Lovemaking takes heart as much as it does technique. It's the same with lists for budding writers. They do not guarantee that drama, exciting plot moves, or human emotion will ever be a part of your story. Without context, they only increase the chances that the unwary writer will end up neck deep in clichés.

There is no guarantee. All we can do is learn enough about literature (read a lot of books!), drama (see a lot of plays, or read them if we have to!), film (see a lot of movies and TV!) and yes, games (play a lot of games!), to help us begin to recognize clichés. Then we must bring our own life experience to the equation: *our* emotions, *our* dreams, the poetry of *our* souls. If we don't succeed—and even great writers fail often—we at least will have tried. If we don't try, we are doomed to a Sartre-like hell where our efforts at storytelling continue to be shrugged off with the words, "It's only a game."

CHAPTER 8

Respecting Story

I N ADDITION TO THE importance of respecting the characters we create, granting characters purpose beyond the designer's convenience makes it easier for us to tell our stories. By the same token, respecting the story makes it easier for us to design our games. I've already suggested some ways of respecting the story even before we reached this chapter, and I want to briefly recap them before we move on.

- Give the story a reason for existing by providing it with a compelling theme. Start with that theme or discover it early.

- Develop the story in concert with gameplay. Don't try to tack either one on to the other like an afterthought.

- Balance the story with the gameplay. The same amount of player time needn't be spent on both, but both should be built with the same craft and care.

- Ensure that the story fits the medium.

- Make the story worthy of its characters.

Now let's examine some more ways to respect story and make it as gripping and entertaining as our gameplay.

WILLING SUSPENSION OF DISBELIEF

> Water, water every where
>   And all the boards did shrink;
> Water, water every where,
>   Nor any drop to drink.
>
> *Samuel Taylor Coleridge, The Rime of the Ancient Mariner*

There's no better place to start respecting story than respecting the audience we tell it to. The player who hits the ESC key to skip the story in a game may be able to sit for hours

DOI: 10.1201/9780429284991-12

watching a movie in a theater. They are a captive audience. They paid money, and unless the film in their opinion is excruciatingly unworthy of their time, they are liable to forgive quite a few lapses in entertainment.

Watching TV, on the other hand, they may hit the menu button (a remote's escape key) just as much, and they are doing it for the same reason they do in a game. The material is unable to capture their attention. Maybe the exposition is too long or too wordy. Maybe the characters are stereotypes, or the story is a quagmire of clichés, so they don't have to watch. They already know what's going to happen.

We need to give the player some credit, though. If they find a TV show worthy of their time, the remote is put down and the popcorn is picked up. If they find a story in games worth following, they might enjoy it enough to keep their finger off ESC. What can we do to ensure this? Absolutely nothing. What can we do to at least make it possible? Understand our responsibilities as authors to the concept of "willing suspension of disbelief." We try very hard to provoke our audience/player into willingly suspending their disbelief. It is important to know, or at least sense ways to help players suspend disbelief; and conversely when we're doing something that fights against that desire.

Often erroneously shortened, leaving off that all important first word "willing," the phrase "willing suspension of disbelief" comes to us from Samuel Taylor Coleridge (1772–1834). Coleridge was a maverick. Abandoning Cambridge University, he and his friend, fellow poet Robert Southey, attempted to start a commune in Pennsylvania, but the effort failed. Before long, Coleridge put radical politics on a back burner and settled down to doing what he did best: writing poetry.

The poems Coleridge is most remembered for are "The Rime of the Ancient Mariner" and "Kublai Khan," both written when he was 26. He suffered facial pain most of his life and, as was the fashion of the day, was prescribed opium for the pain. His inspiration for "Kublai Khan" reportedly came to him in an opium dream. Along with another friend, William Wordsworth, Coleridge is considered one of the founders of the Romantic Movement in poetry. In his middle age, opium addiction consumed Coleridge and drove away all who were dear to him. He still managed to work, turning out a book of prose dissertations called *Biographia Literaria* that included literary critiques and theory and in which he writes about how the volume of poetry co-published with Wordsworth that contained "The Rime of the Ancient Mariner" came about.

Their plan was to co-write and publish a book that represented what they considered "the two cardinal points of poetry, the power exciting the sympathy of the reader by a faithful adherence to the truth of nature, and the power of giving the interest of novelty by modifying colours of imagination." Wordsworth, not surprisingly, chose subjects from ordinary life. Coleridge goes on:

> In this idea originated the plan of the 'Lyrical Ballads'; in which it was agreed, that my endeavours should be directed to persons and characters supernatural, or at least romantic, yet so as to transfer from our inward nature a human interest and a semblance of truth sufficient to procure for these shadows of imagination that willing suspension of disbelief for the moment, which constitutes poetic faith.

Today, over 200 years later, many who know the origins of "willing suspension of disbelief" think Coleridge was speaking of drama. He wasn't. He was talking about a depiction of events outside the norm that is still persuasive enough to capture a reader or audience. Appreciation of reality is replaced by faith.

How do we approach this when writing events set outside the world an audience or player knows to be real? We need to believe in the world we create and respect it: make sure its laws are consistent and logical. Aspects of the game world should all feel like they belong in the same universe together. If we take care to do this, the player has enough points of reference in the world and its fiction to latch on to that they are more willing to accept those points that are alien to them.

This approach encourages us to immerse the experience in as much real-world detail as possible. See the section later in this chapter on verisimilitude for other ways these details can help our stories. We should also try—as much fun as we think it may be—not to break the fourth wall, first introduced in Chapter 3: Respecting Characters.

THE FOURTH WALL REVISITED

In live theater, sets are built, furnishings placed, and props arranged to create the illusion that a fourth wall exists to the actors, but the audience is permitted to see through it. When it first came into vogue, this invisible fourth wall was framed by the proscenium arch (Figure 8.1). The proscenium arch takes its name from the construction of playhouses in ancient Rome, the word "proscenium" translating as "in front of the stage." The modern

FIGURE 8.1 Theater stage with the fourth wall invisible.

stage version developed during the Italian renaissance, which explains the elaborate carving that often surrounds the arch, emulating an ornate picture frame.

The term "fourth wall" has easily migrated to other entertainment media. Early film directors framed their action as if viewed through a proscenium, and movie theaters were traditionally built with prosceniums and curtains. Today, even though the arch may survive only in older theaters, the term remains. The fourth wall is easily defined by the movie screen, the screen of a television set, a computer monitor, a mobile phone, etc.

It remains metaphorically important when we discuss "breaking" it. Here we are speaking of breaking the illusion that the characters are unaware of our observation, or interference in the case of games; or that the fiction's creators are unaware that their work is being performed for an audience.

As mentioned in Chapter 3 there are, of course, times when the fourth wall is purposely broken. For example, Shakespearean soliloquies spoken directly to the audience.

VR can thrust a player through the fourth wall into the game world. When the player turns their head, the player-character does, too. Of course, it's hard not to be aware we're wearing goggles to make the illusion work.

So, when we say we want to make the interface as transparent as possible, we are speaking of the fourth wall. We mean to keep it as simple as possible, to interrupt the immersion as little as possible. Let's look at three other traps the writers of games can fall into when they don't respect the story.

THE TRAP OF CUT SCENES

I've alluded to this trap before because it is so common. Cut scenes, or cinematics, are used as connective tissue between levels or missions, eye candy rewards at the completion of a hard challenge, such as the defeat of a boss mob and so on. Boss mobs rightly deserve a death worthy of their difficulty.

Many designers of games today still seem to think cut scenes are the only way to tell story and reveal character. The writers they hire, particularly if they're refugees from Hollywood, are more than happy to agree with them. Cut scenes are exactly what they are used to. A movie is nothing more than a series of cut scenes. And we've seen repeatedly that movies can be great at telling stories.

Let's first examine the good points of cut scenes. They do have much to recommend them.

- First, as stated earlier, when we write cut scenes, we're on familiar territory. They follow the conventions of film language without the need for interpretation or translation into interactivity.

- Cut scenes are easily accessible to players who are familiar with this type of storytelling, having grown up with it in television and the movies.

- They can be produced independently of the rest of the game and by a separate team. This can free up resources and help keep development time down. If they're animated, the animations and graphics can be much richer. *The Legend of Zelda: Breath of the Wild*'s memories are a good example (Figure 8.2).

FIGURE 8.2   A memory awakened in *The Legend of Zelda: Call of the Wild*.

The term cut scene may have been coined in 1987 by Ron Gilbert, one of the designers of *Maniac Mansion*. Ron called scenes in the game that "cut away" from gameplay as cut scenes. The *Wing Commander* games in the 1990s were a pioneering effort in advancing story through cut scenes. The very nature of cut scenes at that time required them to be segregated from the rest of the game. This was their greatest strength and, in terms of immersion, their greatest weakness. It was difficult enough molding story and gameplay into a single entertainment experience without this segregation.

More recently the distinction between scenes of gameplay and cinematics has blurred. While some games explicitly remove true control as in *Bioshock*, others give players some control during cut scenes with varying degrees of success.

Even if cinematics appear to fit seamlessly into the same world as gameplay, players still know the difference. And many games still change their look to alert players that now it's time to watch, or time to engage in dialogue. Separating story and gameplay, no matter how skillfully disguised may seem easier to do than integrating them. But it hurts storytelling in several ways.

- As we've discussed, it requires the player to shift gears to enjoy both. Gameplay is an active experience; storytelling in cinematics often becomes passive, just like other media.

- The sequences don't just feel different in delivery, try as hard as we often do to integrate them, they can look and feel different.

- It reinforces Myth #2 from Chapter 1 "Myths and Equations," that games and stories don't mix.

- It discourages the search for ways to tell story within the gameplay. If a writer is convinced that cut scenes are the answer, why try other methods?

- It fosters the belief that story and gameplay don't need to be developed simultaneously, that story can be added later to gameplay, or gameplay to story, with impunity. This makes balancing the two difficult.

Let's take it in stages and see if we can wean ourselves from the trap of cut scenes. To answer the first point, remember what I wrote earlier about the shortening of attention spans of passive audiences? Does anyone think the same isn't true of game players? Yet cut scenes, because they are more expensive—that second team isn't cheap—can become bloated in length to justify the time, money, and effort put into them.

Many writers and designers recognize the dangers of cut scenes. There are more and more attempts to disguise them, to integrate them into gameplay, but it is a rare few who can eliminate them entirely. Take a look at games designed by Tim Schafer like *Monkey Island* and *Grim Fandango*. Tim is very proud of the fact the stories are told without cut scenes.

Just as we often force players to read paragraphs of text in some games, with cut scenes we can force them to sit through sequences that are drawn out to justify their inclusion in the game. By making a special case of the cut scene, we encourage producers to ask, "Why, if we're spending all this money on well-known actors and big production values, are the cut scenes so short?"

Why indeed? Snagging an ensemble of stars like Pierce Brosnan, John Cleese, and Judi Dench to voice their characters adds immeasurably to the illusion that 2004's *Everything or Nothing* was another big-budget addition to the James Bond franchise. One of the reasons it works is the actors don't just show up in cut scenes. And, lo and behold, storyline and dialogue almost measure up to a real Bond movie. That shouldn't be surprising since they were written by Bruce Feirstein, cowriter on three Bond feature films.

This game is an absolute rarity. It still relies on cut scenes where we find the story, but at least the voice actors and dialogue cross over into the game. If you're using their voices anyway, the first step on the road to recovery is to create cut sequences that resemble cut scenes but are sandwiched into the action with the same game engine that drives gameplay.

The *Metal Gear Solid* games, notable for their attention to story, rely heavily on cut scenes and long game engine noninteractive passages that pull gameplay to a halt, still segregating it from the storytelling. *Metal Gear Solid 4: Guns of the Patriots*, released in 2008, was almost a movie interrupted occasionally by gameplay. The *Final Fantasy* series uses both cut scenes and game engine scenes as well to advance the story. *Bioshock* went so far as to knock the player down to witness the first cinematic appearance of a Little Sister and her Big Daddy. Ouch!

Using the game engine alone is the route many Japanese console games like *The Legend of Zelda: Ocarina of Time* took. It immediately answers the second difficulty on our list. While the player may be forced to stop play for the same length of time as with a regular cut scene, the sequence is within the same game world as gameplay. Also, it is much easier to limit the length of the scenes because no additional team is necessary to create the

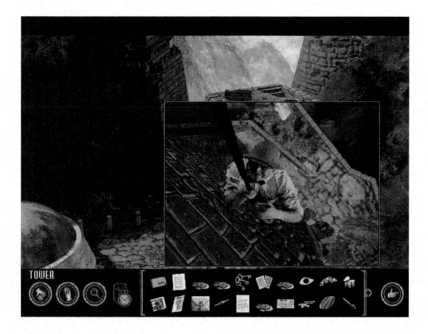

FIGURE 8.3   *The Riddle of Master Lu* cut scene.

sequences. Shorter scenes equal less player fidgeting. This is a good thing! It means they may keep those fingers off the ESC key!

Beyond the opening and closing sequences, there were few cut scenes in *The Riddle of Master Lu* (Figure 8.3). Instead, there were cinematic moments built with the game engine, such as exchanges of dialogue or eye candy rewards for the completion of puzzles, like a building blowing up and a flood of mercury inundating a villain. There were also brief windowed close-ups of characters, their use mandated by the slim video capabilities of 1994 when game production began.

Whenever possible, these sequences were mercifully short. There were exceptions, and I should have known better: a couple of excruciatingly long exposition scenes, one in particular between Ripley and the Baron where they sat still almost the entire time. This broke so many of my personal rules: put exposition in action, or at least keep the characters moving; keep such scenes short; don't write wordy paragraphs... on and on, why didn't I know better? And if I knew better, why didn't I do something about it? Ah well, every time we sit down to write, it's a learning experience.

So, the next step is to keep our cut scenes or game engine sequences short as in *Uncharted 2*, just like the other media we're emulating. *Half-Life* and *Half-Life 2* used game engine-driven sequences that are little more than a brief appearance of a character or an overheard snatch of dialogue to support the game's story. When we use the game engine to drive them, sequences might be no more than a split second long: a Spockian raised eyebrow on the part of an NPC or a shouted command. Once we pare them down this far, we should notice something else.

The next step is to create a continuum of scene length from full sequences to single cuts. At the short end of that vast range, we have scripted moments that barely interrupt gameplay at all: moments of character revelation, like a quick frown the NPC thinks we haven't noticed; moments of storytelling, like a sidekick remembering the legend of the haunted castle while you are both swinging across the moat on a rope; moments of story-telling *and* character revelation, like an NPC choosing door number two before the player-character decides which of the three doors to open.

And once we've noticed this, the next step is to put as much of our storytelling and character revelation into game moments as we can. This is the ideal. Right now, we haven't discovered enough ways to put the entire story there, because we've been distracted by cut scenes. But it's okay. Writers of movies and television don't always discover the perfect attack to every scene. We will explore a few approaches to integrating storytelling and gameplay in the next chapter. I expect the readers of this book will find more. Some of you probably have already.

It's a worthy goal. Every time we try to reach this ideal, we're rewarded by story and gameplay that are not at odds with each other but that complement each other and are balanced. This won't work if you try to add on story to gameplay already developed. It won't work if you try to sandwich gameplay into a locked-down story structure. It works beautifully if story and characters and gameplay are developed simultaneously.

Abandon cut scenes? No. I frequently use cinematics, or at least cinematic-like game engine sequences, as teasers or rewards or to cover transitions. They can still function to provide some context and continuity in games where levels are rigidly separated, for then the gameplay is as segmented as the story. But one day, we may see a game where there are no discrete levels; where the only pauses in the action are those chosen by the player; and where the immersion is as complete as the best films and books. Story integrated into gameplay will take us there, not story stuck in the ghetto of cut scenes.

When players become accustomed to these cut moments, they will relax and expect them. Then the longer cut sequences will seem all the more palatable. You should design and write them with the same care that the gameplay is designed, and there is only one entertainment experience awaiting the player, not two.

THE TRAP OF TOO MUCH BACKSTORY

The heading of this section must sound so unfair! After all the trouble we've taken to create three-dimensional characters with psychological and sociological dimensions, and all our efforts to create a consistent game world that is logical and faithful to its own rules—how can we fall into a trap of too much backstory?

It's far too easy. One of the telltale signs of amateur writers is that once all the research is done and the character profiles are written, they can't abandon all that work, so they try to shove as much of it as they can into the product it is meant to support. This can be as deadly in a game as it is in a screenplay or book. The only writer I've ever seen who was able to successfully bring off this approach was Jane Jensen in her Gabriel Knight games (*Gabriel Knight: The Beast Within*) where *if* the player wants to, they can seek out all the research material in appropriate places inside the game world, but if not, they can move on with their hunt to find the werewolf. Remember the interactive news in the film *Starship Troopers*? "Want to find out more?" The same principle.

For the rest of us, it's better to follow the advice of screenwriter and novelist William Goldman. Goldman is the screenwriter of many great films including *All the President's Men, Butch Cassidy and the Sundance Kid,* and *The Princess Bride.* He is also the author of the nonfiction *Adventures in the Screen Trade,* a book that contains a now famous quote about Hollywood: "Nobody knows anything."

After doing the research for a project, Goldman cuts away all the fat from his screenplays, leaving only what is essential to the telling of the story. If the characters don't reveal themselves in dialogue and action, paragraphs of description won't help. If convoluted explanations of events the player has been a part of are necessary, we've failed to expose the story. Once we've done the research for the game world our characters will inhabit and where our story will play itself out, it will come alive on its own, or it's fundamentally flawed.

There is a second trap of too much backstory. That is the mistaken belief that backstory and story are the same thing. For all its virtues, the adventure game *Myst* does not have a story. It has a backstory that is gradually revealed through the gameplay. The only effect the player can have on the "story" is to decide the fates of the two brothers at the very end. This is only a problem when we mistake backstory and story. If we can recognize the difference, a game may get along just fine with only backstory, as *Myst* did. Notice it's an old school adventure game, though, not an action game.

Backstory is often added to single-player games to explain all the shooting and running around. It establishes the antagonist and what they've been up to. Just as in the Golden Age mysteries where most of the story is a static unraveling of a murder committed early on, the player spends their time in the game making things right again. The much better approach is to establish the antagonist who has an ongoing plan for evil that must be foiled. Villains who wait for the hero to come after them are not worthy antagonists in an action game, and by their inactivity, they weaken the protagonist.

Some designers and writers of massively multiplayer worlds recognized fairly early on that if they relied only on backstory, their worlds were static and gameplay was repetitive. *Asheron's Call, Earth & Beyond,* and *Horizons* all attempted to feature ongoing stories. Games like *Everquest, Dark Age of Camelot,* and *World of Warcraft* that did not recognize this in their initial designs were faced with finding other, often more expensive, means to retain player's interest like additional creatures, higher loot, and more locations to explore. These worlds were much more likely to depend on expansion packs than those that incorporate ongoing story. We'll explore this in more detail in Chapters 18 and 19.

THE TRAP OF LETTING PLAYERS "DISCOVER" THE STORY

This trap can be found in single-player games, although because of their size, it is most egregious in virtual worlds. For that reason, my main example will be taken from a virtual world.

I remember quite a few years ago then *Everquest* lead designer Bill Trost was quoted at one of the game's official fan get-togethers that he was frustrated that players were complaining about the lack of story in the game, insisting there was a full, rich "storyline" in *Everquest,* and that people were simply failing to uncover it. Bill was the keeper of the lore (backstory) of Norrath, the world where *Everquest* was set, and he, with the help of others, put a lot of work into that lore. No wonder he was frustrated. What went wrong?

When I left *Everquest* after playing it for almost two years, I wrote a critique of the game signed by my character name, Skyrain Dreamweaver, the same character I've played in most of my adventures in virtual worlds since then. I understood Bill's frustration and was sympathetic, but this was my response.

> This is such a page from the amateur writer's scrapbook, it needs to be mentioned. Successful writing is (1) inspiration and talent and (2) the ability to present the work to the audience so that it can experience it. If you fail at number two, one is meaningless. Stop blaming your audience if they don't get it!
>
> People are simply playing the game you designed. If it isn't the one you wanted to design, or thought you designed, then change it.

I'd only recently begun work on my first virtual world, *The Gryphon Tapestry,* and in retrospect, my comments were phrased a bit too harshly, but I was speaking as a player who had his own frustrations about the game and as a writer who knew better than to hide his story from his audience.

Games that rely only on lore or backstory fall easily into this trap. As game designers, we realize everything we can make interactive, such as an obstacle or puzzle, everything we can give the player to do, instead of just being told, is a good thing. Virtual worlds in particular need all the "content" they can get to feed the voracious appetites of players. Therefore, on the surface it seems logical to treat backstory the same way, like the clues in some great mystery that must be unraveled, or the extra backstory Jane Jensen made available for the inquisitive to peruse.

There are a couple of differences. Gabriel Knight's game world was much more contained than the vast continents of Norrath. And Jane didn't make any attempt to hide where that backstory was located. By planting bits and pieces of the lore on NPCs and in books scattered through the game world, the *Everquest* designers were deliberately hiding it from players. They assumed players would be interested enough to track it down. And a few were. I remember a couple of fan sites where the collected lore was slowly being gathered.

Unfortunately, as we'll discuss in Chapter 17, not every player of a virtual world is an explorer. Some are just there to kill things and acquire phat l00t. I *am* an explorer, and I couldn't find enough of the lore to make much sense of it. I had to go to those fan sites outside of the game world to fill in what gaps I could.

This is similar to a blunder designers of adventure games can make. We called this a *pixel* hunt and strove mightily to avoid falling into *that* trap.

Some adventure game designers have the mistaken belief that they can add complexity to their games by adding the step of *finding* the puzzle,

Pixel: an abbreviation of the term *picture element,* describes the smallest component of a digital image.

forcing players to move their cursors ever so slowly over almost every pixel that a scene is composed of. This practice does not create complexity or depth of gameplay. It succeeds only in frustrating players. One solution is the "smart" cursor that changes in some way to indicate it's hovering above an interactive element on the screen. Today we have many "hidden object" games whose main gameplay is this. Not my favorite style of play!

Another solution, even more player friendly, was used in *Horizons*. In that game, crafters were required to gather the materials they needed from the world in order to make goods. This included mining, chopping down trees, and harvesting plants, among other activities. Not all rocks or trees or plants were harvestable. Some were permanent fixtures of the background. Every one that *was* usable was highlighted as the cursor passed over it. This was true of other interactive features in that world as well. In *Star Wars: The Old Republic* interactive objects were also highlighted until they were gathered or destroyed. Oddly, in many cases if the player waited around long enough, the easiest objects to reach—those that were not guarded by the more dangerous mobs—would reset themselves, allowing players to skip intended battles and still complete missions.

A disconnect comes from turning the exploration, puzzle-solving, or interaction that should occur *after* the material is located into impediments in the search. If we're afraid our puzzle or obstacle might be too easily overcome, or that our backstory may be too thin, we may be tempted to add such "complexity." We not only run the risk of obscuring our story, but we may also fail to expose it to players at all.

The best solution is to reveal backstory through exposition brought to light during the action of an ongoing story. If we have no real ongoing story, it's far better to at least provide pointers to where the backstory can be found. Instead of hiding it, make a big deal of it! Have your three-dimensional NPCs tell players that historians discovered a book previously thought lost, or that archaeologists have excavated some ancient ruins. This does not have to be an added element. These may just be static pointers to locations and objects that have always been, and always will be, part of the game world.

VERISIMILITUDE

The setting of your game can be a mining colony in the far reaches of space, but we can people it with characters whose motives and desires match our own or those around us. If we propose a land where pigs fly, we can still be aware of gravity. No matter how outlandish the conception of our world may be, it is essential that we give the player enough hooks to create the illusion of reality that we refer to as *verisimilitude*. If we don't, we leave the player floundering without a point of reference they can grab on to.

> Verisimilitude: the appearance of truth or the quality of seeming to be true. It mimics reality enough to be perceived as real.

Maintaining verisimilitude forces us to avoid creating our worlds and stories on the fly, a sign of weak writing in any medium. I've met more than my share of writers who are convinced this style of writing is the only way to go. I was one of them once upon a time. I'll admit it's the most fun. My first plays and screenplays were written this way, making things up as I went along, and they were vastly entertaining. To me. I was constantly being surprised by the twists and turns in my own stories and delighted by the unusual choices my characters made. But how indulgent! And how contemptuous of your *other* audience! When one of my screenplays ended up on Robert Redford's desk, he was not impressed.

We don't want to get hung up on reality. We can't duplicate it, and we shouldn't want to anyway. Moment to moment reality is dull. It's not drama. But we must apply verisimilitude to every aspect of our games to give players the necessary veneer of reality they require. They will thank us for it, because it allows them to hit the ground running—and playing— in any world we devise.

EXPRESSIONISM

My favorite movie of all time is expressionist. No, the film is not *The Cabinet of Dr. Caligari* or *Nosferatu*, classics of German expressionism from the days of silent movies. It is *Night of the Hunter*, the only film ever directed by actor Charles Laughton (1899–1962). Released in 1955, it is a gothic fairytale starring Robert Mitchum and Shelley Winters. Written by noted film critic and

> Expressionism: a 20th-century art movement begun in Europe that stresses the expression of emotion and the inner vision of the artist rather than the exact representation of nature.

novelist James Agee, the story is set in the depression. A Bible-quoting serial killer murders a woman, and then pursues her two children for some bank robbery money. That's pretty much the plot.

The film is an allegory of good and evil, as the famous tattoos on Mitchum's knuckles aptly proclaimed (Figure 8.4).

It is composed of one haunting image after another: the car at the bottom of the river with its ghastly passenger; the journey of the children down-river in the skiff with the various wild creatures in the foreground of the shots; the silhouettes of farmhouse and a lone rider on a mule. It is also one of the scariest motion pictures ever made.

It was adapted by Agee from a novel by Davis Grubb and transformed by Laughton into imagery so vivid it is almost unique in filmmaking. It isn't literal. It's far from realistic. Audiences often have difficulty knowing what to make of it. What I bring away is the completeness of its vision in every frame: theme, style, performance, photography, music. If its

FIGURE 8.4   Robert Mitchum is a wolf in sheep's clothing in *Night of the Hunter*.

spell touches you, there's no letting go. It's something I strive for in every game I work on, even if it's only a moment or two where the player is transported from this world, oblivious to time passing, captured heart and mind.

[Agee deserves his own mention as a writer who loved the English language and wrote prose that flows like poetry. His novel "A Death in the Family" won a Pulitzer Prize.]

SYMBOLISM

Both Joseph Campbell and Carl Jung tell me they would be delighted if your game writing used symbols. They are a shortcut to the human heart and mind I just spoke about capturing. It allows you to do great chunks of storytelling in the composition of a single scene or the objects within it. No need to be all that subtle. Just as great stories are wasted if nobody can find them, symbols should be accessible.

> Symbolism: a movement in art at the beginning of the 20th century. More generally it means infusing objects or actions with significance beyond the literal.

In *Mirage*, a movie written by Peter Stone, a psychiatrist washes his hands of Gregory Peck's plight as he apparently does the plights of all his patients, by... washing his hands. But if we're going to use symbols, we must respect them, the same as we should genres. If we laugh at them, they lose their potency. Symbolism isn't just for high art and literature, as the above example should prove. It is another storytelling tool waiting to be utilized by the writer of games.

CONSISTENCY OF THE WORLD

This isn't the first time I've mentioned consistency, and it won't be the last. It's so important that, even though the concept is woven throughout this book, it deserves its own heading. We've talked about consistency of character and of style. It is a key to helping the player become willing to suspend their disbelief, preserve the fourth wall, and create verisimilitude.

It also helps us as writers. Once we settle on a theme, or a group of characters or a story or a style, everything else falls into place, if we're faithful to that element. And when all the elements are consistent with one another, we don't sit staring at the blank page on the monitor hoping for an idea. They suggest themselves, thanks to the consistent structure we have built and maintain.

Tim Schafer's *Grim Fandango* and *Full Throttle* are examples of beautifully consistent writing and game design. Arena, story, incidents, characters, puzzles, artwork, and music all combine to create and heighten the unique moods. In the first, the player-character is Manny Calavera, travel agent to newly arrived souls in the Land of the Dead from Mexican folklore. The second is the game version of a biker movie, funny and deliberately low-brow.

Many of the games we remember most fondly win a place in our hearts because of consistency. Whether it is the theme or story or characters that we remember most, we remember them because they are reflected in all aspects of the game. Consistency can make good games unforgettable.

SETTING

Two households, both alike in dignity,
    In fair Verona, where we lay our scene,
    From ancient grudge break to new mutiny,
    Where civil blood makes civil hands unclean.
    From forth the fatal loins of these two foes
    A pair of star-cross'd lovers take their life;
    Whose misadventur'd piteous overthrows
    Doth with their death bury their parents' strife.
    The fearful passage of their death-mark'd love,
    And the continuance of their parents' rage,
    Which, but their children's end, naught could remove,
    Is now the two hours' traffic of our stage;
    The which if you with patient ears attend,
    What here shall miss, our toil shall strive to mend.

—William Shakespeare, Romeo and Juliet

Here Shakespeare describes the setting for one of his plays. The classic example of the importance of setting in literature is the heath, a vast expanse of fallow rolling hills, sudden steep defiles, and rugged coastline that made up the fictional county of Wessex in England's west country that is as much a character of the novels of Thomas Hardy (1840–1928) as Bathsheba Everdene of *Far from the Madding Crowd* or Tess in *Tess of the d'Urbervilles*. Hardy, a master of setting, is said to have written his settings as if they were major characters in his stories. This is the same general location as the famous moors of detective fiction on display in *The Hound of the Baskervilles* by Arthur Conan Doyle (1859–1930) with their windswept tors, fog-gripped hollows, and bogs that can suck a horse under in seconds.

In drama, we "set the stage" for the action of a play with every bit as much care as a gleaming diamond is set in a golden ring. Today Broadway audiences applaud the set as the curtain rises on a play with the same enthusiasm they applaud the actors after the curtain's final fall. The baroque setting of Andrew Lloyd Webber's *Phantom of the Opera* is a faithful adaptation of its source novel, recreating the Paris Opera House down to the massive crystal chandelier that swings menacingly out over the audience and plays its own role in the musical's climax.

But the setting need not be so elaborate. In the play *Waiting for Godot* by Samuel Beckett, we have a stage empty except for a withered tree. In his adaptation of Herman Melville's *Moby Dick*, Orson Welles was faced with recreating an epic chase at sea on a live stage. Wisely understanding he could never hope to duplicate the scope of the action the way a film can, Welles used minimalist sets, such as a series of hanging ropes that swayed back and forth to indicate the pitch and yaw of the whaling vessel *Pequod* rolling in the waves. He then directed his actors to sway in concert with the ropes. The effect was almost mesmerizing, and apparently *too* realistic since several theatergoers reportedly became queasy during the performance!

In films, we have countless examples of setting being instrumental: the Italian village of *Il Postino*; the tiny town invaded by a Hollywood film company in David Mamet's *State and Main*; John Ford's favorite location, Monument Valley, lovingly rediscovered by Sergio Leone in *Once Upon a Time in the West*; and the very different cornfields we get in *Field of Dreams* and *Signs*.

A setting is not necessarily only geography. It can be a time, such as the depression, beautifully realized in John Steinbeck's *The Grapes of Wrath*; or the castles of the British royal family in *The Crown*; even a style of filmmaking as in *The Artist*. The 2011 French film is a beautiful example of consistency of world, too: a black-and-white silent film about making black-and-white silent films. Rarely have setting and theme blended so seamlessly.

A setting can be an event like the title celebration in *A Wedding* directed by Robert Altman, or the violence surrounding the 1968 Democratic National Convention that became the backdrop for *Medium Cool,* directed by cinematographer Haskell Wexler. In *The Good, the Bad and the Ugly,* the American Civil War was no more than a constant irritation to the three men intent on recovering a fortune in buried gold coins.

There is another term I've mentioned before that encompasses all these different types of settings. That's an "arena," used by Hollywood writers and producers to immediately communicate setting, types of characters, even the style of a story. The arena of *Full Throttle* is not just its seedy bar, junkyard, or demolition derby racetrack. Those are settings. But the arena for that game provides hints to the writer about where Ben, the biker player-character, will feel most at home. Arena is the complete milieu or environment of a story.

Another setting that deserves its own heading is weather.

WEATHER

A lot of people like snow. I find it to be an unnecessary freezing of water.

—*Carl Reiner*

What would a murder mystery set in a gloomy old mansion be without a thunderstorm raging outside? Think of the blizzard that traps the handful of scientists and military men fighting off the bloodthirsty alien in *The Thing from Another World*. Weather is often used as an obstacle as well as a setting. The plane that can't take off due to a storm; the ship that is lost at sea; or the Victorian gentleman lost in a London fog, so major a weather phenomenon in England they named a raincoat after it.

We don't have the problems with real-world weather in games. Our technical hurdle for a long time was that any moving pixels on the screen could slow down our game action. That's not true any longer. Weather is no longer just a change of scenery; it can affect gameplay in many games these days such as *Sea of Thieves* where your primary mode of travel is a sailing ship. *Red Dead Redemption 2* gives players everything from snowstorms to dust storms. Compare this to *Everquest* in 1999 where developers added fog to limit the player's field of vision. It was so successful that in the first few weeks after the game's release, players complained bitterly they were getting jumped by mobs or losing their way—surely the idea—but their complaints were heeded, and the effect was rolled back. I liked the added danger, but others were more vocal.

It does add one more thing for the artists and sound effects teams to deal with. I worked on two games where weather was placed suspiciously late in the production schedule, and eventually dropped due to time constraints. You thought I didn't notice, huh guys?

I think the real problem for us writers though is that unless the genre or arena suggests it: haunted house mystery, ski-lodge, desert, it doesn't occur to us to add weather to enhance our stories. It's obvious what a great obstacle it can be, but weather can also affect the mood of a story in more subtle ways.

A storm on a distant horizon can be symbolic. Steaming tropical jungle, high humidity, and afternoon rainsqualls are used to great effect to heighten the romance between Guy Hamilton (Mel Gibson) and Jillian Bryant (Sigourney Weaver) in *The Year of Living Dangerously*. Nothing like khaki shirts stained with sweat to conjure up all sorts of images, not all unpleasant.

Raymond Chandler (1888–1959) evokes the hot dry wind that blows westward over Los Angeles in this famous passage from the short story "Red Wind":

> There was a desert wind blowing that night. It was one of those hot dry Santa Anas that come down through the mountain passes and curl your hair and make your nerves jump and your skin itch. On nights like that every booze party ends in a fight. Meek little wives feel the edge of the carving knife and study their husbands' necks. Anything can happen. You can even get a full glass of beer at a cocktail lounge.

Throughout the course of a game, weather can be used simply to alter the look of the graphics for a change of visual. It is a setting, just like a physical location, a time, or an event. It can become an obstacle or a plot point. It can create different moods and evoke emotion. Weather is the writer's friend.

SCOPE AND SCALE

I saved the biggest for last. Just as the correct style is important to a player's buying into a story, the correct scope helps, too. Independent movies often betray their low budgets when they attempt to tackle subject matter too broad in scope for them to handle. We wrestled with this in *The Riddle of Master Lu*, trying with very flavorful, if limited locations, to recreate the feel of Ripley's continent-hopping adventures.

Some stories work best in intimate settings, and they can get buried beneath the spectacle of an epic. *Doctor Zhivago*, the 1965 film directed by David Lean and adapted from Boris Pasternak's best-selling novel by Robert Bolt, is set against the backdrop of the Russian Revolution. But it is not about that revolution. It is a love story. For that reason, the massacre of the students and the cavalry charge across the ice—sequences that were featured in the trailers—are actually very brief. Lean and Bolt took great pains to keep the revolution in the background so that it didn't overwhelm the love triangle of Zhivago (Omar Shariff), Lara (Julie Christie), and Tonya (Geraldine Chaplin).

Contrast that with 2001's *Enemy at the Gates,* the Jean-Jacques Annaud film that opens with the epic scenes of the battle of Stalingrad in World War II. The scope and scale of that film overwhelm and render inconsequential the love story between Vasili Zaitsev (Jude Law) and Tania Chernova (Rachel Weisz). Tonya and Tania are both nurses with their own stories, but the characters are worlds apart in how well served Tonya is over Tania.

Scope was another aspect of game production that was for a long time hampered by technical limitations, and certainly it still requires a lot of effort. But scope and scale rarely cause the technical issues they used to, at least for the big-budget games.

Not only are our graphics processors more powerful, but developers also have become very clever counting polygons, reusing models and skins, and so on, so that settings are much less elaborate than they might appear. It's important for the writer to understand what the game's budget will allow. It does no harm to think aggressively at first and let your imagination roam through sandstorms like the latest film version of *Dune* or dive from the tallest of buildings in *Assassin's Creed* games (Figure 8.5).

Just be aware that even a game with the budget of a major motion picture being built by multiple studios around the world may find itself overreaching. Writing to the budget is difficult in the best of times. It can be deadly to developers who dream too big and cannot recognize when that is happening. Be prepared. Never forget a lesson we'll discuss in Chapter 12. Be ready to scale back and even drop entire story elements when the ship date plows closer and closer like a sandworm.

Luckily not all games require great scope and scale. Players have learned that bigger isn't always better. One look at the quantity of games for iPhone and Android shows us that smaller games can become major hits. And writing for these games presents its own challenges. Big-budget games from Rockstar and Ubisoft tell huge stories backed by expensive production values. But smaller games like *Life Is Strange, Valiant Hearts,* and *The Lion's*

FIGURE 8.5   An impressive blast from the past: *Assassin's Creed 2.*

Song can tell stories that are just as compelling and dramatic and intimate as their more expensive cousins. In Chapter 19 we'll discuss how to meet the special challenges "smaller" stages for our stories present us.

Even though many technical considerations that limited us a few years ago have been overcome, that's no reason to choose a scope of game that doesn't fit our story or gameplay or device. Our choice should be based on the same things that inform our other choices, like style and setting. We should choose the appropriate scope or scale to tell the story and bring the gameplay to life, no more and no less.

CHAPTER 9

Bringing the Story to Life

NOW THAT WE HAVE respect for the story we are telling; have learned some traps to avoid; and have looked at some of the issues that should be taken into account as we write, it's time to take those stories and bring them to life. We'll be looking at drama again. Our friends William Archer and Lajos Egri will offer guidance. And we'll explore opportunities within the game design to tell the story.

FORESHADOWING

Foreshadowing is used to create anticipation and suspense. The idea is that whether or not something exciting is happening at the moment we foreshadow, there are exciting things to come.

> Foreshadowing: the practice of hinting about action or revelations to come.

> Had I but known then what I do now, I might never have married a man I didn't really know, and settled down to domestic life with him in that fog-bound house of stone…

So many gothic romances from the late 18th to early 19th centuries began with similar words that they became known as the "Had I But Known" school of writing, shortened to HIBK. And of course, modern bodice-rippers (a euphemism for a sub-genre of period romance novels) are not immune to HIBK either.

This is foreshadowing at its most obvious, a hook telling the reader flat out that however many pages of sunlight and roses the book may start out with, sooner or later there are going to be bumps in the night and a plucky, nightgown-clad young woman, holding her candle aloft, will haltingly descend into a dank family crypt; climb a creaky stairway to a high, windblown gable room; or timidly tip-toe into a sealed-off wing, there to confront even danker and creakier family secrets whose florid descriptions are guaranteed to run on as much as this sentence.

Most television shows and limited series start with what we call in screenwriting the *teaser*. The teaser can be direct action, without foreshadowing, other than it promises the entire story will contain such action. It can also be more subtle, as the wheels are set in motion for what is to follow.

DOI: 10.1201/9780429284991-13

FIGURE 9.1   Teaser to a *Blacke's Magic* episode.

Figure 9.1 is not only a great place for a producer to stick his name, but the drag race on an abandoned runway also creates the climate for the even more dramatic landing of a plane with no one on board. Both elements foreshadow the bizarre nature of the mystery to follow *and* contain the clues to its solution.

In *Play-Making* William Archer stresses the importance of "carrying forward the interest of the audience…" and lays out this principle: "A good first act should never end in a blank wall. There should always be a window in it, with at least a glimpse of something attractive beyond." When he uses the word "attractive," he doesn't mean "pretty." He is using the word in its basic sense of something that will attract the audience enough so that they don't pack up and leave when the first act curtain falls.

Archer uses an excellent example of foreshadowing from the end of the first act of Oscar Wilde's play *Lady Windermere's Fan.* Lady Windermere has discovered that her husband has been calling on a certain Mrs. Erlynne, and then discovers Lord Windermere has written many large checks made out to Mrs. Erlynne. Her husband then enters, and he asks her to add Mrs. Erlynne to the guest list of a party they are giving. When she refuses, he fills out the invitation himself. Archer points out that this alone foreshadows trouble ahead when the two women meet, but the act isn't over yet.

The first act of the play is set on Lady Windermere's birthday, and at the beginning of the act, her husband has given her an ostrich-feather fan. When he sends a messenger off with the invitation, she announces, "If that woman crosses my threshold, I shall strike her across the face with this fan." Foreshadowing in spades, but the curtain still doesn't fall.

Lady Windermere rings for her butler and instructs him: "Parker, be sure you pronounce the names of the guests very distinctly tonight. Sometimes you speak so fast that I miss them. I am particularly anxious to hear the names quite clearly, so as to make no mistake."

Archer admits, "… for my own part, I can aver that, when the curtain fell on the first act a five-pound note would not have bribed me to leave the theatre…."

If foreshadowing occurs at the beginning of our story, it can be Campbell's "call to adventure." The reason for the call will have been dramatic enough already. Both the setup and the call foreshadow the excitement to come.

Of course, there is no rule that says foreshadowing needs to be confined to teasers or first acts. Just like the old movie serials we'll be looking at later, every last scene of a Netflix limited series ends on a cliffhanger designed to ensure we'll want to watch the next episode. This foreshadowing has been so successful it has led to serious binging of viewers. No more waiting until next week as in network episodic TV, or even waiting until commercials run. Interestingly some limited series like Hulu's *Only Murders in the Building* now deliberately set a week-by-week delivery of episodes to prolong a series' run just as if they were on network TV. As French writer Jean-Baptiste Alphonse Karr wrote in 1849: "Plus ça change, plus c'est la même chose." (The more things change, the more they stay the same.)

In foreshadowing characters may share "What if?" speculations on what may happen if certain actions are carried out. Or some character will make the obvious mistake of relaxing. "Well, looks like the worst is behind us!" Not.

In games, we want the player to keep playing after the first level is solved, so we don't end with the defeat of the boss mob for that level. We want to reveal to the player, or remind them, that this opponent, as tough as it was, is only the minion of a more dangerous foe. We can do this in many ways, such as through the dying threats of this lesser villain; a message that is triggered upon his death to "bring out the big guns"; our sidekick or mentor announcing he's just received word that the antagonist has already made his countermove: killing, kidnapping, or besmirching the character of someone; revealing that the prize sought at the end of this level has already been sent on; or any number of other escalations of the encounter that foreshadow more and bigger conflicts to come.

There are other types of foreshadowing. I'll foreshadow where I'm going with the next few paragraphs. One of these types is our new best friend from the last chapter: symbolism.

In 1922, a mild-mannered former campaign manager for President Warren G. Harding named Will Hays was picked to head the newly formed Motion Pictures Producers and Distributors Association that is the forerunner of today's Motion Picture Association of America (MPAA). The association was created to counter public indignation at immorality in Hollywood, as well as its movies, and to clean up the image of both that had led to local censorship laws across the country. However, the association did little to clean up Hollywood's act, and film became increasingly risqué with the arrival of sound in 1929.

In 1930, the association created the Production Code that remained in effect until 1967 when it was replaced by the MPAA's ratings system that remains with us only slightly modified today. But it was in 1934 that an amendment to the code established the Production Code Administration and required all motion pictures to get a certificate of approval before they could be released. Hays appointed Joseph Breen, a gentleman with an enthusiasm for censorship, to head up the new office. One of Breen's first acts was to force cuts in *Tarzan and His Mate* that featured a body double for Maureen O'Sullivan who played Jane skinny-dipping. The sequence has since been restored. Mae West was another casualty of censorship. Her bawdy banter ("Are you packin' a rod, or are you just glad to see me?"), much of it written by her, was heavily edited and her career never recovered.

The new code was also responsible for all those twin beds seen in movies after 1934 and all through 1950s television. The intention was to discourage audiences from wondering what those squeaky-clean couples got up to after the lights went out. We're just lucky it didn't prevent future generations from being born. I'm proud to report that I was responsible for removing one of the last sets of twin beds: those from the bedroom of Mike and Nancy Kerr on *Edge of Night* in 1983.

As with all censorship attempts, the creative forces immediately began to find ways around the Production Code. One of the most obvious was the lovers' clench where the camera would discreetly tilt up and off the action, but we were meant to assume that they didn't stop there. And believe it or not, here's where symbolic foreshadowing comes in. The writers and directors of the time were not content to infer that the couple had sex. They wanted to indicate whether it was good for both participants.

They did this by tacking something on to that tilt up. If the lovers were stretched out on a soft bed of grass beneath a tree, wind would detach a leaf from that tree. The leaf would eventually flutter down toward earth. If it landed in a bed of blossoming flowers, the audience knew there were rosy times ahead for the young lovers. If it landed in a mud puddle, it suggested the coupling had not gone as well as expected. If the wind picked it up and blew it away in the face of darkening storm clouds, watch out! The approaching storm was often used to foreshadow dark times ahead—metaphorically as well as literally.

Foreshadowing may be accomplished through simple action: the discovery that the door behind which we earlier heard disconcerting growls is found to be mysteriously unlocked. All the dogs starting to bark before an earthquake. The bubbles that roil the surface of the Black Lagoon before the creature pops his head out to grin at Julia Adams.

Notice that in some of these examples, foreshadowing can be used to excite anticipation for something that will immediately occur, as well as events that may be a long time in coming. You and I know we have great conflict and action coming in our games, and foreshadowing is a way to let the player in on the secret.

POINT OF ATTACK

"… the curtain rises when at least one character has reached a *turning point in his life*." states Lajos Egri. "We must start a play at a point of decision, because that is the point at which the conflict starts, and the characters are given a chance to expose themselves and the premise." Remember when Egri speaks of "premise" to translate it to "theme."

> Point of attack: the term used to mark the moment that is picked as the opening to the story or scene. It is *never at* the very beginning of the plot.

The Fellowship of the Ring appears to begin at the beginning. All is quiet in Hobbiton. War clouds do not loom. Yet Sauron is already rebuilding his power base and has dispatched his Nazgûl to search for the ring. It doesn't begin on an average day either. Bilbo has already planned his disappearance from his birthday party. A turning point in his life has been reached. A decision has been made.

FIGURE 9.2   Sly Cooper about to do what he does best.

It might seem like Campbell's hero's journey always begins at the beginning. And, in fact, the quest often does start here when the hero answers the call to adventure. There may be the "refusal of the call," as when *Shane* declines to help the homesteaders, but we know that sooner or later heroes must face their destinies. The quest may be beginning, but the plot is already in motion. A village is raided, a spell is cast, and the Holy Grail is already missing. Evil forces are gathering behind the scenes. Calamity has struck, or the decision of a character will cause it to strike.

The story of *Sly Cooper and the Thievius Raccoonus* did not begin when the Thievius Raccoonus was stolen, or even when Sly decided to get it back. It began after he had begun his quest. We don't find him sitting around with his sidekicks, working himself up into a lather over the theft and vowing to right the wrong. We discover him on the rooftop of police headquarters, about to do what he does best: break and enter (Figure 9.2).

There *is* a montage of still pictures that precedes this and does explain some of the backstory; however, this exposition could just as easily have come out during the early action.

In almost every action game, the first moves of the villain have already been executed before the player picks up their controller. The player may know little of the details of the villain's plans, but something is obviously afoot. It's not all that difficult for us to find the appropriate point of attack for our game. It's much harder to find the best point of attack for a scene.

The second script I wrote for *Charlie's Angels* was an episode called "The Jade Trap." I received a copy of my first draft back from producer Leonard Goldberg with the following note written in the margin: "Make this scene more witty, clever, and sophisticated." After much consternation and gnashing of teeth, I finally removed the entrance of a character at the top of the scene, and all exits at the end. The scene now started in the middle and ended still in the middle. Simply by changing the point of attack and leaving off the goodbye, the scene became wittier, cleverer, and definitely more sophisticated. Leonard caught that the scene was dragging, and his note reflected that, even if his admonition was a bit vague. He was pleased with the rewrite. If only all rewrites were that easy!

This solution worked because in film we can choose the entrance and exit points for our scenes with great care. We can cut in to a scene and out of it again. We can remove all sorts of pace-deadening material, like waiting for characters to enter a room or exit it. Unfortunately, when writing games, we are often forced to begin at the beginning of scenes, even if it's unnecessary and undramatic. In graphical games, we are at the mercy of contiguous space. Stage productions can turn the lights off or drop the curtain to accomplish the same thing as a cut, but Egri's take on transitions in drama is worth repeating. Here he is speaking about all sorts of transitions: changes in characters and relationships or from scene to scene:

> Shall we record every movement of a transition? The answer is no. It is not necessary. If you suggest a movement in transition, and this suggestion throws a light on the working of the character's mind, we think it is sufficient. It depends on the dramatist's ability, how successfully he can compress his material in transition, giving—or suggesting—the whole movement.

Remember? The audience fills in the blanks.

When adventure games jumped from text to graphics, players explicitly guided the player-character from room to room. We opened all the doors, walked the PC through them, encountered an NPC loitering there only to discuss story or puzzles, then walked all the way back across the room and out the door again. This exists today in almost every game. Cuts do occur in single-player games as we transition from level to level, but in general we must traverse the virtual space of a level in the same way that we do in real life. As we know, drama does not equal real life. How then can we capture the dramatic urgency that point of attack can give us? By not taking the space or the progression of our game story quite so literally.

I remember in one of the earliest of the *Star Trek* graphic adventure games once players had explored an area, they were able to use the point-and-click interface to jump to distant locations as long as they could see them. This shortcut successfully removed at least some of the literal traversing of the space. Today many games allow player avatars to run through their worlds' vast spaces or find a horse or a police car to speed things along.

When a player-character transitions between two rooms, we do not have to see every step that they take. Film directors have three main choices when deciding how to cut between scenes. The first is the establishing shot, a wide angle that gives the audience a feel for the next location where the action will take place. Another is to cut to a close-up of a significant object in the next scene; for example, a hand turning on a light, a meaningful *objet d'art*, or a prop. The last is a matching cut that can be literal or simply thematic, such as a cut between two visually similar actions—a book slamming shut in a library to one being opened in a dorm room—or a cut from a waterfall to a shot glass being filled in a bar.

Since we try not to dictate the direction a player must look, preferring to give them more freedom of movement, the matching cut is most difficult. The establishing shot doesn't do much for us since most of the exploration and action in games takes place in wide angles, so we'd expect to see our character enter a new room. But the second, the close-up, has possibilities.

It is a perfectly reasonable jump in a game to move from directing the PC to open a door, to a brief cut of that same PC's hand flicking on a light switch. In this case, if the room were in darkness, it is the next step in a progression the player must take anyway and would not be jarring provided such cuts were used consistently throughout the game.

In an action game, as soon as a player-character moves into a new area, an immediate attack by an enemy serves to thrust the player directly into the scene. It shouldn't be such a fierce attack that the player has no chance of survival, but a lower-level enemy that can be dispatched after the player has gained their bearings is a good way to cut literally to the point of attack.

Massively multiplayer games and battle royales face the same dilemma, and it is not so easily overcome as in single-player games. The problem lies in one of perception. All multiplayer games are thought of as virtual worlds with a very literal geography. Opportunities for cutting are few and far between. Yet transitions between zones, entering or leaving cities or buildings, modes of transportation such as teleports and vehicles, all give us chances to cut out nonessential movement. The key is a more flexible view of the virtual world that allows for dramatic license. It is important to note that not all of these are appropriate in battle royale games. Maps are smaller than MMOs (Massively Multiplayer Online) and the setting is very self-contained.

We can also use NPCs to help us cut to the point of attack of a new scene or encounter. In real life, we drop phrases like "Let's cut to the chase" or "I'll get right to the point" into our conversations if time is limited or our need to say something is urgent. An NPC can replace the usual pleasantries of "Hi, how are you, brave adventurer?" and "I have many fine baked goods for sale today" with "I'm sorry if I seem distracted, but my dog disappeared" or "Aren't you the bold adventurer who rid the village of those werewolves awhile back?" We are "cutting" to the point of attack.

As Egri concludes, "It is imperative that your story starts in the middle, and not under any circumstances, at the beginning." I would only add that we can say the same thing for our scenes and encounters, too.

THE OBLIGATORY SCENE

William Archer suggests it may have been Francisque Sarcey (1827–1899), a French journalist and drama critic, who invented the phrase *scène à faire*, or obligatory scene. Another possibility is Augustin Eugene Scribe (1791–1861), French playwright, librettist, and founder of the Society of Authors,

> The obligatory scene: a scene that must be written, otherwise the audience will feel extremely dissatisfied.

generally credited with perfecting and popularizing the "well-made play," as well as perfecting and popularizing author's royalties, an achievement that made him rich. And yes, his name really was Scribe.

Sarcey describes the obligatory scene in a play called *Les Fourchambault* by Emile Augier:

> … it is precisely this *expectation mingled with uncertainty* that is one of the charms of the theatre. I say to myself, 'Ah, they will have an encounter! What will come of it?' And that this is the state of mind of the whole audience is proved by the fact that when the two characters of the *scène à faire* stand face to face, a thrill of anticipation runs round the whole theatre.

Whoever came up with it first, Archer likes it a lot. His own definition is "a scene which, for one reason or another, an audience expects and ardently desires." It is currently considered to be an old-fashioned notion. Egri dismisses the concept of an obligatory scene with "every scene in a play is obligatory." He's right in one sense. Every scene, every character, we write should move the story forward, and as Egri says, "prove the premise." Certainly, in a network television series, we quickly learned to write only critical scenes. We had little time in our 22 minutes (half-hour show) or 47 minutes (hour show) as it was to indulge in the luxury of writing scenes that weren't essential to the story or character revelation. Better to do both in every scene.

I agree that no moment in our story should fail to support theme, story, character, or all three at once. However, *some* scenes are far more important than others, and we do notice their absence. One of my favorite American authors is William Faulkner, and *Intruder in the Dust* is one of my favorites of his novels *(Absolom, Absolom* is the other). While in general I dislike unnecessary remakes of movies, I've always wanted to do a remake of the 1949 film version of *Intruder in the Dust*. Faulkner is said to have written the entire novel over one long, drunken weekend. It is for this reason I forgive him for leaving out an obligatory scene.

The scene in question is two old ladies standing off a lynch mob bent on hanging an innocent Black man accused of murder. That the lynch mob will be coming is foreshadowed, as is the timely disappearance of law officers. Yet because the story is told through the eyes of a young boy not present to witness it, it happens offstage like action in a Greek tragedy. It would have been easy to put the boy at the scene to witness it. It is a major dramatic confrontation the reader has been prepared for and is expecting.

You probably remember a similar scene from the film version of Harper Lee's equally superb novel *To Kill a Mockingbird* when Gregory Peck waits in the rocking chair for a similar mob on a similar mission. In that story, also told from the point of view of children, the kids *do* witness the confrontation (Figure 9.3).

If we're going to go to the trouble of foreshadowing a critical moment in a story, we'd better deliver it. If we're going to create two characters in opposition, they had better clash. This need is so deeply felt by writers and their audiences that to not deliver the scene is to betray the audience's need even more than the stories. In movies as diverse as *The Towering Inferno*, *Heat*, and *Runaway Jury*, the same obligatory scene in each is not a necessity for the story or the theme, but because of the casting. Paul Newman and Steve McQueen, the two reigning stars of the time, were only in one movie together, *The Towering Inferno*. To not have a scene between them (there were two) would have betrayed audience expectations. The same holds true for Robert DeNiro and Al Pacino in *Heat* (they were both in

FIGURE 9.3　Gregory Peck in his finest hour faces a lynch mob in *To Kill a Mockingbird*.

Godfather II, of course, but could never have met) and Gene Hackman and Dustin Hoffman in *Runaway Jury*.

General Gordon and the Mahdi never met face to face during the siege at Khartoum, but in the film of *Khartoum* they do. It was felt necessary to place these two characters in opposition in the same room (or, in this case, tent) at least once, even if it meant altering history.

It's easy to spot obligatory scenes. They are the high points of drama and conflict in a story. And they're usually easy to spot. Is there any question what the obligatory scene is in *Rocky*? If Rocky and Apollo Creed never got into that ring together, the movie screen would have been studded with Milk Duds and Jujubes.

Inherit the Wind's obligatory scene is historically accurate. William Jennings Bryan (Matthew Harrison Brady in the play) did take the stand to be questioned by Clarence Darrow (Henry Drummond in the play), although there is much debate over the difference between the play and the actual trial transcript. But it was an obligatory scene the entire play was leading up to.

The obligatory scene benefits from not being exactly what the audience expects. Because it is so highly anticipated, any twist we throw into it is all the more powerful, as long as it doesn't violate the reason the scene is obligatory to begin with. At the end of the western *The Professionals*, written and directed by Richard Brooks (who received academy award nominations for both), protagonist Henry "Rico" Fardan (Lee Marvin) learns that his mission to rescue the kidnapped wife of powerful land baron Joe Grant (Ralph Bellamy) has been a lie, and it is Grant who is the true villain from whom his wife was only trying to escape. The confrontation between Fardan and Grant is the final obligatory scene in the film. Up until now, this being an action movie, obligatory scenes were primarily resolved in gunplay and explosions, and a movie with less on its mind might have ended with a shootout. Instead of taking the gold offered as his reward, Fardan sends Grant's wife off with her true love again, resulting in the following exchange.

GRANT

You bastard!

FARDAN

Yes, sir. In my case an accident of birth.
(he swings up into his saddle)
But you, sir, you are a self-made man.

And Fardan with his wounded comrades rides off into at least a metaphorical sunset. Brooks chose to punctuate his obligatory scene not with bloodshed, but a memorable exchange of dialogue, one of my favorite ending lines in a movie.

We are faced with including obligatory scenes in every game we make. If, like the casting examples we promise something on the box, it better be in the game, or players will revolt. Protagonist and antagonist inevitably must meet for the final showdown.

In my Agatha Christie games featuring Hercule Poirot, if the detective and culprit did not meet, *and* if the culprit did not wither beneath the damning evidence thrust into his face, then readers, filmgoers, and players would revolt. In video games, there can be literally hundreds of obligatory scenes: every level boss must be confronted. Every quest-giver must be satisfied that the quest has been completed, whether the result is satisfactory or not.

In *Dark Side of the Moon*, there were two chief villains going about their nefarious deeds with entirely different agendas. Both were responsible for the loss of many lives, although only the first did any actual murdering. He is dispatched in the old-fashioned way with the expected confrontation, final exposition, and resulting fireworks. The second villain is only encountered in passing as Jake, the player-character, tries to escape the unstable moon. The player is given a moral choice of effectively executing this man by ceiling a door and cutting off his escape or permitting him to live by opening the door and letting justice take its course. Either way, the scene is obligatory.

Obligatory scenes occur in every level and every quest we write, not just in the endgame. Yes, as Egri argues, *every* scene should be necessary, but some are more so than others. Those are the true obligatory scenes. We set them up like jokes. Every joke has an A and a B side. The A is the setup. The B is the punch line. Leaving out an obligatory scene is like forgetting the punch line of a joke.

CRISIS, CLIMAX, AND RESOLUTION

Lajos Egri defines crisis as "a state of things in which a decisive change one way or the other is impending." Archer, distinguishing drama from fiction, says the "essence of drama is *crisis*." He argues that the dramatist "deals in rapid and startling changes," what our old friends the Greeks call the *peripeties*, and what we today call *reversals* (see the "Reversals" section). Archer then goes on to defend drama in my favorite quote of his:

It may be thought a point of inferiority in dramatic art that it should deal so largely in shocks to the nerves, and should appeal by preference, wherever it is reasonably possible, to the cheap emotions of curiosity and surprise. But this is a criticism, not of dramatic art, but of human nature.

—William Archer, Play-Making: A Manual of Craftsmanship

Writing in 1912, he sums up precisely why we writers of games have more to learn from drama than prose fiction. Because if there's anything we're good at, it's "shocks to the nerves," and I'm not talking about vibrators built into our gamepads. We already begin with the ability to provoke the adrenal gland through the intensity of gameplay, something other media must work harder to achieve. But all mammals have adrenal glands. It's up to us to take that ability and add to it something a bit more profound and human.

We have our crisis then. A major change is going to occur. Only one? No. As we move through the story, crisis follows crisis, each one escalating tension and suspense. Every one of these crises needs an additional element: a climax. Egri says, "crisis and climax follow each other, the last one always on a higher plane than the one before."

The word "climax" does not refer to the very end of a story that is followed by the denouement. The actual word is taken from the Greek and means "stair." That gives us the hint about its meaning. Each crisis demands a climax, a point where the rubber band of crisis has been stretched excruciatingly taut and finally snaps: that moment of confrontation, accusation, conflict, violence. And that climax then begs resolution, the final stage begun with multiple crises.

Resolution is simply the outcome of the climax that is a result of the crisis. The story is built from this three-step dance. Every one of these crises has reached a climax and has been resolved, only to have the stakes raised higher, and the next crisis always looming as even more profound.

They don't have to follow one another in lockstep fashion, one immediately after the other: Crisis A followed by Climax A followed by Resolution A followed by Crisis B followed by Climax B followed by Resolution B (Figure 9.4).

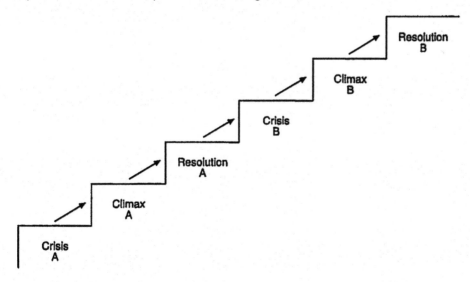

FIGURE 9.4 The stairway of crisis, climax, and resolution.

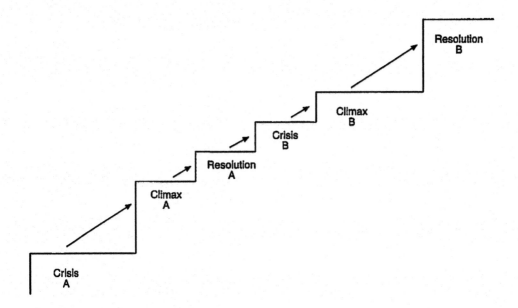

FIGURE 9.5 The stairway with time expanded.

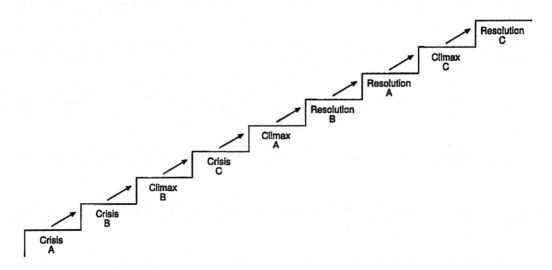

FIGURE 9.6 The stairway with crises, climaxes, and resolutions of different lengths.

There can be a great deal of time between a crisis and the moment it reaches a climax, and the same between climax and resolution (Figure 9.5).

Even more interesting is that multiple crises may play out in parallel with one or more great crises stretching past many smaller crises, climaxes, and resolutions (Figure 9.6).

This overlapping of different sets of crisis, climax, and resolution is at the heart of soap opera structure. You never finish all your stories on the same day if you want to seduce viewers to tune in the next day. Overlapping of stories like this can be at odds with distinct levels in single-player games and monthly deliveries of new content in virtual worlds, and care must be taken that the levels and episodes (or longer) are not too formally presented. We'll discuss the latter problem more in Chapter 17, when we examine "The Trap of Episodic Structure." Once the needs and limitations of the structure are understood, however, many variations and combinations are possible in a single game story.

Watch how novelist and screenwriter Alistair MacLean tightens the screws by piling crisis upon crisis in *The Guns of Navarone* or *Where Eagles Dare*. Both are textbook examples of this style of action writing.

However the dance plays out, we know by the end of the game that the player's protagonist character will have triumphed time and again against ever fiercer obstacles. And still all the player's best laid plans; all the new skills and gadgets the player-character has acquired; all the allies the player may have recruited; will still not seem to be enough to defeat the strong antagonist we've set in opposition against them.

Story and gameplay are not at odds here. They complement one another. They are working together with one noble goal in mind: to take the player and wring them dry of energy and emotion.

REVERSALS

It's as good a definition as any. I was a scrawny kid in high school: six feet two and weighing less than 140 pounds. But I wasn't all that bad at reversals when we wrestled in Mr. Brown's gym class. I needed to be to survive!

> Reversal: when the defensive wrestler comes from underneath and gains control of their opponent, either on the mat or in a standing position, while inbounds.

In storytelling, of course, a reversal is a sudden turn of events or fortunes. In writing television and movies, we focus on what we call the third-act reversal, borrowing the three-act structure from drama. Alan Ball, academy-award-winning writer *of American Beauty*, as well as executive producer on both *Six Feet Under* and *True Blood*, sums up his feelings about such things when discussing network meetings he endured getting notes for three earlier TV shows he wrote and produced (*Grace Under Fire, Cybil*, and *Oh Grow Up*):

> There always seem to be twice as many people as needed at every meeting. The networks have so many people who have to justify their jobs that they sit in on meetings, trying to come up with some kind of accepted feedback. They use all of these recycled buzzwords they learned in some storytelling seminar that I don't even understand: 'We need a third-act reversal here' or 'Let's telescope the action here.'
>
> —*Alan Ball, Fast Company*

I mention reversals because, yes, they can be used to good effect. It was a deliberate parody of the third-act reversal in *The Riddle of Master Lu* when a villain knocks Ripley down, then shatters the fourth wall by emptying his inventory. I also included in that same game a shop that sold everything an adventurer might need, but it was never open. Yes, sometimes being a game writer or designer requires a sadistic frame of mind.

Just throwing a reversal into the third act guarantees nothing. In fact, it has become so formulaic in screenwriting (thanks, I suppose, to those same seminars) that audiences can pretty much feel one a comin' in sort of the way birds get skittish when a storm approaches. How do we use reversals without their becoming clichés? Carefully set them up with the barest of clues, clues that are big enough, however, for the audience to remember and not feel cheated.

The great thing about our audience, the player, is that they aren't inundated with third-act reversals enough to spot 'em when they're coming, because *games don't have third acts.* Or at least not as we think of the term. I'm not going to go into all the business of breaking stories down into three acts. Enough people do it already. You won't see a special heading for it in this book. Just know that what is meant by a three-act structure is this:

- Act One: Introduction

- Act Two: Complication

- Act Three: Resolution

Ah, resolution! There's a word we know! The odd thing is that drama, where the notion of three-act structure originated, has long since wised up and gone to two acts, something network executives, the occasional aspiring writer, and other seminar attendees (even game company executives now unfortunately) are never told. Plays used to be five acts.

In the broadest sense, yes, game stories have an introduction. It's usually that cut scene up front. Then for the rest of the game all we have is Act Two. Finally, we have the endgame: Act Three. My act three reversal in *Master Lu* actually occurs right before the endgame, so I guess I cheated.

A game's structure cannot productively be defined by acts. Or if it is, every level should be one. And what are the acts in a virtual world? The introduction is hidden somewhere in the backstory. Complications are littered about the world waiting for players to trip over them, and there is never, ever, a third act. If we need three things to define story structure, we already have crisis, climax, and resolution. We start in the *middle* of our stories. We start with a crisis. We don't need no stinkin' acts!

This gives us far more freedom than those hapless screenwriters! We can have reversals in every level if we want. We can throw planet-shaking reversals at thousands of players at once in virtual worlds any time we please. In a single-player game, we set up an expectation, then reverse it. Things are finally going the player-character's way when all of a sudden the plot slaps them upside the head. Reversal. Or the converse: that new horde of mobs descending to finish off the PC actually turns out to be needed allies. Reversal. Call it a twist if you like (I know I do), although twists can be other things besides absolute reversals of fortune: a plot turn that sends us still forward, but in an entirely new direction; a character revelation that changes our perception of the character; a dance popularized by Chubby Checker.

ARCS

This term gets bandied about in seminars as well, but it has more merit. It is a good visualization for story and character tracked over the life of a game. Character arcs describe the

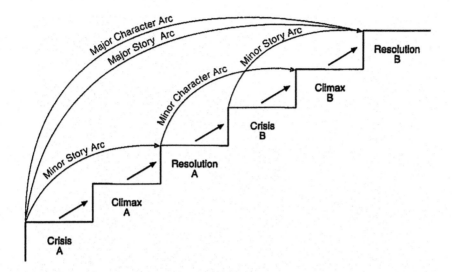

FIGURE 9.7   Story arcs climbing the stairway to drama.

growth and development of the character. Nothing too surprising there. Story arcs, however, are each one composed of crisis, climax, and resolution. And like those three building blocks, arcs can be found in any structure, three-act or thirty-act.

Egri, talking about the theater of over fifty years ago, tells us that: "The shortest scene contains all the elements of a three-act play. It has its own premise, which is exposed through conflict between the characters. The conflict grows through transition from crisis and climax. Crisis and climax are as periodical in a play as exposition is constant."

Periodical is a great word. Look again at the staircase in Figure 9.2. Let's add the arcs like gravity-defying Slinkies. Periodically a new step is mounted. Exposition occurs on all. And over that staircase of crisis, climax, and resolution, we can draw our story arcs, as in Figure 9.7.

They overlap beautifully. And that's what we need through our thirty levels or neverending escalator of virtual worlds. Be sure you can track all the character arcs for your major characters. Minor characters may not need them. Be sure you can lay out on a chart all the overlapping story arcs of your game. If you can do that, all the levels or chapters or episodes in the world can't disrupt the player's interest.

EXPOSITION IN ACTION

My mentor at CalArts, Sandy MacKendrick, had a cousin named Roger McDougall who was a writer (*The Man in the White Suit*, *The Mouse That Roared*) and composer.

(Roger is also known, by the way, for having been diagnosed with multiple sclerosis in the 1950s, but his doctors decided not to tell him what he had. He was bedridden by the time he learned the truth, did a lot of reading, put himself on his own strict diet, and recovered. Sandy used to chuckle and shake his head in amazement every time he told the story. Notice how this paragraph of exposition stopped *my* story.)

Sandy told us that Roger had a simple definition for "exposition in action." Every time a character walked into a room, they should have a gun in their hand. Sandy used *Odd Man Out*, the film that made James Mason a star, as an example where this rule was followed

FIGURE 9.8   Following my mentor's advice in *Dark Side of the Moon.*

almost literally. Mason plays an IRA leader on the run, and he does wave a gun around quite a bit while trying to explain himself (Figure 9.8).

A kinder, gentler definition of "exposition in action" is exposition that doesn't stop the forward movement of the story. Mystery writers have it easy. The investigation of a crime is both exposition and the story's primary action (not necessarily physical action remember). We also get to save the biggest barrel of exposition to empty at the very end.

Action movies (now it means physical action!), on the other hand, can survive on very little exposition; and we can extend Roger's definition from "gun in hand" to include "cars in chase," "bombs being defused," "monsters on the prowl," and many more situations that give us a nice cover of suspense or adrenaline rush to sneak some plot in. Drama with nonphysical action like courtrooms, medical operations, chess games, corporate takeovers, and the like can use exposition in action in precisely the same way.

How can we keep the exposition from interfering with the action?

- **Reserve it for cut scenes.** You can do this, but you still run the risk of bogging down your cut scenes with it. Besides, we like to tell our stories as part of the gameplay and that is our action.

- **Stick it into the action as a game engine sequence.** Better, but the risk is still there.

- **Keep it to the point.** Even if there is important secondary exposition, save it. Tell only what absolutely needs to be told for the player to understand what's happening.

- **Keep it brief.** A few lines interjected here and there. No action, however rousing, will cover paragraphs of exposition.

- **Break it up.** Create "cuts" with action, comments from another character, or a lapse of time. Let's assume a player-character, a knight named Edmund. Let's give him a sidekick named Baldrick, and a primary antagonist, a villain named Melchett. In the game they inhabit, we can lay in one piece of a chunk of exposition at a time. Start with a scout who declares, "Someone who looked like Melchett was seen on the battlements of Level's End Castle!" Then as player-character and sidekick ride out (player is steering the horses): "If it is Melchett in that castle, he'll be guarded." They fight their way through an ambush on the forest road (player is actively fighting). "Funny, these aren't Melchett's men. I wonder if Lord Percy has interested himself in the affair." As they approach the castle (steering horses): "We can't just ride up and knock on the gate, Sir Edmund. We need a cunning plan." "I have it, Baldrick. The moat is swimmable." Upon breaking into Melchett's bedchamber (player clicks on a crumpled form on the bed): "Melchett!" "He's been strangled!" "He wasn't master here, but a prisoner! But whose…?" In the same breath: "Lord Percy!"

The common practice of having NPCs spew out information in paragraphs not only cheapens the potential for the character ("I know I'm a self-made man, Pamela…") but it fights against the pace of the game.

And exposition does not have to be in dialogue. No, I'm not suggesting essential exposition be stuck into long paragraphs in an in-game book or journal either. Let's follow Edmund and his sidekick's adventures *without* dialogue: A dying messenger hands the player-character a blood-stained note. It reads "Someone who looks like Melchett has been seen on his castle's battlements." As the player-character prepares to mount up, his sidekick appears with extra weapons. A hanged man swings from a gibbet at the entrance to the forest with a sign on his chest that reads "Death to all brigands!" The ambushers are wearing the Lord Percy family crest. The player-character and sidekick must kill two guards at the bedchamber door, both wearing that same crest. A portrait on the wall bears the name Melchett. The dead man on the bed is the same.

Sure, no dialogue at all is stretching it. But study Hitchcock's mastery of exposition without dialogue for many clues on how to accomplish it. Remember the playground scene from *The Birds*? Exposition is fluttering down onto the jungle gym behind Tippi Hedren. In the same film, the sequence where she sees the man lighting a cigarette while gasoline spreads at his feet doesn't need the brief dialogue it contains.

Look for opportunities for exposition in geography (length of journey, possible hazards, time elapsed), weather (clothing needed, obstacles), body language (fear, aggression, love, hate), décor (wealth, a character's self-esteem, interests, hobbies, professions), wardrobe (wear and tear, armor or not, elegant, seductive), and any other nonverbal cues that will not stop action. This is one way where having three-dimensional characters really pays off.

Don't stop the story, or the action sounds obvious. Yet it is one of those concepts, like "Your uncle the Duke" exposition, that often seems to get lost in the shuffle when the writer actually writes. "Your uncle the Duke" is another gift to me from Sandy MacKendrick. It is a phrase that describes exposition artificially shared between two characters only for the benefit of the audience. The characters should both already know the information.

Sandy's example went like this: "You know your uncle the Duke?" to which the only reasonable reply is "Of course I do. He's my uncle." But we see this all the time. "Remember when I told you…?" "When we started this venture you promised me…" "Don't try to back out now. You told me…" And on and on and on.

In the next chapter, we'll move from concepts that games share with other entertainment media to a few that are quintessentially our own.

CHAPTER 10

Games

Charting New Territory

M ANY OF THE IDEAS we've been discussing come to us from other media, mainly the theater, television, and film. Some of these thoughts needed translation; others could be used as is. Now we're going to turn our attention to some of the concepts that games bring to the table. Here no translation is necessary since the concepts were developed while writing game stories.

What about characters? Did computer games add nothing new to writing characters? Actually, we did, so we're going to first jump back in time to the section of the book where we looked at characters and affix the following addendum.

CHARACTERS REVISITED

The most obvious new idea video games brought to characters was the ability for the audience to become the player and take part in the action. That is the entire point. Video games are not passive. They are active. Until now the closest thing to this experience that other media have provided has been the actor playing a role. The audience usually has had no part in this. There are exceptions, and they are worth noting as examples that people like being part of the action, even when there is no video game in sight.

In Chapter 6 I mentioned *Tamara*, a play set in an Italian villa before World War II where the "theatre" was an American Legion Hall on Vine Street in Hollywood, and several rooms had been dressed to re-create the rooms in the villa. The audience had "passports" stamped upon entering the building, were eyed suspiciously by actors playing customs agents, and questioned. Unfortunately, the audience's part in the play ended there.

Once inside, the actors moved freely from room to room, followed by the audience. Several scenes took place simultaneously. The audience could choose to follow any characters they wished but were asked not to interrupt the scenes. Another problem was that the play had been written with a golden path. Audience members following the "correct" actors got more of the central story.

DOI: 10.1201/9780429284991-14

FIGURE 10.1   *The Mystery of Edwin Drood*, a Broadway musical.

Most audience members knew which scenes to witness, either through word-of-mouth or repeat visits. I went back a second time and deliberately chose the path less traveled, and it did make all the difference. I saw some interesting vignettes but missed most of the main action of the play.

The Mystery of Edwin Drood, the novel that remained incomplete at Charles Dickens's death, has been completed by others many times. Most are novels that take up the tale where he left off in a pastiche of Dickens' style. In 1985, a musical version of *Drood* debuted (Figure 10.1). Not only did it break the fourth wall repeatedly, by allowing actors to step out of character and address the audience, but at the end the audience was asked to vote for whom they thought the killer was.

The idea of allowing the audience to vote on the outcome of a mystery or courtroom drama had been used before several times. The best-known example was *The Night of January 16th* by Ayn Rand. Rand is best known for *The Fountainhead* and *Atlas Shrugged*, and the school of philosophy that is called objectivism. Even in this minor effort, though, a very ordinary mystery, her favorite theme of the individualist versus collectivist was in evidence. The audience was invited to vote on the guilt or innocence of the accused. It was made into an even more ordinary movie in 1941 that dropped that gimmick.

Audience members shout sketch ideas to improvisational theater troupes. Performance art, too, may invite audience members to become a part of it. The late 1960s and early

1970s gave us Guerilla theater, spoofed by Brian DePalma in the "Be Black Baby" sequence from the 1970 film *Hi Mom!*. "Be Black Baby" is a fierce satire, and unfortunately remains relevant today. The fictional play within the film offered a role reversal where white audiences were given the opportunity to feel what it was like to be treated as the oppressed minority. In the most memorable moment, a battered and brutalized upper Manhattan couple stagger out afterwards, praise the play, and vow to tell all their friends to come see it.

Films, of course, have also dabbled in game-like structures, alternate plotlines, and so on, such as *Sliding Doors*, *Groundhog Day*, and my favorite *Run Lola Run*, but true audience participation in films has been limited to a few failed experiments like *Mr. Payback* and *Ride for Your Life* where audiences pushed buttons to vote on which branch of the story to follow next.

TV has even gotten into the act with numerous unsold pilots and short-lived game shows like *Whodunnit?* with Ed McMahon. My only limousine ride ever with the eternally young Dick Clark (1929–2012) occurred when we went to pitch one of these interactive mystery ideas to CBS. You've never heard of it, trust me. I suppose even today's "reality" TV series like *Antiques Roadshow* and *Real Housewives* have something in common with the earlier attempts, but with a limited cast of "real people" characters.

On a smaller scale in the 1980s, possibly inspired by *Tamara*, there were dinner party events featuring actors in character that allowed various levels of interactivity with their audiences. These were private parties, not money-making events. I attended one at a house in the Hollywood Hills where guests were greeted by a body drowned in a hot tub and after a catered dinner we watched as one of a Simon & Garfunkel-like duo was electrocuted by his guitar and plunged into the swimming pool.

Such experiences led to commercial events such as *The Dinner Detective* franchise founded in 2004, which has today grown to over seventy-five locations in the United States. The audience gets to interact somewhat with actors and get a dinner in the bargain. There are many of these murder mystery dinner troupes performing in several countries. Mohonk Mountain House in the Catskill Mountains has hosted a fun murder mystery weekend with surprise guests like famous authors since the 1970s. There also are of course plenty of boxed murder mystery party games that allow guests to play characters.

All these examples should indicate that casual participation is an extra level of fun beyond passive media. But none of these comes close to what we do. The player becomes—or at least drives—the player-character. Audience and actor are truly one.

Another aspect of characters that video games didn't invent, but die-hard gamers have embraced, comes to us from tabletop role-playing games like *Dungeons & Dragons*, *Call of Cthulhu*, *Vampire: The Masquerade*, and countless others. In these games and their progeny, computer role-playing games (CRPGs, shortened these days to RPGs), players build their characters using attributes like strength, dexterity, and intelligence. Each attribute, represented by a number indicating the points in that attribute the character has, affects the character's ability at certain skills like swinging a sword, dodging bullets, or casting magic spells. A Game Master, the person in charge of storytelling, will determine the outcome of gameplay with die rolls, adjusting to decisions made by the players.

In tabletop games, these are the only aspects of character the Game Master determines. The rest—accents, character traits, and so on—are added by the players themselves. This explains why computer RPGs for a long time did no more with characters either unless they were NPCs. Gradually, more and more of the character work we've been studying in other media was adopted.

The most interesting idea video games can call their own evolved out of this. We can allow our other characters, the actors not played by the player, good old NPCs, to react to the player's actions. I've given numerous examples of this from the funny rejoinders voiced by units in *Warcraft* when we click on them too many times, to the programmable charts that can track subtle changes in the ebb and flow of relationships between player-characters and NPCs.

What do we have to look forward to? Interesting experiments by academics have suggested there are very real benefits to using even the limited artificial intelligence available to us today. It's a lot of work to write interesting character and dialogue for every one of possibly hundreds of NPCs. And NPCs who mouth identical phrases throughout a game are at odds with encouraging the player's willing suspension of disbelief. But minor characters, akin to characters in interesting limited-subset AI experiments like *Façade* (2006) and *Prom Week* (2012), can help fill out our cast lists without the tedious task of writing each one individually. It's something to keep in mind the next time you face those hundreds of blank pages.

Time now to step out of the Way Back Machine and return to our present topic of storytelling.

PUZZLING DEVELOPMENTS

Obstacles are common to all dramatic media, and puzzles are one of the obstacles that gamers often face. The difference is that puzzles the audience must solve are the province of interactivity alone. We might think that mystery novels share puzzles with us; and it's true when we talk about the game the writer plays with the reader and the puzzle of the crime. Clichéd dialogue like "There's still a piece missing." and "It all fits!" refer explicitly to the puzzle aspects of a mystery story.

But the enjoyment of the mystery is not only that "game." The reader need not figure out the puzzle of "Whodunnit?" at all to enjoy it. Even more significantly, the reader can continue from the beginning to the end of the story without hindrance, whether they solve anything or just enjoy going along for the ride.

Too often, puzzles can end up as little more than obstacles to story progression, bearing little resemblance to dramatic obstacles, a gap the Professor Leyton games and the Phoenix Wright: Ace Attorney franchise attempted to bridge. Both spawned movies and TV series and even went head-to-head in *Professor Leyton vs. Phoenix Wright: Ace Attorney*, a title that truly "says it all."

Bob Bates is currently a consultant for several leading game companies. His most recent solo efforts are the game *Thaumistry*, and a novel, *The Ritual*. I've already quoted from his book *Game Design: The Art and Business of Creating Games*. Here's what Bob has to say about puzzles:

In traditional media, the hero of a story has obstacles to overcome. In games, these obstacles become puzzles.

Good puzzles contribute both to plot and character development. They draw the players further into the fictional world by encouraging them to explore the environment and to delve below the surface of the people they encounter.

Imagine, for example, that the player enters a room and discovers a door blocked by a teenage boy who is sitting cross-legged on the floor, his eyes staring vacantly into space, tears streaming down his cheeks.

To get through the door, the player will have to get past the boy. But who is he? Why is he crying? What will it take to get him to stop? To learn the answers, players will have to talk with the boy, or with someone else, or learn something about his background, or look around the setting to find something that might make him feel better. All these activities enhance the story. The backbone of good fiction is character, and the best puzzles are those that involve the desires and motivations of the characters who populate the game.

As you approach the problem of puzzle design, think about the hero you have created and about what they need to accomplish. Then think of reasonable obstacles that the villainous forces of the game might place in the hero's path. When you create puzzles that spring naturally from the characters and settings of the game, and when players learn the solutions through exploration and conversation, you'll find yourself with puzzles that contribute to, rather than hinder, the flow of your story.

Another way to write character is to create puzzles that, like dramatic obstacles, grow your player-character by revealing nuances of their character. It's done in a similar fashion to other media. The most obvious is to offer a moral choice to the player as part of the puzzle, as in *Dark Side of the Moon*, where the player decides whether to watch the villain die or rescue him and hope the courts punish him as he deserves.

Another obvious possibility is to require some skill or knowledge that the player-character may be known to possess, but that has not been utilized before. If that skill or knowledge is detrimental to another character, the player must decide whether to use it or not. And that can affect the relationship between PC and NPC. It's often an interesting idea to offer an alternative solution to the puzzle so that there is no real right or wrong solution.

A bit more subtle puzzle would be one where all the repercussions of solving it are not immediately apparent. The player only learns after they are past the puzzle that while opening the water valve has helped them, it has drowned some creatures they were trying to help. Reversal! Then present them with a similar puzzle where the result might be the same!

The puzzle can provide exposition. A series of bombs are constructed in such a way that provides clues to the manufacturer or to their whereabouts. An ingenious trap suggests engineering skills the villain may have that were previously unknown. The player can now be on the lookout for similar traps. Foreshadowing!

Every good story puzzle is a crisis that leads to a climax and a resolution. Back to those bombs for the obvious example. The player knows: "If I don't defuse this, that house nearby will be utterly destroyed!" Crisis. Climax follows: "The player chooses the blue wire!" Wrong one. The player runs for his life and makes it to safety just as the bomb explodes... causing a landslide... that buries an entire town.

Other story elements that puzzles can expose include the fleshing out of backstory: "Ah! So that's where that stolen concrete truck went!" More foreshadowing: "Notice anything odd about that demolished bridge? It wasn't blown up. It was *chewed*." Symbolism: "Every obstacle that Hitler fellow throws in my path reeks of his belief in Aryan supremacy."

The point is once puzzles are recognized for the excellent character revelation and storytelling tools they are, a whole other set of options are opened up for the writer of games. Imagine the joy when you can remove great masses of exposition that swell your cut scenes and scatter them among a few puzzles.

QUESTS

Quests, missions, tasks, errands ... they go by many names, but they are one of the primary means we have for telling our stories in games. And we're going to look at them in detail. They are structured like stories, or at least story acts. And as Egri says of scenes in the quote in the "Arcs" section in the previous chapter, they should each contain all the elements of the larger story. There is no need to demote the storytelling to a cut scene when you can play it out in the action of the game.

All quests share common elements that reveal themselves in a series of steps. In parentheses I'll tie them to Campbell's hero's journey.

- A request is made to the player that they accomplish something. (Departure: the call to adventure)

- The player decides whether they'll accept. They often *do* have a choice. They can turn down the request. (Departure: refusal of the call)

- They *may* be handed a special weapon or device or spell. In *Dark Age of Camelot*, there is a Hibernian quest called *Treasure Hunt* whose ultimate goal is a hidden gem. From components collected by the player, an enchantress fashions a Necklace of Finding that will pulse with power when the player nears the hidden gem. (Departure: supernatural aid)

- The player sets out. (Departure: crossing the first threshold)

- The player *may* experience a variety of adventures. (Departure: Belly of the Whale and most of Initiation)

- The player accomplishes their goal. (Initiation: the ultimate boon)

- The player returns to the NPC or to other aspects of the game that were put on hold. (Return: all subheadings)

Quests can be given to players in all sorts of ways: a mission assigned in a pre-level cut scene; an NPC within the game who may offer a quest when the player selects them, or they may accost the player on their own; an entry found in a journal; a looted object. There are more, but they all fall into two categories: pull and push. Pull quests are uncovered by an overt action of the player. Push quests are thrust upon the player while they are going merrily about their own business.

Push is used to solve the challenge of making sure the player is aware of content, and it does not rely on their stumbling over it or force them to go looking. The quest should not be to find the quest. At one of my tutorials, my guest Chris Klug, now an Assistant Teaching Professor with Carnegie Mellon's Entertainment Technology Center, shared a subtle push technique that I like a lot. Here are several variations on the principle.

Part of the routine in virtually every virtual world is killing mobs and looting them. Players then make use of what loot they can, give away what they can't, or sell it. They can sell it to other players in virtual worlds. Both single-player games and virtual worlds can also provide merchants. So, a game could introduce a special item or class of items not seen before. When taken to a merchant, the looted item would trigger a result beyond the usual, "I'll give you 10 silver pieces for that." Instead, the merchant can become interested in the special loot, and might relate a snippet of story; suggest someplace the player-character might look for more information; or ask the PC if they'll take on a quest to find similar items or learn more about the looted item.

This idea offers a surprising twist to the normal routine of the player. Any twists in the routine can make gameplay less repetitive. It also offers the possibility of more unique adventures to follow.

Tasks and Errands

Let's first look at the differences between these. Definitions are not standard from game to game, so I'm flying by the seat of my pants here. The simplest of quests are called tasks or errands because of the trivial nature of the work involved. Not all the above bulleted quest steps are included.

These tasks and errands are usually *FedEx quests*. FedEx quests are the most straightforward and prevalent of *all* quests in computer games.

They are divided into three similar types:

> FedEx quests: get their name because they resemble how Federal Express and other delivery services work in real life.

- **The errand is a straightforward delivery or pickup.** In one variation, the player is told by NPC1 to pick up an item from NPC2. In the second variation, the player receives an item from NPC1 and is told to deliver it to NPC2. In both variations, either or both of the NPCs may give the player a reward.

- **The second type involves combat.** NPC1 asks the player to slaughter a specific creature to receive a reward. There is no NPC2. The player proves to NPC1 that they have completed their task by looting (removing from the mob's carcass) a possession or a body part, such as a hide or tooth.

- **The third type is an "escort" quest.** Instead of an item, you are tasked with delivering an NPC, usually either someone somebody else wants to kill, or someone who must be escorted through hostile territory. Escort quests are different from the first two, because the NPC is mobile and vulnerable. If they die, the quest fails. Even trickier are NPCs with minds of their own who will attack targets far more powerful than they are, or who will heedlessly march into danger. One notorious example of an escort quest is from *World of Warcraft* where you must protect an absent-minded professor named Remtravel (sleepwalking?), who is searching for a fossil at his dig site and is oblivious to nasty creatures called troggs that try to munch on both him and you. If not balanced carefully, escort quests can be extremely irritating because players have no control over the NPC's actions. Yet, they do provide a change of pace from carting inventory items around.

The item or NPC in all three cases is called a *token* by designers.

> Token: a piece of data used to measure the player's progress in a game.

When the item—such as a letter or a box of chocolates in a delivery errand, or the looted tooth of the great white tiger in a kill task, or an important witness in need of protection—is given to the player-character, we say the token has been passed to the PC. This tells the game engine that the PC has it in inventory, or in the case of an NPC, that it is attached to the NPC in some way. When the player hands over the item or delivers the PC safely, the token is removed from the PC and a reward is given to the PC.

We can also track a player's progress by flipping *flags* rather than tracking tokens.

> Flag: a signal, symbol, character, or digit that is used as an indicator of the player's progress in the game.

Once the player arrives at a certain physical location in the game, for example, the state of the flag is changed to indicate that. This may trigger an encounter or other happening in the game world, but it may also just be filed away by the program code for later use.

The virtual world *Horizons* contained an early quest for scouts where the player-character is asked to go "scout" for enemy activity at a series of locations. The player goes to a location and a flag is flipped to let the program know that when the player returns to the quest giver, a reward is to be paid out or the player is to be given the next in the series of assignments.

Horizons also featured an interesting *suite* of *one-off* tasks under the umbrella title "Trials of the Gifted." Like the scout example listed earlier, these tasks cleverly teach various gameplay mechanics to players within the fiction of the world.

> Suite: a word taken from music to describe a group of connected puzzles or quests.

In one test, the Test of Endurance, the player-character is weighted down so they can barely move, and then asked to walk a certain distance. In a second test, the player is required to use a sprint command to speed the player-character's progress. A third test involves the use of a resurrection command. The Test of Knowledge only required that the player visit several NPCs to learn about the history of the world. The final test involved solving riddles.

Along with suites and one-offs, another approach to quests can be found in *Star Wars: The Old Republic*. These are called *chains*. They can be as simple as a second FedEx quest granted by the same NPC to secure an additional item or items the NPC needs. They can contain changes of direction and offer moral or ethical choices that can change the initial objective. In *SWTOR*, they can be entire storylines for individual characters as we'll see.

> One-off: a term borrowed from manufacturing where it means a fabrication process where only a single part is produced. I use one-off to indicate that they are meant to be played only once.

> Chain: describes a series of activities or encounters linked together like a chain.

Whether tokens or flags were used to track progress, and while they may contain FedEx elements, these are not restricted to FedEx in overall structure. They can go far beyond it. I mention that because I once had a brief online debate in an email list I belonged to with another game designer who believed there was only one type of quest because the mechanism for tracking progress by the game engine is virtually identical in every quest; and it's important to understand quests at that minute level. I remember having a similar discussion with another game designer even earlier (at a GDC party aboard the Queen Mary actually). He insisted that all puzzles were "lock-and-key."

Both observations are correct as far as they go. But they are as counter-productive to the creation of quests and puzzles as stating that there is only one plot, a variation on "Boy meets Girl. Boy gets Girl. Boy loses Girl." To me this is like saying you've detected that words are made up of letters, and that discovery of this fact will somehow make you a better writer.

As I wrote during the exchange of posts, "it leeches out all meaning and context; gets us nowhere in finding new ways of doing things; and makes it look like there are none." And "to reduce all quests to the same simple mechanism is to follow a postmodern reductionist path where there is no reward at the end but an empty canvas: not art, not life."

It is far more valuable to writers and designers to go the other direction, expanding instead of contracting, categorizing tasks and errands like these as "activities" (scouting), "trials" (endurance, speed), "knowledge" (game mechanics, history), *"mini-games"* (riddles), and so on. Finding unique qualities in various quests and giving them workable descriptions is far likelier to produce a greater variety of more interesting quests.

> Mini-games: complete little games within the world of the larger game.

In general, tasks and errands are composed of only two or three steps. Whether they're one-offs or repeatable, even in this basic form they can be used in storytelling in a variety of ways.

- **Backstory on the world of the game, its history, and its historical figures can provide a context for tasks and errands.** The *Legend of Zelda: Breath of the Wild* and (it should not be surprising!) the *Lord of the Rings Online* have many quests that refer or illuminate extensive backstories.

- **Exposition on a region and its inhabitants can be revealed.** When the player enters a new location or level, the tasks they're offered can reflect the interests of the new characters they meet, the culture of the area, primary concerns the inhabitants have, and so forth.

- **Characters can be introduced and play different roles in different quests, becoming more fleshed-out in the process.** An NPC who has an item another NPC wants the player to pick up (Task 1) might also need alligator shoes for his store (Task 2). That same NPC may be a neo-Nazi (Task 3) and a spy for alien invaders (Task 4) who is unfaithful to his wife who wants him killed (Task 5), so that she'll reveal the whereabouts of the plans for the new railgun design she stole from her lover's briefcase (Task 6). These are not quest suites but *intersecting simple tasks*. Look how much you've learned about the character of the NPC in the process of doing a few.

- **The items obtained can have more than one use and can lead to other quests or some other form of storytelling.** The Better-than-Average Grail may be used in a later task to heal a wounded soldier.

Tasks and errands are not always one-offs even in single-player games. Players can repeat simple errands for cash in order to purchase better supplies, for example.

In *The Riddle of Master Lu*, one of our mini-games required the player to hunt down curious exhibits to stock Ripley's *Odditorium* in New York, the forerunner of the *Ripley's Believe it or Not!* museums found all over the world from Orlando to Hong Kong (Figure 10.2).

FIGURE 10.2   The Odditorium was in constant need of bizarre new exhibits.

Matrix Quests

The number of quests in a video game can be astronomical, but let's look at a popular low-level mechanism for quests that can create the illusion of "many" quests with a lot less effort than one-offs.

I call these *matrix quests*, but this is another animal in games that goes by many names. Alternates include generated quests, table quests, and systemic quests. In real life Robert Ripley traveled the world to acquire bizarre objects and stories for his Odditorium. This made it a perfect location to launch matrix quests in *The Riddle of Master Lu* game.

While they are very helpful for quickly adding a lot of content, matrix quests should not be relied upon as the entire quest system. Even with random variables, they can quickly become redundant and boring, and players soon figure out what is going on. Once they do, willing suspension of disbelief and the immersion that should follow will suffer.

In structure, matrix quests are simple FedEx quests, either delivery or kill. Both types of quest are built on the same matrix. Table 10.1 is a matrix for delivery quests.

Any NPC from Column A gives a player any item from Column B to deliver to any NPC from Column C. The engine doesn't choose until the player queries it for a quest. Even a dozen NPCs or items in each column provide a reasonable number of permutations. A basic system will simply randomize the variables, but this could mean that the game engine could choose the same NPC and item many times in a row, immediately revealing the shallowness of the enterprise. Shuffling variables so that any resultant combination (NPC1/Item3/NPC6, for example), will not occur again until all other permutations have been exhausted, goes farther to preserve the illusion of there being many "new" and "different" quests.

In *Dark Age of Camelot*, they were called *tasks*. In *Star Wars Galaxies*, they were called *missions*. Similar to other science fiction MMORPGs like *Anarchy Online* and *Earth & Beyond*, the missions in *SWG* were given by mission computers as well as NPCs. Such missions also occur in *Star Wars: The Old Republic*. These should not be confused with missions in single-player action games that correspond to the more elaborate quests we'll look at shortly.

There is absolutely no reason storytelling can't occur in matrix quests. Enough permutations, artfully conceived and written, can conceal the underlying structure. A matrix quest sophisticated enough to replace one-offs hasn't appeared yet and keeping them bare bones will reveal their inherently repetitive structure.

Matrix quests can be given more variety simply by creating different matrixes, depending on the profession of the player-character or the region where the quest givers can be found. Multiple matrix quests can have crossovers to interconnect them with each other.

TABLE 10.1   Matrix for Delivery Quests

Column A	Column B	Column C
NPC1	Item1	NPC5
NPC2	Item2	NPC6
NPC3	Item3	NPC7
NPC4	Item4	NPC8

In soap operas, we have what are known as "crossover sets." These are sets of public places where our many characters, dragging their own storylines with them, can run into each other to exchange exposition or complicate each other's stories. In games, crossover locations can include NPCs in some proximity to one another who can access different menus. A single NPC can be a character in several different tasks.

The more variations we can incorporate, the better chance we have of disguising the simple structure of matrix quests, and we can still benefit from the ease with which we can increase the content of our game worlds.

QUESTS AND MISSIONS

True quests or missions are more elaborate and can be of varying lengths, number of steps, and styles. The missions of a combat game are intricate quests to secure or hold strategic objectives, rescue hostages, uncover nefarious plots, and so on. An epic quest in an RPG can be a series of tasks stretched across an entire continent or galaxy.

Quests and missions can come in all sorts of interesting shapes and forms. Here are some examples from real life: run with the bulls in Pamplona; play bingo for cash; return home from the Trojan Wars; gain the respect of a parent; help Jews escape Hitler; prove that chivalry isn't dead (*Don Quixote*'s quest); face your personal demons on a reality TV show about your love life; finish this book. Each has a reward for overcoming one or more challenges.

Knowledge can be more important than items in a quest. Story, backstory, secrets, geography, ethics, character traits, universal themes, and so forth can all be tracked the same way we track items with tokens and flags. "Secrets?! But wait, Lee! Hours after a game is released, walkthroughs are available online!" If the knowledge is untracked and can be used by anyone, you're out of luck. But obtaining the combination to a safe from a website wouldn't be enough if the combination were random. Players can't skip steps if those steps are flagged.

It's trickier in virtual worlds to protect secrets but still possible. In *The Gryphon Tapestry*, we had a system for trading game secrets. The trick was to take what was thought of as intangible—in this case, knowledge—and make it tangible. An analogy would be an attribute like strength. In real life, we can measure someone's strength by making them bench press weights, adding more until they can no longer lift them. We simplify this in games by assigned numerical values.

In real life, we gauge knowledge by testing and scoring those tests. In games, we simplify this by assigning values to discrete bits of knowledge. The *TGT* system used tokens masquerading as knowledge. First, they were attached to various skills, so not everyone could use all secrets. And there were levels of rarity. Some secrets could be shared by many people. Others, once learned, were the player's for life, and the token was no longer tradable. Still others could not be permanently learned. They required the secret (token) to be possessed by the player-character, just like the "physical" Journeyman Boots in *Everquest*, for example.

Once secrets are formalized in a single system, the rarest grow in stature and can be coveted and sought as much as uber loot drops. They can be as ordinary as magic spells or as unusual as evidence. Hearing gossip that an NPC might be a smuggler isn't proof of anything. But a piece of evidence proving it can be used—it can be held over the NPC as blackmail or delivered to the police.

Types of Quests

To populate our game world with quests or missions, we use a variety of types; otherwise, the quest system is repetitive and boring. Single-player games can offer any type of quest without fear, so the writer of single-player quests can view the following types only with an eye to increasing variety. Virtual worlds must be a bit more thoughtful about their use. The ramifications can be earthshaking. For this reason, I'll be going into more detail about virtual world applications.

Quests can be categorized in many ways:

- **Number of steps or length of the quest.**

- **Unique components, such as activities, knowledge, or mini-games.**

- **Overall complexity or difficulty.** The difficulty may be due to how hard individual puzzles are or the sheer number of them.

- **Ease of execution by the writer/designer: how fast they can be constructed.** This is obviously affected by all three of the above bullets.

- **Repeatability.** In the sense that a single player can replay the quest more than once; multiple players can do it; or both.

- **Single or multiplayer.** This is different from the previous bullet and refers to whether the quest is designed for a single-player or multiplayer game. A more special consideration is whether the quest is truly multiplayer. Just because it's in a multiplayer game doesn't make it so.

- **Usefulness in storytelling and character revelation, of primary interest to writers.**

- **Effect on the world.** An important factor that can influence all aspects of the quest design.

- **Value or effort versus reward for the writer/designer.** A group of quests that are easy to execute, but have little impact on the game, might have equal value to a single massive quest that significantly alters the game world.

Given all these possible ways to sort our quests, I'm faced with a challenge: how to create some sort of hierarchy that makes sense. I'm going to hedge my bets and stay flexible, but you'll see there is something in what follows of a hierarchy from "small" to "large." For each class of quest, I'll highlight as many of the above features that the level supports. I'm indebted to discussions I had a few years ago with Chris Foster, now Game Director at Hidden Door, where they're using machine learning to build a cooperative storytelling platform. These discussions helped me enormously to refine classes of quests.

1. **The simplest class of quests: tasks or errands.** As discussed, one-offs are simple delivery or kill tasks of only two or three steps. Example: "Take this cloth to the weaver in the next village, then return to me for your reward." They also can be infinitely re-playable and fill out the content of the game. Example: "The entire town is plagued by rats. I'll give you a copper piece for every rat you kill!" Writing each individual task is a huge waste of time. Designers often supplement these with matrix type systems. The danger is in relying on them too heavily or presenting them so obviously that their structure is revealed. In virtual worlds, the only effect on the game world is the player's acquisition of a reward. These tiny quests can deliver story, background, and character in small bites.

2. **The second class is comprised of variable quests.** They can save us some time in single-player games. Example: "Find the members of the rebel forces trying to assassinate the mayor of the village and eliminate them." Each target is a quest or level with different challenges that must be overcome in different ways, but all follow a similar structure. In virtual worlds, the scope of the quest can be expanded without changing the structure. Example: "Find the Romulans who have invaded Middle Earth disguised as elves and eliminate them!"

   These quests may be re-playable or not, but at the very least they provide enough targets and variables that they can seem to be. Also in virtual worlds, they will not affect the world if they can be repeated, except for player rewards. These can be more ambitious in character and storytelling *because* they aren't infinitely re-playable. Example: set kill limits. When the player kills ten pointy-eared invaders, more of the Romulan plans might be revealed; they might retaliate; the stakes can be escalated.

3. **The third class of quests is restricted in some way.** The skill or faction the player chose at the beginning of the game may determine which side of a battle they find themselves on. Example: *Star Wars* games differ in gameplay and story depending upon which side of the force the player chooses. There may be entirely unique quests offered. Example: If you chose to play a Ninja, you may get the quest to assassinate a warlord, but shouldn't be surprised if you're not asked to participate in palace politics. This can add to the re-playability of the game by offering unique gameplay for different initial choices. Examples: "A wily wolf is killing the local livestock. No swordsman can catch up to it. Maybe your arrows will be faster!" or "The space station is holding a baking contest, but to enter you must be able to at least bake fruit tarts" where fruit tarts require a skill level of ten in baking. These quests generally can be a step backward in complexity from the second class because they already have the unique feature that restricts participation, which lessens the impact that some resources may go unused in single-player games. In virtual worlds, they are usually variations on lower-level quests because designers may not want to limit access to major plot points or unique characters. Deliberately restricting access to story points and characters can make for some lively player discussions at the pub, so I would do it with pleasure. They may affect other players if the quest involves a competition, but need not affect the world at large.

4. **The fourth class of quests is an advance in complexity on the first three levels.** They may still be repeatable but are more commonly seen as one-offs. They offer as reward a unique item: gun, spell, whatever. Whether repeatable or not, these can delve more deeply into story and characterization than the first three levels because of their additional complexity and length.

   These quests can get very involved, if we'd like. Instead of a straightforward path for the player, there can be twists and turns. An NPC encountered later in the quest may require a subquest before they'll aid the player. Another may insist the initial quest giver lied and may try to get the player to switch allegiance. The nature of the quest object might be unknown. In the movie *Romancing the Stone*, the stone was a huge emerald. In the sequel, *Jewel of the Nile*, the jewel was a person. More sophisticated structures also exist. The quest may not be linear, but rather modular, allowing the player to experience the steps in any order. When you think of a quest with many steps, perhaps dozens, this is the level. It is the most complex of nonworld affecting quests.

5. **The fifth class of quests adds interest because it is the first to affect the world beyond the player, if only in a limited way.** Here the focus is on rewards that are not just transient items, but become temporary or permanent fixtures of the world, such as plaques commemorating player accomplishments; souvenirs players can display in their homes; articles about player achievements in in-game news reports; or town criers announcing the deeds out loud.

   While these affect the world, they do nothing to really change story or gameplay. These rewards can be attached to either one-off or repeatable quests, although to avoid clutter, the world-affecting reward should probably be limited to the first time a player completes the quest. The benefit is of high value because the quest complexity level should be higher than the preceding levels. The player achievement can be shared. Either the player can call attention to it, or even better, the *world* calls attention to it. Opportunities for ongoing storytelling are limited deliberately because the player can take the stage instead.

6. **The sixth quest class is like number five.** The world affect is somewhat larger but temporary. This could be a quest for a single player-character or a group. We call this a "flip-flop" quest because the game state is not permanently changed. One questor completes the quest, setting State A to State B. Another questor completes the quest and State B is reset to State A. For example, a player aligned with the green faction might free a green NPC from the blue jail. Celebration in Greenland, outrage in Bluesville. The quest is in context with the game world and can provide additional limited storytelling and character revelation, but won't contribute anything to an ongoing story.

7. **The seventh class of quest is the big brother to six.** Here the world effect can be much larger, but is still temporary and flip-flop. To maintain imbalance, the key to this situation, there should always be an odd number of opposing factions. A good example of this was *Dark Age of Camelot* where players were divided into three realms in

opposition: Avalon, Hibernia, and Midgard. Players of each realm periodically took over the castles of their enemies and stole artifacts to increase their powers at the expense of their foes.

This "capture the flag" gameplay can only swing back and forth with power ebbing and flowing. This swing can take months, but it will happen. No realm can ever completely conquer the other two, or both game and revenue stream would end. Unfortunately, just like its smaller sibling, this class of quest does not contribute to the ongoing story in a virtual world. It's just as well. The game structure is static. There is no ongoing story to tell.

8. **The eighth class of quest is important to us because it is created specifically to support ongoing story.** These quests may be added as part of the opening of a new playable area; in an expansion product sold separately; or as a part of monthly episodes. *Star Wars: The Old Republic* contains distinct quest chains already embedded in the game for each class of character.

   The distinction between this class and number nine is that the quest does not trigger new content. The new content is given to players as part of the episodic update, and the quests tied to it are a part of that. It is obviously a great way to contribute to the advancement of the story and character. And while you will see later I consider this type of episodic update a trap for writers and designers, it is certainly putting focus on story and character, and for that we can be grateful. The game world can be affected, but again, it isn't so much the quest or the players doing the affecting. There are some exceptions to this, but this formal presentation of new material can lessen player immersion. Far superior is our next class.

9. **The ninth quest class is the event quest, the first to allow players to affect the game world in a big way.** It is a tremendous opportunity for telling the ongoing story that lies along that large arc we drew in Chapter 9, "Bringing the Story to Life." These quests alter the world, not just for a single player or a small group, but for everyone. These quests are not re-playable unless the new state achieved can be added to. For *Disney's Virtual Kingdom* (a virtual world that was never built), I created Class 5 quests where players received a brick with their character name on it as a reward. That brick could be used to rebuild a castle or build a bridge to a new island. That new island was a new playable zone. Additional zones accessed from the first island might have required more bridges to be built.

   I first proposed this idea several years ago in an online discussion on storytelling in virtual worlds. I suggested that instead of just bringing a server down for a few hours and updating the content when it came back up there could be a new zone where none had been the day before. The world change could have been brought about by the actions of the players. We know we're going to have to add new content, so why not give the players the chance to do it? I gave as an example a huge quest that *Dark Age of Camelot* could implement, which would require players with varying skills weeks to accomplish, but at the end of it the players would have released the content, not the developers. Nothing came of that suggestion, although a couple of years later I was able as a player to see the concept in action in *Horizons*. I was part of an effort contributed to by hundreds of players that opened four new zones and freed the race of satyrs. That race became a playable race. The selling of the idea to players was problematic, and the execution of the idea was rocky, but the concept was proven with flying colors. It was the most profound sense of community I have felt in one of the massive virtual worlds. And the excitement with which players entered into the quest to free the satyrs was intense. In theory, players were moving the ongoing story of the game forward. The event need not be on that grand a stage. Any new content developers want to add to the virtual world could be done in a similar manner.

10. **The tenth and last quest class I'm going to talk about is the ultimate quest of the virtual world, and hopefully the never-ending quest.** Here the journey is more important. The Holy Grail is never found (or lost again as in the third Indiana Jones movie), but the experience is fulfilling and entertaining nonetheless. Most massively multiplayer games have never-ending quests because to complete the quest would essentially end the game. Yet games like *Asheron's Call*, because they provided ongoing story, could ride on never-ending quests the way soap operas ride on never-ending stories. In *Horizons*, players were involved in an ongoing struggle with the Withered Aegis, an undead army that threatened to overrun player-controlled lands. As mentioned earlier, *Horizons* can still be found online. I expect the Withered Aegis will never be defeated. If the quests and the stories that drive them overlap (again like soap operas), multiple huge story arcs can survive just as long. Remember some soap operas (and now virtual worlds) have been running for *decades*.

Puzzles, learning skills, quests… killing stuff, forming clans or guilds, politics, achieving wealth or fame… any of these can form the foundation that we can build story upon.

Imagine your surprise if, by clever use of puzzles and quests and other gameplay mechanisms, you can remove *all* the character development and exposition from your cut scenes and then cut the cut scenes.

REWARDS

Just a further note about rewards. They've come up more than once already. Rewards add to the "fun" factor of the experience. These rewards can be eye candy, a cool dramatic scene, or a plot or character twist that launches us into the next act. Action games are full of such rewards. They give the player the satisfaction of victory that compels them to play more. Just as we sprinkle reminders to players throughout the game about what they need to accomplish, we sprinkle rewards to pat them on their backs and to suck them back into the game with renewed energy.

Rewards can be plot devices on their own as we've seen: loot that propels us into a new story or quest; or increased faction with an NPC who will now share new revelations with the player. They are another tool that writers of games can pull out of their hats to reveal their characters and tell their stories.

THE STORY UP TILL NOW

"What did that NPC say to me back at the hamburger stand?" "How many objectives of this mission have I completed?" "What was the town the villain threatened with destruction next?"

Over the years, we've come up with several ways to remind the player what they've done. I introduced a few of these earlier: journals, diaries, a tape recorder or notebook that is often a part of the interface. I prefer to use a "game world" place to stash them. The journal might rest on my desk in my in-game home. The tape recorder is a part of my inventory. But however it is done, it is much less likely to break the fourth wall than the player-character returning to an NPC and having the NPC repeat a conversation, as if it hadn't occurred.

In one of the early games I worked on, *Once upon a Forest*, important clues were noted in a journal that one of the characters kept. In another, *Dark Side of the Moon*, this was handled by the V-Clips ((V for Video) in the VDA, the Video Digital Assistant), an extrapolation of the PDAs of the time (Figure 10.3). Remember those? We call them cell phones now.

The method used is not nearly as important as the concept of keeping it within the context of the game fiction. Anything we can do to preserve the fourth wall and aid in the player's willing suspension of disbelief, however small, is worth doing!

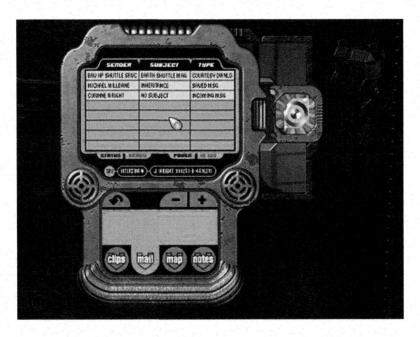

FIGURE 10.3 The Video Digital Recorder from *Dark Side of the Moon*.

CHAPTER 11

Story Anatomy

Here are three topics that didn't precisely fit in any of the chapters, but that bear thinking about as we write our games. We'll look at the other side of emotional game moments; sort through some ideas on how to share our themes with players without beating them over their heads; and look at the many and varied roles comedy can perform in games.

HEART: PLAYER EMOTION

Entertainment in games can spring both from the gameplay and the heart. Remember the example I gave in Chapter 5, "Character Traits," when I talked about the emotions our characters feel? It was the quest from *Earth & Beyond* where a Jenquai NPC you'd previously helped offered a new opportunity to intercept a Progen shipment of weapons. You went to the coordinates given, but the ship there was carrying children, not weapons. I chose not to blow the ship up and returned to the NPC, who was furious with me, calling the children of our enemies "weapons."

We discussed the NPC who gave out the quest and his revelation of character through emotion. The quest evoked emotions in me, the player, as well: surprise and sympathy upon learning what the ship's true cargo was; the consternation aroused trying to decide what to do; and my anger at the NPC's response. His remark about the children of our enemies being weapons resonates with echoes of our own planet's troubled politics: conflicts between peoples that have been going on and on and seem today farther from being resolved than ever. That sent a chill down my spine. All those emotions in a short one-off (non-repeatable) quest.

That quest in *Earth & Beyond* will stay with me as long as Floyd's death in *Planetfall*, and another moment from another Infocom text adventure game, Brian Moriarty's *Trinity*. Very early in the game an elderly woman, crippled and deformed, handed my player-character an umbrella in Hyde Park that would be of critical use later in the game. Hours later, my player-character traveled back in time to Hiroshima right before the atomic bomb was dropped. There I met a little girl, and I realized that she would become the old woman who gave me the umbrella in Hyde Park. I was shaken. Shock, pity, a feeling of helplessness over what was about to happen to her and what it would mean, sadness, all washed over me in a second or two.

DOI: 10.1201/9780429284991-15

Emotion lies at the core of all great literature, drama, films, and TV. What touches us—what illuminates a truth about the human condition—is at the heart of what entertains us. Mark Barrett remains convinced that the medium of interactive entertainment can be as expressive and emotionally affecting as literature and film, notwithstanding an abundance of evidence to the contrary. Check out his blog at Ditchwalk.com/docs/. Here he gives a succinct definition of emotional involvement:

> What is emotional involvement? It's believing in a false reality, the same way you believe in a movie when you watch it, or a novel when you read it. Books are a collection of paper pages that you hold in your hand. That's reality. *The Lord of the Rings* novels are fantastic journeys you take in your head. That's emotional involvement.

By combining freedom of movement with the capability to move quietly, then placing the player-character in a world full of shadows and heavily armed guards, the player can be induced to experience the same sense of exposure, risk, and fear that the in-game character would be experiencing in that narrative context.

A game like *The Sims* creates emotional involvement by encouraging the player to take responsibility for the welfare of on-screen characters. The player's investment of time and energy creates an emotional bond between the player and those in-game characters in the same way that caring for a child or a pet or even a plant creates a bond. Once the bond is strong enough, in-game events and threats that impact the health or welfare of the in-game characters can produce a wide range of emotional responses in the player.

Games like *ICO* (and several missions in *Splinter Cell*) give the player both an in-game character to play as well as an NPC to take care of with that player-character. Add additional narrative context or more simulated elements to the game world, and the potential for even greater emotional involvement is clearly real.

The Last of Us is a great example of using both techniques to create strong emotional involvement. *The Last of Us 2* experienced a backlash from some players because of that success in the first game. Everybody has emotions except for asocial personalities who can only mimic them. But the ability to communicate these emotions so that an audience may feel them is a talent. It's the same with story ideas. Everyone has them because everyone has an imagination to a greater or lesser degree. Story ideas are a part of children's make-believe. But bringing those ideas to life for others to enjoy is a talent.

Why is emotion in computer games so elusive? I've been told it's because gaming attracts people who aren't very much in touch with their emotions to begin with. Players and creators alike are suspicious of emotion and fearful of it. All stereotypes may start with a grain of truth, and the computer geek is no different. But it *is* a stereotype, and therefore no more valid an observation than all actors are immoral or all writers drink way too much bourbon. (I never drank bourbon. When I drank whiskey, I drank scotch.)

A more plausible answer may be that performing artists are trained to lose their inhibitions. They learn to infuse their art with their personalities, as in music, or strip away their own characters so they can inhabit the personas of others as actors. Writing, art, and programing are the main creative pillars of the games we make and are far less social

FIGURE 11.1   An orchestra's structure is evident in the arrangement of its musicians.

pursuits than performance art, but they too require a dialogue between the artist and their emotional center and game creators are rarely given any training to get in touch with their emotions.

Another possibility is that the nature of collaboration in the computer games industry is somewhat different from other collaborative mediums. There are two models in music worth looking at: the orchestra and the rock band. Both are collaborative, but they approach their collaborations very differently.

An orchestra is highly structured. There is a conductor, a strict hierarchy of musicians such as first violin, second violin, and so on. Even if the orchestra is going to perform an original work, the music is written down. The various members are allowed to interpret it for the instruments, but they are guided by the conductor who always has the last word for the sake of the overall presentation (Figure 11.1).

A rock band is a far looser collaboration (Figure 11.2).

Paul McCartney and John Lennon wrote the bulk of the Beatles' songs, but George Harrison and Ringo Starr both composed as well. The essence of collaboration in a rock band is that everybody has the chance to interject ideas. These ideas are tried, wrangled over, and ultimately accepted or discarded. The process can lead to music every bit as successful as a symphony written by a single composer on his Steinway grand. One of the hottest developers out there is called Rockstar after all. But the rock band model requires a spectacular amount of talent or talents not often found. It is also fraught with pitfalls that the tighter structure of the orchestra attempts to avoid. With talent comes ego. With great talent often comes great ego. McCartney's solid populist approach and Lennon's far more eclectic tastes finally clashed once too often, and the Beatles were no more. McCartney has revealed in a 2021 interview that one day Lennon simply announced to the others that he

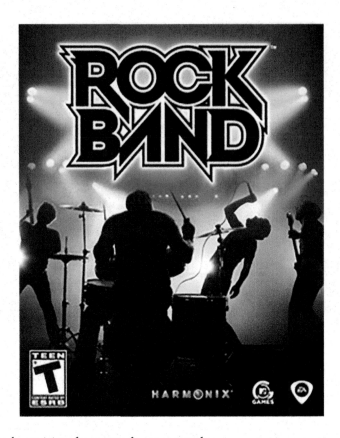

FIGURE 11.2 Rock musicians have a tendency to wander.

was leaving. Rock bands break up over differences of opinion on the type of music to play, the style of play, and so on, whether they write their own material, just perform songs written by others. It's far easier than an orchestra breaking up over creative differences.

The film and television industry is firmly orchestral in the structure of its collaborations. But the game industry is still a young industry, both in terms of the average age of its members and its relatively short time on the planet, and you'll find far more posters of BTS on the walls of cubicles worldwide than you will Jaap van Zweden, the music director of the New York Philharmonic. So, it shouldn't be any surprise that computer game collaboration is a lot more reminiscent of rock bands.

In film, every artist or technician knows their job. They each create and contribute in their own area of expertise within the structure of the production. A costume designer is usually content to design costumes. Of course, they may move on to write, produce, or direct. They earn those opportunities based on additional skills they displayed on productions apart from their regular duties. They are not rewarded for their efforts as a costume designer by being given the chance to try their hand at a job they may be interested in but for which they have no talent. Pay, benefits, and rewards are focused on advancement and recognition *as a costume designer.*

In games, everybody wants to help with the fun stuff. And developers, bless 'em, are often happy to comply. In our industry, we have the concept that everybody needs to buy into the idea before an original game can be built. This often means allowing everyone to contribute directly to the vision in all areas, not just those for which they are qualified. I remember my first job at a game studio, coming out of a meeting and being told in absolute seriousness by one of the programmers that he thought it was the duty of management to see that he had a good time making games. In movies, if you don't buy into the director's or producer's or (rarely!) writer's vision, you are gone.

I need to stress here that writers and designers shouldn't stifle input from anyone. I try to listen to every idea that comes my way while I'm designing. If the interest is there, I'll use the idea as a teaching tool to help people grow into writing or design, and mentor them in any way I can. But it is dangerous when everybody on a new production team *assumes* they will have an equal say in its development.

This rock band approach to game design can result in good games. But with all those different personalities squeezed into the conference room for hours at a time, all having a voice in what the game will be in order to commit to it, it should be obvious that a lot of emotion can emerge. Whether an idea makes it into the game, though, is another thing. And any overriding vision that we may find in creation (expressionism) or interpretation (an orchestra) will have difficulty surviving.

Whatever the explanation, while emotion that touches players is showing up more in games, it is still hard to find, and here I mean the *range* of emotions found in other media. This is a major reason games are treated by critics as well as the general public kind of like *The Beverly Hillbillies:* tolerated because they make a lot of money but laughed at or ignored by the majority.

I'm not going to try and make a list of ways to mechanically insert emotion into games. I don't work from such lists as I write. The lists are a part of me *in context*, and ready to be drawn upon, because the emotions are mine. Read the lists if you must to jumpstart your memory. Better to make up your own list. Read books, watch films and television. Watch as other human beings interact with each other, and how you interact with other humans. When you are moved in a way that is meaningful to you, a way you might like to move others, remember it.

If you aren't having any luck sharing the emotions you feel through your writing, you might do well to get some professional help. "Wait," the outraged reader will cry. "Is he saying I need therapy?" Not necessarily. Try an acting workshop at your local college instead. Most workshops will include training in improvisation, as well as exercises in funny faces and making yourself cry on cue. I've been an actor on-and-off for many years. To cry on cue, I think of the dog I grew up with, Peppy: a half-Dalmatian, half Labrador who was jet black except for a splash of white on his chest (Figure 11.3). When I use that image of Peppy (called in acting *sense memory*), I'm not pretending to cry. The emotion is absolutely real. And it is mine.

> Sense memory: recalling an object not present to create its reality for an actor.
>
> I remember how Peppy looked; how he felt when I petted him; how he smelled. Then I use a second technique called *emotional memory*.
>
> Emotional memory: recalling significant events that evoked emotions at the time to re-create those emotions in a performance.

FIGURE 11.3 Peppy at play.

I grew up in a small town called Olmsted Falls, Ohio. There were no leash laws in those days. Dogs ran free. I remember I was around ten or eleven the night Peppy didn't come home. He was gone for hours. At last, very late he finally came limping and stumbling up to the door, bloody and whimpering. He'd been hit by a car. The vet was close and even at that hour he came to help. He bandaged a broken leg and cleaned some other cuts. I sat on the floor with Peppy the rest of the night, his head in my lap. That's the night I invoke when I want to cry on cue as an actor.

Marriage and having kids can be two more great ways to get in touch with our emotions and to force us to examine them. The emotions can surprise and overwhelm us. Whether we can learn from them, and translate them into our work, is something else. If you can't find any emotional moments in other media, or life, or aren't interested enough to try looking for them, writing is probably not for you.

Once we can draw upon our own emotions and can make others feel them, we aren't tied to the themes and interests of the present day or even this planet. If we can write three-dimensional characters and interesting stories, we can take on any subject matter set in any time or in any place—real or unreal. All that's left is researching the details or imagining what it would be like.

Games are very good at capturing the mood of their intended audience, their interests, and their outlooks on life. It's a direct copying from life in the present. Little interpretation is necessary. They are fast, slick, and more often than not, relentlessly hip and cool. But individual games will last only if they hit that ever-moving target. What is hip and cool today isn't tomorrow. To pursue the present is to get lost in the past, a past only hanging on as nostalgia.

If we want our work to endure as *Hamlet* endures, it is essential that we attempt to get beyond what is hip and cool at the moment, and tackle some more lasting human values. Emotion is a good place to start.

MIND: SHARING THE THEME

Okay, we've settled on a theme we want to explore in our game. We write characters orchestrated to illuminate the theme. We allow it to drive our story. But how do we protect ourselves from turning our entertainment into pedantry?

We can't forget that our first and foremost goal is to entertain. As soon as we lose sight of that, all our good intentions mean nothing. It's also not enough to let the gameplay be the fun part while we teach. Classrooms are littered with enough educational games that try to combine uninspired gameplay with obvious teaching. I tackle that rocky marriage elsewhere in *The Multiplayer Classroom* books.

It's easy enough to say that we should support the theme with every character and story situation, but how do we put that into practice? Few TV series rely on a single storyline to carry an episode. There is always a main story, what we call the A story. Our A story may not be able to sustain itself for the entire episode, and some padding may be required. Also, there are often other characters who must be serviced, but who are not prominently featured in every story. For them, we write B stories, smaller stories that play out in only two or three scenes in an hour, or "runners," which are brief story moments that are scattered throughout the show.

Rarely do all of these relate to one another except incidentally. There are exceptions, of which the British courtroom comedy-drama *Rumple of the Bailey*, written by John Mortimer, is a textbook case in point. Mortimer wrote *all* of the episodes for the series, and every one had a central theme. Mortimer knew he had a limited time in which to expose the theme, yet he faced the same problems all series writers do in servicing all the characters every week. His solution was to ensure that every story—A, B, or simple runner—supported a single theme.

If the main criminal case Rumpole was involved in centered on infidelity as a motive for murder, Mortimer's theme might be that infidelity can be destructive to everyone involved, no matter how peripherally. You can bet that at least the temptation of an extramarital affair would be highlighted elsewhere in the same episode, perhaps involving one of Rumpole's fellow barristers in chambers. Rumpole's wife Hilda might be angry at Rumpole defending a philanderer because her best friend suspects her husband of having an affair. The barmaid at Rumpole's favorite pub might lay into her husband the barman over his flirting with a customer.

I've mentioned how *Seabiscuit* explored its theme that everyone has value in just about every scene in the film. The dozen or so stories in Richard Curtis' *Love Actually* openly revel in the fact that they are explorations of the many facets of love. It's not enough—and, in fact, way too unsubtle—to have a single character sum up a theme for the audience. It's like those awkward moments when the title of a film is disingenuously dropped into the middle of a defenseless conversation in order to explain it.

But when we have the luxury of all the characters (at least the major ones) and all of our plot points (at least the major ones) reflecting our theme, our job is done for us. We don't have to worry about the player getting it. They can't avoid it. And if it is subtle enough, they won't mind.

Let's look at *Sideshow* again. I named the player-character, David's best friend, Joel, named after my own childhood best friend, Joel, who committed suicide in his early 20s.

I felt guilt over that, as well as sorrow. My guilt was not that I could have prevented it, but that we'd allowed ourselves to grow so far apart, I didn't know why Joel took his own life. I only had stories, a few bits and pieces that seemed to explain it, but didn't really. The loss was all the greater for my inability to understand it, and therefore come to terms with it.

Even though my favorite theme memory and the past's influence on the present is in abundant display in *Sideshow*, the main theme is of guilt and what it can do to us. I made it more explicit. David feels guilt over his best friend's death when they were kids because he was present at Joel's death, and David feels that his own cowardice prevented him from saving his friend.

The very first scene (yes, a cut scene, I admit it!) shows the accident as David and Joel ride on a roller coaster. Joel's showing off causes him to lose his balance. David watches as he plummets to his death. Might he have helped? Was he a coward? The moment is ambiguous.

So, we start with the incident that inspired the guilt and then see it is a reoccurring nightmare of David's. These moments, without any dialogue referencing David's guilt, still strongly suggest a motive for his current actions. But David's is not the only guilt. It is partially guilt that has turned Dr. Adams into a bitter old man. Guilt plays a part in why another character, Kathy, has transformed herself into the stereotypical old-maid librarian. A more recent and ongoing guilt haunts the chief of police.

Sounds like we have enough guilt to satisfy any jury. But the key is not to bury the player in it. I give them enough things to do, including thwarting an attempt to take over the world. I don't dwell on the theme, but it crops up enough that an accumulation of moments is enough to get the point across. Here David is telling his old friend about his writing career.

* * *

DAVID

I do mostly local stuff for a couple of weeklies. In Boston. That's where I live now.

KATHY

Gee, I never would've thought you'd be a writer. Joel was the storyteller. You liked to take
things apart, see what made them work…

DAVID

People change.

* * *

People don't change, of course. Not that much. David had become a writer more because it was Joel's aspiration than his own. We talked about using NPCs to reveal character. As in *Sideshow*, we can simultaneously reveal the theme to both the player and the player-character through the comments and observations NPCs make. Those comments may not even refer directly to the PC, but if we've layered in enough hints, the player will take the comments to heart.

And, of course, as the plot reaches a crescendo, you know David will be faced with a similar moment to the one we saw in the opening scene and will be given the chance to redeem himself. Character is revealed through action more than words.

We don't have to be serious when we treat serious themes. Comedy is another road to the same destination.

FUNNY BONE: ROFLMAO!

Something familiar,
Something peculiar,
Something for everyone:
A comedy tonight!

Stephen Sondheim, A Funny Thing Happened on the Way to the Forum

Communication between human beings on Reddit and online games is still predominantly accomplished with text. Many ways to streamline all that keyboarding have been developed, such as acronyms like the elaborate ROFLMAO, which stands for Rolling On Floor Laughing My Ass Off. This indicates to those reading that whatever remark prompted it was even funnier than a remark that prompted only LOL (Laughing Out Loud). We love our comedy in entertainment. And games are no exception.

Comedy games are not as common as action games. Often, they are aimed at younger audiences. But we have had our share of comedy games from *Monkey Island* to *The Stanley Parable*, *Goat Simulator*, and the *SouthPark* games.

We've talked about comedy quite a bit so far here and there, but how games treat comedy deserves some closer study. Self-referential and anachronistic comedy are both popular. As we've seen, winking at the player is fashionable, regardless of context or the fourth wall. And we have lots of examples of wacky, off-the-wall comedy (Figure 11.4).

Comedy can be liberating to the writer/ designer, which explains its appeal beyond the obvious. Hal Barwood calls this the "Three Stooges take on design" because the player is invited to settle into the mindset of a game world where its internal logic is illogical. We

FIGURE 11.4 *Goat Simulator* is not all that behaviorally accurate, but still fun.

FIGURE 11.5   *Barry* is dark comedy with a sharp point.

then can get away with all sorts of situations and obstacles and puzzles that wouldn't work at all in more strait-laced games. Hal points out that "the skateboarding, plum-bouncing, chair-riding, and pirate-ship-flying sequences in *Rayman I*" are great examples of the freedom comedy can give us.

In Chapter 7, "Once Upon a Time," I discussed comedy as a counterpoint to heavier material to either give the player some relief from flying body parts or to provide a contrast that highlights the noncomedic action of the game by placing it in stark contrast to the comedy. No matter how grim a game's premise, there is usually room for the appropriate kind of comedy, one that doesn't break the fourth wall. Players will welcome it.

I mentioned in my text bite on Aristophanes that he wrote very edgy comedy, prickly social satire that makes plays like *Lysistrata* work for audiences centuries later. We have little of this in computer games. We seem to leave the edgier humor to other media. It is comedy with a sharp point. It cuts the mighty down to size; gets in the face of its audience; and enthusiastically breaks taboos. The HBOMax series *Barry* is a good example, moving from laughter to shock in a heartbeat (Figure 11.5).

Comedy doesn't get much edgier than the satiric film *Dr. Strangelove, or How I Learned to Stop Worrying and Love the Bomb*. From the Nazi scientist's arm with a will of its own, to mad General Ripper trying to start World War III because he believes commies made him impotent through fluoridation to its uncompromising finale (Figure 11.6), the film shoves the audience's face into the absurdity and horror of nuclear war. Memorable one-liner from writer Terry Southern: "Gentlemen, you can't fight in here! This is the war room!"

We rarely find the searing humor of *Dr. Strangelove* or even *Lysistrata* in games yet. Just as we avoid tragedy, we don't set our sights on comedy so intense. To do so could alienate players who might be thrown by it.

But earlier I did give a few examples of provocative humor that can be found in games. They are worth looking at more closely. In Steve Meretzky's adventure game *Space Bar*, in addition to the main player-character, players drive several different avatars in flashbacks. As Steve explains:

FIGURE 11.6 Riding an A-Bomb to glory in *Dr. Strangelove*.

> You play an incredibly *incredibly* wealthy and jaded alien businessman who is putting together a consortium to buy an entire planet. One entity is interested in minerals; one in harvesting the oceans for fish; one in lumber rights; etc. Once the deal is done, the entire population of the planet will be relocated, and the planet completely broken up for its component parts. In addition to being a really interesting puzzle (putting together the best possible consortium to make the highest possible offer), it was supposed to be an indictment of out-of-control corporate capitalism and its complete disinterest in human suffering while trying to max the bottom line.

We can see some of this same greed and exploitation at work in *Tropico*, where the player is again invited to play the role of unblushing capitalist pig.

In *Space Bar*, the main player-character is Alex Node, a human being on a planet where humans are a minority. In a reverse twist on the film *Alien Nation*, the PC is a police officer partnered with a Marmali, one of the majority race. Alex's partner is a friend and treats him with respect. But as Steve says,

> every other Marmali you meet (including your Marmali boss, the police chief) consider humans to be incapable idiots—whereas it's the Marmali who are a bit on the dim and lazy side. It's played for humor but with the hope of getting people not used to being a member of a minority group to think about what it would be like.

And there, as we'll see in the next section, is the crux of the matter. Steve hoped the player might think of more than how to solve the puzzles or to complete the game.

Another example is *Grim Fandango*, set in the Land of the Dead. Writer/Designer Tim Schafer has said it was inspired by a folklore class at Santa Cruz and film noir, such as *Double Indemnity* and *Gilda*. *Grim Fandango* isn't the only game to use film noir as its inspiration. Remember the hard-boiled detective games in Chapter 7? But the list of successful noir games remains short. Very few go beyond a superficial copy of the genre.

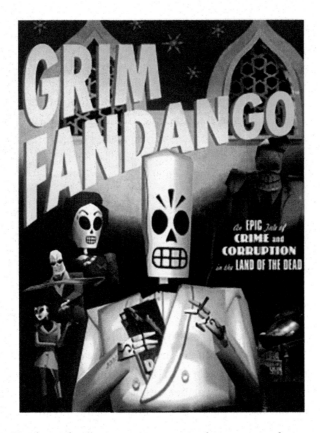

FIGURE 11.7 *Grim Fandango*: humanity can turn up in the strangest places.

Mimicry is not mastery. It looks at its subject from the outside, without respect or understanding. Even in its fantastic setting, *Grim Fandango* (Figure 11.7) succeeds where others failed because it gets at the human core—the small, mundane victories and evils that film noir loves to explore.

The *Grand Theft Auto* series from Rockstar are not comedy games, but they use some sharply observed parodies of American culture to both heighten the impact of their violent themes and to provide some relief from them.

Comedy can be used in many ways to help us in our writing and to tickle our players. Cheap laughs are easy, though. It's much more important to take the time to mold the comedy until it fits the fiction of the game world. A wacky, anachronistic game world like the one in *Katamari Damacy* can mean freedom for us and fun for the player. The wrong kind of comedy can destroy all our efforts at immersion.

We also run the risk of slipping into ruts in the types of comedy we use. Meaningful themes that make the player think about the world around them can be present in comedy as well as any other genre. We just have to decide to do it.

CHAPTER 12

Editing

I N 2008, I WROTE a pitch document for a Syfy Channel reality show pilot called *Danger Game*. The premise was simple. Remember the 1997 movie *The Game* with Michael Douglas and Sean Penn? Douglas is a rich businessman who has lost touch with his humanity. For his birthday, his ne'er-do-well brother gives him an invitation to a strange, very expensive, alternate reality game where he is humiliated, chased, battered, bewildered, and more. You are never quite sure what is "real" and what is part of the game. In the end, Michael Douglas's character learns some painful life lessons and emerges a better man.

A company from London who was beginning to set up shop in New York City was attempting this in real life. *Danger Game* would follow wealthy clients through similar thrilling adventures, but the audience would also get to see how the puppet masters behind the scenes operated and reacted when the real world intruded, and they were forced to quickly change their plans. It's important to realize that many perfectly intelligent and talented people have no clue about how to construct and sell a TV show that must play by rules often dictated by players playing in the real world in real time. Nor do the executives trying to understand what they're buying.

I wrote draft after draft of the document trying to find a comprehensive middle ground that indicated the fluid nature of the experience yet explained apparently linear story beats that led to a conclusion where the client, a real person this time, learned their own life lesson. All the rewrites weren't enough. The network just didn't understand the concept. The show was never produced.

> Alternate reality game: a game that takes place in real time in the real world.

I have covered my classes which were designed as alternate reality games in *The Multiplayer Classroom: Designing Coursework as a Game* (Second Edition, CRC Press, 2020). Details on four alternate reality games that I wrote and designed for others (*Skeleton Chase 2: The Psychic* (Physical Fitness), *The Lost Manuscript* (Chinese Language & Culture), *Secrets* (Culture and Identity on the Internet), and *The Janus* Door (Cybersecurity)) are covered at length in *The Multiplayer Classroom: Game Plans* (CRC Press, 2021). There you will find extensive details of each game, including complete game design documents.

DOI: 10.1201/9780429284991-16

Editing may never save a project when there is no common purpose or knowledge between developers and publishers. But more often than not it can bring a game to life by clarifying the original idea so all can understand it. And even more than writing a first draft, editing requires craft as much as it does talent. Writers have brushes with reality after we write our first drafts. Rewriting will be necessary for a whole host of reasons ranging from the creative to the technical. Often, a creative solution won't be possible technically, or a technical solution will require a compromise that harms the original material. Experience teaches us to keep one ear cocked at the Victrola's horn like the pooch in the old RCA ads, to hear as much reality as we write even then. (See Figure 12.1.) Later drafts require the cold harsh light of reality to illuminate our thinking.

(For the dog lovers among us: the name of the dog was Nipper, first immortalized in an oil painting in 1895 and a notable fixture on the Albany, New York skyline today. Check out his interesting history sometime and win a few bets in bars.)

We need to start with some sense of what is achievable to minimize the rewriting later. In TV we learned to write to the limitations of the show. The budget for *Charlie's Angels* allowed us, on average, a guest cast of only seven. *Edge of Night* had six standing sets circling the soundstage. Given the time the production crew had to work between the end of shooting one day and the beginning of rehearsal the next morning, I was allowed a change of only one or two sets per day.

Something similar is true in games. This is where that knowledge of programming and art comes in handy. Writing something that cannot be created with our technology, or at least can't be done in the time we have to produce the game, is a waste. We shouldn't trust other team members to do our jobs for us. We need to learn what is possible, what is probable, and what is impossible, or at least know who we should ask.

Sometimes, we get it right the first time. Sometimes, we don't. Editing a game design is no different than debugging program code. Creativity counts, but knowledge and craft come into their own. This chapter will address some of the issues that we face when we take off our creative writer hats and put on our craftsman editor hats. We'll start with collaboration. Without it, we would never be forced to edit at all.

FIGURE 12.1 The dogged writer tries to keep one ear tuned to reality.

COLLABORATION

Making games is a collaborative process. It is often a different type of collaborative process than movies or television, much more indulgent and freeform. Movie and TV production teams are orchestras. Game developers are rock bands. It's "everybody into the pool" collaboration.

At no point is this more dangerous than when the design is being written. We've had all the blue-sky meetings. We've marked up the whiteboards for weeks. Notes have been diligently typed and grudgingly agreed upon. Now it's time for all those less fun details to be hammered out.

There are two ways this can occur. One writer/designer can create a design document based on the notes, supplementing them with one-on-one discussions with the leads responsible for various parts of the design. The other is for design leads to write up their own sections and hand them off to a writer/designer to mold into a single document.

I've worked with game developers who prefer the first and game developers who prefer the second. The first is the quickest and the safest. Almost everyone wants the second. Why? Well, the writer thinks he's getting help with the writing. Everybody else thinks they are writers. It looks like a match made in heaven.

It isn't until the nonwriters face that blank screen that all those great ideas dry up and the words form themselves into sentences that don't quite mean what they meant to say. This is the point at which the writer/designer—in the worst cases, just a poor staffer who is expected to do little more than collate—is forced to go from lead to lead with either hat or whip in hand and try to get the material out of them.

In either case, as the design morphs over the months of production, the keeper of the design document will be tasked with maintaining it and distributing updates back to the rest of the team. At one developer, I introduced the system of colored pages we use in television and film so that team members could tell at a glance which updates were the most recent. All the team members had to do was insert the new pages into their copies of the design document. This created very colorful stacks of paper on desks, file cabinets, and floors.

No one wanted to take the time to insert new pages into binders. This baffled me at first until I realized that what no one really wanted to do was take the time to *read* the changes. Coming from an industry where this task was accepted as essential, I was astounded. I watched as various teams went their merry ways, creating assets that no longer matched the current design requirements, then calling acrimonious meetings to blame each other for the wasted time and effort. I spent my time answering question after question that was already answered in the design document.

I tried emailing executive summaries highlighting design changes. Nobody read them. The changes continued to be hashed out in large, time-consuming, face-to-face meetings, or by people poking their heads into my office. If they didn't come to me, I hunted them down, and checked to see if what they were working on resembled the design in any way.

In TV and film, we at least have a continuity person, a script supervisor, whose job it is to see that all work is indeed correct and recorded. I've seen a similar position at only a single developer in the past decade. She also answered phones, did copying and distribution, kept the break room stocked, and distributed T-shirts.

These days our design documents are built using a variety of tools from Microsoft Word documents to Excel to HTML to wikis to Google Docs, flowcharting programs, and more. The structure of game design documents varies wildly depending upon a host of factors, including publisher guidelines, developer preferences, style of development (agile, waterfall), type of game, and so on. We're saving a lot of pink and blue trees. Nobody else that I've seen uses colored pages. And rarely does everybody read more than bits of their pieces, no matter what form the document takes. Games get made with things in them lead designers are surprised to find. Senior creative leads face player questions with, "I'm not sure how that works. Let me ask."

What can we as writers do about it? Nothing. Trust me, I faced this situation when I entered the game industry and more times since then than I'd like to say. It has to be a top-down decision in a company that can put aside for the moment the thrill of finally getting that first lump of venture capital deposited. That there is a structure to the team and procedures that will be followed has to be communicated to each interviewee before they are hired. The interviewee must then sign in their own blood that they will respect the structure and follow the procedures and understand that failure to do so means they can summarily face a firing squad.

Otherwise, executives and publishers better just shrug and go with the flow. Stop wondering why so many deadlines are missed, games don't resemble their specs, features don't work, or are missing. It's the culture. Rock 'n roll.

In addition to collaboration between all team members, we can look at the special collaboration between writers and designers. Just as there should be a single keeper of the design document to at least attempt continuity and consistency, there needs to be a "keeper of the vision." The creative buck must stop someplace, or different opinions and disputes can cause the process to grind to a halt. When a final decision must be made, the keeper of the vision makes it.

This keeper of the vision can be a single individual, or it can be collaborators. In the fluid nature of such things, writers, producers, programmers, and artists may all be designers. The important thing is to establish a hierarchy with checks and balances built in. If your keeper of the vision owns the company, all the writers, designers, and producers in the world may not be able to provide any checks and balances unless their boss is enlightened enough to welcome them.

In recent years, Hollywood has seen collaborative teams of family members writing and directing like the Coens (*Fargo, No Country for Old Men, The Ballad of Buster Scruggs*); and the Duffer Brothers (*Stranger Things*); and creative partners like co-writers on *The Big Sick*, Emily V. Gordon and Kumail Nanjiani. Nanjiani also acted. Writing and directing teams are a much more popular collaboration today than just a few years ago. Lead actors are frequently listed as Executive Producers these days. But writers have collaborated for centuries.

Remember drug-addicted Sam Coleridge who gave us the phrase "willing suspension of disbelief?" Here's the longer passage in *Biographia Literaria* the earlier quote was taken from. It's a rather long quote. You may be tempted to hit the ESC key, but I thought it was an interesting view into collaboration between writers 200 years ago.

"During the first year that Mr. Wordsworth and I were neighbours, our conversations turned frequently on the two cardinal points of poetry, the power of exciting the sympathy of the reader by a faithful adherence to the truth of nature, and the power of giving the interest of novelty by the modifying colours of imagination. The sudden charm, which accidents of light and shade, which moon-light or sun-set diffused over a known and familiar landscape, appeared to represent the practicability of combining both. These are the poetry of nature. The thought suggested itself (to which of us I do not recollect) that a series of poems might be composed of two sorts. In the one, the incidents and agents were to be, in part at least, supernatural; and the excellence aimed at was to consist in the interesting of the affections by the dramatic truth of such emotions as would naturally accompany such situations, supposing them real. And real in this sense they have been to every human being who, from whatever source of delusion, has at any time believed himself under supernatural agency. For the second class, subjects were to be chosen from ordinary life; the characters and incidents were to be such, as will be found in every village and its vicinity, where there is a meditative and feeling mind to seek after them, or to notice them, when they present themselves.

In this idea originated the plan of the 'Lyrical Ballads'; in which it was agreed that my endeavours should be directed to persons and characters supernatural, or at least romantic, yet so as to transfer from our inward nature a human interest and a semblance of truth sufficient to procure for these shadows of imagination that willing suspension of disbelief for the moment, which constitutes poetic faith. Mr.≈Wordsworth on the other hand was to propose to himself as his object, to give the charm of novelty to things of every day, and to excite a feeling analogous to the supernatural, by awakening the mind's attention from the lethargy of custom, and directing it to the loveliness and the wonders of the world before us; an inexhaustible treasure, but for which in consequence of the film of familiarity and selfish solicitude we have eyes, yet see not, ears that hear not, and hearts that neither feel nor understand.

With this view I wrote the 'Ancient Mariner,' and was preparing among other poems, the 'Dark Ladie,' and the 'Christabel,' in which I should have more nearly realized my ideal, than I had done in my first attempt. But Mr. Wordsworth's industry had proved so much more successful, and the number of his poems so much greater, that my compositions, instead of forming a balance, appeared rather an interpolation of heterogeneous matter. Mr. Wordsworth added two or three poems written in his own character, in the impassioned, lofty, and sustained diction, which is characteristic of his genius. In this form the 'Lyrical Ballads' were published; and were presented by him as an *experiment*, whether subjects, which from their nature rejected the usual ornaments and extra-colloquial style of poems in general, might not be so managed in the language of ordinary life as to produce the pleasurable interest, which it is the peculiar business of poetry to impart."

One of the best movie directors ever was Billy Wilder (1906–2002). In 1934, Wilder came to Hollywood from Galacia, an Austro-Hungarian province now a part of Poland and western Ukraine. He arrived with little knowledge of English. Yet while neglected by film critics because of his deliberately unobtrusive directorial style, he became known for films featuring acerbic wit and riveting dialogue. It was suggested at first by those who didn't know him that since English was a second language, his collaborators provided the verbal brilliance. But Billy was a writer himself. And the wit was every bit as much his.

Billy gave us: "Let me get out of these wet clothes and into a dry martini," a line sometimes mistakenly attributed to humorist Robert Benchley. He told actor Walter Matthau after a take, "That's fine. We're on the track of something absolutely mediocre." To his fiancée: "I'd worship the ground you walked on if you lived in a better neighborhood." When producer Sam Goldwyn asked him to arbitrate (settle a dispute) on a film directed by Otto Preminger, Billy replied, "I'm sorry, Sam, but I wouldn't dare disagree with Otto. I still have relatives in Germany."

With the major exception of Raymond Chandler, Billy had great luck with his collaborators. Chandler wrote classic mystery novels like *The Big Sleep* and *Farewell, My Lovely*. He would seem to be a perfect collaborator on the now classic film, *Double Indemnity*. But Chandler annoyed Billy by trying to think up complicated camera angles instead of writing dialogue. Billy's other two major collaborations were twelve years with Leigh Brackett (*Sunset Boulevard*, *The Lost Weekend*), and twenty-five years with I.A.L. Diamond (*Some Like It Hot*, *The Apartment*, *Witness for the Prosecution*, *The Private Life of Sherlock Holmes*). In an American Film Institute interview, he and I.A.L. Diamond were asked how they collaborated. Billy said this:

> I'm already very gratified if anybody asks that question, because most people think the actors make up the words.... We meet at, say, 9:30 in the morning and open shop, like bank tellers, and we sit there in one room. We read *Hollywood Reporter* and *Variety*, exchange the trades, and then we just stare at each other. Sometimes nothing happens. Sometimes it goes on until 12:30, and then I'll ask him, "How about a drink?" And he nods, and then we have a drink and go to lunch. Or sometimes we come full of ideas. This is not the muse coming through the windows and kissing our brows. It's very hard work....

I highly recommend seeking out interviews with Billy Wilder and I.A.L. Diamond for informative and very witty looks at one of Hollywood's most famous and successful writing teams.

My primary mentors in my days as a writer in Hollywood were both writing teams. The first were Ron Austin and Jim Buchanan (*Mission Impossible*, *Harry in Your Pocket*) who were one of two production teams on the second season of *Charlie's Angels*. My second pair of mentors were Dick Levinson and Bill Link (*Columbo*, *Murder She Wrote*) who watched over me like guardian angels on *Blacke's Magic*. Dick passed away in 1987 at the young age of 52, Bill died late in 2020, not long after receiving the Mystery Writers of America's Lifetime Achievement Award.

Jim and Ron would work in different ways. Particularly in the beginning of their career, they would write together. Jim suggests this was due to "insecurity." He says, "For most the togetherness eventually drives you both bonkers." They preferred to support each other in whatever way was necessary at the time. Jim would be writing one episode while Ron directed another. They would toss around some story ideas, then one would go off and write the script, the other acting as a critic or rewrite person. On the next script, they would reverse the roles.

I also talked with Bill Link while preparing for this chapter in an earlier edition of this book. He began with a quote from Oscar Hammerstein: "Collaboration is the same as marriage only without the sex." Bill and Dick wrote together. As he put it, "Every sentence came out of the two of us. It was a ping-pong game." This was true no matter what medium they were writing in.

"Dick typed and I paced. Luckily, we were both morning people. We'd write from 10 a.m. to 1 p.m., then spend the afternoon producing. We were happy if we turned out five good pages of screenplay in a morning." If they hit a rough patch, they would go to their separate homes and sleep on it.

Great believers in the power of the unconscious mind, as I am, they knew that if the creative mind tries too hard, it gets stressed. And when you are filled with stress, there is no room for creativity. Bill said that one of his best times for solving writing problems was 3 a.m. He'd wake up with the problem on the tip of his brain, roll it around a bit, write down the solution, and go back to sleep.

Some collaborations are between very different types of writers who complement each other. For example, one may be strong on dialogue, and the other is very visual and good with action. He and Dick were different. They were like two halves of the same coin, both working on every aspect of the project with one exception. When they went into a meeting to pitch an idea, Dick would do the talking.

Bill had two other thoughts. He believed very strongly that the earlier in life two writers begin their collaboration, the stronger it will be: "We met on the first day of junior high school. We evolved as people together. We were best friends from the day we met until the day Dick died."

Bill and Dick were lucky in another regard, too. When Dick married, then later Bill, both of their wives liked the other writing partner. But it isn't always like that, Bill warns. If one partner gets married and if the single partner and the new mate don't get along, trouble can arise. He's seen it many times. The new husband or wife can become jealous of the time the collaborators spend together. They can decide that the spouse is doing all the real work for only half the money. Divorce can follow, or what's worse the breakup of the writing partnership. Or... doesn't this sound like a situation for a mystery show you might have seen?

Don't look for only one way to collaborate. There isn't one. Every team must reach its own style of collaboration, and writers who are not part of the same team from game to game must be flexible enough to adapt to one another. It helps to immediately establish ground rules. Some of these will help with full team collaboration as well.

- **If the keeper of the vision is not an individual, keep the core group as small as possible.** The more people you add with the ability to veto or filibuster, the more likely your progress will keep grinding to a halt just like politics. And your team may only have a very short time to get it right.

- **Create a hierarchy.** Everyone must understand the hierarchy and abide by it. Respect chains of command. Don't wander into a junior artist's cubicle to ask a question unless you have established with their lead that it's okay to do so. This isn't just polite; it facilitates communication and prevents nasty surprises.

- **Establish procedures.** What form will the design document take? How will revisions be tracked? How many rewrites before a draft is submitted to the rest of the team? Who gets to make the final edit? Who gets to read what? How are notes produced and shared? Strict procedures actually do not limit you. They free you. They provide security. They guarantee that the fluid creative process can continue smoothly because at the end of the day you always know what the next step is.

- **Assign roles.** Respect those roles. There will always be overlap. Roles may shift and change with time. But keep them clear. A junior programmer who's been with the team for two days needs to know their decisions are subject to review. The keeper of the vision must remember that creating the game is above all else a collaborative effort. They are not the commandant of a POW camp.

- **No matter how passionate the creative wrangling becomes, don't make it personal.** Keep it courteous. We live in an increasingly rude world. Whatever culture or environment you have been brought up in, don't carry it intact into a collaboration like Pigpen with his dust cloud. Be willing to adjust to the temper of your colleagues. It's the difference between being perceived as a professional or a candidate for day care.

- **When the keeper of the vision says it's time to move on in the discussion, everybody needs to move on.** Right then. And with no hard feelings. Leave the inevitable but nonproductive anger and frustration in the room. Take the passion with you and apply it to your work.

- **Assign a single individual or a tiny team to maintain the design document.** They will have to ride herd on all those leads who need to contribute to the document in one form or the other. Give them the authority to do so.

All, *all*, of the structure we may balk at in the beginning of pre-production will free us during the production. It's not a paradox. Everyone will know their job and what to expect. Even in rock bands, the lead guitarist would think twice about banging on the drummer's drums.

ADAPTING TO THE ENGINE YOU END UP WITH

There's a lot of enthusiasm at the beginning of a new game. If it's the first one, we know we want to be competitive, but we may not be quite sure what we're capable of. If it's yet another in a long string of hits, we know the customers will want us to top our previous efforts. In those halcyon blue-sky days, we sit around that long conference table and decide what it is we want to do, and then try to figure out if we can do it. We never get it quite right.

In our tech-driven world today video resolution gets more powerful every year and CPU speeds increase every quarter. We know we want to take advantage of those advances. Sometimes we are working from specs that have been proposed, knowing we'll have to tweak once they are finalized.

If we're designing for the next generation of an Xbox, PlayStation, or Switch the problem is the same. The time between new hardware releases in consoles has increased in the past decade. That relative stability can give us some breathing room if we're aiming at the current machines. But even then, we are constantly trying to squeeze as much out of our target platform's capabilities as we can to cope with intricate and ever-changing technology, developers enter the twilight zone of educated guesswork. It is a realm of imagination. There are signposts up ahead, but who can tell for sure where they point?

There are many potholes in the road called production. Capital dries up. Personnel changes. The bar is set too high. Promises, based on wishful thinking, are made, but are unable to be realized. In the cubicle by the window, the tech director starts to sweat.

Meanwhile, in the corner office, the lead designer is taking a break playing *Monster Hunter Rise*. The producer (who also has a nice office but is never in it) swings by to see the tech director and after a brief conversation whispered at the tops of their lungs, he heads for the lead designer's office, smile fixed firmly in place.

The writer in a cube by the restrooms is happily scanning the blue skies of the sequel. Suddenly, there's a shadow on their monitor. The writer, brain deep in alien worlds, for a moment assumes someone is just waiting for a free stall inside the restroom. They never get visitors this far into production. Then they look up. It's the producer. The producer wonders if the writer would mind joining a quick meeting in the lead designer's office. It's been a while since the writer has been in an office with windows, but finally the writer looks away from the view and focuses. The game has been designed for an engine that cannot be completed in the remaining development time. The writer is a professional who has heard this all before and never contemplates jumping out the window to see the view close up.

This type of editing is difficult because a game engine's influence is felt in every aspect of the game. The editing process is going to feel like correcting a mistake in knitting where you must pick apart rows of interlocking loops one at a time. For example, let's say you were planning on letting the player-character swallow an occasional flying pill, but now the aerodynamics are never going to happen. For every spot where flying occurred, a substitute, dialogue, and action must be rewritten for it.

It may require multiple solutions. If you already have the animation for climbing a ladder, that impassable cliff can be made climbable, maybe with the addition of special climbing shoes. Getting from the roof of a tall building to a room several floors below may now require lowering a window washer platform. Whatever alternatives you come up with, if you can keep within the spirit of the story and the character, you should be okay. Faced with a technical reversal, like a scaled-back game engine, is no time for the writer to panic. It's a time for invention, or re-invention. And it's as inevitable as breathing.

STOPPING THE BLEEDING WHEN YOU CUT LEVELS AND AREAS

Another gotcha that will getcha sooner or later is the need to cut entire blocks out of your game. While it may be an aesthetic decision only, this issue occurs more often when it becomes apparent that a key milestone will not be met. The only alternatives to such radical surgery are beyond the writer's job description: extending the deadline and adding more people. Both cost more.

Luckily, adjusting the amount of content is a challenge that television writers face daily. We've talked about how shows sometimes need to be padded. There's an infamous episode of *Moonlighting*, which was so short that actors Bruce Willis and Cybill Shepherd were filmed seated on stools talking to fill out the time at the end of the program.

More often, shows need to be cut. When I first started writing *Edge of Night*, it was necessary that I write the first two weeks of the transition between the former head writer's ongoing storylines and the beginnings of my own. Overlap, remember? There was no time to learn how daytime scripts differed from nighttime. Daytime scripts developed from live television. Nighttime scripts evolved from movies. They have very different formats. I had a few examples to work from. That was it. I wrote two weeks of scripts and shipped them off even before I moved to New York.

Something went horribly wrong. Nick Nicholson, the show's executive producer was not only talented and experienced but a very courtly gentleman. I can imagine how he truly felt when he phoned me the morning they were rehearsing the first of my shows, but what I heard was:

"How are you, Lee?"

"Great, Nick! How are you? Shooting my first script today, aren't you?"

"I'm splendid, thank you! Yes, yes. Thank you for getting the scripts to us so quickly. We're looking forward to welcoming you properly to the show next week."

"I'm looking forward to that too."

"Oh, there was one thing…. The scripts you sent us are somewhat long."

"Somewhat? What is somewhat?"

"Oh, this show we're rehearsing right now is about one-third too long…. Think you could cut it a bit before we tape this afternoon?"

One-third too long. Cut two weeks of episodes by 33%. Make sure it all still flows, characters are properly introduced, exposition is not lost, and do that all on the first show, the one all the others depend on in the next few minutes…

"Sure, Nick… Um…. May I get back to you?"

"Of course, of course. Soon as you can, my boy. I appreciate it!"

So, while Nick probably turned to the Writers Guild Directory and called the show's attorneys to see how solid my contract was, I set to work. Actually, it wasn't that hard. Here's why.

I had been a story editor and writing producer long enough to know that there's very little time in television to get sentimental about your own work. If you don't cut it, somebody else will. And writers are like auto wrecking yards. We never throw anything away.

If a good part gets lost among the stacks of rusting gas-guzzlers, it'll eventually find its way back into a working vehicle. I transfer the passion I put into the scenes to begin with into the gusto with which I slash big X's through page after page like Xorro.

Craft plays a huge part in cutting entire levels or areas or characters in a game, because if the game has been solidly constructed, every element supports and is supported by others. Pull one out and the entire structure can collapse. This is something nonwriting producers and executives have trouble understanding. All they know is it's cheaper to cut pages than any other solution to meeting milestones.

But the experienced writer knows the most important task is to determine what can be removed entirely and what should be repurposed elsewhere. Again, we must be ruthless. But we also need to not cut away too much until there are gaps in story or character development.

Let's look at a fairly simple example. We faced the challenge of losing an entire level in *Wild Wild West: The Steel Assassin* (Figure 12.2). It was an elaborate variation on PacMan where the player uncovered critical exposition by completing puzzles while avoiding guards in a warehouse full of theater and circus props and costumes. Because of the patrolling guards, puzzles could only be finished in bits and pieces. Learning the guards' routine was essential to figuring out in what sequence to do which steps. Part of the exposition uncovered led to the next major section of the game: a rundown mining town in Nevada. Figure 12.3 illustrates the place in the overall game structure of this one level.

By disassembling the level into its components, I saw that the cut was not as disastrous as people thought. None of the gameplay could be used because just transferring assets wasn't going to help our time and resource crunch. So that was filed away in my junkyard for possible use in another game. A look at the characters in the level revealed there were no major characters beyond Artemus Gordon, the player's current avatar, present and nothing critical to Artemus's character was discovered, so no character arcs were affected. I knew we couldn't cut a block of exposition and simply insert it in another level because that would only inflate the storytelling there. So, I next sifted the exposition. I identified two pieces of critical exposition and two pieces of important exposition. All else was discarded. This left me with the following:

1. Broken Hope, Nevada, the name of the town where the shipment Artemus was following was headed. (This was critical. It pointed the player to where the investigation should go next.)

2. An item (key) indicating the gang had access to Ford's Theatre where President Grant was scheduled to appear. (This was critical. This showed that the gang was much farther along in their plans than was suspected and would provide a possible way into the theater for Jim West.)

3. A note revealing that the guards knew about Artemus and had orders to kill him. (This was important because it indicated that Artemus could not con his way past the guards here. They would shoot first and ask questions later.)

4. An item (watch fob) linking the guards to the assassin of Lincoln known as "The Bull." (This was important because it meant the guards were not just a bit more zealous than normal guards but received their orders from the criminal organization.)

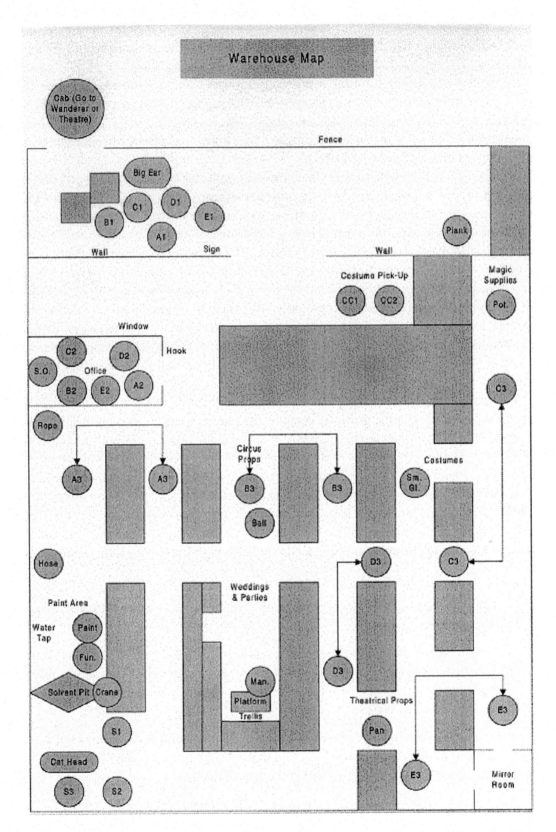

FIGURE 12.2 The level that never was in *Wild Wild West: The Steel Assassin*.

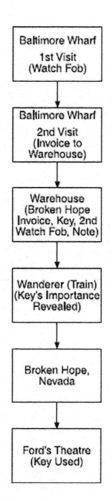

FIGURE 12.3   Game structure with warehouse level intact.

The first important item, the note, was dropped. No more level, no more reason to warn the player. The second important item was duplicated elsewhere in the game, so it could be dropped. The first critical item, an invoice with the name of the town that was the shipment's destination, was moved earlier to an office safe in the second wharf level, effectively bypassing the need for the warehouse level between that one and Nevada. The second critical item, the key, was transferred to the pocket of another bad guy earlier in the game, but *not identified* until the following location, which was aboard the Wanderer, the player-characters' train. Figure 12.4 shows the game structure after bypassing the warehouse level.

I deliberately chose an easy example here. The more a level or area of the game was connected to the others, the more work was needed to make certain it could be dropped. The more discrete the affected areas of the game were (meaning they were independent of one another), the easier they would be. We wanted both types of locations, though, and we'll explore this idea when we talk about game modules in Chapter 14, "Modular Storytelling." Whatever…the modus operandi for the editing process is exactly the same:

- **First, trim all excess fat.** We instinctively know what some of it is: a joke or character beat or subplot that stands on its own, or only reinforces other material. That goes easily.

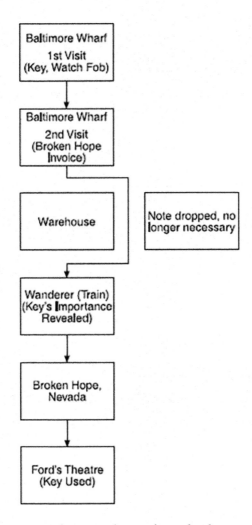

FIGURE 12.4   Game structure now bypasses the warehouse level.

- **Preserve any genuinely entertaining moments, if possible, even if they aren't entirely necessary.** Entertainment is entertainment after all. If you can't, save them in your junkyard.

- **Gameplay can sometimes be moved.** If you have a level a bit lighter than others, see if you can work it in there. No place to put it? Save it in your junkyard.

- **Identify how the level affects character arcs.** Look at the moments of character revelation with the level removed. If there is a jump in the growth or development of that character, that jump needs to be fixed either in the level before or the level after.

- **Separate out all the specific points of exposition.** Determine which are critical and which are expendable.

- **Don't treat the exposition as a single block that must be shoved into another level, doubling that new level's expository load.** The prisoners of war in *The Great Escape* mixed the darker tunnel soil into their gardens so it wouldn't be noticed. Do the same thing. Spread the exposition out over several levels. Even if there are two or three points tied to a specific moment or object, break them down. Don't assume they all must be moved as a group. It is much less disruptive on other levels to spread them out.

Happily, not all editing is the result of calamity or outside pressure. There is actual rewriting and editing we could and should do on our own.

POLISHING DIALOGUE

> The search for the *mot juste* is not a pedantic fad but a vital necessity. Words are our precision tools. Imprecision engenders ambiguity and hours are wasted in removing verbal misunderstandings before the argument of substance can begin.
>
> *Anonymous Civil Servant*

As is often the case with these things, *le mot juste* is not the entire term. It drops an important word. The complete phrase is *le seul mot juste*. And that gives us its true definition.

> Le seul mot juste: describes the one correct word to express meaning or to prompt the desired reaction.

If a description of action or a line of dialogue is not clear to the reader or audience, or does not affect them as it was intended, it usually means the writer has failed to find *le seul mot juste*. An amateur writer may not notice that what is in their brain failed to make it to the page. They think they've expressed themselves fine and can become defensive when someone questions them as to their intent.

A professional should know, even if no one has given them a note, when a word or phrase is not exactly right. When writing dialogue, we will recognize that a joke can be funnier; an argument more intense; an expression of love more passionate; a putdown more savage; an apology more heartfelt. That's when we rewrite, or to use a kinder, gentler word, we *polish*. All writers polish. It can happen at three different moments while writing: instantaneously, immediately, and revisitation.

I expect that because I have written for most of my career to extremely tight deadlines, the moment I begin transferring thought to page I'm already polishing it. It's instantaneous. When I try to picture what I do, I think of computer programs that crack passwords and how they're portrayed in movies. Sometimes recognizable words or at other times random characters are displayed on a computer screen, then replaced at a dizzying speed to suggest it is only a matter of time before the program comes up with the correct password. Of course, as speedy as this is, our brains work far faster. I'll start to type the word, stop, delete it halfway through, and then type its replacement, barely aware of the steps my brain took me through to prompt the substitution.

Once I manage to get the line of dialogue or a sentence in this book on the screen in front of me, I'm already re-reading it, even as I begin to construct the next line in my mind. This parallel processing means that I can be writing something new at the same time I'm polishing both instantaneously and immediately. If I see a better choice, I make the change, then start writing the next sentence.

If I sense a change is needed, but *le seul mot juste* still eludes me, I may leave the word out or throw in an approximation, write for a while, and then return to it. Revisiting can occur when I know a polish is needed, or not. In the latter case, it is a part of the natural process of re-reading an entire scene or chapter to make sure I'm saying what I want to say. This revisitation can occur moments, minutes, hours, days, weeks, months, or even years later, if I've put the entire project aside. Remember the piece of dialogue between Dr. Adams and his daughter from *Sideshow*? Here's how it *really* went in the original:

* * *

NANCY

Dad, you love this town, and you know it.

ADAMS

That's right, my dear. I love watching all the children I brought into this world smoking or drinking or cholesterolling themselves into early graves.

NANCY

(to David)

This is an ongoing debate…

ADAMS

Or piling into trees at 90 miles an hour. Or ingesting chemicals that turn their brains to jelly. Fascinating profession: medicine.

NANCY

We save lives.

ADAMS

And we learn far too much! And the thing we learn that cuts the deepest is that we'll never know enough to stop them. Or ourselves. We're all on the same ride… to oblivion… and we're all determined to make that ride as short as possible!

* * *

I count at least five edits: three conjunctions dropped to increase the intensity; a punctuation mark changed to indicate more emotion; and an extra space deleted as a copy edit. There are also two spaces after periods instead of just one, a holdover from my typewriter days. If you don't know what a typewriter was, you'll have to look up that definition on your own.

One trick to help you recognize that *le seul mot juste* has not been found is to watch out for *tombstoning* when you're polishing.

> Tombstoning: refers to the over-repetition of individual words or phrases in a sentence or paragraph.

The word was originally a printer term referring to a mistake in laying out a page. If all the stories and illustrations are laid out in identical columns one next to the other, the repetition makes the layout boring. Don't confuse tombstoning with deliberate repetition to drive home a point. In the next paragraph, tombstoned phrases are in italics:

Parents asked if there were mosquitos at the lake. *Camp counselors told parents* there were no mosquitos at the lake. *Parents asked if* their children would learn to fish. *Camp counselors told parents* their children would learn to fish. *Parents asked if* there were any serial killers hiding at the camp. *Camp counselors told parents* the only serial killer at the camp disappeared many years ago.

This is repetition for effect (again follow the italics):

One camp counselor promised the kids badges if they swam to the raft. *There were none.* He promised them hotdogs for dinner. *There were none.* He promised he would show them a scary movie before lights out. *He didn't.*

Here the repeated phrase is deliberately used like a hammer. Even when the words change in the last sentence, the rhythm of the hammer is well established.

Don't get hung up on correct English in dialogue. You may have noticed how little discussion of "correct English" there is in this book. The *seul mot juste* has nothing to do with it. In the opening voice-over to the various *Star Trek* series, "to boldly go" is a split infinitive, but it *sounds* stronger than "to go boldly." Complete sentences can slow pace to a crawl. Find the point of attack the same way you would in a scene. Cut away the connective tissue as I did the conjunctions in Dr. Adams's dialogue.

The search for *le seul mot juste* is as critical to writing as the search for the North Pole was to scientists. But unlike scientific exploration, the search can be rewarding even if we never make it. Just making the attempt, digging out the dictionary or thesaurus if we have to, can be worthwhile. Even if we fail to find the *best* word, we may find a *better* word. And every time we do that, we're one step closer to clarity and emotional impact. We just need to know when to stop searching.

No discussion of *le seul mot juste* would be complete without mention of Gustave Flaubert (1821–1880), its most famous stalker (see Figure 12.5). Flaubert would spend days searching for a single word. *Madame Bovary,* his best-known work (and a very readable

FIGURE 12.5 If Flaubert had tried to paint a self-portrait, we might never have known what he looked like.

novel), took five years to write. Part of learning to be a writer is learning when to stop searching and move on. Maybe the reason Flaubert suffered from nervous ailments, drank heavily, and frequented prostitutes was that he realized his search was endless.

Once upon a time in my former life, I found myself at a party in the Malibu Beach Colony. I was searching for a glass of drinkable chardonnay when I fell into conversation with a blow-dried, deeply tanned man in his 30s who introduced himself as a fellow screenwriter. This is the moment during most Hollywood parties where strangers begin the profoundly religious Credit Ritual Dance. "I'm writing/directing/acting in that new buddy cop flick over at Warner's. What have you written/directed/appeared in lately?" He told me he had been working on his first screenplay for the past three years. That was the extent of his writing career. I realized then I was either talking to somebody with a trust fund or one of the waiters. I wanted to shake him, but instead I smiled politely and nodded my head a lot as he detailed the adventures in writing he was experiencing week in and week out. I did ask one question, "When will you know it's done?" "Oh!" he assured me, "I'll know!"

Maybe it's the relentless search for *le seul balance juste* when game developers say they'll "release it when it's done." Instead of the implied perfectionism, it feels more like a self-indulgent excuse for missing milestones. It certainly is no more a guarantee of quality than a product that actually ships on schedule.

I don't think I've ever had that much freedom, so maybe that's why I'm not more tolerant of it. From the mini-plays I used to write at Boston University for my fellow actors to perform and my fellow directors to direct in our classes to the tight and unrelenting deadlines in television, I've always known that there comes a time to stick a fork in it and give thanks you have something to eat.

As you polish your dialogue, imagine David Mamet sitting on the pallid bust of Pallus by your chamber door. This is your last chance to take it beyond the colloquial to something that rivets the attention. Write words that pierce the brain, not those that go in one ear and out the other.

Less is more. In this day and age, unless a character is written to be wordy, keep the dialogue lean. Then when you want a character to burst forth into an impassioned speech, it is all the more compelling because of the contrast.

Actor John Crispin Blake in my play *The Man Who Came to Murder* is entirely too fond of hearing himself talk:

* * *

BLAKE

Language is so much a part of my life I must try to remember that to most mortals speaking is merely a hurdle in the race to make one's needs public, whereas to me a single word is a banquet in and of itself.

MILLIGAN

I get it. The word's your oyster.

* * *

His male nurse, Milligan, jumps his small expressive hurdle and is content.

Even if dialogue seems in character, mix up the length of the individual lines. In a long speech, or only three or four lines, if each sentence is close in length to the others, it creates a monotonous rhythm. If you missed it in the polish, a good voice actor will instinctively try to break it up for you. Let them.

Remember not to allow your characters to be too self-aware or to explain themselves in too much detail. Show them in action. If a character's dialogue is reminiscent of a patient on a psychiatrist's couch, you're in trouble, that earlier scene I shared from *The Lion's Song* notwithstanding.

COPY EDITING

The dialogue itself is better than in most adventures, although it reads as if it was translated from another language by a non-native English speaker. Also (a pet peeve of mine) it's poorly proofread; when a game company spends presumably hundreds of thousands of dollars developing a title, why can't they pay a professional sub-editor a few bucks to look over the text?

PC Gameworld review of Post Mortem (2003)

Language evolves. Words become extinct or their meanings change. At any given point in time, however, there are distinct rules for language usage. To ignore them is to surrender in the battle for communication without firing a shot.

> Copy editing: proofreading the review of style, spelling, grammar, and punctuation in a written document.

Copy editing is obviously important in a book. But there is a feeling in the games industry that it's not important. There appear to be several reasons for this.

- **People think computer spelling and grammar checkers catch everything.** They don't. They're particularly bad at sensing context. My apologies to Microsoft and Apple, but they miss tons of errors. Style sheets are just as dangerous. Human beings have built-in computers that do a far more reliable job.

- **Many of our documents are seen only internally, so why bother with the time or expense?**

- **Just as everybody thinks they can write; they seem to feel the same thing about grammar and punctuation.** They don't notice how sloppy some of the documents they produce really are.

- **Instant messaging apps like Twitter, Tumblr, Facebook Messenger, WhatsApp, and yes, PvP games have increased both the volume of communications we must process, and the speed required for input.** Spelling and grammar suffer accordingly. Kids are being raised by the Internet just as generations ago they were raised by television. Their opinion is that they're correct when they think there is only one way to spell "there."

There are three reasons that copy editing should be a routine step in the production of our documents, even if they are only online dialogue scripts, design, and technical documents.

CATS : ALL YOUR BASE ARE BELONG TO US.

FIGURE 12.6 *ZeroWing*, a game that cries out for a translator.

The first is clarity. The farther our words stray from their true meanings, the greater the obscurity of our pronouns; the longer our run-on sentences, the more likely it is that readers will misinterpret our meaning. R.D. Laing already told us how difficult it is to communicate. Why make it worse?

The second motivation for copy editing our documents is impression. There are few stronger signals we send to those around us than our use of language, either written or spoken. Whether we like it or not, we are judged by phrases like "He don't know nothing." and "Me and her went to the store." And the same holds true for all those double negatives and misspellings in our business documents. Let's give ourselves the benefit of the doubt: most are simple typos. If we had more time to check our writing, we would clean it up. But we don't, and nobody considers how busy your schedule was if your writing is full of errors.

The third is force of habit. Let's say you still think impression isn't that important in internal documents but do think it's vital in communications outside the company. If the bulk of your writing is only design-related, and you don't bother to copy edit and one day you're given the assignment of writing an external proposal, those same errors you unconsciously slide past in one may come back to haunt you in the other.

"All your base are belong to us" was part of a new English language introduction written for a port of the Japanese game *Zero Wing* on the Sega Mega Drive (Figure 12.6). It's become a classic of bad translation. But there are examples in many games, including those developed in English-speaking countries, of text that cries out for copy editing.

If the job is left to some poor programmer trying to insert 200 text files into a level at 3 a.m., expect mistakes. Have someone re-read the text in the game. And what happens if that design document you wrote is suddenly requested by a potential investor?

Few game developers can afford copy editors any more than they can afford a continuity person. But please when you hire someone for a position, check their written communication skills. *Read something they've written.* Having a few people who can spell or understand grammar will pay off in the long run. Not taking the time to copy edit can backfire in more than industry hilarity at your expense. It could cost you a contract with a publisher or a line of credit you need to finish the game.

The Roots of a New Storytelling

T HE FIRST EDITION OF this book was published almost two decades ago. Which should explain why some examples of games, movies, TV shows, etc. are unfamiliar to the current reader. I still include older examples because they are good, hopefully clear, examples and worth knowing. Which brings me to the title of this chapter. Despite its (or my) antiquity, new ways of storytelling, often but not always, peculiar to video game writing, are still not entirely understood. And while we do see writers of video games exploring some of the same ideas in more recent games, many don't realize they are reinventing the wheel. Knowing where ideas begin and how we can use them is an important part of being a writer. And no, I do not mean the ideas in what follows began with me. Some began centuries ago, as you will see.

C++ and Java are both computer languages that support *object-oriented programming*, a type of modular programming with more formalized rules. It may seem like a strange way to introduce a discussion of a new type of storytelling, but the paradigm is remarkably similar. In OOP, data structures become objects that include both data and functions. Functions are parts of a program that perform specific tasks.

> Object-oriented programming (OOP): a programming paradigm in which independent modules of code are built to interact with each other.

In modular storytelling, the modules are objects that include both data (story) and functions or tasks performed on the story, like the passing of tokens, setting of flags, and tracking of player actions. The idea is to bring the telling of story in games into line with how gameplay is constructed. Both can be programmed as modules. Story can be written as modules.

Modular storytelling has its roots in the distant past, as we're about to see and, at its simplest, combines two key concepts: episodic storytelling and nonlinear storytelling. In a way, it is a wedding of the two fields I know best: video games and television. It gives us a

DOI: 10.1201/9780429284991-17

basis for creating games where story and gameplay are never at odds with one another but complement one another. Let's take a look at the roots of modular storytelling.

THE ODYSSEY

Homer's *The Odyssey* is three stories in one: Odysseus, King of Ithaca, and his 20-year journey home from the Trojan wars; his ever patient and faithful wife Penelope fending off suitors for her hand; and Odysseus's son Telemachus's growth from boy to man. To keep things simple, we'll focus only on the events that make up the main story that gives the epic poem its name.

- After leaving Troy, Odysseus's ships are caught in a storm and land on the island of the Lotus-Eaters where many get high by munching on the plant, and decide to just hang, rather than continuing the journey. Odysseus manages to get enough of them straight to set sail again.

- The ships stop at the land of the Cyclops, one-eyed giants. After one of the Cyclops, Polyphemus, traps them in his cave and dines on a few of the crew, Odysseus and the surviving crewmen blind him with a large stick, and escape by hanging on to sheep let out to graze. Unfortunately for Odysseus, Polyphemus is the son of Poseidon, God of the Sea.

- At the island of Aeolus, King of the Winds, Odysseus is given a bag of all the bad winds that would hamper his progress. But within sight of home, some of his crewmen (thinking the bag is filled with treasure) open the bag, blowing the ships far off course.

- The goddess Circe on the island of Aeaea turns a number of Odysseus's crewmen into pigs and falls in love with Odysseus. Odysseus, after spending only a year with her, learns from Hermes how to undo the spell, and the ships set sail again.

- Odysseus journeys to Hades to seek counsel from the prophet Tiresias, who tells him he will never reach home unless he earns Poseidon's forgiveness.

- Odysseus fills the ears of his crew with wax, so they won't be seduced by the Sirens' song. He wants to hear it, so they tie him to the mast of his ship.

- Two hazards confront Odysseus simultaneously: Scylla, a six-headed monster, and Charybdis, a ship-devouring whirlpool. Six crewmen are sacrificed to Scylla to bypass Charybdis.

- On the island of Helios, God of the Sun, crewmen give into temptation and eat some sacred cattle. A thunderbolt from Zeus kills the crew and destroys Odysseus's last ship.

- Odysseus is rescued by the sea nymph, Calypso, who wants to be his bride. With the help of Athena and Hermes, Calypso is persuaded to release Odysseus and give him a small boat.

- Poseidon unleashes a storm that demolishes Odysseus's boat. With the help of Athena, Odysseus reaches the island of the Phaeacians. They transport him in one of their ships home to Ithaca where a few more adventures await.

Even though this appears to be pretty straightforward storytelling, it's easy to see how we might classify each of the separate events as a module, connected to the others and complete in itself. This is important because I have a confession to make. This isn't the way Homer told his story at all. The point of attack is far later in the story. The correct order of events goes like this:

- Odysseus is held prisoner by the sea nymph, Calypso, who wants to be his bride. With the help of Athena, Calypso is persuaded to release Odysseus and give him a small boat.

- Poseidon unleashes a storm that demolishes Odysseus's boat. With the help of Athena, he reaches the island of the Phaeacians. There he reveals his identity and shares his previous adventures in *flashbacks* as follows:

- After leaving Troy, Odysseus's ships are caught in a storm and land on the island of the Lotus-Eaters where many get high by munching on the plant, and decide to just hang, rather than continuing the journey. Odysseus manages to get enough of them set straight to set sail again.

- The ships stop at the land of the Cyclops, one-eyed giants. After one of the Cyclops, Polyphemus, traps them in his cave and dines on a few of the crew, Odysseus and the surviving crewmen blind him with a large stick, and escape by hanging on to sheep let out to graze. Unfortunately for Odysseus, Polyphemus is the son of Poseidon, God of the Sea.

- At the island of Aeolus, King of the Winds, Odysseus is given a bag of all the bad winds that would hamper his progress. But within sight of home, some of his crewmen (thinking the bag is filled with treasure) open the bag, blowing the ships far off course.

- The goddess Circe on the island of Aeaea turns a number of Odysseus's crewmen into pigs and falls in love with Odysseus. Odysseus, after spending only a year with her, learns from Hermes how to undo the spell, and the ships set sail again.

- Odysseus journeys to Hades to seek counsel from the prophet Tiresias, who tells him he will never reach home unless he earns Poseidon's forgiveness.

- Odysseus fills the ears of his crew with wax, so they won't be seduced by the Sirens' song. He wants to hear it, so they tie him to the mast of his ship.

- Two hazards confront Odysseus simultaneously: Scylla, a six-headed monster, and Charybdis, a ship-devouring whirlpool. Six crewmen are sacrificed to Scylla to bypass Charybdis.

- On the island of Helios, God of the Sun, crewmen give into temptation and eat some sacred cattle. A thunderbolt from Zeus kills the crew and destroys Odysseus's last ship.

- Odysseus is rescued by Calypso.

- After he tells his tale to the sympathetic Phaeacians, the flashbacks end and they transport Odysseus in one of their ships home to Ithaca where a few more adventures await.

Remember Homer did not make up *The Odyssey*. Nor did his surviving version necessarily follow earlier variations. This was the order he chose when his version of the story was written down for the first time. Novelists often use a similar flashback structure to that used in Homer's version. Instead of straightforwardly tracking the story from one incident to the next, we leap ahead in time, and then describe the intervening events.

Here is the end of Chapter 16 from my mystery novel *Impossible Bliss:*

> Inside, a dark shape huddled over the bookcase next to Wagner's desk. Shepard felt for a light switch, found it, and flipped it up.

The action in Chapter 17 continues without missing a beat:

> Light flooded the living room. The figure whirled. Bruce Wagner glared at him; a small sheaf of papers clutched in his hand.

Chapter 13 in the book starts after a time lapse:

> Wednesday morning the Carmel Valley hills were blue and green, already heated by an advancing sun. Shepard tried to concentrate on the phantom melody that refused to become a song while he drove out the valley road toward the Carmel Rancho Racquet Club.

In the third paragraph, I begin to fill in any important events with a flashback:

> Before he headed out to the tennis club, Shepard had tracked down Charlie Revere in the tiny lounge at the back of the station. Crammed with vending machines, a couple Formica-topped tables, and a clump of molded plastic chairs, the lounge also served as ready room and general gathering place for on-duty officers.
>
> 'Any luck with the Sea Orchard Fish Company?' he asked the young, red-headed man.

This low-level nonlinearity is just a different method of beginning the chapter to interject some variety into the structure and rhythm of the storytelling. The choice of the point of attack is critical. Choose the right spot, and the audience still experiences the story in a natural flow. Choose the wrong point of attack, and the flashback will seem gimmicky and artificial.

One other feature of the epic poem deserves mention: this is the reappearance of characters first encountered early in the story. Poseidon sets his traps for Odysseus after learning what Odysseus did to his son, Polyphemus, and then wanders offstage for much of the voyage, only to return, and unleash his direct fury when he sees Odysseus still afloat. Athena and Hermes show up on more than one occasion to help Odysseus out of a tight jam. If *The Odyssey* were a computer program instead of an epic poem Poseidon, Athena, and Hermes would be functions, not gods.

Janet Murray in her interesting book, *Hamlet on the Holodeck*, goes into some detail on the bardic tradition supporting *The Odyssey* and *The Iliad* that I brought up in Chapter 2, "The Story Remains the Same." Here she describes Alfred Lord's analysis in *The Singer of Tales*, concluding:

[The bards'] success in combining the satisfactions of a coherent plot with the pleasures of endless variation is therefore a provocative model of what we might hope to achieve in cyberspace. To do so we must reconceptualize authorship, in the same way Lord did, and think of it not as the inscribing of affixed written text but as the invention and arrangement of the expressive patterns that constitute a multiform story.

So, we can bid bon voyage to Odysseus, keeping in mind our first roots of a new storytelling:

- Stories in other media are not always linear.

- *The Odyssey's* story is episodic and therefore easily modular.

- The way reoccurring characters function in the epic poem structure facilitates modular storytelling.

- The bardic tradition allows for improvisation on the strict patterns and themes of its storytelling.

THE CANTERBURY TALES

Fast-forward almost twenty centuries to the Father of English Literature. Geoffrey Chaucer's *The Canterbury Tales* are separate stories within a connective framework: a pilgrimage (Figure 13.1). Each narrative is intended to be equivalent in length and stature. There is no attempt to raise the stakes in the stories from "The Knight's Tale" through the odd last tale "The Parson's Prologue" and "Chaucer's Retraction" where the author apologizes for writing of such mundane matters. The tales were unfinished remember. Chaucer intended to write a hundred more, and there is much evidence to suggest that even the "completed" tales were in various stages of editing. They are divided into ten sections, or fragments. The most well known of these, "The Wife of Bath's Prologue and Tale," appears in the third fragment.

Because the stories are separate entities framed by the journey of the pilgrims, as opposed to the fairly linear narrative (even though much is told in flashback) of *The Odyssey*, Chaucer had much more latitude in the order which they were presented. Of more interest in our own historical pilgrimage then is the nature of the connective tissue.

Medieval scholar G.C. Coulton wrote in 1908:

Even more delightful than any of the tales told by Chaucer's pilgrims is the tale which he tells us about them all: the story of their journey to Canterbury. Nowhere within so brief a compass can we realize either the life of the fourteenth century on one hand, or on the other the dramatic power in which Chaucer stands second only to Shakespeare among English poets. Forget for a while the separate tales of the pilgrims—many of which were patched up by fits and starts during such broken leisure as this man of the world could afford for indulging his poetical fancies;

FIGURE 13.1 *The Canterbury Tales.*

while many others (like the Monk's and the Parson's) are tedious to modern readers in strict proportion to their dramatic propriety at the moment—forget for once all but the Prologue and the end-links, and read these through at one sitting, from the first stirrup-cup at Southwark Tabard to that final crest of Harbledown where the weary look down at last upon the sacred city of their pilgrimage. There is no such story as this in all medieval literature; no such gallery of finished portraits, nor any drama so true both to life and to perfect art. The dramatis personae of the Decameron are mere puppets in comparison; their occasional talk seems to us insipid to the last degree of old-world fashion.

—G.G. Coulton, Chaucer and his England

The frame for the stories, a common structure, as we saw in Chapter 7, "Once Upon a Time," is a looser example of an over-arching story than the more complete narrative structure of *The Odyssey's* three storylines. Yet this fragile connective tissue feels familiar to our contemporary eyes. It is identical to the separate stories or episodes we see in television framed by an over-arching story.

It is also very similar to the over-arching stories we write for our games. What are the individual quests if not separate stories linked thematically to the overall story in an RPG?

The briefings and other story beats between levels and missions in our action games, however elaborately they are produced, are just as insubstantial. They are made more so by their disconnection from the gameplay. It is, in fact, how this connective tissue is viewed by game writers that often *forces* the game stories to be linear, not the stories forcing the gameplay to be linear.

It should be obvious that if *The Canterbury Tales* were a game, and the stories levels, only the barest of changes in the framework that collects them would be needed no matter what order we chose for them to be played. It seems, though, that what we gain in flexibility of storytelling is balanced by a loss of depth in the over-arching narrative. Let's take that concern to the next stop on our pilgrimage.

DON QUIXOTE DE LA MANCHA

A much smaller jump in time, a little over two centuries, brings us to what we learned in school is the first true novel in western culture. During a discussion in an Internet newsgroup a couple of years ago, somebody said that a free-form, modular approach to storytelling *might* generate coherent story, but asked how it could ever approach great art or literature? I might have used *The Odyssey* as an example or *The Canterbury Tales*. But in answer I chose *Don Quixote de la Mancha* by Miguel de Cervantes Saavedra (Figure 13.2). Written in 1605, it is rightly considered a work of immense literary and artistic achievement.

My first introduction to *a picaresque novel* was *Gil Blas* by Alain-Rene Lesage. Set in Spain, but originally written in French at the beginning of the 18th century, the novel was a major hit, translated into many languages, including Spanish, which explains why it was force fed to me in my fifth-grade Spanish class.

The episodic nature of picaresque novels makes them unusually well suited to the study of storytelling in games, as well as to the more particular form called *modular storytelling*. Let's take a deeper look at *Don Quixote de la Mancha*.

Picaresque novels: originated in 16th-century Spain and are composed of a loosely constructed series of episodes connected by a central character. Examples also include *Tom Jones* by Henry Fielding and *Moll Flanders* by Daniel Defoe.

In the book, a somewhat befuddled Don Quixote imagines himself a heroic knight, and sets off to prove that chivalry is not dead. He experiences several adventures in his quest, the first alone before he meets up with a servant/sidekick, Sancho Panza. Together, they meet Dulcinea, a serving girl Don Quixote mistakenly believes to be a highborn lady. The three set off together.

Up until this point in the story, the episodes follow a predictable linear path as the Don announces his intent and collects his compatriots. Compare this experience with the early stages of the hero's journey of Joseph Campbell or a player-character collecting party members in a single-player RPG. But now the episodes take on a new quality. Each is fairly equal in terms of emotional intensity, and each can be considered as a module as well as an episode. No tricks like I played with *The Odyssey* this time. Here the modules are in the order presented in the novel.

FIGURE 13.2 Picasso's Don Quixote. Compare this to his paintings in Chapter 2!

- Don Quixote tilts at (attacks) windmills, mistaking them for giants.

- Don Quixote rescues a "princess" from her two captors (actually friars).

- Don Quixote becomes involved in a tryst between a servant girl and her lover.

- Don Quixote scatters a flock of sheep, thinking they are two opposing armies.

- Don Quixote disrupts a funeral procession, imagining it to be a parade of monsters.

- Don Quixote is prevented by Sancho from fighting a monster he hears in the night (it's only the roaring of a windmill).

- Don Quixote seizes a barber's bowl, thinking it to be a famous golden helmet.

- Don Quixote encounters a chain gang on their way to the galleys.

- Don Quixote fights for Dulcinea's honor.

What follows is a series of several scenes that again work best in linear order, leading to yet another series of modules. (The book was written in two parts with ten years separating their publication.) Finally, in true epic style, a character from an earlier module returns.

On his deathbed, Don Quixote comes to his senses, bemoans his foolishness, and renounces chivalry. The irony and moral of the story is that his noble-hearted nature, however misdirected, *was* the true essence of a chivalric knight. He dies without learning the truth.

What is the best remembered moment of the novel? Tilting at windmills. The phrase (along with the word *quixotic*) entered our language and has remained for four centuries. *When* does this episode occur in the novel? It is the *first* module in the story. And what is the implication to us? The novel would have reached the same emotionally satisfying conclusion no matter what order the modules were in. The picaresque novel can be thought of as modular storytelling, with only one path mapped through the modules. There is no need for a golden path for the story to be enjoyed to its fullest.

If Don Quixote were a game, the modules I listed previously could be played in *any* order with the tracking of variables to make sure that the dynamic world would always make sense to the player. In Figure 13.3, I've deliberately mixed up the incidents. The sequence is irrelevant.

Here we have an over-arching story that is far more substantial than *The Canterbury Tales*. The meaningful narrative, complete with compelling theme, moving climax, and ironic conclusion, is there before us. Each episode in Don Quixote's quest supports that over-arching story. The *order* of the modules is unimportant.

FIGURE 13.3 *Don Quixote* structured as modules.

MOZART, GAME DESIGNER

Yes, *that* Mozart. We're pausing for a musical interlude. In 1787, Wolfgang Amadeus Mozart designed *Musikalisches Würfelspiel* (Musical Dice Game). It consisted of 176 minuet measures and 76 trio measures. The order in which they are to be played is determined by dice rolls. The random numbers generated are then played based on a chart (Figure 13.4). If you

WOLFGANG AMADEUS MOZART

Musikalisches Würfelspiel

Table of Measure Numbers

	Part One									Part Two							
	I	II	III	IV	V	VI	VII	VIII		I	II	III	IV	V	VI	VII	VIII
2	96	22	141	41	105	122	11	30	2	70	121	26	9	112	49	109	14
3	32	6	128	63	146	46	134	81	3	117	39	126	56	174	18	116	83
4	69	95	158	13	153	55	110	24	4	66	139	15	132	73	58	145	79
5	40	17	113	85	161	2	159	100	5	90	176	7	34	67	160	52	170
6	148	74	163	45	80	97	36	107	6	25	143	64	125	76	136	1	93
7	104	157	27	167	154	68	118	91	7	138	71	150	29	101	162	23	151
8	152	60	171	53	99	133	21	127	8	16	155	57	175	43	168	89	172
9	119	84	114	50	140	86	169	94	9	120	88	48	166	51	115	72	111
10	98	142	42	156	75	129	62	123	10	65	77	19	82	137	38	149	8
11	3	87	165	61	135	47	147	33	11	102	4	31	164	144	59	173	78
12	54	130	10	103	28	37	106	5	12	35	20	108	92	12	124	44	131

Table of Measures

FIGURE 13.4 Mozart's musical dice game.

download a recorded version of *Musikalisches Würfelspiel*, you will only be hearing one variation out of thousands.

Okay, the attribution of this game to Mozart has been called into question. But I'm going with it. It totally fits my picture of him. And the game itself is real. And modular.

While we're on the subject of music, two colleagues of mine at Rensselaer Polytechnic Institute, composer Michael Century and artist Shawn Lawson, created an iPad game that used the iPad's built-in accelerometer to create some Goldberg Variations Bach never thought of. We'll have another musical interlude in the next chapter.

CHARLES DICKENS AND PUBLISHING IN PARTS

A little over two and a half centuries later, our quest takes us to Victorian London where Charles Dickens polished episodic structure to gleaming art. His long novels, written as serials, have a much more defined linear structure, yet there are modules in any of them that could be experienced in different order. The Victorian novel is a far more sophisticated form than the picaresque. Its structure may not appear at first glance to suit our purposes as well as *Don Quixote*. But remember that Cervantes was there at the birth of the novel. Is it any wonder that his structure speaks most easily to us here at the birth of interactive storytelling?

Let's consider Dickens for a moment. Of immediate interest is the fact that he wrote his books in biweekly or monthly installments called *parts*. Dickens wrote episodically a long time before TV.

> Parts: the first issue of many Victorian novels. They consisted of a few chapters bound in paper. *The Mystery of Edwin Drood* had seen the publication of six parts composed of twenty-three chapters at the time of Dickens' death.

Take Scrooge's ghostly visitors in *A Christmas Carol*, published in 1843. After we get past Marley's introductory spirit, each episode is a distinct module; each is a complete story with its own conclusion and moral; and each supports the main over-arching story and the theme "greed is bad." With a bit of shifting around, couldn't those visitations transport us to the same satisfying conclusion in another order? Or as a game in *any* order? Scrooge could very well have been visited first by the Ghost of Christmas Present, seeing the dinner party given by his nephew, and hearing what his contemporaries really thought of him; then terrified by his grim future; and finally taken back to the moment when he made a decision that started him on his pursuit of wealth above all else.

The movie *Betrayal*, written by Harold Pinter, begins with the breakup of a relationship, and then takes us backward to the moment the characters met. Their meeting is warm and witty and full of promise, but we know where the relationship is heading; and that knowledge infuses every moment with the melancholy of lost love.

A Christmas Carol, because of its structure built around the three visitations is an easy example. Let's take a more complex Dickens novel, my favorite actually: *Bleak House*. Dickens' intent was the unmasking and ridiculing of a venerable institution of English property law called the Chancery Court, responsible for all matters pertaining to inheritance and property.

Bleak House, published in 1852, was loosely based on a case in Chancery Court involving the estate of a man who died intestate in 1798. The case was not settled during Dickens' lifetime. In fact it was still not resolved in 1915 and had by then cost over £250,000. The Chancery Court's reputation was so bad there was even a boxing hold called "Getting in Chancery," which involved your opponent locking your head under one arm and pounding it repeatedly with their other fist. In the famous children's rhyme used by Agatha Christie in *And Then There Were None*, we find:

> Five little Indian boys going in for law;
> One got in Chancery and then there were four.

To illustrate the dreadfulness of Chancery, Dickens introduces us to a bucket-full of characters, all affected by its insane intricacies. Each story is carefully threaded through the novel. It would appear impossible on the face of it to start rearranging things. But this novel too was written as a serial. And Dickens did not have every twist and turn plotted in advance. How he wrote is almost identical to how daytime serials are written today, as we'll see shortly.

In *Bleak House*, it is possible to pluck an entire thread from one place in the book and plop it down whole in another. Here the story *threads* are the modules. They consist of multiple A stories, B stories, and runners populated by sharply drawn characters (Figure 13.5).

- Esther Summerstone, narrator of much of the book, carries the over-arching story that ties together the others.

- Richard Carstone and Ada Clare are wards of the court, their love tested by the ongoing intricacies of the Chancery case.

- Sir Leicester Dedlock and his wife, and her search for her lost illegitimate child.

- Inspector Bucket's investigation of the mysterious death of lawyer Tulkinghorn.

- The love triangle of Esther and John Jarndyce and Doctor Woodcock.

- Selfish Harold Skimpole's luxuriating in the generosity of others.

- Mrs. Jellby's philanthropic concern for the rest of the world at the expense of her family.

- And many more.

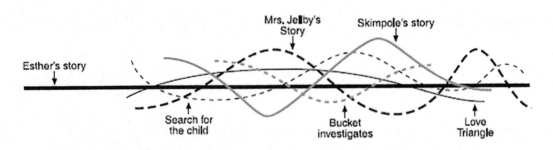

FIGURE 13.5 The modules of Bleak House are threads.

All in some manner support the horrors of the Chancery theme. But instead of existing as discrete chunks, they are woven through the entire structure precisely the way they're woven in episodic television. We have our tokens and our flags ready in games to help us mark players' progress. With the tracking of remarkably few variables, our own story threads can be juggled in just the same way.

What is necessary is the mindset to be able to see the steps in each thread as separate from steps in the other threads. Dickens demonstrates in book after book that he was able to see his complex stories as individual strands making up the whole. It's a skill anyone writing daytime serials today must also possess. In fact, it's precisely the skill needed in editing when we must cut a level or zone, but don't want to create a jump or discontinuity in the narrative.

Often in this book, modules will be depicted as separate boxes of story for the sake of clarity, but we mustn't forget that this is only the simplest form they can take. Threads are another. It's time now for us to continue our journey forward in time some fifty years, but to take a step backward in terms of the sophistication of modular storytelling.

SATURDAY MORNING AT THE MOVIES (MOVIE SERIALS)

In 1909, only thirty-nine years after Dickens' death, the Clarendon Company of Great Britain produced what is believed to be the first movie serial, a series of one-reel episodes featuring Lieutenant Rose, RN. Four years later in 1913, an American company, Selig, released *The Adventures of Kathlyn*, the serial that established the formula that was to last for decades in movies, radio, and television. *The Adventures of Kathlyn* introduced the ending we call the *cliffhanger*.

Cliffhanger: an exciting end to a chapter or episode that derives further suspense from leaving the audience uncertain of its outcome.

Characters were often literally left hanging from cliffs at the conclusion of the weekly chapter of a movie serial. The audience had to dangle for seven days before finding out their fate. Less than a year later, one of the most famous serials of all time, *The Perils of Pauline* starring Pearl White, was released.

The serial or "chapter play" became a staple of Saturday mornings, playing before the regular matinee feature and for a reduced price. As befits a young audience out for thrills, the stories were unsophisticated and repetitious. Stretched out over twelve to fifteen weekly chapters, each peppered with car chases and more hand-to-hand combat than a hockey game, the 20-minute episodes always ended with a cliffhanger. The basic premise of the story was set up in Episode One and remained unresolved until the final wrap-up. In between the structure of the episodes was identical. The villain would attempt a dastardly deed, and the hero would heroically counter it; or the hero would close in on the villain, only to have the villain slip through his fingers at the last second.

In a twelve-episode serial, only two episodes, the first and the last, needed to be shown in that order. Writers would often come up with cliffhangers before any other material for an episode. They would make lists of possible cliffhangers, even borrowing stunt footage from other serials or regular movies and tacking it on to new episodes. The cliffhangers and their resolutions were the connective tissue. If we retain the concept of their flexibility, ready to be dropped into any episode, the ten intervening episodes could be shown in any order. Even given the linear nature of the medium, we shouldn't be surprised to hear that projectionists occasionally got the reels of film mixed up, and audiences often never noticed.

What made these episodes *feel* modular even if they weren't? Several things:

- **The repetitive action.** Watch a few serials, particularly those from Republic Studios in the 1940s. Many are now available streaming or on DVD. Even though they may differ in locations, the fistfights are virtually interchangeable, the climaxes impossible to tell apart.

- **The blandness of the characters.** None stand out enough in the audience's mind to overshadow any others.

- **The static relationships.** The banter between hero and heroine was established in the first episode and remained the same until at last they're permitted one token clench before the final fadeout.

- **The infinitely spawning bad guys.** Villains seemed to have an inexhaustible supply of unquestioningly loyal minions at their disposal. And just like the mobs in our games, they often looked alike. This is because the same actors played multiple parts. A clean-shaven thug killed in Episode Three would often show up again in Episode Six sporting an unconvincing mustache. And most of the action heroes were doubled by the same incredible stuntmen like David Sharpe. Shot with the camera pulled back to blur their features, the combatants looked like the same people from fight to fight in serial after serial because they *were* the same.

- **The pendulum story moves.** Neither hero nor villain ever gains an insurmountable upper hand until the finale. The balance of power simply swings back and forth like clockwork.

Yet the audience *was* entertained. And as the serial plot meandered its way toward the denouement ticket sales swelled. Something very interesting was occurring: a synergy we'll talk more of in Chapter 14, "Modular Storytelling."

The Saturday morning serials fit the modular storytelling mold as well as anything we've looked at so far. We can thrill to Captain Marvel fighting the re-spawning forces of evil in repetitive modular episodes that, except for the first and last, really can play in just about any order (Figure 13.6). Pass a few tokens, wave a few flags and Shazam!

DENNIS WHEATLEY'S CRIME DOSSIERS

During the 1930s, as movie serials were beginning to reach their peak of popularity, a significant experiment in storytelling took place. For many years, epistolary novels had been popular.

Bram Stoker's *Dracula* was structured as a series of journal and diary entries. Agatha Christie's

Epistolary novel: a novel composed of reproduced letters or other documents supposedly written by one or more characters.

FIGURE 13.6 Captain Marvel in thrilling black and white! (Republic).

The Murder of Roger Ackroyd is told in the form of a journal penned by one of the main characters, a sort of Watson to the detective, Hercule Poirot. In 1930, Dorothy Sayers, one of the best of the Golden Age of Mystery writers, published *The Documents in the Case*, a mystery told entirely through various interview transcripts, letters, and police reports.

In 1936, prolific mystery and fantasy writer Dennis Wheatley collaborated with J.G. Links to produce four unique books: murder mysteries consisting of loosely bound documents and physical clues such as torn photographs (one was *very* racy), telegrams, locks of hair (reportedly contributed by nuns!), real matches, and even bloodstains. The solutions were sealed at the back of the book. The precise nature of the collaboration would seem to have been Wheatley plotting the mystery stories and Links fabricating the various documents and procuring clues. He must have known a lot of nuns.

The first of these, *Murder Off Miami*, barely managed to be published. The original publisher Hutchinson's had little faith in the idea. Booksellers thought it too much of a novelty to sell. Wheatley personally hawked the book to bookstore owners throughout London. Once it reached the public, the book was an immediate success, spawned three sequels, and several imitators (Figure 13.7).

In 1983, a gimmicky mystery novel *Who Killed the Robbins Family?*, edited by Bill Adler and written by Thomas Chastain, left off the last chapter and offered a $10,000 cash prize to

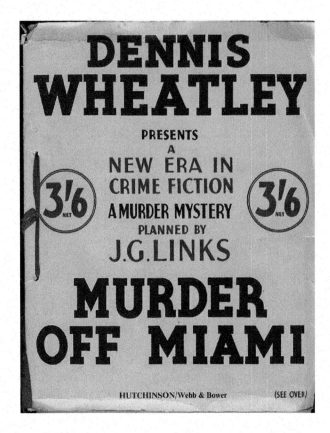

FIGURE 13.7 *Murder Off Miami*, interactive storytelling circa 1936 (Hutchinson).

the first reader to solve the mystery. Later that same year, I was approached by my friend, Otto Penzler, editor, publisher, and book dealer, to write two books in the same vein for Warner Books but patterned after the Dennis Wheatley Crime Dossiers. It would have been prohibitively expensive to produce books with actual clues, so Otto's plan was to include reproductions of documents and photographs of clues and suspects.

At the time, I was head writer of *Edge of Night*. I used my knowledge of soap opera production (yes, my scripts were shorter by that time!) for the first book, entitled *Death in Broad Daylight*. Unfortunately, our fortunes were tied to the success of two books in an earlier series that more directly imitated *Who Killed the Robbins Family?* Their sales were disappointing, and our series was never published.

I bought back the rights to the two stories I'd written, and *Death in Broad Daylight* eventually did see the light of day as an Internet mystery, an early alternate reality game in 1996. The game offered a $5,000 prize for the correct solution. Players were able to access several websites, such as a fan site for a fictional soap opera, a police department website, and a library. More mysteries were planned, framed by the search for missing photographer and amateur detective Joshua Light, whose files provided the stories. That's the author of this book as the absent Mr. Light hiding behind the camera in Figure 13.8.

The *Crime Dossiers* by Wheatley and Links remain for me the first attempt of what we call today interactive storytelling. They presented the evidence of the case and invited

FIGURE 13.8 *The Light Files: Murder Off Miami* in the Internet age.

readers to construct the story in their minds. The game of solving the crime was every bit as important as the story. Even though the copies of the books were all bound identically with the pages and clues in the same order, readers flipped back and forth through the pages, rechecking alibis and studying clues.

This format translated beautifully to the Internet where aspiring detectives could follow dozens of links between documents and photographs. Not only was the structure not linear, but the course of the story was entirely determined by the choices of the reader/player deciding where to go next. The home page of the mystery, now called *The Light Files*, deliberately gave no clue which links were considered by us to be important. Because of the unique nature of our medium, we can create three-dimensional story structures just as we do three-dimensional characters. Each fictional website was a module, and each document or map or photograph on it were modules *nested* inside it.

Take another look at Figure 13.3. That is a two-dimensional structure. Now imagine drilling down inside each one of those boxes to find the modules that form them, and inside those modules still others just like the human body is made up of cells that are made up of molecules that are made up of atoms that are made up of subatomic particles... modular anatomy. In the next chapter, we'll take these two-dimensional roots from other media and watch them blossom into something rich and strange.

DAYTIME SOAP OPERAS

The thriller wasn't the only genre of serials, or chapter plays, that evolved. Radio introduced listeners to soap operas that dared to turn Republic serial climaxes into climaxes of a very different sort.

First appearing in the 1920s, radio serials blossomed in the 1930s and made a successful transition to the 1940s, thanks in large part to a former schoolteacher named Irma Phillips. Her first soap, *Painted Dreams*, was on radio. It ran for thirteen years but is pretty much unknown today. Not so another of her soaps. *The Guiding Light* is the only American soap to make the transition from radio to television. It premiered in June of 1952 and ran until September 2009 almost sixty years later. It's in second place as the longest running soap on TV in the Guinness Book of World Records. First place goes to *Coronation Street*, a British soap, and as of this writing, still going strong. I wonder if any of our virtual worlds will top that record.

> Soap operas: daytime serials that replaced the frantic action of movie serials with frantic domestic issues and were often sponsored by soap manufacturers.

Today very few daytime soap operas remain. They air every weekday, day in and day out, fifty-two weeks a year. They mark a major step in my development as a writer. *Edge of Night*, debuted in 1956, was the soap known as much for its murders as its love triangles. I was head writer for its last two years: 1983 and 1984. I came to *Edge* from primetime (nighttime) television where my specialty was mystery writing. I thought I was used to deadlines. Primetime television schedules were harried enough, but we at least only had to do one show a week, and every year we went on a weeks-long hiatus between the last episode of one season and the beginning of preproduction for the next season. Seasons, thanks to Netflix, Amazon Prime, and other streaming services, are an endangered species. Series are scattered throughout the year to meet the constant demand for new product. The hiatus can occur at any time of year and is usually much longer.

The episodes my staff and I wrote one week were shot the following week and broadcast the week after that. There was no time to be sick. If I wanted a vacation, I wrote faster, getting at least an additional week ahead. I averaged 500 pages of writing every month. That included long-term story arcs, weekly breakdowns (story outlines of episodes), and two to three scripts per week.

Our characters in primetime episodic television remained for decades relatively static from episode to episode. They might face many different crises each week, but their roles in the show rarely changed unless there was a contract dispute. Today continuing stories are a staple of many TV shows. Characters in soap operas, thanks to the challenge of producing five episodes a week grow, develop and change over time. One character might be a "bad girl" for years on a soap only to evolve into a loving wife and mother. Good guys could suddenly turn rotten. Child actors grew up. Romantic leads grew old. All of this demands a significant concentration on character.

Even with all those pages of writing, every single scene cannot move the story forward. The average viewer sees only two to three episodes every week. We needed crossover sets and coffee-table scenes ("More coffee, Madge?" "Thank you, Betty. Did you hear what happened between Jared and Kate last night?") to keep the audience up to date. Beyond that, the sheer amount of new content necessary is enough to send you screaming away in a straitjacket. (Sound familiar, massively multiplayer world writers?) So, there are far more A stories, B stories, and runners. Any given character might be integrally or peripherally involved in four or five stories at once.

The other major mistake I made in my first few weeks on *Edge* (in addition to the long scripts) was the speed with which I told the stories. I'd been hired to bring a swifter, night-time pace to the show. Unfortunately, I left the audience blinking in the dust. So many major incidents happened in so short a time, the producers had to force me to apply the brakes. My scenes were much shorter than what they were used to. There was much more intercutting. Easy enough to write. But it meant the crew was racing across the soundstage trundling those huge video cameras and trying to do it silently while another scene was in progress. It took us about six weeks to settle into a pace that both the audience and the crew could survive.

Daytime TV couldn't rely on matching the production values of big budget television shows, let alone movies. We might occasionally head off on location, but those times were few and far between. You know what shooting on location was called? A remote. We set one scene on the roof of a fictional TV station. We shot it on the roof of our own studio. It was 50 feet away. It was still a remote. In soaps, the story and the characters must carry the interest of the audience. There is little else. That was what I loved and feared the most.

I loved it because on *Edge of Night* I was able to take a relationship from the moment two people met through to their wedding night eighteen months later. I could weave a score of stories together, bouncing characters off one another in unexpectedly dramatic and ironic ways. I learned that when you have that many stories running simultaneously, the best stories were the simplest. Their construction would add all the complexity I needed.

I feared it because the deadlines were daily, and the need for content was relentless. The weight was all on me and my small staff of two or three co-writers. Yes, it could be frightening, but it was also the most exhilarating writing experience of my life. One of the reasons I'm attracted to massively multiplayer games is the similarities between them and soaps. Yet nothing has come close to challenging me the way soap operas did.

I'll be returning to soap operas when we get to Chapter 17, "Storytelling in Virtual Worlds." In the meantime, here are some more roots for the new storytelling in general.

Soap operas are the most advanced example of individual modules connected by story since Charles Dickens. Unlike Dickens, we not only have story threads as modules tied to an over-arching story, but we also have multiple threads tied to multiple stories; and we have the simpler episodic structure of Chaucer and Cervantes and movie serials as well. Variety is not only the spice of life; it is one of our most valuable tools. Anything we can do to hide the underlying repetitiveness of our gameplay is good.

Soap stories can last for months, just like our games. Also, one of the points of taking the steps of a story and making them interchangeable modules is to give the player freedom of choice and movement, yet still guarantee them that the story will not only make sense but remain compelling. Soaps give us models like coffee-table scenes, crossover sets, and simple stories woven together to make them seem more complex, yet at the same time comprehensible.

EPISODIC TELEVISION

By way of introduction, I should point out that designers have been playing with the concept of episodic games for a few years now. The thinking seems to settle on three ideas.

The first is a suggestion to release single-player games in smaller increments, or episodes, to provide an ongoing experience to the player. The benefits would be lower production costs and hopefully equivalent price points; the ability to reuse assets and engines without the radical overhaul the demand for next-generation graphics requires; and to enable the developer to produce more product in a shorter period of time.

Television producers often make pilots that become the opening episode of a TV series. More money is lavished on these than a typical episode to make them look as good as they can, much like an original game followed by occasional releases of new content. Since we already have periodic releases, all this episodic model seems to give us is a cheaper original game. Even with all the talk promoting this idea, I haven't seen notable successes created like this. I provide it here for completeness.

Next, we have the episodic release of content in virtual worlds. We first began to see this in monthly updates for MMOs like *Asheron's Call*, *Earth & Beyond*, and *Star Wars Galaxies*. This wholesale adoption of the episodic model of television seems so logical on the surface, but is such a big trap, I devote an entire section of Chapter 17 to it.

The third idea is of most obvious use in our discussion on the roots of a new storytelling, and I've already alluded to it: modules=episodes. Today much of fictional storytelling on TV contains elements of the serial, but is serialized to lesser or greater degrees, giving us the whole range of examples of modular storytelling we've been discussing:

- The individual stories loosely attached to a framing story in *The Canterbury Tales* is the model for television series that use only a premise and arena to frame weekly episodes. Many situation comedies (sitcoms), as well as dramas and especially detective shows with a different crime every week. There are continuing relationships, but if there is an over-arching story, it's kept more or less in the background. In *The Mandalorian*, the stories of individual episodes take prominence, but all illuminate the ongoing mythology of the series and the *Star Trek* universe.

- The more ambitious story that arcs over Don Quixote's adventures can be seen in series like *Nancy Drew* and *Bosc*. Here, the individual episodes are still the focus, a sort of scary monster of the week but each season has a clearly over-arching story that connects the episodes.

- The intricately woven story threads of Dickens are found in dramatic series and comedies that—no matter what their genre—emulate the structure of daytime soaps. In *Locke & Key*, the over-arching story takes prominence, and individual episodes are often simply steps along its course.

All these types of episodic structures can be found in our games. The first two are mostly the province of single-player games. The planned structure for *The Light Files* Internet mysteries with one over-arching mystery framing the individual episodes.

There is the over-arching story to which levels or missions are attached. The strength of the connective tissue varies. The complexity of the third example might overwhelm the gameplay of many single-player games. Less is more. Simpler is better. We can make the stories seem complex, while keeping them simple. Despite its seeming complexities *The Legend of Zelda: Breath of the Wild* story and ultimate player goals can easily be explained.

There can also be a continuing story that bonds a series of games such as another RPG, *Baldur's Gate*. The player's search for identity and the results of that search carry through the entire series. That seems to continue in *Baldur's Gate 3*. Hopefully, someday we can play the full game and judge for ourselves. Many series seem to start from scratch each episode with only characters and relationships intact much like the TV series *Castle*.

The third example comes into its own in massively multiplayer virtual world story structures as intricate as any daytime soap. The trick is, of course, to keep them modular enough that linearity doesn't overwhelm the nonlinear world of the game. Again, we'll look at virtual worlds in Chapter 17. Now it's time to take these roots of a new storytelling and grow something.

CHAPTER 14

Modular Storytelling

Indeed, naturally I think that a film should have a beginning, middle, and an end—but not necessarily in that order.

Jean Luc Goddard (French New Wave filmmaker)

The roots of modular storytelling are deep and long. Even in linear media, there are different story structures than the ones we trot out time and time again.

In Geoff Ryman's novel *253*, based on his 1996 website, we are given brief character sketches of the riders in one train traveling between stations in the London tube. On the website 253 sketches of riders are hyperlinked, meant to be read in any order. Even the print version is supposed to be read in any order, just as the documents in *The Light Files*. The writing isn't strong enough, and Ryman squeezes his narrative into a linear event near the "end," but up until then it is an interesting experiment.

Akira Kurosawa, one of the world's greatest directors, made a film in 1950 called *Rashômon*, with several of the roots we've been discussing embedded in it. I highly recommend viewing it. (Avoid the wild west remake released in 1966 with Paul Newman and Claire Bloom.)

In Kurosawa's film several people seek cover from a rainstorm at the Rashômon Gate near Kyoto. To pass the time, they discuss a shocking crime that has occurred nearby. A woman allegedly has been raped. Her husband has been killed. This story frames flashbacks told from the points of view of the three participants: the woman, a bandit, and yes, even the dead husband speaks through a medium!

The bandit claims he didn't rape the woman; it was consensual sex. He does admit killing the husband. The woman claims she was raped by the bandit, but her version suggests she may have killed her husband. The husband's spirit supports her claim of rape, but says he committed suicide. All these stories have the ring of truth about them. And there's a fourth version. One of those gathered at the gate, a woodcutter, says he witnessed the crime. Yet his account seems to draw on parts of each version, and his version is the most suspect of all. Did he really see anything?

DOI: 10.1201/9780429284991-18

Rashômon isn't a mystery story. Sherlock Holmes doesn't step out of the rain and clear the matter up. Instead, it is a meditation on the nature of truth and perception. No matter how much we may think we know the truth, in the end, we can never be sure. Look at what this single film gives us:

- A framing story right out of Chaucer.

- Flashbacks that relate different versions of a single incident.

- A narrative that does not move from A to B to C but converges on a single point on the horizon. Yet no matter how fast we run toward it, it stays distant and undefined.

- Characters revealed not by self-awareness, but by the descriptions of others.

- R.D. Laing's theories of perception in action.

Quentin Tarantino's *Pulp Fiction* and the *Kill Bill* duo are examples of films where the order of the story has been rearranged to foreshadow, provide ironic juxtapositions, and keep the level of the action rising. In *Kill Bill Vol. 1*, we know early on that The Bride (Uma Thurman) will kill O-Ren Ishii (Lucy Liu). But the sequences leading to that confrontation play out on a broader canvas than her first mano a mano fight with Vernita Green (Vivica A. Fox). By mixing up the linear sequence of events, Tarantino builds to that final series of spectacular battles in traditional style, even while his story bounces giddily back and forth in time.

If we decide that all linear media story structures are the same just because pages follow each other in the same order in a book, or movie action is nothing more than light shown through a succession of frames all in the same order each time, we are narrowing our focus far too much—just as if we say all puzzles are lock-and-key or all quests are FedEx.

I'm going to propose another analogy. Imagine a set of 26 children's blocks, each with a different letter of the alphabet on it. If the child stacks the blocks in order from A to Z, we have a linear progression of the alphabet. If we allow the child to stack the blocks in any order the child wishes, the presentation of the alphabet is no longer linear. Yet the stack is the same height, and all the letters of the alphabet are still there. If the steps in a story progress from A to B to C and so on, it is the picture most people have when they think of a linear story. If it doesn't matter what order they are presented in, the story is nonlinear.

Some people don't even recognize modular story structure as story structure at all. Like film direction that concentrates on what is in front of the camera (Billy Wilder), rather than the camera itself (Brian De Palma), modular storytelling is transparent and should go unnoticed by the player. We'll set our stage for modular storytelling by looking at the common forms that narrative takes in games.

THE YOKE OF NARRATIVE

In Chapter 7, "Once Upon a Time," we talked about the golden path, the concept of an optimum path through a video game. The golden path will only seem a viable or inevitable part of a game design if it is tied to a limited definition of linear storytelling. If books, plays, and movies can break the bonds of linear storytelling, why shouldn't the most nonlinear medium of them all?

This blind adherence to tradition is a result of incomplete knowledge on the part of some of the first practitioners of storytelling in games. Then those that followed them simply copied the ideas. As Richard A. Bartle says in his book *Designing Virtual Worlds*, "Too much virtual world design is derivative. Designers take one or more existing systems as foundations on which to build, sparing little thought as to why these earlier worlds were constructed the way they were."

This is not just true of virtual worlds, but of game design in general. You may hear an echo of my comparison of Picasso's mother and daughter from Chapter 2, as Richard goes on to say, "Question the paradigms, avoid stagnation. You have to understand a system before you can challenge it, but that doesn't mean you have to accept it."

There are two traps in game design here: parroting an idea without knowing why and discarding an idea without bothering to learn it. The first trap is, as Richard states it, pretty clear. It's like aspirant clockmakers who notice that a clock ticks and chimes, a pendulum swings, and hands move; and then try to copy it without bothering to study the gears that make it all work. The second rises from a combination of ignorance and arrogance.

The ignorance takes two forms. One is a failure to learn how other media have explored storytelling for centuries. The second is an assumption that because video games add the additional element of interactivity or gameplay that even if game writers and designers knew the old rules, they couldn't possibly apply them to games.

The arrogance also takes two forms. The first is that games—even those with shoddy storytelling techniques, cardboard characters, and clichéd plots—have sold quite well thanks. There wouldn't appear to be any need to improve. The other is that because a designer who is not an experienced writer can't see the trap in discarding concepts they haven't bothered to learn, or even knew existed, no one else can either. This middle-management style of arrogance that forces creators to work within the limited imaginations of their employers has been the bane of artists from Mozart to Orson Welles. If employers don't understand, or can't do something, they assume it can't be done. "Too many notes, Mozart!" "I'm re-editing your film, Orson!"

As a result, we are all saddled with this yoke of narrative in games, even though it need not exist. We have stuck our heads into it almost without complaint. "They're only games, after all." Yet we have progressed, as we'll see in this look at the story structures we must choose from today.

TRADITIONAL STORY FORMS IN GAMES

In the earliest text adventures, we saw the beginnings of an exciting possibility: gameplay and storytelling emerging into a single entertainment experience. It was nonlinear, much like the web form we'll come to later in Figure 14.4, with the boxes being the rooms and the arrows interconnecting tunnels. The player could explore many different rooms of *Colossal Cave* in whatever order they chose. Other areas of the cave were opened upon solving puzzles.

Colossal Cave (aka *Adventure* and *Adventure in the Colossal Caves*) was first written and programmed (in FORTRAN) by Will Crowther circa 1975; then it was expanded and distributed by Don Woods in 1976. Crowther was a caver, and his game was always intended to simulate the exploration of a cave. In fact, *Colossal Cave* does exist. It's a section of Mammoth Cave in Kentucky, reimagined in a fantasy setting. And at that it succeeded well. The game is loaded with references to actual features of the cave system, and caver jargon is used throughout.

True, the puzzles were only that, and not dramatic obstacles, and they weren't always consistent with the loose fantasy fiction of the world. Other characters, like the troll and the thieving pirate, were nothing more than puzzle elements, and the "story" was more an environment or arena built on some backstory. Yet it was the start of a promising trend.

Then graphics arrived, and we got distracted by the pretty pictures. The graphics improved year by year, but the stories stayed sketchy. When we attempted to develop the stories, they seemed to get more and more linear. However many areas there were for the player to explore, the stories started to fall into a familiar, comfortable line.

Video forced us into a truly linear path from which we have never recovered. The best video seemed to offer was branching storylines, covered in a moment. *The Riddle of Master Lu* and *Dark Side of the Moon*, I'm proud to say, avoided both linear and branching. Too bad that fact went largely unnoticed.

So even though our first attempts at computer games with at least story "elements" like *Colossal Cave* and the *Zork* Trilogy hinted at nonlinear storytelling, their influence faded, and the torch was kept lit but flickering by other text adventure games until graphics snuffed it out. Gameplay and stories headed down two very different paths.

In the diagrams that follow, the boxes indicate any number of moments in the progression of a story. They may be scenes, levels, locations, character encounters, puzzles, or any of the various storytelling devices we talk about in this book. They are all points where story is advanced. The arrows indicate how players can move from story point to story point.

Traditional (Linear)

Storytelling, even with its variations, is still to a large extent linear in other media. There's no reason for it not to be. Other than standard techniques like flashbacks, which rarely fail to advance the story in a single direction, most books, movies, and television tell their stories in lines, straight or otherwise. One major example of a writer/director of movies who does experiment with nonlinear storytelling is Christopher Nolan. Check out *Memento*, *Inception*, and *Tenet*. These movies require that attention be paid. It took Nolan a decade to bring *Tenet* to the screen.

The storytelling of many games is linear, following discrete paths with signposts along the way, as in other media. Some games moderate this slightly. *The Legend of Zelda: Breath of the Wild*'s open-world style of storytelling allows the player to interrupt one quest to solve another. Progress flags are set so the player can return to the same place. Some quests differ depending upon the order they are played, but more likely they are withheld completely until some other goal is accomplished. Finding and photographing various locations on the huge *Breath of the Wild* map trigger flashbacks that fill in the game's backstory. Capturing these pictures can happen in any order. But the choice of order does not affect how the player chooses to play the rest of the game.

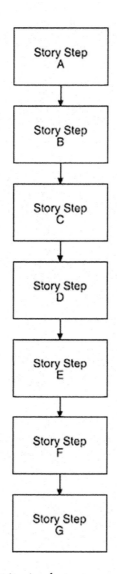

FIGURE 14.1   Linearity: storytelling at its simplest.

In Figure 14.1, the story starts at A, proceeds from obstacle to obstacle until B is reached, then in the same manner to C, all the way to the end. The arrows point inexorably in one direction from the introduction to the endgame. It looks a lot like a stack of children's blocks, doesn't it?

This is how writers of games saw other media telling stories like this, and the first attempts slavishly copied the structure. Why not? The traditional linear story structure has a lot going for it.

- It is time-tested.

- It is successful in a variety of media.

- It is familiar to the writer and comfortable to the player.

- It guarantees authorial control over the progress of the story.

- Traditional stories enjoy the added benefit that lots of people have had experience writing them. The difficulties are limited to the same craft issues found in other media.

Figure 14.1 also looks a bit like our python from Chapter 7 standing on its tail. If we increase the size of the lettered boxes, that's exactly what it is: balloons of nonlinear gameplay connected by narrow one-way funnels like those found on crab traps to ensure there is no turning back. The most obvious limitation to this structure is that it ends up forcing gameplay and storytelling into a linear structure. This construction could be obvious, as in level-based games, or disguised as in the python structure.

It's a fair question to ask why linear gameplay is such a nasty thing. Designers can track and control the player's advancement in the game, advancing their skills at a rate balanced with the increasing difficulty of gameplay, making sure they don't get too powerful too quickly. Even though the two may feel quite different when they're implemented, they are structurally similar. It would therefore help to foster the illusion that the story and gameplay are part of a single entertainment experience.

But there are too many factors working against that illusion. The storytelling is predominantly passive, and the gameplay is active. They are often segregated from one another by the use of cut scenes, long game engine scenes, pages of text, and so on. Why add one more immersion-breaking element?

Linear structures are completely at odds with what players want to do in games. Linear structures force them on to rails or limit them to small areas in obviously larger worlds. In a linear adventure game, a single puzzle can stop a player's progress dead. We know we need to limit them, but why choose a tactic that makes it so obvious?

Players want freedom. The more freedom, the more real the game world feels to them. When we start holding up signs saying, "You can't go here" or "You can't do that," and they know in the real world they could go there, or do that, we're rubbing their faces in the fact that the game world is actually a very limited subset of the real world. Indiana Jones isn't going to visit every exotic locale on Earth in every film. The audience knows that. They accept the illusion that he is able to. We have to exert ourselves to create that illusion.

Some years ago, I worked on an interactive storytelling project for a very well-known company and with a lot of money behind it. It would also feature some cutting-edge technology. There was no gameplay as such, only narrative, so the player controlling the avatar was called a "user." I want to support any efforts in interactive storytelling. The fact that more than one person could move independently through the narrative interested me. It was doomed from the start for several reasons, only two of which are pertinent to our discussion. The team in place when I arrived had made two assumptions that were absolutely wrong.

First, their way of maintaining the illusion of a world beyond the areas of the game was to herd and punish the avatar. We often feel as if our player-character is being dragged from point to point through linear stories, but in this case, the dragging was literal. The avatar was first asked by NPCs to go someplace or remain someplace or do something. If the player tried something the narrative didn't support, the NPCs would grow more insistent. If the player remained recalcitrant, the NPCs would manhandle the player's avatar, physically moving it, or the engine would remove the avatar's ability to move.

At the very beginning of the narrative, the avatar was somewhat at the mercy of outside forces. But very soon the player would move on to sections where taking them prisoner, or holding them in place, wouldn't work at all.

Snatching control from the user whenever it was expedient, and at moments when it would be obvious to the user what was happening and why, would be calamitous. Users would get angry at being forced to march from moment to moment in the story. They were being treated like incarcerated felons.

Their second assumption was that users would "understand" that this straight-jacketing of the avatar was necessary and go along with it. All I could think of were the thousands of forums out there pelted with posts from gamers when designers make a mistake. I tried to show them other ways of limiting the game world that weren't so invasive, that worked within the context of the story and the world, but the creative lead remained adamant. I was only one of a series of designers that told the creative lead this. The game was never released.

Players want freedom of choice and action. Linear storytelling clearly limits their choices and actions. They want the world affected by their actions. It's a technical task to add bullet holes in walls and make most objects destructible. It's a writing/design task to create moments of story and character based on their decisions. Luckily, a number of writers and designers realized the corner linear storytelling was pointing us toward and looked for alternatives. The first alternative was branching storylines.

Branching (Linear Thinking)

> The branching story is a great idea, poorly implemented (see Figure 14.2). The game frequently loses track of exactly what information you have learned. This means you're presented with conversation options like "Tell me all about X" when you've never heard of X at all! Similarly, the nonlinearity of the plot means it's possible to advance along one storyline past a point of no return before you've collected essential items from another area.
>
> *PC Gameworld review of Post Mortem (2003)*

I entered the games industry as the result of my frustration with two games. The first I mentioned in Chapter 6, "Character Encounters," was *Return to Zork* in 1993. The other was *Sherlock Holmes: Consulting Detective* released in 1992, one of the first games on CD-ROM. In *SH:CD*, players moved through the story by interviewing various characters in full-motion video (FMV) clips of live actors. You found these characters by selecting locations from a menu. The story was linear. The presentation was not. To use our analogy of the children's blocks, players could select a character on Block D before Block C, even if the questions they were given to ask that character were dependent on the conversation on Block C. Look at the date on the review quoted above. Over almost three decades later, game designers are still making the same mistakes.

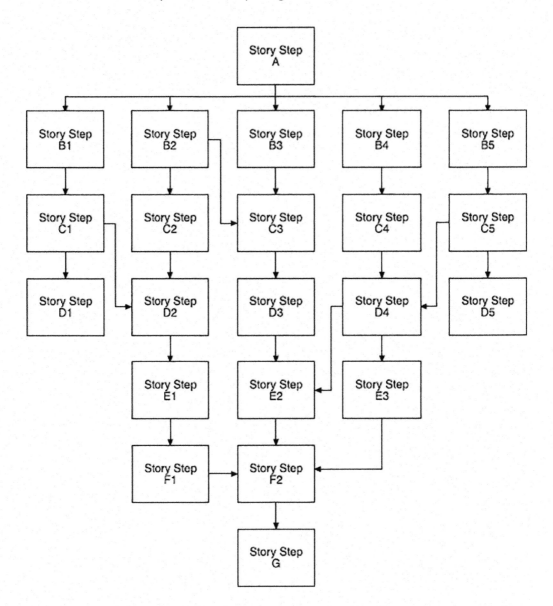

FIGURE 14.2 Branching: the perennial answer to interactive storytelling.

A far more fundamental mistake also occurs on a regular basis. Branching stories have been with us since text adventures, yet every few years another company arrives on the scene, announcing they've solved interactive storytelling. Their solution is always branching storylines. The theory goes that branching is not only "interactive," but it encourages repeat play.

Branching breaks down into two main types: single point branches and games structured with many branches. The first is most often seen in the endgame where the storyline will happily proceed on its linear way until the conclusion where players will be faced with a choice that sends them into one of several alternate endings. These endings may be of equal value, or one may take precedence over the others, completing the golden path.

My favorite example of this is *Titanic: Adventure Out of Time*, Andrew Nelson's adventure game from 1996 that got a big boost from the release of a certain movie one year later. It was a beautiful-looking adventure game with a fanatical attention to historical detail. What made the alternate endings work so well was that Andrew had real history to play with. In one ending, players could even prevent World War II from occurring. Each ending was equally interesting. There was no golden path ending. There was no entirely happy outcome. Given the nature of the material, this isn't surprising. *Blade Runner* is another example of an older game with interesting alternative endings.

A rarer type of single point branching is when the branch point is located at the beginning of the game as in Hal Barwood's *Indiana Jones and the Fate of Atlantis*. Another of my sidebar contributors, Noah Falstein, was a co-designer on the game. He suggested custom-tailoring gameplay to a player's preferences by giving him a choice of how he wanted to play the game: as a lone adventurer; with an NPC companion; or as an action game hero. The choices were carefully integrated into the fiction of the game world. Quite a bit of additional work was needed to support all three paths, although some assets were reused.

However, most games use branching storylines simply for additional interactivity or to encourage playing the game more than once. There is, in fact, anecdotal evidence to suggest that most players don't replay the games to try out different paths or endings. This is probably because many branches are there just to be branches. The story may shift slightly, but the differences are not meaningful. I'm not saying the choices may not result in significantly different gameplay, but that they do not expose the core themes or emotional stakes of the story very often.

In the Xbox game *Tom Clancy's Splinter Cell: Pandora Tomorrow* (actually written by J.T. Petty), there are multiple branches in story progression, as well as multiple endings to the story. These can involve ethical decisions on the part of the player to the point of questioning and even defying orders. NPCs react to players' decisions, and the game difficulty adjusts as their attitudes to the player-character, Sam Fisher, change. The branches are meaningful therefore both to the story and game mechanics.

Meaningless branches make branching meaningless. Story branches that require the player not only to think, but to feel as well, are the best use of the form. The verdict is still out on whether they encourage repeat play.

I would much rather see games that are so dramatically compelling and fun to play that they are played multiple times for those reasons. We don't watch *Casablanca* over and over again to see if Rick and Ilsa will finally wind up together. We watch because the characters touch us; the ethical choices are meaningful; the story is engaging; and the theme of self-sacrifice for a greater good is a powerful one. Also, the film's sense of humor is timeless!

Games that rely on branching for their entire story structure can still be found everywhere in video games. Every few years someone claims to have discovered the key to interactive storytelling. It's invariably branching. George Santayana's quote succinctly explains why: "Those who cannot remember the past are condemned to repeat it." Besides amnesia, why does branching remain so popular? A number of reasons:

- **It is time-tested.** Maybe not as long as linear storytelling, but it's been around now for decades.

- **It has been somewhat successful despite being tied so closely to FMV.** Remember *Night Trap* (1995)? *Silent Steel* (1995)? *Black Dahlia* (1998)? *The X-Files Game* (1999)? (Note: *The Riddle of Master Lu* and *Dark Side of the Moon* both contain FMV. There is branching only in the dialogue trees of Lu, and none in DSOM.)

- **It's still locked into paths.** There can be a golden path and less satisfactory paths.

- **It's familiar to the developers of games.** There are still many who think it is the only way to tell interactive stories.

- **It's familiar to the players of games and the reviewers of games.** They recognize that even the limited choices branching gives us are more interactive than linear traditional storytelling provides.

- **There is still authorial control over the progression of the story because branching is really just a form of linear storytelling.** Each branch is still a stack of blocks piled from A to B to C and so on. Over the course of a game with the most branches imaginable, the story progression is still headed in the same direction from beginning to end.

People who are locked into linear story structures in games and are fearful of branching don't understand a fundamental principle involved. They fear the branches will keep spreading like some massive genealogical family tree.

When I took over the job as head writer of *Edge of Night*, I was told that a huge chunk of stations carrying the show were going to be dropping it in a few months no matter how successful we were. It was the last soap of the afternoon because of its title. And that time slot bumped up against the period when network programming gave way to local programming. Our half hour was coveted by local stations for cheaper programs, reruns, programming more geared to school kids, and for many more reasons. And sure enough, that September our station coverage took a major hit. *House of the Dragon* would not have survived the loss of that many stations.

I had been flirting with interactive storytelling since 1981 when I wrote a pilot for a television series that Atari was involved in. The story involved a family who could use their large-screen TV as a gate to other worlds. The plan was to release episodes based on games and to base episodes on Atari games.

When *Edge of Night*'s ratings dropped solely from the loss of the stations in 1983, we tried to figure out what we could do to attract new viewers. The 900 number was a brand-new phenomenon at the time. I suggested allowing the audience to vote, and then taking stories in the direction they preferred. The reaction was similar to what we still find in games over almost four decades later. They pictured multiple story branches headed in all directions; scenes being shot that would never be aired (remember we only had a couple of weeks lead time); and they saw this all happening in real time: phone calls tallied, scripts hastily rewritten, and stories that were out of control, at the mercy of the viewer. No more authorial control!

I pointed out that our lack of lead time, and the nature of soaps, actually made the idea workable. I'd learned my lesson. I understood about coffee-table scenes. I knew there were times to slow one story for a couple of weeks or more and allow an overlapping story to get up to speed. Given our short lead time, it would not have changed the pace of the show at all to create a suspenseful branch point; slow the pace of that storyline while we focused on another story (this also increased suspense); tally data on what the viewers wanted to see; write the new scenes, shoot them, and have them on the air a couple weeks later. My writing time for an entire episode averaged less than 3 hours. The writing time of a few transition scenes would be insignificant.

When they asked about out of control story branches and horrors! abdicating authorial control and allowing the audience to dictate story, I drew a diagram for them. It didn't look like Figure 14.2. It looked like Figure 14.3.

Instead of letting all those housewives, law enforcement officers, and convicted felons write our stories, I would present them with choices that I could fit back into the overall story arc. Any experienced writer knows that even if you're moving from A to B to C, there are many alternatives you can choose to get there. If we offered the audience a choice once a week in different stories (there were many being told in the show at any given time), we'd still only be giving them two or three choices in stories that ran for several months.

Well, it didn't happen. We opted to refocus on some core characters and up the stakes in their lives. It would have been an interesting experiment, particularly in light of TV shows like *America's Got Talent* where viewers can vote whether participants can stay or must go.

Branching is all about illusion. No authorial control is given up. In solo boxed games, writers don't have to adjust to players. We may have to write more, but not as much as one might think. Entire scenes and swatches of dialogue, if they are not seen by the player when they first appear, can be positioned in any number of places.

Video games still use branching in dialogue trees where its use is not as outdated as it is in overall game and game story structures. But even here, there are more sophisticated structures we can use. My use of dialogue branching in my earlier games led me in parallel with other designers (I'm not the only one tackling this stuff after all!) to the next level of sophistication in story structures: the web.

Web (Simple Nonlinear)

Kenneth Millar was a mystery writer who lived in Santa Barbara, California. He was the direct stylistic descendant of Raymond Chandler. Under his pen name of Ross MacDonald, he wrote intricate hard-edged detective novels featuring his detective Lew Archer. Paul Newman appeared in the film adaptation of the first Lew Archer novel, *The Moving Target*, with the character name changed to Harper to fit in with Newman's other hit "H" films like *Hud*, *Hombre*, and *The Hustler*. The screenplay was by William Goldman.

Millar constructed intricate murder mystery plots around one of his favorite themes: the decay and corruption that lay beneath the surface of seemingly ordinary American

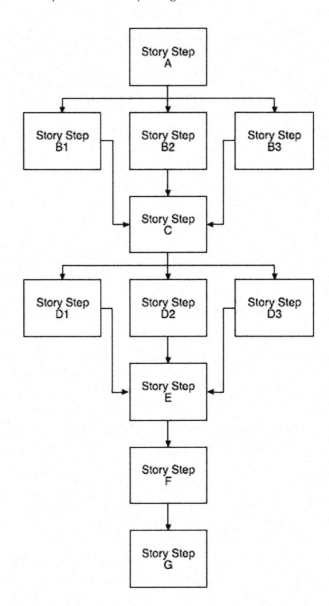

FIGURE 14.3 Retaining authorial control in branching stories.

families. He would walk along the beach every morning, a spider weaving his stories like webs, spinning out long strands, then connecting them again and again in the most unexpected places. He didn't know until the last minute which of his many characters was the culprit. So cunningly were the characters trapped in the web that any one of them could have done it. This image of his stories as webs has remained with me till this day.

When I played those first text adventure games, I mapped every room on graph paper. I still have some of those maps filed away. I remember one particularly difficult game built with ASCII "graphics" on my green phosphorescent monitor. It was called *Asylum*. You started out trapped in a padded cell. It took me forever just to figure out how to escape from that cell! I would never have been able to complete it without drawing a map.

Any of you who have mapped games, whether early adventures and RPGs or some text MUDS still with us today, will recognize Figure 14.4. In our maps, the squares were not story points, character encounters, levels, or scenes; they were called rooms. These rooms could be indoors or outdoors. They might be only part of a bigger room within the game world like a ballroom divided into subrooms such as the entry, dance floor, banquet tables, and stage. The arrows indicate the exits from and entries into these rooms.

These maps not only kept me from getting lost in the game (particularly in mazes!), but they were also a map of the game's structure. When I became interested in the design of games, I realized that, thanks to mapping, I had a good first leg up on how games could be structured. It wasn't until I'd actually had a couple games released that I realized that they

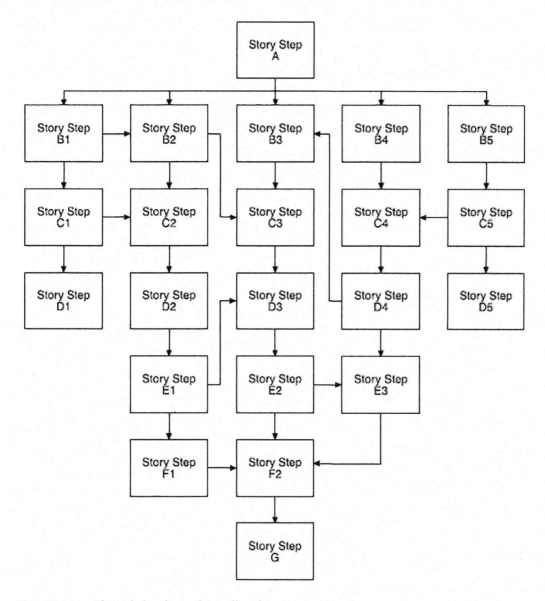

FIGURE 14.4   The web: less linear but still with strings attached.

could also be maps of story structure. Here are the main items of interest about the web story structure:

- **It is the first truly nonlinear storytelling form, even though it is not a very complex one to imagine.** For the first time, the progression from A to B to C is no longer clear. You can go from A to C to B. By allowing progression in more than one direction, it breaks the linear pattern. It is definitely the beginning of a new paradigm.

- **Webs are still fairly new.** It's hard to find examples of them at all in many types of games. We do find webs in console action games that don't depend on explicit levels but open new areas after players complete certain tasks. When these areas can be opened in different orders, as in treasure hunts or sandbox games, the web structure is present.

- **It still feels familiar to gamers and reviewers because they mistake it for branching.** This indicates that it's working because they don't recognize it.

- **For the first time we loosen the author's grip on the story, which is why you don't see writers unfamiliar with web structure embracing it.** The more perceptive light fires to push back the darkness it suggests. Others don't even notice it.

- **It is more difficult to write than its two predecessors.** An entirely new element has entered the mix.

- **It moves us one step closer to a structure that resembles true nonlinear gameplay.**

- **It provides a useful transition from linear thinking to true nonlinear modular storytelling.** The story is designed in the same way that gameplay is designed.

The Riddle of Master Lu was built with a few huge modules. Within those modules, it was business as usual. The dialogue was structured as branching dialogue trees. It wasn't until *Dark Side of the Moon* that I was able to put the web structure to use in the dialogue trees. Some of that game's structures are not modular but web. This was necessary when I had to limit the paths players took to reach certain goals. I don't necessarily see this as a flaw in the game's design, although sometimes it revealed flaws we were unable to correct.

In *Dark Side of the Moon*, there are several unfortunate choke points that must be completed in order for the player to progress. What is worse, a couple of them are not obviously connected to the player being able to advance. As far as I'm concerned, this is as bad as forcing players to hunt for pixels and search for the story. I apologize to the players. I screwed up.

Hopefully, an example of the corner I painted us into will illuminate one of the challenges that nonlinear storytelling presents. At the beginning of the game, the lower levels of the mining colony were inaccessible to the player-character Jake. The reason for this was technical, not story related. Because of all the FMV involved, the game first shipped on six CDs (later it was released on a single DVD as well). At the time (1997), that was a lot to load onto a player's hard drive, although they had that option. Assuming that most players would be swapping disks, I needed to find a way to minimize that as much as possible.

I divided the disks according to mine level, so that players knew that if they needed to take an elevator ride, a new disk would probably be required. So, for a technical reason, there were sections of the game that were modular, but they were stuffed into a python-like structure (sort of the reverse of *The Riddle of Master Lu*). To work within the belly of the python, I backed up a step to the web structure of the following puzzle.

It was necessary to receive a Proof of Claim, Jake's right to his uncle's mine, before he could proceed to lower levels of the mine. But the mining clerk was never in his office. Furthermore, players had to find out where the clerk spent most of his time: a gravity dice table. Like lotto players, the clerk played a certain "lucky" number every time, and that number was the very one needed to enter into the security keypad to gain access to his office. The problem it created was the fact that there was no indication that it had any connection whatsoever with the player's inability to access the lower levels. That's sloppy puzzle design. Knowing that I had to create a choke point, I should have reworked the puzzle so players could connect it to its reward early on.

This type of puzzle structure is not uncommon in adventure games. And you can get to the important information by several routes, but it remains a web, not true modularity. True modular storytelling (and puzzle design as we've seen *is* storytelling) would have removed that chokepoint. It took another six months for hardware to catch up with the design. If we'd been able to release on DVD to begin with, such artificial choke points (there weren't many!) would have been unnecessary. Given the size of today's hard drives— gigabytes giving way to terabytes—even DVD search times are a thing of the past.

It was not a real python structure, of course, because the choke points were not one-way. As each obstacle was removed, the player had access to a greater part of the game world, until eventually all locations in the world were "open," at least in the sense that the player knew how to access them. So, the web structure fell away to reveal modules underneath.

One benefit of such choke points was that, even though they were a nuisance to the purity of my concept of modular storytelling, they were helpful as flags. As soon as the game engine was notified the player had accessed a new area, any situations, puzzles, character encounters, and so on connected to that new step in the story could be flipped to a new state. Characters who could once reliably be found only on an upper level could now appear in new spots. Jake's status changed within the story. He moved from a busybody to a fugitive from a murder charge, and colony announcements changed to warnings to be on the lookout for him. Consequently, the nature of puzzles left unresolved were changed.

I'm giving you clues here to which method of storytelling I overwhelmingly prefer. Let's move on now to a new storytelling.

Relinquishing Control

We will pause here a moment for readers cringing at the above heading. Writers have fought for centuries to retain control over their work. Editors, critics, network and studio executives, governments, and of course audiences have all attempted at one time or another to bend our art to fit their concept of what art should be. Is it any wonder then that a concept like Relinquishing Control might send a few screaming for the exits? Ah, excellent! I see more than I expected are ready to soldier on. Let's have an unflinching look at true nonlinear storytelling.

Modular (Nonlinear)

The thrust of the last few chapters has been toward an integration of story and gameplay. It makes sense that the closer the way we construct our stories comes to the way we build our games, the better chance we have for that integration. Even though I've tried to prepare the way for a modular concept of storytelling, there are several scary issues we need to address. Let's look at Figure 14.5. What's missing? All those comforting little arrows.

It might seem more accurate if we drew the diagram with two-way arrows from every box connecting to every other box. I didn't do that for two reasons. The first is that it would look like a hairball. I didn't want readers to take it as a personal challenge to trace every one of the connections. The point should be clear without them. The story can progress from any single box (module) to any other single box with two exceptions: the first box and the last. A game has to begin somewhere (point of attack!) and end somewhere (final resolution!), or at least a single-player game does. Virtual worlds don't need that last box.

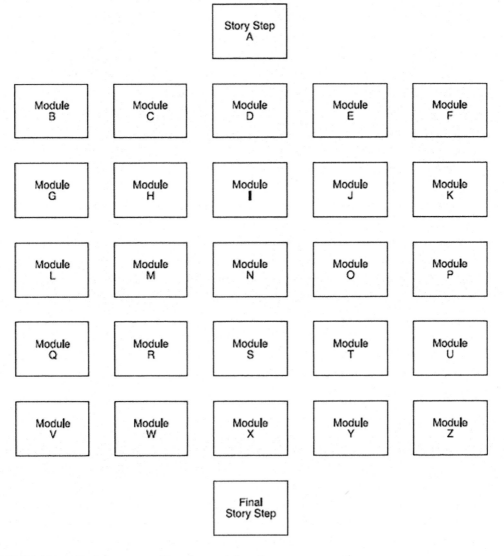

FIGURE 14.5   Modular: storytelling that matches the way gamers play.

The second reason is that I want to wean us from the idea of paths. This concept, firmly established by the first three storytelling forms we've looked at, fails to acknowledge how the gameplay in many games is already designed. In some sandbox games, like the *Grand Theft Auto* series, a linear story winds its way across the landscape. In a game like *The Legend of Zelda: Breath of the Wild*, the gameplay is already laid out in modules. You start the game in a large area with a number of locations to explore. There are no real boundaries at the edges of the area. Players can move over a lot of territory in any direction they choose. The boundaries are created by the level of mobs waiting to kill the player and a map that doesn't immediately reveal itself. The physical world of the game doesn't continue in a linear way, it expands in reaction to player choices.

There are no true choke points. This is why linear quests and storytelling seem so odd when we encounter them in MMOs. How did they get there? Why do designers think they're good ideas? It's due to the parallel development path they took to solo player games. Their pedigree stems from tabletop role-playing and small MUDs, not text adventure games. Text MUDs and text adventures look very much alike if you examine obvious things like the text format, player input, maps, and so on. They are really quite different. In Chapter 17, "Storytelling in Virtual Worlds," and Chapter 18, "Storytelling in Small Games," we'll look at the challenges their independent history has created for them.

If we can get beyond the idea of paths being the way a player moves through a game, we'll be able to progress to new paradigms. Paths promote linear thinking. Do all games need to be nonlinear? No. I don't believe that any more than I think all games should tell stories. What I'm saying is that if you choose to make your game linear, don't do it because you think it's the only way to tell your story. Don't copy the paradigms of the past before you understand them. Once you do understand them, you hopefully will be able to see how they can be repurposed. Remember Picasso's mother and daughter!

Okay, what distinguishes modular storytelling from the first three forms?

- **It is unfamiliar to many designers, particularly those who routinely segregate story and gameplay.**

- **Its structure is not immediately apparent.** Without all those comfortable arrows in the diagram to hang on to, it can look frighteningly vague.

- **There is apparently no authorial control.** It looks as if the direction the story takes is totally at the whim of the player. Players may love this, but writers don't.

- **It can be difficult to grasp.** It requires a new way of looking at story, especially for someone who is not already experienced in constructing linear stories. You didn't read that wrong. I'm not suggesting it should be easier for someone not tied down to the old "outdated" ways. Look around. It's one of the core themes of the book.

- **Modular storytelling requires much more effort.** Once the mind clicks over to how it is done, there are other factors that we begin to look at in the web form, the first nonlinear structure. However, we are used to those issues from gameplay design. They are not as foreign as you might think. It is the application of them to storytelling that is not obvious.

No other structure is better at integrating story and gameplay than modular. Those boxes in Figure 14.5 can be of any size. They can be entire scenes if you like, or brief moments captured in the rush of gameplay. All that is required of them is the same thing required of any step in a story—that it moves the story forward.

But what is forward? No matter what order the story steps are experienced by the player, the momentum is always from the story's beginning to the story's end. The player may jump around on the diagram from box to box, but eventually they will find themselves where the author has always wanted them to go.

J.T. Petty, in an interview with Amazon.com circa 2004, said,

> At the stage of interactive narrative we're working with now, I feel like we still need to control the narrative pretty strictly. I've never been a fan of multiple endings; they make me feel as if none of the endings are actually valid.

But he then appears to contradict himself: "With current technology and innovations, I think the best we can do is create the illusion of narrative control and create the most manipulative/sympathetic situations possible."

He is expressing the anxiety a lot of writers have when faced with interactivity. He's obviously intrigued by its additional challenges enough to try branching but seems to think multiple paths are his best storytelling tool. Anything beyond that is unexplored territory.

While there is apparently no authorial control in modular storytelling, there really is. Now that we know the story still starts at A and will eventually end at Z, we should be able to relax a little. What's next? Adjusting the modules. Not only are they different sizes, but the modules are also dynamic. Just as we break down the elements of a scene or level to see what we need to save if we're dropping it, we do the same in modules to see what components are tied to that particular story step, and which are more flexible. Most are flexible.

Setting remains tied to a specific module. We don't change a module's location from a corporate office in Manhattan to an Iraqi desert oasis. Physical action is tied to the module, just as it is often tied to the setting. Most puzzles remain constant for the same reason, although we can see where the game engine might lock or unlock a door and place a key in a scene, depending on previous player actions.

Characters may or may not be tied to the module. If an NPC is mobile, they're free to sit in our digital green room like an actor until they are called upon to make their entrance. We'll maintain the illusion for the audience that they have a real-life offstage, just as we do in plays. "Where has that no account brother of mine gone off to?" "Probably gambling at the casino again!" No, the closest he'll come to that is playing cards backstage with the actor playing the character he murdered in the first act.

Most importantly, as we saw in our discussion of cutting levels and areas, almost all story steps can be fluid. As we discover when we edit and must move story elements around, exposition works in a surprising number of places in any given story. Remember that the player's perception is that the story is always moving forward along a single linear path. Modular structure is entirely invisible to the player.

Now that we've freed the necessary steps of our story from being tied to any individual scene, we need to track the player's progress. We do that in the same way we track player progress in any other part of our game like skills or quests or acquired items. We pass tokens. We set flags. Even though the player has been successfully derailed and is now wandering freely through our world, every action they take, every choice they make, is dutifully tracked.

The backpack is a classic game device for inventory. We know it holds far more in a game than it would in real life. It is a game convention we accept. Think of the player-character hiking through our story carrying a backpack containing the various objects, story steps, and NPC character developments possible in the story. It's a database just as it is in the inventory analogy. The game can pick through it at any moment and find out where the player has been; what the player has done; what the player has learned; what NPCs think of the player-character; and so on.

Having that information, the game can automatically salt the next module the player visits with the next step along all those "paths." If the player fails to experience all the possible elements now available to them in one module because of their progression through the story so far, those elements remain in the backpack as the player moves to the next modules and then they can become available again. None of these variables in the backpack need to be tied to any of the others. Some may, but it's not necessary. We may need a specific story step to reveal growth in an NPC, but even that is fluid.

This might sound like we could be tracking unwieldy numbers of variables. This isn't true. The number of story steps and character revelations in any scene are very few even in the most complex stories, or audiences could never follow them. In our stories that are simple, even when they're disguised as complex, the number is very manageable. The challenge comes in testing all the possible variations and making sure they track appropriately.

It may take a certain kind of personality to handle as much of this as possible during the writing. As J.T. Petty says (and remember he's only talking about branching!):

> I've got my sock drawer organized according to the Dewey Decimal system. Low-level compulsion comes to me pretty naturally and keeping track of the narrative threads is usually pretty satisfying. The script format we came up with for the first SC [Splinter Cell], the documents we call "Mission Bibles," are also helpful, (especially since the level designers have to know the various threads as well as or better than I do).

I have that same compulsive nature and feel the same satisfaction when the pieces of a story or conversation match up like dominoes.

Time for an example. In Figure 14.6, we see a portion of Figure 14.5 magnified so we can better see the building blocks that make up the module. This is one possible story progression based on choices made by a player named Jane. The letter P stands for permanent features. The letter D stands for dynamic features that are present dependent on player actions.

In Figure 14.7, we see the same story as it is experienced by another player named Dick, who made different choices. (Their dog Spot doesn't play computer games.)

Even though Dick and Jane have made very different choices in where to go and what to do, both find themselves at exactly the same point in our story. *They have experienced all the material we've created for them.* Yet we are maintaining authorial control. In a virtual

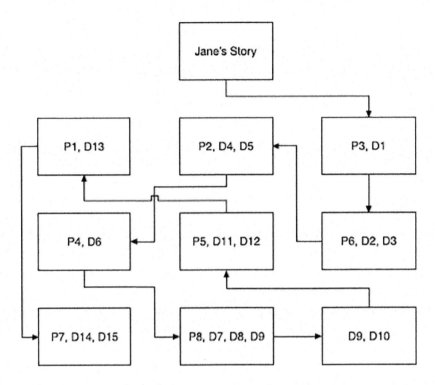

FIGURE 14.6   Jane progresses through the story.

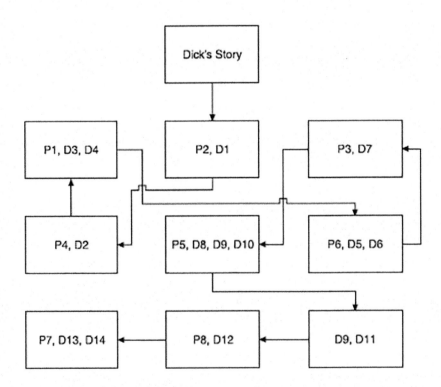

FIGURE 14.7   Dick progresses through the same story.

world, of course, Dick and Jane may be simultaneously involved in the same quest, following it from step to step at an identical pace, and still never meet. The divergent experiences prompt a lot of discussion at the in-game pub.

Another question may have occurred to the reader. Maybe we can tell stories in this fashion in our games. But isn't modular structure too loose to give us compelling stories? The answer to that question lies in Chapter 13, "The Roots of a New Storytelling," and is scattered throughout this book. It was that question that prompted me to rediscover *Don Quixote de la Mancha*. That story would remain great literature no matter in what order we followed its picaresque adventures.

We don't want to throw out all that we've learned on how to write stories, but we do need to look at them with different eyes. Divorcing story steps and character development from setting happens every day when writers rewrite. If it's raining, shooting at a practical location may need to be rescheduled to an existing indoor set. If an actress in a TV series becomes pregnant, that may need to be written into the storyline or disguised. I've had to do both. With two different actresses. At the same time. Physical action scenes were altered or shifted to other characters. Actors' contracts sometimes dictate story moves. Mike Muscular is asking for too much money? Involve the character in an auto accident, keep him a helpless paraplegic for a couple of heart-wrenching weeks, and then write him out. Writing for a television series requires being aware about how dynamic and flexible story (and careers!) must be.

But if you were paying attention in the earlier chapters, you know there are some other issues to be dealt with. What about rising action and tightening the emotional screws? What about the crisis, climax, resolution trio? What about reversals?

These are dealt with in several ways. I realized how flexible we could really be with story and character while working on *Dark Side of the Moon*. The word to describe the effect I saw is *synergy*.

To explain this effect, I developed the following example that I give at my tutorials and lectures. I call it "A Bad Day at the Office." Please remember

> Synergy: occurs when two or more substances, organisms, or elements combine to produce an effect greater than the sum of their individual effects.

this is one example of a way to escalate tension or suspense in a modular story structure. It is by no means the only one!

Suppose in the course of any workday, six bad things can happen. These are not earth-shaking, such as getting fired. Nor are they so minor as to pass beneath our emotional radar. All are of a similar intensity, somewhere in the middle ground between minor irritation and total calamity. A misunderstanding with a coworker, a meeting that went nowhere…whatever.

Okay, one of these happens to you. You go home, and your significant other asks how your day was. Balanced against that one bad thing is an entire day of good, or at least neutral incidents. So, you reply, "Pretty good!"

Suppose three bad things happen. Depending on your outlook on life, you might reply, "So so." "Not bad." "Not so good." Etc. The cup is either half full or half empty.

Suppose all six happen. You would say you had "a bad day at the office."

Now, these six things could happen in any order. And none is of a higher intensity than any other. One of the reasons *Don Quixote* is such a good example is because each of the incidents in the main part of the book have a similar emotional level. Yet, simply by juxtaposing them in a single day or story or game, then adding them up, something interesting happens.

The resulting emotion is stronger than any one of the individual pieces. Synergy. This phenomenon is the real world's gift to us, the writer of games. It is a gift our linear media colleagues would never appreciate. They have no need for it. We can manipulate that synergy in a modular story. At the end of a game session in which we rescued a child from bullies; helped a baker deliver his pies; defeated a bandit in combat; solved an intriguing puzzle; and completed a mission that required stealth and ingenuity. We can say we had a great time no matter in what order we experienced those modules.

Here's another way to tackle some of the storytelling challenges we face. And it's the solution to the question I posed at the end of the section on web story structures. Which form do I overwhelmingly prefer? Modular storytelling, right? No. I prefer none of them— and all of them.

In the sentence length of your dialogue the types of characters you use to populate your world; the quests you create; and in so much more, variation is everything. It keeps the player interested. And it's no different in story structures.

While I may prefer modular for overall game structure because of its flexibility and how closely it mirrors the way gamers like to play, it is not the only possibility. The web structure got me out of a corner in *Dark Side of the Moon*. I also use it in most of my dialogue trees.

Branching is still a viable alternative for dialogue trees, especially for exchanges with minor characters or "conventional" dialogue (bartering with merchants, talking to town criers) where the exchange follows fairly strict rules. Branching also can be useful for presenting players with meaningful choices that can pose ethical and moral questions or altering the player-character relationships with NPCs.

Linear story structures are perfectly fine for cut scenes, if we must have them. They are more effective when used sparingly in the nonlinear structures web and modular. Want to guarantee an immediate climax and resolution to a crisis? Tie all three together and move them as a single piece. We can also use choke points (either one-way or two-way) to guide players to an important story goal.

Reversals aren't the problem they may first appear to be, any more than interim rewards are. They can be attached to specific modules or allowed to float freely, ready to be plucked from the backpack at emotionally satisfying moments. We always control the removal of items from the player's backpack. It's an illusion that the player is in control of the story. They are only in control of their own actions or how they experience our story. Just like the magician who forces a card on an audience member, we can force moments on the player at will.

In *The Gryphon Tapestry*, we, of course, had random encounters with adversaries or mobs like bandits, wild animals, and magical creatures we could choose to fight, negotiate with, or run from. Sometimes, however, for story purposes, we wanted to force an outcome of a battle. To the player, the battle seemed as random as any other. The messages describing the action were the same. Yet we knew whether the player was going to win or lose. Writers are magicians. We manipulate and misdirect, and the audience loves us for it.

We've been discussing modular storytelling in only two dimensions. Like our characters and our game worlds, modules can be three-dimensional. I've mentioned the third dimension once before. Let's enter it now.

NESTING MODULES

Just as modules contain static components like setting, and dynamic variables like story steps, they can also contain other modules, as illustrated in Figure 14.8. The largest module can be the entire game world. Within that game world can be as many stories, characters, quests, encounters, puzzles, and so forth that our time, budget, energy, and brain capacity can support. And each of those can be made up of even smaller modules.

A small module, such as an encounter with a minor character, may contain a module consisting of exposition, faction, advancement, reward, or any number of things.

Nesting modules is also a way to retain a familiar level structure but with a more flexible appearance. Treasure hunt games can present us with several areas that may be entered from the very beginning of the game. Maybe we can't progress very far at first, but as soon

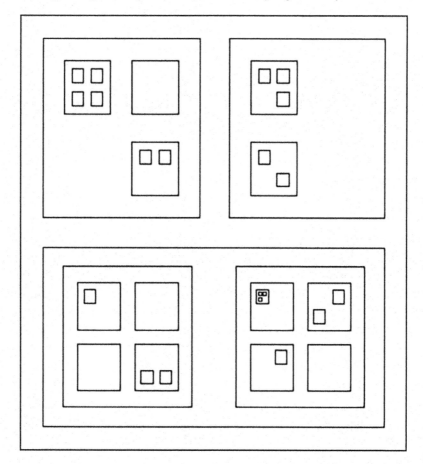

FIGURE 14.8 Nested modules.

as we acquire the necessary item or skill or knowledge, we can proceed a bit further. These areas can be nested modules with components also broken down into modules, which are variable depending upon what the player has accomplished and experienced.

It would be an interesting experiment to see how far we can drill down in this third dimension. How far you want to take the nesting of modular structure remains dependent upon many factors. Take it only as far as it adds value to your game. And remember variety is the spice of life!

SYSTEMIC STORYTELLING

Game writers need all the help we can get to fill the world of the game. Everything from conversation to combat is designed as a system so that every joke or sword swing doesn't have to be coded individually. Object-oriented programming allows us to create reusable modules that interact with each other. Story can be built module by module.

> Systemic storytelling: a game system where individual sections of the narrative are molded together by the game engine reacting to player choice.

We've seen in the past few years much exploration into systemic storytelling. It's a natural concept: constructing stories in the same way games are constructed. The FedEx quest matrix discussed in Chapter 10 is a crude example of systemic storytelling.

Hal Barwood wrote and designed two entirely systemic storytelling games: *Indiana Jones and his Desktop Adventures* in 1996 and *Star Wars: Yoda Stories* in 1997. The plots were randomly generated at the beginning of each play session. Locations, items, and even the length of the game were all shuffled to provide a different experience every time. Greg Costikyan explored the possibilities in 2007: http://www.electronicbookreview.com/thread/firstperson/storyish.

Modular storytelling by its very nature requires systemic storytelling just as game design needs systems. It exists somewhere between those matrix quests, which can span huge worlds, if we choose, and AI experiments like *Façade* and *Prom Week*, which work their magic by strictly limiting the world. On the one hand, we can't rely entirely upon systemic narrative and gameplay, or the game becomes far too repetitive and mechanical. On the other hand, the subsets of life explored with AI quickly become claustrophobic. In each case, the illusion evaporates.

I've been wrestling with the power and the challenges of systemic storytelling since 1995. And the exploration continues today whenever games seek to tell stories.

A Gamasutra interview with Patrick Redding in July of 2008 concerning *Far Cry 2* also includes comments from yours truly and some other game writers (http://www.gamasutra.com/view/feature/3727/redefining_game_narrative_.php).

Some theoretical musings from Justin Keverne in two Gamasutra blog posts in 2011 can be found here: (http://www.gamasutra.com/blogs/JustinKeverne/20110602/7717/Framework_for_Systemic_Storytelling_Part_1.php).

If we can stop being lazy and get past cinematics and long speeches to spend some serious R&D time on systemic storytelling, we'll quickly realize we have only scratched the surface of the possible.

STRUCTURING CHAOS

Those writers with faint hearts may want to skip over this section. It strays outside the scope of the book, and I only include a couple of brief ideas to tickle your brains. But if moving beyond linear or even branching feels too much like diving into the ocean from a cruise ship at sea, you aren't going to want to dive in with the following lead weights attached to your boat shoes. I'm not going to go into much detail, but with apologies to Stephen Hawking, I wanted to share with you my forays into some theory that reminds me of attempting to connect quantum mechanics with the theory of relativity. (In 2020, astrophysicists probing white dwarf stars have reported evidence in their data of both Einstein's general theory of relativity and quantum mechanics!) Still with me? Okay, don't say you weren't warned.

A few years ago, I began messing around with chaos theory. The theory was popularized by Dr. Ian Malcolm, Jeff Goldblum's character in the first two *Jurassic Park* films.

We are seeing chaos theory applied to studies of the weather and attempts to predict stock prices. It seems like it could be put to good use in politics, too. My first brush with chaos theory was many years ago when I had a screen saver that drew terrain by using fractals.

The term *fractal* was coined in 1975 by Benoit B. Mandlebrot, a mathematics professor at Yale. It

> Chaos theory: describes the complex and unpredictable motion or dynamics of systems that are sensitive to their initial conditions. Chaotic systems follow precise laws even though they appear to be random. Chaos theory discovers and maps a high level of order and pattern in what was assumed to be random activity.

refers to objects built using recursion (each iteration is a reduced version of a previous iteration—sorry I warned you) where part of the object is defined and part is variable. Despite the apparent randomness of each individual screen of that screen saver, I could set several variables such as mountain height and the ratio of landmass to water.

It seems to me very likely that instead of concentrating on what we traditionally consider A.I. storytelling or what we conventionally think of as structured writing, chaos theory offers us the best of both worlds. A modular structure built as a fractal would have a top level consisting of a row of seed modules chosen by the author. They could contain all the ingredients of story and characterization we used when we wrote our stories: characters with traits that would set them in opposition to other characters; settings that supported story; values assigned to conflict that when added up would create a climax.

These ingredients are not just tossed at random into the mix, however. They are very deliberately chosen to steer the story into a recognizable genre toward a satisfying, if undetermined, conclusion. Furthermore, the structure is tweaked with specific authorial story moments triggered when a critical mass of ingredients is reached. Turn the heat up on a pot of water, and eventually it boils.

Here we will pause for our second musical interlude. I mentioned a former colleague, Norbert Herber, back in Chapter 3 whom I worked with on a planned virtual world called *Londontown*. Norbert created a soundtrack for each player, based on rules, which is the musical equivalent of fractal seeds. Gone were the looping files of yesteryear.

I have gut instincts about writing and storytelling. They almost always pay off. And I have a gut instinct that there is something very useful here for the storyteller in a medium that embraces freer story structures that other media only flirt with. I'm done now. I said it was just a brain tickle.

ADVENTURES IN A NONLINEAR WORLD

Modular storytelling can help us integrate story and gameplay *and* create a game environment the player is free to explore. It's not theory. It's proven. Every day we're seeing examples of it in games. Most examples are small. I use it all the time. You may have sensed a greater freedom of action but have not pinned down exactly how it was achieved. Or like some of the reviewers who played *The Riddle of Master Lu*, you may never have noticed.

Sophisticated story can survive the demolition and separation necessary to the process. This is also proven. It is being done daily in other media every time we rewrite. We can maintain authorial control over the story and its steps, even as we unbind those steps, and let players encounter them as they choose. The order is irrelevant.

Tracking the progression of the player and mapping our story moves to that progression is something we do routinely in gameplay.

Modular storytelling allows us to throw off the yoke of narrative we've been harnessed with for decades. It gives us a chance to tell our stories as part of a single experience that is both narrative and game. It's past time to stop bussing our players back and forth between story and gameplay. It's time for true integration.

PART IV

Games People Play Today

INTERLUDE IN A TWISTY MAZE OF PASSAGEWAYS

> go east

The tunnel narrows here to a low east-west crawl.

> go east

This is a large cave. Stalactites hang from the ceiling, glistening in the light from your brass lantern. A solitary figure sits on a nearby boulder, shoulders slumped, head in hands. The figure's T-shirt and jeans look remarkably like your own.

> look

There is a lost adventurer in the cave.

> talk to adventurer

The adventurer stirs and looks up, blinking at the light. "Hello!" he exclaims. "Another one, eh? Lost as I am, I expect."

> talk

"I've been wandering these passages for who knows how long, existing on little more than spring water and blind fish. I took a wrong turn back in 1976 I think it was. What year is this?"

> talk

The lost adventurer looks stunned. "That long? I was a young man when I went astray, and now...well I'm not so young now..."

DOI: 10.1201/9780429284991-19

> talk

"All I can tell you about is our immediate surroundings. At least I think I can." He points behind you to the west. "Back the way you came is the real world…somewhere. Further to the east you'll find action, if it's action you crave. South of here more adventure awaits. To the north, you'll find children playing, and in the room beyond them are adults dressing up and pretending to be people they are not. Climb up through that hole, and you'll find simulated countryside and sky. But don't be fooled; it isn't real. You may find it a worthwhile strategy to lower yourself into that crack in the floor over there, although I've heard what sounds like clashing armies down there."

> talk

The lost adventurer scowls. "Parsers haven't improved much in all these years, have they?"

> talk

"That's easy for you to say. But I see no point in beating about the bush, if there were a bush nearby. Here there are only games. It's best if you pick one direction and see if it suits you. If you get bored, you can always try a new one. Just remember you're now lost like I am in a twisty maze of passageways. There's no returning to the real world. Would you like me to show you how to catch blind fish?"

CHAPTER 15

Game Types

As I mentioned in the introduction, the word "genre" gets misused a lot in our industry. In this book, I've tried to make the distinction between genres of games that break down the same as they do in other media and types of games that are uniquely our own. We'll get to genres in Chapter 16, but first let's look at the types of games that lend themselves to storytelling.

Throughout the book, I've discussed issues that are common to character creation and storytelling across various game types. Each type of game presents unique challenges and opportunities. Before I look at them in alphabetical order, I'm going to dispose of one amazingly popular type, just to get it out of the way:

CLICKERS

If you like to play tennis where you occasionally swing the racket, but never actually need to hit the ball, where you win with no effort whatsoever except occasionally clicking something, these are for you. Welcome to the exciting world of Idle games or Incremental games or Clicker games. You might well wonder why this category needs three names. All are more concerned with rapid rewards for minimal effort. I'd rather collect lint as a hobby. These are barely games and if you want story, you're better off poking a Kindle, listening to an audiobook, or turning the pages of a real book.

Note: there are many similar concerns in the next two categories that follow, Action and Adventure. Indeed, there can be crossovers between all of them. Action-Adventure games are a popular category. So read through all the game types that follow.

ACTION

Action gamers, particularly those who play shooters, demand a greater adherence to real-world physics than any other type of game outside of simulations. No longer are the only objects that can be affected by the player those that are obstacles or otherwise related directly to the plot. Now bullet holes pockmark walls. Anything in a room that can be damaged in the real world by automatic weapons fire can now be damaged in the game world. Innocent civilians can get caught in the crossfire.

DOI: 10.1201/9780429284991-20

This makes it easier to hide which objects are puzzle-related, a temptation we should resist because it puts us right back in the realm of hide-the-pixel puzzles. We need to believe enough in our obstacles, and the challenges necessary to surmount them, that we don't conceal them from players. This requires two different classes of objects: those that are just collateral damage, and those that are meaningful.

A balance must be struck between immersion and ease of gameplay. If we're using a reticle attached to the cursor to target, unless it's the dot from a laser sight, we're already moving from the real world to game convention. If it glows a bit brighter when it moves over an important object, it's not intrusive, and the player accepts it. Think of it as a visual representation of instinct or experience in the game world, depending on who the player-character is. If the PC is the member of a SWAT team, experience would tell them which objects in a room would be more important than the others. If the PC is one of Alfred Hitchcock's innocents on the run, then it is the survival instinct, or senses heightened by fear, whatever we need.

All this additional detail means that something has to give. In the case of action games, we limit the world. The player does not have free access to the entire city of New York in an action game set there. Not every floor of every high rise will be accessible and loaded with gameplay. We pare back scope just as we do in television and movies. The only medium that allows us the entire universe and all of its inhabitants is prose. But even there, novelists are constantly making choices of where to cut back. At least for them, the reason is not budgetary but focusing and heightening the drama.

It's also worth considering the moral and ethical issues that are raised. I'm not talking now about the explicitness of the violence in the game or sexual content. I'm talking about the choices we are giving the player. In the section on adaptations from other media in Chapter 7, we talked about making sure to stay true to the morality—or lack of it—of the adapted characters. In Chapter 13, "The Roots of a New Storytelling," we discussed using branching to introduce ethical choices. These are specific issues we address as we write and design. But in a game world where almost anything can be destroyed, we're backing away from making the decisions, and leaving them entirely in the hands of the players.

Should players be able to gun down or run down innocents in the street? No. Never. This creates a serious dilemma for storytellers. One solution might be the smart cursor approach. Just as we alter the targeting crosshairs to point out important objects, we might disable them entirely when passing over an innocent NPC. This keeps a character "good," but at the expense of the very shooting range challenge designers are trying to emulate.

We may not care if players think we're condoning such activity. I hope we do. And if we do care, then there must be consequences for players who recklessly take or endanger life in the game world. The best place for those consequences? Address them within the fiction of the game. It is a thematic solution. It doesn't break the fourth wall. It gives us another opportunity for storytelling and character revelation.

There's another moral issue: the killing of other human beings. For decades, the *Star Trek* franchise has been accused of xenophobia. The good characters are all human or at least humanoid with recognizable human values. The bad characters are often heartless humanoid aliens like the Romulans, or outright nasty non-humanoids like the pool of tar that ate Tasha Yar. Gene Roddenberry vigorously fought this sentiment. Over the course of the series, more benign aliens were discovered, and more humans turned murderous for balance.

Movies and television can easily accommodate the slaughter of human beings by other human beings for one major reason. The audience isn't doing the slaughtering. In games, the player pulls the trigger. To avoid dealing with the moral issues this raises, we have several fallback positions.

- **The *Star Trek* solution.** Nobody cares if you're blowing away slimy creatures with five eyes.

- **The historical solution.** Nobody cares if you're defending democracy from Nazis. You must be careful of race, of course. In World War II combat games, you can kill Japanese soldiers. Today they are our allies. I can't imagine any mainstream developer creating a game that pitted real-world races against one another in violent conflict.

- **The foreign nationals solution.** Nobody cares if you're taking down armed hostiles from a nation bent on the destruction of your own country.

- **The generalized terrorist solution.** Nobody cares if you're terminating with extreme prejudice terrorists who owe no national allegiances, if you avoid references to religion.

- **The generalized criminal solution.** Criminals are bad guys. They deserve punishment as long as the punishment fits the crime. Slaughtering shoplifters in a department store might raise some eyebrows. *Grand Theft Auto: Vice City* was dealing with criminal gangs modeled on reality. Despite the protests, there's no evidence that the developers were trying to say all Haitians are criminals any more than a theme of *The Sopranos* was that all Italians are in the Mafia.

- **The mindless evil solution.** It doesn't matter who the antagonist is if they are hellbent on destroying all the good things in life like children playing; butterflies flitting; lovers walking hand-in-hand on a sunny day in the park. I feel like I'm going to break into song… it's okay. Luckily, the urge passed. Of course, the mindless evil solution also pertains to all of the antagonist's minions if they remain indistinguishable from one another, spawning as needed like ants from an anthill you've poked with a stick. If they *are* distinguishable, all the better. Yet another opportunity for us to write zealots, traitors, weaklings, snitches; adversaries who are honorable, greedy, clever, stupid, sentimental, humorous, long-winded….

- **The fantasy solution.** *Disney's Toontown Online*, an MMO for kids and families ran from 2003 to 2013. It allowed players to cause the bad guys, humorless robotic cogs, to break down, by using gags (jokes) for weapons. In virtual worlds, races become things like elves or Wookies. If there is PvP combat, players can play different races that are at odds with each other and kill each other. It's an interesting dynamic we'll look at in Chapter 17. For the record in June of 2021 the game was resurrected by fans as *Toontown Unwritten*.

Action games require pace, more so than any other type. As in action movies, we must keep our dialogue and stories lean. Robert Ludlum had 900 pages in which to tell his stories. With a couple of exceptions, the plots were so convoluted that they did not translate well to movies, let alone games.

We don't have 900 pages. We don't want them. Every time we brake for exposition, we interrupt the race to the climax. That doesn't mean we have no twists. Surprise is an important part of storytelling. But we make it easy on ourselves as writers by creating twists that explain themselves even as they occur, rather than requiring elaborate explanations. Here is an example:

Mission briefing for Bitsy Boom, crack NSC agent: the player-character is told by her superior that there's a traitor in the NSC. There are three suspects. She'll have to storm an enemy safehouse to get the truth. Her superior gives her the escape plan to use once her mission is complete.

- Twist #1: A guard looks at her ID and lets her pass an early checkpoint (exposition in action).

- Twist #2: A higher level spy shakes her hand, believing she is the enemy's inside contact (Twist #1 explained in action).

- Twist #3: Bitsy is assigned to hunt down the spy that has infiltrated the safehouse. (We already know Bitsy has been asked to hunt down herself.)

- Twist #4: Bitsy is contacted by her superior and told the three suspects are all dead. She must abort her mission before the enemy realizes their mistake (brief exposition).

- Twist #5: Her cover is immediately blown. Everybody's gunning for her (exposition in action).

- Twist #6: Bitsy overhears the safehouse boss getting instructions. The real traitor is still alive (exposition in action).

- Twist #7: Bitsy finds bad guys waiting along her secret escape route, kills the safehouse boss, and automatically loots a significant clue from his body (exposition in action).

- Twist #8: Bitsy escapes only to find herself under arrest by her fellow agents. She's accused of being the traitor (exposition in action).

- Twist #9: Bitsy confronts her superior with the clue. He was the spy after all. (Brief exposition ties clue to superior.)

- Twist #10: Bitsy's superior escapes and swears revenge (exposition in action and beginning of transition to next mission).

That's ten twists in the simple linear storyline of a single mission. None of the twists requires more than a sentence or two of exposition at the worst, and some are instantaneous. All should heighten the player's interest, yet none are so complex as to baffle the player. There is a very clear through line.

One of the conventions used in balancing an action game is that health is often automagically restored. If the player can find enough health packs or bandages or healing plants or whatever the game world's fiction allows, their effect is nothing short of miraculous. The bad guys can spawn as many of their number as necessary to create the necessary challenge in each level. The player is stuck with the PC and counters like health points and lives. We discussed the death of the player-character in Chapter 4, "Character Roles." This instantaneous health thing, though, is also a bother. It is a purely game solution to game balance that does not take story and character into account.

Like alternatives to player death, one solution doesn't appear to fit all unless it is stated as simply as: make it true to the game fiction. In a science-fiction or fantasy setting, such miracles may find justification. In a game set in the present day focusing on stopping Columbian drug runners both in the U.S. and on their own turf, if we want to preserve as much of the fourth wall as possible, it's much better to place things like health in context.

A more realistic metaphor is the number and severity of wounds. Bandages staunch the bleeding, but a counter is activated, increasing the suspense. If the player doesn't complete the mission in a certain amount of time, the wounds become debilitating, and the mission fails. Miraculous recovery can then occur *outside* of the game world.

Again, it's all about balance. If the player heedlessly rounds a corner and comes face to face with the muzzle of a Kalashnikov, whatever happens next to the PC is deserved. If we go for suspense instead of shock, we can warn the player that there is a hostile around the next corner. We can give the PC the ability to peek or provide a security mirror or sound effects.

Usually, there is no explanation whatsoever as to why hallways are littered with such items. Yet it is a simple matter to place them in context when the scene is set for a mission. The level is the scene of an earlier failed firefight. Bodies and weapons are still strewn about. The level is a warehouse where military supplies are stored. An earlier operative has planted the necessary tools here and there. These might be stashed in specially marked containers among similar containers that belong in the location. Scooping them up on the move is still permitted.

The *Half-Life* series was groundbreaking in its painstaking efforts to keep such conventions grounded in reality. The use of the biohazard suit gave the player-character a shell that had to be recharged, the equivalent of regaining health and armor. Weapons and ammo were found in supply cabinets. This attention to the reality of the experience is stunning in *Call of Duty: Vanguard*, released in November 2021, where it's possible to break through destructible obstacles and fire blindly without targeting. When the effort is taken to place such activities in the context of the narrative's fiction, we all win. The game mechanics no longer fight against the storytelling; they are part of it. But… but Zombies in *Call of Duty: Vanguard*? Really?

Shooter and stealther action games can take a couple of different forms: solo games for a single player-character and squad-level games where the player either controls several characters or the computer controls them. Most of what we've been focusing on so far are solo games. Squad-level games where the computer is in control of team members allow greater chances for storytelling and character because of the additional interaction.

The player has their own Greek chorus tagging along to comment on the action; create relationships with the PC for the purposes of generating emotion; and offering updates to mission briefs, opinions, and jokes. We can create an emotional attachment between any PC and NPC. If we're told we must free hostages, we can give them context that is emotionally charged like recognizable human plights: they've been tortured, or their families were victims of genocide; they are elderly or children. There are lots of buttons to press, but the relationship remains static. When the NPCs are squad members, the relationships are continuing and can ebb and flow.

Once we've rescued hostages, we may still need to get them to safety, triggering an escort quest where the NPCs become unofficial team members, and possibly can now be directed. And, of course, they are all available for exposition, complaints, heroics, and humor.

Action games aren't all shooters or stealthers. Traditional sports games rely on the game itself for their storytelling. This isn't a rule carved on a stone tablet. It is a convention. A story involving a sports team is very viable, if players indicate interest. The same holds true for racing games and extreme sports.

There are as many solutions as our imaginations allow. Too often, if it fixes our gameplay problem, we stop there. The key is to think about a story context, as well as a game context, for our game design issues. Once a solution fits into the game world and is consistent with the fiction of the world, the problem is truly solved for both parts of the entertainment equation.

ADVENTURE

Even if you couldn't already tell, it should come as no surprise that my first games were adventure games. When I entered the industry in 1994, adventure games were where you wanted to be if you were interested in story and character. Role-playing games caught up with them first, then action games, and finally, strategy games. But by their very nature adventure games ruled the roost.

There are a lot of theories as to why adventure games plummeted in popularity. To a certain extent, all of them are true.

- **Developers of adventure games grew complacent, and our games stagnated.** Puzzles were the chief obstacle, and their nature rarely changed. Monotony is not a primary goal of entertainment.

- **Failed experiments in FMV limited the flexibility of our gameplay.** The quality of the FMV was far below the standards of Hollywood production, even when Hollywood got involved.

- **Improved graphics gave *Myst* and adventure games in general a new lease on life.** People wanted something to show off their new video cards. But as graphics chips added memory and CPUs became faster, adventure games did not look so good when placed alongside action games.

- **The demographics of the marketplace and our gaming culture changed.** The first kids' games were adventures or interactive picture books. Soon the early kids' games were also action games. As they grew older, many players weren't interested in slowing down their entertainment.

- **The fortunes of adventure games were tied to the personal computer, and for many gamers, the computer is not the machine of choice at the moment.** Consoles reign.

- **The industry is cyclical.** RPGs were once dead, buried beneath thick manuals, and far more options than the average player could ever hope to learn or care to use. Then *Diablo* revived them with its RPG-lite style of play. Strategy games were on the outs until real-time strategy games like *Warcraft* and *Command and Conquer* appeared. Again, simplicity was in. Adventure games were never sold as simple games. Theirs was the challenge of the crossword and the chessboard.

In the last edition of this book I wrote, "Pure adventure games are currently a small niche, but they aren't dead." Today they are far from dead. You won't see as many on the major consoles, but we can find them for your cellphone, tablet, computer, and the Nintendo Switch. One of the games I wrote for recently that I'm most proud of is *The Lion's Song*, an adventure game. The game I'm currently working on is an adventure game. Many of the games I've cited in this book are adventure games. I hope I'll always be able to say that.

Let's look at challenges unique to adventure games. We find puzzles in all types of games these days, but they remain at the core of adventure games. For that reason, more care should be taken in: (1) treating them like dramatic obstacles, and therefore opportunities for story advancement and character revelation; (2) making them logical within the fiction of the game world; and (3) keeping them thematically consistent throughout a game.

Adventure games give us the chance to construct more interesting puzzles than simple "find the key" exercises. The players have the time to appreciate them. Let's look at time for a moment. We have four kinds of timers at our disposal in game design.

- **First is *real* real time.** The player is sitting at their computer, and the clock on the wall is ticking. Few games use this timer. Virtual worlds occasionally do.

- **Second is game time.** The player-character is within the game world, and a clock in the game engine is ticking. If a shooter or strategy game measures the passing of time, this is the timer they use.

- **Third is event time.** The player-character is within the game world, and there is the *illusion* that a real clock is ticking. Events are actually in control of the passage of time. The player may be given a limited amount of time to finish a mission, but in fact, may have as much time as they need. Or the clock may only advance as the player does. To create suspense in an early game I used Event Time. The player-character finds themselves locked in a trunk and dumped into the middle of a lake. Every time the player completed one step of several in the necessary escape sequence, the level of water in the trunk rose, increasing the tension. The last step in the escape could only occur once the trunk was completely filled with water and the player-character was holding their breath. Yet they would never drown. Event Time can be used to create the illusion that the NPCs are going on with their lives even if the player-character is not present. It will appear as if it is just a lucky break that the PC seems to arrive at the most dramatic moments.

- **Fourth is turn-based.** The game *explicitly* doesn't advance until the player completes their move. All strategy games used to be built as turn-based. *Civilization* is a good example. Action games are usually "real-time." Adventure games are often turn-based to give the player time to think.

Turn-based and event time give adventure game writers an added opportunity to tell their story and reveal character. The game convention allows the player to sit there if they want, mulling over an obstacle. Designers occasionally add game time puzzles, but they remain unpopular with players. There are times when adventure gamers do not want to be rushed.

Another challenge is the same as action games, but different. That's pace. In action games, we don't want to interrupt the pace. In adventure games, the pace must lag to give us time to think and solve puzzles. Adventures allow for far more flexibility in game engine storytelling because of the changes in pace built into their design.

Writing an action/adventure hybrid? Adjust the pace to the gameplay. Allow time for thought, to solve a puzzle, or even if it's just prep for a battle. Games can give the player time to prepare for battle by pre-programming moves when they see a firefight up ahead as in 2016's turn-based strategy game, *X-Com 2*, then watch as the action plays out on its own. Or the game can surprise the player with a surprise attack when they least expect it, giving them just enough time to select a weapon if they're lucky. Remember as you write and design that you may be appealing to two very different sets of players: fighters and puzzle-solvers. You cannot afford to alienate either group. Some games will offer the player a choice between the two at the beginning of the game by offering different difficulty settings and puzzle solutions.

How can we create pace in an adventure game? By varying the difficulty of puzzles. Start out with simple puzzles to settle the player into the game and then increase the challenge. Then when the game is approaching the climax, simplify once more. Not only does this increase pace, but the player also will think the game has made them smarter. This is not a bad thing. It will look good in the advertisements: "Our game will increase your I.Q.!" It's certainly every bit as true as announcing that the game will put you in the middle of a movie.

Another way to create pace is by narrowing the world. Adventure game worlds are like action game worlds: subsets of the real world. *And Then There Were None* takes place on a lonely island of the coast of Devon. *Murder on the Orient Express* is set for the most part on a snowbound train. In *Evil under the Sun*, we return to a different island off the Devon coast. All are confined arenas (Figure 15.1).

Because adventure gamers don't require that every bottle on a bar be destroyable, attention can be paid to those elements of areas that are directly connected to plot and gameplay. This focus is of great benefit to the storytelling and presenting the theme. And this allows us to expand the world a bit more. Adventure games adapt well to the modular story structure. Then as story threads are tied off, the size of the world can shrink, to compel a faster race to the finish.

FIGURE 15.1   *Evil under the Sun*: Hercule Poirot works on his suntan.

In *Dark Side of the Moon*, we had a perfect context for narrowing the world during the course of the game. The moon was becoming unstable and was going to explode. Earthquakes shook the mining colony. Shafts caved in. Passages players once explored were blocked. In the final rush to escape the moon, there was only one route open to the PC, Jake. This kind of situation is like all those action movies that are structured the same way. Movies don't like to give their characters multiple ways to escape from danger. That leads to discussing options, not action. Give them one option, make it seem impossible, and then force them into it. That's how movies increase suspense and pace. Adventure games can do the same thing. (So can action games, of course; the need simply isn't as great. The pace of the game is already there.)

Narrowing the world need not necessarily mean only its geography. Another related way to increase pace is to reduce the number of tasks to be performed; the number of characters to interact with; or the player-character's inventory.

A villain emptied Ripley's inventory near the end of *The Riddle of Master Lu* as a third act reversal. I broke my own rules by allowing the actions of an NPC in the world of the game to break the fourth wall when the villain bent over a fallen Ripley, and as he rifled his pockets, the player saw the inventory display on the interface vanish item by item. My reasoning went like this: it was a third act reversal scene we've watched over and over again in movies and television, and I wanted to spoof that. Also, the game convention of inventory was directly related to possessions, so theoretically anyway, a villain in the game world should have access to the PC's possessions. And finally, by the end of an adventure game, the player usually has a huge puzzle-solving arsenal at their disposal in inventory. I wanted the player to start from scratch for the endgame.

Adventure games have always had more opportunities to tell the story built into them than any other type of game. This has given adventures an advantage over other types of games in thought-provoking themes and rich characters for years. This has now changed. Today all types of games introduce the player to thought-provoking themes and vivid characters. All it takes is the will and the craft to do it.

MULTIPLAYER

Esports like MOBAs feature player versus player (PvP) tournaments for significant cash prizes. PvP games like these are outside the scope of this book. However, many action games, strategy games, and

> MOBA: multiplayer online battle arena.

RPGs feature PvP gameplay. Virtual worlds belong on this list as well, but their differences are significant enough to warrant a couple of chapters on their own.

The only multiplayer type of game that really interests us as writers here is cooperative multiplayer where two to four players share a console, or two and up play over a network or online for fun, not cash prizes. PvP here pretty much eliminates the need for story, even when played in the world of a non-PvP world. The game that sports a PvP version of its single-player world will feature that same world, but it becomes little more than a backdrop. In cooperative multiplayer games the players work together. Computer-controlled team members are routinely replaced with human beings, although this doesn't need to be the case. There's no rule that says you can't have both. There's no rule you cannot have story either.

Cooperative players can experience any encounters or plot twists together. An interesting variation allows players to separate. On consoles, the screen must be split, and therefore both players can experience firsthand what one is doing. Over a network connection or the Internet, players can retain full screen. This is much more "realistic" because players must communicate their adventures to one another.

Once cooperative players can split up, the storytelling becomes a greater challenge, but the rewards are commensurate. Players can immerse themselves more easily, relaying information, or calling for help. The story can be made up of areas and incidents that can be played separately or together with differing results. Players may encounter the same NPCs at different times and form dissimilar relationships with them.

Whether the stories are linear, branching, Web, or modular doesn't really matter. Diverging gameplay allows us to explore alternatives; come at obstacles from different sides; and experience many more variations on single-player play. It promotes more socializing—and remains fertile ground for storytelling between the game and the players and between the players themselves. "Did you explore the old mill yet?" "Hey, the grocer in town has a sale right now on grilled thief fingers. They'll open almost any door!"

MODS

Mods can be found in any of the preceding game types: action, adventure, role-playing, and strategy. Theirs is a unique place in the games industry because they can be produced by players and fans of a commercial game as well as by its original developers.

Many games allow modding these days, including everything from *Minecraft* (obviously!), *The Elder Scrolls: Skyrim* (a real blessing while we wait for a sequel!), *Stardew Valley*, *The Witcher 3: Wild Hunt*, *Grand Theft Auto V*, *Civilization V*, *Fallout: Las Vegas*, and even *Doom*. These games all allow players to design their own takes on those worlds with their own stories, many of which are also multiplayer.

Building a new level for a successful commercial game, or an entirely new game, with assets provided by the developer, has become an excellent way for

> Mod: short for modification. A verb meaning to create new content from an existing commercial game by programming, or by using software provided by the developer. A noun used to describe the result, which still requires the original game software to run.

budding young game writers and designers to show what they can do. Modding software now ships with many game titles and is often very easy to use. Much modding software consists of drag-and-drop menus supported by a scripting language, which is much easier to use than a hard-core programming language like C++.

Companies benefit in two ways: they might have the makings of a successful expansion pack, sequel, or franchise dropped into their laps. Mods are also great audition pieces for future employees. For example, Bioware asks writers to use the company's modding software to create a level or piece of a game. This allows them to test not only the writer's ability to write dialogue and descriptive prose, but also the equally important skill of understanding game logic. Many famous novelists and screenwriters have crashed and burned on the beaches of the game industry because they couldn't grasp how to tell their stories to an active player with a voice in the narrative structure.

Some of my colleagues insist that a game designer must be a programmer, but I disagree. It's easy for me to disagree. I don't code. But I do understand game logic, and my design documents and scripts often use the most basic terminology: IF, ELSE, THEN, etc. Potential, future top-ranked game designers, and especially future top-ranked game writers, are out there right now modding, and they will be able to prove their worth to a sometimes reluctant industry through the results of their labors.

ROLE-PLAYING

Just as weapons and ammo litter hallways in shooters, treasure boxes have been left lying around by careless mobs in many dungeons. It's one of those conventions copied, but not thought about very much. As in shooters, simply finding a reason for the litter is sometimes all that is necessary. The game mechanic may remain the same: click on the box, and it opens. Either the contents go directly into inventory, or the player can choose which items to take. But answering the design question without addressing the fiction of the game world is to needlessly treat the storytelling as a second-class citizen.

Character exposition in computer RPGs started as simply the stats and abilities the player-character or other party members were granted. The advantage of strength a warrior enjoyed over a wizard, or the ability the wizard had to cast spells that the warrior lacked, were the only differences in character. This is a direct result of the development of RPGs from tabletop games where it was the players who gave their characters personality and dialogue.

Over time, however, RPGs began adding more typical character traits. In contrast to RPG-lite games like *Diablo*, three RPG franchises embody for me the current state of affairs in RPG character development beyond stats and abilities: *The Legend of Zelda: Breath of the Wild* from Nintendo, *Dragons Age* from Bioware, and *Elder Scrolls* from Bethesda. Ken Rolston, designer of *Elder Scrolls III: Morrowind (2002)* and *Elder Scrolls IV: Oblivion* (2007), describes how to reveal character through environment.

"To have weight, a primary character requires exposition. Obvious methods of exposition, like dialogue, are perceived and resented by the player as awkward and manipulative. Dialogue, in particular, appears awkward and manipulative because it is, in a game, so far inferior in flavor and freedom to its real-world counterpart.

Visual cues to character are discovered by the player through the player's free and unconstrained exploration and observation, and, as such, are more subtle, less awkward and obtrusive, and more unconsciously acceptable in shaping the player's response to the character.

Caius Cosades is the player's first and most important informant and patron in *Morrowind*. He is a spymaster, an agent of the Empire and Emperor, and your primary quest giver (Figure 15.2).

Three visual details define Caius Cosades: his bare chest, the skooma pipe beneath his bed, and the book he is reading.

FIGURE 15.2 Caius Cosades from *Elder Scrolls III: Morrowind*.

Caius Cosades is the only character in *Morrowind* with a bare chest. He is an old man, which makes his bare chest seem more peculiar. And it is a strongly muscled chest, which is even more peculiar. He will be your boss. He is an old, creepy guy who lives in one room, but he looks like an old creepy guy who could kick your ass.

The skooma pipe openly visible beneath his bed reveals that Caius Cosades is a drug addict. A spymaster who is a drug addict? That does not inspire our confidence in his judgment as our spymaster.

The book *The War of the First Council* is an historical summary of the political and religious conflicts of *Morrowind*'s major factions, presented in the voice of a serious and reflective Imperial scholar. The old man is a creepy crack addict, but his bedtime reading is serious history.

Thus, by looking at Caius and exploring the items by his bed, we get the impression that Caius Cosades is an eccentric, creepy old man, with a disordered but fundamentally earnest and serious mind.

At first, we have a strong emotional reaction to what we see. The bare chest is odd, vaguely sexual, and repellent in an old man. The skooma pipe is worrying—I'm taking orders from a drug addict?

But the book tempers our uneasy response with a reflection of Caius's mind—a serious mind studying the exotic culture of the foreign country of his posting.

Thus, we begin our relationship with a strong, at best ambivalent, emotional response to Caius Cosades, tempered by an intriguing hint of his mind's inner workings.

These are the features I'm proud of in his exposition.

On the other hand, I'm sorry we didn't take the same care with the other 3,000 characters in *Morrowind*. If we had, we would have rewarded the inquisitive and observant player every time he encountered a new character, and would have taught him to explore and savor their intriguing personalities—before he killed them and went through their pockets."

RPGs were the second type of game after adventures to embrace storytelling. As in the case of RPG characters, RPG storylines matured to fill the gap left by the lack of a human Game Master. In tabletop role-playing, just as players bring their characters to life, it is the job of the Game Master to bring the world and the story to life.

RPGs are perfect for storytelling. In them, the story is authored just as it was when it was written by the GM. The difference is that the GM could react to the gameplay on the fly and adjust to player input like the parent who shifts gears as necessary while telling a bedtime story to a child who bombards them with questions. In single-player RPGs, players don't demand such flexibility (although they do in virtual worlds, as we shall see). This gives writers of solo RPGs the freedom to create elaborate worlds full of interesting characters and thrilling adventures.

There is a trade-off, however. RPGs today are not limited too much by geography. There are entire worlds that will take hour upon hour to explore. Some areas of the world that players would normally be able to visit often do not show up on the map until certain conditions are met. This allows the writers to advance the story in a linear fashion, while the gameplay permits players to roam freely within revealed areas.

Other games open their worlds, but restrict player access by making the challenges in certain regions far too dangerous for low-level player-characters. As players gain in skills and abilities, they can survive these more advanced areas. This recognition of level is used in character encounters as well where NPCs carrying high-level functions in the world can refuse to deal with player-characters until they are stronger.

Such methods are gameplay solutions only thinly disguised as belonging to the world fiction. It is because they can allow open-ended exploration that RPGs have attracted me in recent years as a perfect opportunity for modular storytelling. In fact, the *Might and Magic* RPG series used a simple modular structure for many of the quests. To fill out the world, quests were added that did not advance the story, only the player-character by providing experience points (XP) and items. These quests may have been consistent with the world fiction, but because they were not tied to the narrative, there were no variables that needed to be tracked. So, while the basic structure was there, the designers did not take advantage of all those quests to advance the narrative as true modular storytelling would have allowed.

Because RPGs track so many stats, the stats themselves can be used in storytelling. We've talked about how relationships with NPCs can be affected by player actions in several ways. They can also be affected by player stats. The first time a player-character enters a village, they may be low-level, unskilled, and dressed in cast-off leather. Villagers can treat them with disdain. Perhaps a kindly cleric has sympathy for them and sends them off to do some errands. Later the same player-character, now battle-hardened and wearing shining mail may return. Now they are respected.

Hopefully, the villagers they interacted with at the lower level remember them and are quick to apologize for their earlier behavior. The cleric may react with pride, and now humbly ask if the PC can undertake a much more important mission. The relationships can be further affected by how the player decides to respond to this new state of affairs. They might bully merchants into reducing their prices or shrug off the cleric's entreaty. Or they could find forgiveness for their past behavior and be offered lower prices. Doing the good deed for the cleric could result in no monetary reward but a blessing that increases their odds of surviving. Even though stats are a game mechanic, they can support storytelling, given a chance.

SIMULATIONS

We are going to look at two types of simulations. Combat simulations focus on military equipment, such as planes, helicopters, and tanks. Social simulations focus on social systems, such as families, cities, and industries.

Whereas action games run the risk of alienating players if they cast them as crack pilots and then allow them to crash repeatedly, players of combat simulations accept the challenge. Where action games simplify controls as much as possible yet still try to maintain verisimilitude, simulations take pride in accurately modeling controls, maneuverability, and physics. If a simulation features an Abrams tank, the tank had better look and act like one, or the simulation player will be up in arms.

Combat simulations have become another niche market like adventure games, supplanted by combat in action games. As the games industry has grown, more players are attracted to the razzle-dazzle than the finely detailed environments of simulations. Racing games in particular take great pains to keep controls simple whether the player is at the wheel of a Ferrari, straddling a Harley, or balancing on a skateboard. These more freewheeling action games recognize that their younger demographic wants to be able to do cool things they may not be able to do in real life. Simulations can appeal to an older demographic who takes pride in the mastery of the simulation.

In recent years, simulations have added story, but they face a couple of challenges unique to their game type.

- **First, they are only borderline games anyway.** They must be far more aware of real-world details, even at the expense of action.

- **Secondly, they have difficulty inserting story into the simulation because it can distract from operating controls.** If there are plot moves, they are brief and to the point: a comrade is in trouble; mission parameters abruptly change due to increased numbers of hostiles; new information, not available at the mission briefing, is suddenly communicated to the player.

As a result, if there is any storytelling to be done, it is limited. Some may not even attempt to tell a story from mission to mission in any other terms than a campaign such as the Battle of the Bulge or rescue missions during a natural disaster.

In no other game type do story and "gameplay" feel more at odds than these kinds of simulations. It isn't impossible, but writers need to recognize the rigid limitations of the form. As soon as a simulation begins to concentrate on story, it almost invariably becomes an action game. Today, simulations are mostly developed for educational purposes. Even then educational simulations, very aware that they are teaching tools, may still place their lessons in a dramatic context to better engage the student.

The second type of simulation holds more promise for storytelling, yet ironically its most successful example leaves all the storytelling up to the interaction between game and player. The standard-bearer of this type is the *Sims* franchise. *Sims* adventures would seem a natural next step.

These are social simulations like *Rollercoaster Tycoon Adventures* (2018), *Zoo Tycoon Ultimate Animal Collection* (2017), and even *Game Dev Tycoon* (2020) usually set in interesting and visually exciting industries, such as theme parks and transportation (wait, how did video games get in there?). All such arenas are as ripe for storytelling as they are in other media. Here story can be tied to the fortunes of the player the way they are in RPGs. As the player advances by mastering the simulation, story twists like natural disasters and computer-controlled rivals are obvious. Even *Sim City* added tornadoes and fires to spice up play.

Taking such incidents to the next stage and building an entire story on player advancement makes perfect sense. It is, in fact, the area I've looked at most when my mind turns to chaos theory and fractals. You skipped over that section? Shame on you! Seeding story in social situations is as obvious to me as it is in psychology when researchers confront participants with variables. "What if?" they ask. There are sociologists who deliberately break *Star Trek*'s Prime Directive when modeling cultures to see how they will respond. They are seeding stories the way we seed fractals. Okay, enough about fractals. Let's move on to the next section.

STRATEGY

Strategy games, like all types of games we've discussed here except adventures, did not start out telling stories. They began by presenting players with a broad canvas in contrast to simulation's detailed models. Over time, as action games and simulations began to place their missions in context, strategy games like *X-Com* did the same in 1994.

Civilization (1991), arguably one of the very few games that will stand the test of time and be seen as a classic, presented a diversity of turn-based gameplay that took players from a single wandering tribe to the establishment of a colony on a planet circling Alpha Centauri generations later. It needed no more story than that. Characters were either units or opposing rulers controlled by the computer. This formula has worked well through many sequels including *Civilization VI: Gathering Storm* that in 2019 included the effects of climate change.

The difficulty in integrating story into gameplay in strategy games is the omniscient POV they require. Strategy players need to see as much of the geography as possible. 1998's *Starcraft* balanced its "unit view" somewhat with large-sized character profiles that talked. In 2010, *Starcraft II: Wings of Liberty* reimagined the world of the original, adding new features, and (gasp!) more storytelling. It was a hit with a Metacritic aggregate score of 93. It became the fastest selling RTS of all time.

It's good to remember that stories are not tied to the medium. They can be *shaped* by a particular medium, but they require little more than the ability of the storyteller to touch the imaginations of the audience. That hunter spinning yarns by the fire, or a grandparent telling a story to a sleepy child, are not relying on pictures to advance the story. They aren't necessary. The tribe's artist may have painted the story of a hunt on the wall of the cave, but words came first, not graphics. (The most famous cave paintings in the world were found in France, also home to some of our most celebrated artists. I wonder if there's a connection.)

If the story is compelling enough, the characters involved in it can be the size of ants. They can come alive as characters if we allow them to. Must every unit in a strategy game be treated so well? Of course not. Not every one of the thousands of slaves in *Spartacus* gets dialogue, only the stars like Kirk Douglas and Tony Curtis. But any slave could have a three-dimensional character and a story to tell in the strategy game version of *Spartacus*. We, the writers, get to decide which ones get to step forward and claim to be Spartacus.

Strategy games may not appear to lend themselves as readily to narrative as action, adventure, and role-playing games, but there are still avenues to be explored, just as there are in social simulations. All it takes is a designer willing to try and a receptive audience.

CHAPTER 16

Game Genres

IN THIS CHAPTER, WE'RE going to examine various genres and how well they map to games; to which types of games they are best suited; and which challenges each one presents to the writer. There are hybrids, of course, that contain elements from more than one genre. The *Resident Evil* and *Silent Hill* game series take horror conventions and mix them with science fiction, post-apocalyptic science fiction, and even an extreme kind of tough-love psychotherapy.

This is not meant to be an all-inclusive list. Comedy has been with us since the beginning of this book, and hopefully it hasn't all been unintentional. In particular, we looked at various styles of comedy in games in Chapter 11, "Story Anatomy." The genres that remain are heavily weighted toward *melodrama*.

MELODRAMA

Let's start with a couple of definitions.

Ick. Here's another.

Hmm. Not so bad.

Melodrama is a term I've deliberately avoided up till now, mainly because it suggests a low-grade type of entertainment, and I didn't want to confuse the issue by defending it. If I were to admit up front that most of what we do is melodrama, it might have seemed as if I were saying it's okay to go for the lowest common denominator. Saying "It's just melodrama," is as bad as saying, "It's only a game." We do not deserve to be let off the hook so easily (Figure 16.1).

> Melodrama: a dramatic form that depends on sensation, simplistic plotting, stereotypical characters, coincidence, implausibility, and artificially happy endings.

> Melodrama: a dramatic form that focuses on action, clear plotlines, characters who personify good and evil, plot twists, and morally unambiguous resolutions.

Which is the true definition? Both are, of course. Or the answer lies somewhere in between. A discussion pitting melodrama and drama against one another—Drama good! Melodrama bad!—is as pointless to me as one pitting story and gameplay against one another.

DOI: 10.1201/9780429284991-21

"Lucy! tell me that this man is a madman!"

FIGURE 16.1 Melodrama is not the dirty word some think it is.

Now that you understand the importance of three-dimensional characters, and the care with which stories should be constructed, you're ready to handle the monkey wrench melodrama tosses into the works. Let's bring melodrama out on stage and have a look at it.

The word *melodrama* began life as a description for musical theater. In the 19th century, it attached itself to florid dramas where characters were starkly contrasted and broadly written as either virtuous and good or dastardly evil. The plots were simple, and the acting style over-the-top. The critics twirled their mustaches and sneered at melodrama. Society matrons turned up their noses at it. Common folk lapped it up.

Those last three sentences are melodrama. In fact, most of the entertainment in any medium is melodrama. The pit at the Globe Theatre was home to common folk, and Shakespeare wrote to them as much as he did to the aristocracy in their balconies. Almost all film and television entertainment is melodrama. Drama is still found on the stage, one of the reasons certain plays perform wonderfully in London's West End or on Broadway and then fail when they go on tour. With a rare exception, the *New York Times* fiction bestseller list is a list of melodramatic novels. Today the pit is the mass market, not the aristocracy. If you want to sell big, sell to the pit.

The difference between drama and melodrama to me is in the quality of the execution. Two more definitions illustrate this.

We recognize 19th-century melodrama today as being packed with bathos. And it certainly shows up in popular media where a failure to establish an audience's empathy in characters leads to irritation, not compassion. However, if we can craft characters the audience identifies with and cares about; if we write such scenes with some restraint and sensibility, we can achieve pathos in either drama or melodrama.

> Pathos: a dramatic quality that evokes sympathy, pity, or sorrow. Bathos: a dramatic quality that attempts to evoke sympathy, pity, or sorrow, but fails, often arousing laughter instead of tears.

The lines are blurred, and it is to our benefit to blur them. It may help critics and college professors to draw rigid distinctions, but it doesn't serve writers well. Just as it is counterproductive to analyze to the point where we lose sight of the whole experience, or dangerous to rely on lists without history and context, trying to find the lines of demarcation between drama and melodrama only serves to cut off useful aspects that are applicable to both.

Remember William Archer unapologetically defending drama in Chapter 9, "Bringing the Story to Life"?

> It may be thought a point of inferiority in dramatic art that it should deal so largely in shocks to the nerves, and should appeal by preference, wherever it is reasonably possible, to the cheap emotions of curiosity and surprise. But this is a criticism, not of dramatic art, but of human nature.

Is he yelling at the common folk down in the pit? He wouldn't be that silly. No actor ever won an argument with the pit. Don Rickles, the famous comedian of insults known as "Mr. Warmth" and "The Merchant of Venom," was attacked more than once by audience members over his nearly fifty-year career. The pen may be mightier than the sword, but the fist can often end the joke. What is it called? Ah yes: the punch line.

Archer, writing in 1912, is able to defend drama even as he derides melodrama elsewhere in *Playmaking*, because he sees what the two share in common, yet appreciates the difference in execution. It's *all* in the execution.

Bathos, one-dimensional characters, implausibility, and artificial story construction don't belong in today's melodrama any more than they do in drama. That they crop up all the time is a testament to bad writing, directing, acting, or any combination of those. No one denies that melodrama goes for the throat, yet it can do so with some grace and style, and when it does, the audience welcomes it with a willing suspension of disbelief. A third definition of melodrama would incorporate its heightened drama, but at the same time allow for its human drama as well. I write melodrama. We all do. To do it well is the key.

As I said, almost all the genres that follow are home to melodrama as much as drama. Comedy appears to be the only exception. It has its own versions of melodrama in farce, slapstick, and burlesque. A classic moment in both a murder mystery and a farce is the flinging open of a closet door. In a mystery, a dead body falls out. In a farce, the body is alive and dressed only in underwear.

What are the most popular genres in games? Fantasy and science fiction. Why? The reasons aren't hard to find.

- The roots of many of the first games came from these genres: tabletop games like *Dungeons & Dragons* and films like *Star Wars* were popular at the beginning of the personal computer revolution.

- The audience is no longer as overwhelmingly young and male as it used to be, but a transition to more diversified studios building games remains an ongoing struggle.

- They are overwhelmingly the genres of preference for many game developers attracted by technology, interactivity, and the possibility of creating anything our imaginations can conjure.

There are a couple of more craft-oriented reasons why developers are more comfortable with fantasy and science fiction.

- Fantasy and sci-fi allow us a wider range of solutions to fiction-breaking game problems like player-character death, tissue regeneration, and so on.

- Locales are more flexible. They may resemble real-world models, but the genres allow for all sorts of bending of the rules. It's easier to create an alien world than to duplicate our real one. In games set here and now on planet Earth, we're more likely to spot details that aren't correct, or shortcuts taken to reduce the game world to a manageable size.

Let's look at each of these two genres in turn.

FANTASY

When we speak of fantasy in video games, we mainly mean high fantasy. This is the realm of elves and dwarves and magic handed down to us from various mythologies, such as Celtic and Norse and codified by J.R.R. Tolkien. High fantasy was then borrowed by tabletop role-playing and digitized in role-playing game franchises from *Wizardry* and *Ultima*, *Might & Magic*, and *Baldur's Gates* to *The Elder Scrolls*, *Dragon Age*, and *The Legend of Zelda: Breath of the Wild* (Figure 16.2). We also have massively multiplayed cousins like *World of Warcraft* and *Lord of the Rings Online*. *Divinity: Original Sin 2* is multiplayer, but not massively so.

Curiously enough, when one attempts to define high fantasy, it starts to sound familiar. High fantasy is concerned with epic battles between good and evil; stereotypical *types* of characters; simple plotlines with clear goals; and morally unambiguous resolutions. Do I have to state again that there are exceptions? No? Good. High fantasy sounds a lot like melodrama, doesn't it? It should, and God bless both their houses.

Fantasy is a comfortable genre. We grew up with it via fairy tales; then watched it take over the bestseller lists, thanks to the acolytes of Tolkien, in series such as Raymond Feist with his Riftwar Saga, Robert Jordan and his *Wheel of Time* series, Terry Goodkind and his *Sword of Truth* series, David Eddings' *Belgariad*, and yes, George R.R. Martin's *Game of Thrones*. Interestingly enough, high fantasy has not done as well as you might expect in other media, not at least until Peter Jackson's triumphant return to the source in the *Lord*

FIGURE 16.2   *The Legend of Zelda: Breath of the Wild*, a huge world of adventure with lots of room for storytelling.

of the Rings trilogy of films. In 1999, *Wheel of Time* spawned a video game designed by Glen Dahlgren for Legend Entertainment, and the books have recently been thoughtfully adapted as an Amazon Prime miniseries. Branden Sanderson, who took over writing duties on the franchise when Robert Jordan died, is the source for rumors of another video game based on the books that appeared in 2021, although as of this writing no game has surfaced.

The crossover here is from books to games, an unusual occurrence, but potent enough to drive the sales of many games. The type of game most known for fantasy is, of course, role-playing, although we see the action version in games like *Infinity Blade* for iOS and strategy in games such as *Kingdoms of Camelot* on Facebook.

The first challenge the writer of high fantasy has is facing the conventions of the genre. Fat axe-wielding elves and tall wise dwarves just won't play outside of comedy. No matter whose world we base our game on, or even if we invent a "new" one, we must be respectful of high fantasy's conventions the same way we would be respectful of a license. If we make an exception, we do it because we know the rule, and have a very definite reason to break it.

Being respectful of the source material creates all sorts of challenges. Earlier, I said we expect certain stereotypical types of characters. We need to recognize this as not being a license to write stereotypes. Instead, the skillful author should bring them to better than one-dimensional life.

Plots should not blindly follow the same "small band of adventurers on an impossible quest" cliché. We need our quests in our games but should find other dramatic situations as well. Some authors focus on the politics of their worlds, others on the romantic lives of their characters.

Raymond Feist and David Eddings slavishly follow Campbell's hero's journey in their first books, but were then faced with a similar predicament. Their heroes reach the end of their journeys, but there are still more books to write. In the Riftwar Saga the central character Pug, who sprang from very modest beginnings to say the least, becomes the most powerful wizard in most of the known universes. How does the author put such a character in danger? How do we empathize with him?

We usually avoid answering these questions because our game stories end at the moment of ascension to power or riches, per the "Return" in Joseph Campbell hero's journey. But sequels challenge us again. As our player-characters and other party members rise in levels, we must boost the power of their antagonists. This is not simply a question of game balance, but of story balance as well. If we just keep leveling our characters up, we risk losing the empathy even if we continue to provide danger. In the first couple of books, I cared what happened to Pug. Once he became all-powerful? Not so much.

Many game writers and designers seem to view a genre only from the outside. They copy the conventions without knowing why they are there, or where they came from. Then they find themselves wallowing in cliché. The moves are all there, but something essential is missing: the creative commitment of a writer or designer who doesn't do their job.

Too often, the answer is to cop an attitude and distance themselves: "This material is really beneath me, so I'll just have some fun with it instead." That's practically a direct quote from a game writer/designer. The genre isn't beneath them; they are beneath it. Learning the conventions of the genre and respecting them is a sure sign of an experienced professional writer. They then know when it's possible to add their own vision into the mix and bring that genre truly alive once again.

Other forms of fantasy crop up as well. If high fantasy takes us to hopefully fully realized worlds, low fantasy concerns the intrusion of fantasy into our more rational world—like survival horror, as in the *Silent Hill* and *Dead Space* series.

It's easy to follow the silver bullet, stake through the heart conventions of most forms of fantasy. As Curt Siodmak wrote for the film *The Wolfman*: "Even a man who is pure at heart and says his prayers by night, may become a wolf when the wolfbane blooms and the autumn moon is bright…." It's much harder when you start from an entirely blank page.

Many console games create wacky worlds all their own like *Rayman*, the various *Mario* series, and the many *Spyro the Dragon* and *Skylanders* games like *Skylanders: Ring of Heroes*. These worlds are unique unto themselves and offer the greatest opportunity for the writer's imagination to run riot because they are not based on accepted traditions of the genre. The writer/designer must be particularly careful to be consistent in whatever laws govern their worlds.

The fact that these games are also comedic and whimsical gives the authors some leeway, but it is also a danger. However crazy the logic, it must still make sense in context. A schizophrenic's logic is never crazy to the schizophrenic.

Writing fantasy characters is its own challenge. Suddenly, we are faced with a huge variety of creatures at various stages of sentient evolution that we can interact with. Here, too, it's important not to get carried away when given all that freedom. To keep the characters grounded in emotion and behavior that is recognizable to an audience, and that can therefore create empathy, we *anthropomorphize* them.

> Anthropomorphic: describes assigning human characteristics to nonhuman creatures and inanimate objects.

How far we want to take this depends on the character and the world fiction. But the combination of human qualities with the nonhuman substance of the character can create delightful characters like Yoda or Grogu (terrible name for a cute little Yoda), Ents, Dorothy II from *The Little Shop of Horrors*, even King Kong.

Fantasy will remain popular. No genre connects more directly to our imagination than fantasy. All worlds are possible. It's our challenge to make sure they're believable, too.

SCIENCE FICTION

Science-fiction games share with fantasy an exhilarating unrestraint in their ability to portray alien worlds that stretch our imaginations both as writers and as players. The difference in science fiction, as the term implies, starts with some basis in recognizable science. Flying horses who take wing through magic are replaced by flying saucers that soar thanks to anti-matter drives.

There are many subgenres of science fiction. Just a few are space operas like the *Halo* series and the *Mass Effect* trilogy; alternate realities and parallel universes as in the *Half-Life* games; post-apocalyptic games like *Fallout 3*; computers gone mad as in *Portal* and *Portal 2*; DNA-based time travel as in the *Assassin's Creed* series; and like fantasy the creation of entirely new worlds and cultures like Frank Herbert's *Dune* or Anne MaCaffrey's *Pern* series of books. They also include other types of games like *X-Com 2* (Figure 16.3), in gameplay terms a platoon-based war game where the targets are aliens.

> Space Opera: an often derogatory, dismissive label for science fiction that focuses on melodrama first defined by Wilson Tucker in 1941. The term was inspired by the label "soap operas" for serial dramas, defined in Chapter 13. Today there are many examples in media that embrace melodrama and transcend this limited description.

Many of these subgenres have been strip mined enough. How many stories have we seen in so many media where someone from the future journeys into the past to correct something, or someone stumbles into the future from the past? Do we really want another post-apocalyptic or cyber-punk vision of the future any time soon? I need one about as much as I need another player-character with amnesia. Please… just say no.

If RPGs are the most likely home to fantasy, shooters seem to be most attracted to science fiction these days. It makes sense. Shooter players enjoy the potent weaponry science fiction can provide. As we've seen, blowing away aliens is less ethically problematic than human beings. And difficulties with health and player-character death have more possible solutions.

Science fiction also shows up in strategy games like *Starcraft* and *Starcraft II: Wings of Liberty*, notable among this type of game for their interest in storytelling. Both *Starcraft* games deserve an additional mention for combining gameplay and story in a strategy game. *Starcraft 3* has been teased but don't expect it anytime soon, if ever.

FIGURE 16.3 *X-Com 2*: war in a science-fiction setting.

Adventure games too are comfortable with science fiction. In addition to the confined settings of spaceships and remote outposts on distant planets, the relatively sterile environments can help with puzzles. One way to avoid pixel hunts is to limit the number of interactive objects in an area. This works against immersion when, in an environment meant to simulate the world we live in, only one book on a shelf or only a few items scattered on furniture are interactive. In space, we seem to accept the fact that desks are cleaner; corridors are devoid of plants; all reading material is confined to files on a computer; and so on. We don't need to clutter our settings with noninteractive objects in the name of verisimilitude.

The percentage of interactive objects goes up as the overall number of objects decreases. It becomes that much easier to find the important ones. I used this "less is more" philosophy in *Dark Side of the Moon*. The player needed to be able to purchase items from the company store. One way to do that was to find ore and sell it to Hunter, the owner of the mining colony's casino. I could scatter bits of low-grade ore here and there for players, and because of the lack of clutter, they weren't that hard to find. (Later on, I gave players access to another character's credit card, giving them the ability to buy out the store if they wanted. This was another way of increasing the pace of the game. The necessity of gathering ore was bypassed.)

Whereas high fantasy can be limited by convention, science fiction is limited by its roots. Since science fiction must be at least an extrapolation of some facet of real science, we must be cautious when writing it to make it at least plausible. It is that tie to science that demands more care be taken to ensure a willing suspension of disbelief.

A major reason *Half-Life* worked as well as it did was because of the hard science feel of the Black Mesa Research Facility where something had gone horribly wrong. Gameplay necessities, like guns and ammo and health and armor, are in sync with the reality of such a research facility.

One of the *System Shock* games, RPG-shooter hybrids, takes place on a space station taken over by another computer gone mad named SHODAN. Its sequel is set on a research vessel, the *Von Braun*, bound for Tau Ceti to investigate a mysterious transmission. Here again the game world is based on hard science. Story delivery in the *System Shock* games is surprisingly one-note: messages, data disks, and even psychic transmissions in the sequel. What sets the games apart is the oppressive, menacing atmosphere created by their confined settings, and most importantly, sound that can alert the player to danger ahead. Again, the verisimilitude of the locations helps us to accept the fiction. *Bioshock*, developed by some of the same team members, retains a slavish attention to evocative environments even as the storytelling remains entirely in cut scenes and static messages.

Another challenge for writers of science-fiction games is similar to the concern in fantasy about the level of power of the player-character and their antagonists. In fantasy anything can happen if it's set up properly. The same is true of science fiction. Because science fiction looks at the unknown and asks "What if?," just about anything can descend from the night sky with evil intent.

We ran into this challenge all the time on *Star Trek: The Next Generation*. Too many times we were faced with alien beings that were unlike anything the crew of the *Enterprise* had seen before. And every time an unbeatable alien was beaten by the *Enterprise*, the ship and its crew gained in levels, at least in the audience's mind. So, the most unstoppable, unbeatable enemy imaginable, the Borg, was introduced. (2010's *Star Trek Online* made a serious miscalculation in allowing players to one-shot Borg in the tutorial. So much for unstoppable!) Every story structured like this has what is called a *penny drop* scene.

In *Star Trek: The Next Generation*, the Borg's weakness was realized in the first penny drop scene. They were all linked as one mind, apparently wired in series. Like a string of Christmas lights, you can take out all by breaking one. Then sometime later the Borg reappeared in the *Star Trek* universe. Only now they were able to adapt to the weapons that had previously defeated them. Another penny drop scene was needed. This scenario illustrates another term, *formulaic*.

Science-fiction games fall into formula even more than fantasy: *System Shock II*'s mysterious signal is a perfect example, and its predecessors range from Arthur C. Clarke's Rama books to *Alien*.

We can't make the mistake of confusing formula with convention. This is the same as mistaking a paint-by-the-numbers picture for a school of art. Recognizing formula is not

> Penny Drop: that moment when a character suddenly gets very excited and yells, "Of course! They live on an arid planet! What if we sprayed them with a garden hose???" You've found the one thing that will gain you the result you want. The term comes from that satisfying clink you hear when a coin drops into the telescope on an observation deck, or a vending machine. It is derived from the sound of a coin clanking into a pay telephone. What's a pay telephone? An extremely rare animal hunted almost to extinction by mobile phones.

> Formula: a string of clichés, plot moves so predictable the audience can recite them as the action unfolds.

easy. You attend that writing seminar, rush home to your keyboard, and start pounding out a three-act structure with arcs and reversals in place. The story flows! It may not be until you're fifty pages in that you suddenly realize you've seen it all before. You're not following the conventions of the genre; you're marching to a formulaic tune.

One of the most problematic characters we dealt with on *ST:TNG* was Q, and again it was because of the power the character wielded. How do you combat something that can do anything? You can't. So, Q had to remain, not evil or good, but beyond those: irritatingly arrogant and cavalier, operating on a god-like plane we couldn't hope to understand. Given a choice, I'd much rather write a peasant than a god any day.

Speaking of characters, science fiction adds to the range of fantasy characters. Not only can we create nonhuman creatures, but manufactured entities as well, like robots and androids. Isaac Asimov recognized that not only was there a need to keep the power of robots manageable for the story, but it was also an opportunity for exploring what it might mean to be a robot. For books like *I, Robot* and *The Naked Sun*, he created his often-quoted Three Laws of Robotics:

- A robot may not injure a human being or, through inaction, allow a human being to come to harm.

- A robot must obey orders given it by human beings except where such orders would conflict with the First Law.

- A robot must protect its own existence as long as such protection does not conflict with the First or Second Law.

One of my favorite episodes of *Star Trek: The Next Generation* is "The Measure of a Man" from the second season, written by Melinda M. Snodgrass. The story concerns an attempt to disassemble Data to see what makes him tick, so that other such androids can be made to serve Starfleet. Data at first agrees until he learns that all Starfleet's horses and men may not be able to put him back together again. Wonderful philosophical wrangling surrounds the legal hearing when Data tries to resign from Starfleet to avoid disassembly.

Robots from Steve Meretzky's Floyd in *Planetfall* to computers like SHODAN in *System Shock*, GLaDOS in the *Portal* games, and Melissa from *i love bees*, the alternate reality game created to promote *Halo 2*, are all daughters of *2001: A Space Odyssey*'s Hal.

Notice that all the rogue computer systems in these games have female voices and personalities! What's up with that? Regardless of the sex of software programs, all are great chances for characters not found in the real world, and can be used, as in the case of "The Measure of a Man" to explore very human issues like civil rights.

Fantasy and science fiction share a great attraction for audiences and writers alike because of their seemingly unlimited possibilities, and that's their greatest danger as well. If we don't appreciate that paradox, our games run the risk of inviting players to take a thrilling spacewalk, then snapping off their umbilical.

WAR

War! Huh! Yeah! What is it good for? Absolutely nothin'! Say it again, y'all!

Norman Whitfield & Barrett Strong

Edwin Starr (1942–2003) sang that back in 1970. But you couldn't prove the sentiment by looking at video games.

War games were once the number one subgenre of simulation and strategy games. Simulations of conflicts, campaigns, even single battles like Gettysburg were everywhere. There wasn't just one simulation of Gettysburg on store shelves at the same time either; there were many.

Then, in a trend we've already witnessed in several types of games, half of this genre slimmed down and sped up, reinventing itself for the controller generation while the other half slowed down, settling comfortably into strategic games. Even those are mostly simpler than true combat simulations and can be played without page turning in thick manuals.

A remarkable exception to most of the action or tactical war games, and one I like a *lot*, is *Valiant Hearts: The Great War* (Figure 16.4). A game that teaches the true cost of war, *Valiant Hearts* is disguised as a side-scroller in an interesting setting with characters you care about, including a dog. I cried my heart out at the ending.

Not only do war games come in just about any type imaginable, but each type is also defined by how it approaches combat. Let's start with the real-time strategy game style that we still find. These are omniscient-view games, either in isometric 2-D or true 3-D, giving a view of entire battlegrounds. The strategic war game can be found as a primary component in more general empire-building strategy games like *Age of Empires IV*.

Conflict in the original *Civilization* was indicated by an icon representing an entire army landing on top of another icon and blinking for a second or two. Combat in most of today's strategy games is full of sound and fury: individual units moving independently

FIGURE 16.4 *Valiant Hearts: The Great War* A war game with a valiant heart.

with swords clashing, guns firing, nicely animated explosions, and cameras that can swoop into the heart of the action.

War games can be divided into three camps. The first is based on actual conflicts as were most of the period war games like *Battlefield 1942*, *Battlefield Vietnam*, *Medal of Honor* (1999), and the original *Call of Duty* games, all set during World War II.

Second, thanks to human beings' seemingly built-in need to resolve disputes with bloodshed, we have modern war games, such as the *Call of Duty: Modern Warfare* games, the rebooted 2010 *Medal of Honor*, and *Tom Clancy's Ghost Recon* series. Will an end to war ever be possible? Looking at the world we live in today, I have serious doubts. And if there is war there will be war games.

The third group adds the element of fantasy with strange creatures and spellcasting. In addition to the *Warcraft* games there are many *Lord of the Rings* games.

Story in the first camp is handled mainly as historical background to provide context for the upcoming battle. The second camp adds more story as it searches for new enemies to shoot at. The third either borrows the roots of its stories from other media or must create its own backstory.

For writers, high-level strategy war games, where you manipulate entire units of soldiers, don't provide much challenge. If you go the route of cut scenes and mission briefings, the story is reassuringly linear and segregated from the gameplay. This type of game spares you the chance to get down and dirty with the foot soldiers, so character revelation is at a minimum.

This isn't to say that strategy war games can't be created with more sophisticated stories and characters. We need to see the cost of shattered lives and demolished hopes. But the desire for storytelling beyond context at this level really hasn't been proven, and the audience doesn't appear to be clamoring for it the way they are in the other incarnations of war games. Developers of these games spend their resources on the addition of player vs. player more than on storytelling.

If we zoom in to the next level of war games, however, things change dramatically. Whether first or third person, these are squad-level war games such as Tom Clancy titles produced Red Storm and many others. The player is now down in the trenches, firing weapons and hunting for ammo just as in other shooters. The squad is of two different types. Either the player controls all members, moving from player-character to player-character, or there is some level of AI control.

We find both in PC and console games, plus a necessary hybrid where the player can choose when to drive other characters. This is used in an attempt to retain the strategic element that was otherwise lost when squad-level war games differentiated themselves from turn-based like *X-Com* to real-time games. As stated before, human players can't keep up with computer-controlled enemies. Computer-controlled enemies don't need to take breaks from the almost constant action, so some relief, in the form of AI was needed for human players.

In any of these three cases, though, there are many more story and character opportunities. Now we have comrades in arms with distinct personalities to interact with. Now we build friendships with them, so if one is killed, the player can be touched by the loss. This is not true only for foot soldiers. Squadrons of fighter planes or tanks or ships are treated in the same way. In *Star Wars*, I never really cared about Wedge, another pilot along for the ride with Luke Skywalker, but his death was necessary in the final battle because of what he meant to Luke, even though most of his dialogue comes over the radio. This use of characters heard via in-game earbuds and mics, but not seen, is a staple of war movies in general and can be used to good effect in squad-level games. If we give them voice, we have a chance to give them something interesting to say.

Historical scenarios are popular, covering just about all our modern wars from World War II to Iraq and Afghanistan and in time, I'm sure, Ukraine. Strategy game-type simulation has given way to a cinematic feel of being in the action. Both should mirror as closely as possible real-world tactics.

One PC game deserves mention for taking its cue from the 1987 film *Good Morning, Vietnam* and using music as an immersion tool. The use of music from the 1960s to the 1970s adds immeasurably to immersion in *Battlefield: Vietnam*. This game is one of several that allow players to experience the war in several different roles: from dog soldier to sniper to helicopter pilot. *Battlefield 2042* (2021) features Battle Royale gameplay set exactly one hundred years from the first game in the series, Battlefield 1942, it does not however feature oldies from 2030.

With this technology, we have the tools to make a story-based single-player war game every bit as compelling as a war movie that explores the human side of war beyond the moral calculations of early efforts like *Close Combat*. Out of all the genres, war games can explore themes that are difficult and not easily resolved. There is usually no fantasy or science-fiction patina to soften the life and death issues. In 2004, I wrote that "right now, we're stuck in the safe John Wayne world of *The Green Berets*. Would anyone want to play a grittier game? If it's written with the conviction of the HBO miniseries *Band of Brothers*, I'd say yes."

Today we can wade through that grit if we choose. Evil now hides in shades of gray and enemies can exist behind a smile. We're much more willing to explore the darker sides of conflict, as in *Call of Duty: Modern Warfare 2* where the player-character, Joseph Allen, undercover, assists Russian terrorists in killing civilians at Zakhaev International Airport in Moscow. At whatever level games portray it, warfare is anything but a clean fight. Storytelling in games that allows players to experience war at its most visceral must never lose sight of that.

ESPIONAGE

Stealth and secrecy are our only weapons now. You gentlemen are, I trust, stealthy and secretive.

Alistair Maclean, Where Eagles Dare

Like fantasy and science fiction, there is a lot of crossover between this genre and the next, crime. Because games in this genre are almost invariably action games, there is a lot of similarity with war game first-person shooters, although espionage games are more likely to resemble the play style of *Thief* than *Doom*, where being stealthy and secretive can gain you almost as much as firepower and reflexes.

FIGURE 16.5 *Splinter Cell: Chaos Theory* Spies and stealth, a seventeen-year-old classic.

Yes, *Where Eagles Dare* may look like a war movie, but it's not. Long before Indiana Jones was a gleam in Steven Spielberg's eye, Richard Burton and Clint Eastwood starred in this 1969 super-charged action film about a World War II commando raid on an impregnable German castle perched on a mountaintop, at times literally a cliffhanger. And it is also a workable model for the structure of our espionage games.

What games fall under this genre these days? There is a definite crossover between espionage games and stealth games: a wide range that includes *Thief II*, *Dishonored*, and *Tom Clancy's Splinter Cell: Chaos Theory* (Figure 16.5). Developers of espionage games have become increasingly interested in storytelling as a way to stand out from the crowd (although major licenses and long-running series don't hurt!).

Being stealthy and secretive gives writers the potential for other obstacles than simply enemies to be gunned down. These obstacles then can be overcome in a variety of ways: cracking a safe's combination lock; accessing computer files by deducing a password; borrowing credentials that get the player-character past a suspicious guard; using special stealth moves like the player-character being able to pull themselves over a fence or wedge themselves between two beams in the ceiling; and many more.

Even good shooters are not simply shooters, but stealth games as well. By varying the gameplay, we not only keep the experience fresh for the player, but we also provide ourselves with a variety of different approaches to the storytelling. Let's look at the opportunities presented in the previous paragraph's examples of gameplay.

- **Cracking a safe's combination lock.** Does the character use a digital tumbler detector or a stethoscope? Where did the character pick up safecracking? What exposition does the safe contain?

- **Accessing computer files by deducing a password.** Instead of just finding the password taped to the bottom of the keyboard, provide clues to the password. It will require a search of the office the player might not otherwise bother to make, revealing the character of the computer's owner: Are they married? Any kids? Pets? Birthday/how old are they? What are their hobbies? Hmmm… they're colorblind and have a black belt in karate… might be useful knowledge later on.

- **Borrowing credentials to get past a suspicious guard.** This gains you knowledge about the true owner of the credentials; provides the opportunity for revealing dialogue with an NPC who trusts the player-character; and maybe ensures their friendly recognition of the player-character after the credentials have been destroyed.

- **Wedging themselves between the beams of a ceiling.** Not only may this move save the PC from detection, but it also could give them a chance to overhear NPC conversation in the corridor below them that may include character insights or exposition crucial to the mission.

Because espionage games are set in a world that more closely resembles our own world, rather than fantasy or science fiction, we are constrained somewhat by real-world natural laws and physics (at least as much as the *Mission: Impossible* team would be). It also means that we don't have to police our imaginations as closely. We should automatically recognize when credibility is being stretched to the breaking point.

Espionage games take the player to multiple new locales, everywhere from Paris to Indonesia or Moscow to Cairo. Real locations mean we don't have to make everything up. We can do research. If the game visits Venice, Italy, a gondola would be a natural choice for transportation at some point. The fact that Geneva, Switzerland is home to so many well-guarded and secretive banks suggests an obvious puzzle: breaking into one.

Few genres immediately suggest such an interesting variety of skills the way espionage does. Fantasy and science fiction are wide open. You start from scratch. War is… war. You start with an M16. Espionage makes you as multi-skilled as a human is likely to get.

The major issue for the writer is how realistic the game is going to be. In 1965, *Thunderball*, the fourth James Bond film, was released. That same year saw the release of *The Ipcress File* starring Michael Caine, a far grittier look at the world of espionage. Both films were produced by Albert "Cubby" Broccoli and Harry Saltzman and featured much of the same behind-the-camera talent. *The Ipcress File* wasn't any more realistic, featuring as it did a psychedelic brainwashing room, I paid homage to (stole) for *Edge of Night* almost twenty years later. It was simply done in a realistic style of British cinema popular at the time that also produced such non-espionage films as *Room at the Top* and *The Loneliness of the Long-Distance Runner*. The style meant the characters felt more like real people than James Bond. They weren't all glamorous and neither was their work of stakeouts and prisoner exchanges. Harry Palmer, Caine's character, didn't much fancy being a spy at all. He wore glasses, spoke with a working-class accent, made mistakes, and in the end almost killed the wrong man. Today we have a new, grittier Bond, a trend that started with *Casino Royale* with Daniel Craig and continues in *No Time to Die*, Craig's last appearance in the role.

CRIME

Crime might look like it belongs linked up with the next genre, mystery. But crime games are much closer in structure and gameplay to espionage and non-strategic war games. This genre includes both sides of the law: from the many locales of *C.S.I* to the *Grand Theft Auto* series (Figure 16.6). Cops and robbers. Depending on the game players can play either side of the law.

We don't see crime-based strategy games much, but both squad-level and single player-character are well represented. We let players play criminals because it appeals to the naughty side most of us have within us. 2009's *Grand Theft Auto IV*'s expansion pack *The Ballad of Gay Tony* is unapologetically not politically correct. You can hear the developers giggling maniacally even now. If *all* games *only* gave us the option to be criminals, we might risk encouraging a generation of social misfits. But for the rest of us, playing villains is a fun diversion and release. Inkle's *Overboard!*, mentioned earlier, is our most recent opportunity to be very, very naughty.

Playing honest officers of truth and justice appeals to the hero within us, and is a reaction to the chaotic world we live in. Mysteries may try to deny that world exists. Crime confronts it; knows we're frustrated that we can't do much about it; and hands us the weapons to change that.

This section is shorter than most of those in this chapter because gameplay and opportunities for character and story have been discussed in the sections on earlier genres, particularly war and espionage. Deciding whether hostages are taken by bank robbers or terrorists doesn't affect the mechanics of the gameplay, only the details. The major difference is in the storytelling.

Deciding whether the game casts the player-character as a S.W.A.T. member or a single detective on a homicide case determines the style of gameplay in a shooter, whether the genre is science fiction, war, espionage, or crime. But there are two primary considerations when designing a crime game I want to mention.

FIGURE 16.6 *Grand Theft Auto 5*, 2013's addition to a long-lived crime family of games.

The first is that, of all the genres, this one is the most real and known to us. With a couple of exceptions, usually dealing with 1930s gangsters, crime games are modern day, or near future. We need to get the world right, and we need to get the facts right. If we screw up on police procedure, or on how to handle terrorists, players will know and rightfully be annoyed. Remember our characters and stories don't have to be real, but they must *feel* real.

The second is thematic. Playing cops and robbers is fine, but because crime games are based in a recognizable world, the consequences for actions must be carefully weighed. This is not only for dramatic variety, but also because a game's creators have committed themselves to a point of view. We make choices every time we write. Being aware of that, and making meaningful choices, are the most important and often the hardest part.

MYSTERY

Ah, my favorite genre. I was a mystery writer long before I was a game designer, and a mystery lover long before that. The game I'm currently working on is a mystery. Mystery is the chameleon of genres, showing up in all the others, adapting itself to its new surroundings without missing a beat. There is mystery in every game I've ever designed and most of the TV shows I wrote. Even when I worked in a nonmystery genre like *Eight Is Enough* (family comedy) or *Father Murphy* (family Western), I usually wrote a mystery.

I love traditional mysteries because they are windows on an orderly universe far removed from the uncertainty and injustice that are a part of everyday life. In a well-constructed mystery story, clues are followed to a logical conclusion. There are no loose ends. Good *usually* triumphs, and evil is *usually* punished. This wasn't true of life in the golden age of mysteries any more than it's true today. There is no guarantee of such tidy resolutions in this world. But that's okay because mysteries deal with illusion, not reality.

Classic mystery stories fall into two major camps. *Cozies* evoke quaint English villages with their elderly tea-sipping spinsters and deacons and bicycle-riding constables. Most of Agatha Christie's mysteries are cozies, but even at their coziest, her amateur sleuth, Miss Marple, had a keen edge to her that belied her lace and granny glasses. *Hard-boiled* mysteries originated in the United States. Among the more famous hard-boiled writers are Dashiell Hammett and Raymond Chandler.

Mystery writers are often compared to magicians, and with good reason. We use some of the same techniques, like misdirection and sleight-of-hand. We'll look at some of these in a moment.

Being a mystery writer has helped me in *all* my writing. Traditional mystery structure is unforgiving. You need to know where you're going. The clues must pay off and the motives tie up. At the end of the story, if your reader tosses the book aside or walks out of the theater and goes, "Huh?" you failed.

It's because I'm a mystery writer that I stress such elements of writing as consistency and clarity. You need to play fair with your audience. And this is the primary difference between mystery stories and crime stories. Crime fiction is more firmly based in the real world. It may contain one mystery or more, just as any other genre, but it's sloppier, and in the end, justice is not always certain. Misunderstanding this distinction leads a lot of unaware writers to confuse the two, just as *noir* and mysteries are often confused by the undiscriminating. For the record, Raymond Chandler wrote hard-boiled mysteries with noir elements. Cornell Woolrich caused the French to first use the word *noir* to describe his work because he used *black* in many of his titles. He did not write mysteries. He wrote psychological thrillers that sometimes contained elements of mysteries. Alfred Hitchcock's *Rear Window* is based on a Cornell Woolrich story.

When the mystery has loose ends, or the solution makes jumps in logic, or depends on wild speculation or coincidence, it is doomed. The result can be dissatisfaction in the audience much like when the director crosses the axis for two matching shots (see Chapter 6: Perspective). They may not know what's wrong, but they know something didn't work. It can also be worse.

It's like the feeling we get matching up our socks after doing the laundry, and we are left with a stray. We can usually track down its mate in the washer or retrieve it from that linty space between the dryer and the wall. If a mystery reader flips back through the pages to check on a stray clue (as I suggested you do in the preceding paragraph), the result can be catastrophic if the clue isn't there. The plot is exposed in all its unfair artifice. If a magician's illusion fails onstage, the audience sees the smoke and mirrors used to construct it. "Don't look at the little man behind the curtain!" cries the all-powerful Wizard of Oz. But it's too late. We've seen him.

As I said, mysteries are a component of many games. But as a genre they are fairly rare. They've been with us from very early on. The first was probably Infocom's text adventure *Deadline*.

The Phoenix Wright games are mysteries. As mentioned earlier, 2010 saw the release of *Heavy Rain*, a contemporary thriller, but with obvious film noir aspirations. *L.A. Noire* in 2011 was set in 1947 with its echoes of classic noir films from *Double Indemnity* to *L.A. Confidential*. Both featured crime-solving and action set pieces. 2015's *Her Story* was a mystery. So was 2019's *Disco Elysium*, although it earned my wrath for its amnesiac player-character. What did I say about amnesia? Just say no!

Why haven't mysteries enjoyed the popularity of fantasy and science fiction? I think there are three reasons. All have to do more with we who create games than those who play them.

The first is that mysteries can seem very complex, and simple stories work best for games, as in any other action medium. We need to separate story structure from mystery problem and solution here. The underlying solution to most mysteries is as simple as Mrs. White in the library with the candlestick. The rest is all as much smoke and as many mirrors as we want to use to disguise that fact. The plot moves must be clear even if we don't reveal their true meaning.

The second is that even if you've created a new world for your science-fiction game, as long as you're consistent, you can make up all sorts of natural laws. Spells can be whipped up in a fantasy game on demand. Mysteries force us to plant both feet firmly on the ground. We must play fair.

The third is the reverse of the number one hackneyed metaphor that shows up in so many mysteries. You know the one I mean: the pieces of the jigsaw puzzle line. Please! Swear an oath. Swear now that you will never refer to the clues in a mystery story as "pieces of a jigsaw puzzle" or observe that "we don't have all the pieces" or "the pieces don't fit" or "there's only one piece to the puzzle missing." Swear it.

Thank you. Now that I got that out of my system, back to the reverse. When we write a mystery, we start from the end when the jigsaw puzzle is complete. We then take it apart and plant the clues like Easter eggs throughout the story. We may change a clue, or add more, or alter details in the solution as we write, but we must start with that unforgiving completed jigsaw puzzle. Too many writers attempt to wing it with just the culprit's identity and motive and a vague clue or two. The pieces don't fit. The player notices. Just as stories might be unfairly looked down upon in games, mysteries are looked down upon because they often are not done well. I swear I will never mention jigsaw puzzles again in this book. Amnesia? I might. I don't remember.

Being a fan, I'd like to see more mysteries in games. If you accept the three reasons I've given for our lack of mysteries and are willing to try and make the effort to write one, I have a few helpful hints.

Use *misdirection* in all sorts of ways, refine it, and layer it. Different types of people will play your mystery. Start with a coarse layer of obvious red herrings that the helpful sidekick or another looker on will point at. These are innocent suspects, false clues, motives that could lead to murder but didn't, and so on. The canny mystery writer will often double bluff and point at someone, exonerate them beyond a shadow of a doubt, then reveal they committed the murder after all.

> Misdirection: the magician's best friend, it is the art of focusing a watcher's attention on one place, so they don't see something happen in another.

Create a second layer that waits to trap the clever player who sees through the major red herrings. Then a third, and a fourth if you like. The term *red herring*, of course, stems from British fox hunting. (Oscar Wilde called it "the unspeakable in pursuit of the uneatable.") Early pro-fox activists would stuff burlap bags with smoked (red) herrings and drag them across the trail between the fox and the pursuing dogs, hoping to throw them off the scent.

Want to know who the killer is in far too many books and movies? Wait until the detective's sidekick, or the dumb police officer, lists the suspects. They must, of course, to remind the audience. One of two things will happen. They'll make the mistake of saying, "So, it must be Professor Plum, Colonel Mustard, Miss Scarlet, or Mr. Green. We know it can't be Mrs. White." Who's the killer? Quick! No looking at your neighbor's paper! Or he'll say, "So, it must be Professor Plum, Colonel Mustard, Miss Scarlet, Mrs. White, or Mr. Green." The killer is the same in both cases: Mrs. White.

Somewhere sometime in the dim past (long before R.D. Laing) somebody must have done a study on human perception and concluded we pay a lot of notice to the first item in a list, but then our attention begins to drift. We pay almost as much attention to the second item, even less to the third, and so on until the end when we snap back to consciousness and zero in on the last item to prove we were actively involved the entire time. Mystery writers routinely place the killer's name in the bottom third of the suspect list. It takes a confident writer to double bluff and pick the first or last name.

As for the first case, even if a master of the puzzle mystery like Agatha Christie allows a character to be ruled out because they couldn't possibly have done it, the canny reader will be suspicious and watch that character like a hawk. Once any character has the player's full attention, clues can leap into view. It's a balance we must maintain between being sneaky and playing fair with the player. It isn't easy, but it is essential.

Withhold explanations. In Chapter 9, I talked about the crisis, climax, and resolution triplets. We saw that by stretching the time between any of these we could heighten suspense. The same thing is true with exposition. Every time a detective collects a clue, it's the A side to a joke. The punch line is the moment the meaning of the clue becomes clear. You can't have one without the other.

It's like the classic situation that gives rise to the phrase, "waiting for the other shoe to drop." Where did it originate? Nobody knows. It was called an "old chestnut" in a copy of *The New York Times* published in 1921. It probably originated with some poor soul in a downstairs lodging house room trying to go to sleep who hears their upstairs neighbor getting ready for bed. The neighbor takes off a shoe and tosses it aside. It lands with a thump. The longer that neighbor takes to toss the second shoe, the more excruciating the suspense becomes. The poor soul downstairs will not be able to sleep until the second shoe drops. Human beings, even the less anal ones, need closure. Keeping it from them only makes them desire it more.

A variation on this is *don't try to hide clues*. The best clues are those where you can jump up and down in front of the player and point at them. "Look! A clue!" The player sagely guesses what the clue means and is totally wrong.

The close-up magician who works their illusions right under our noses uses physical dexterity called sleight-of-hand. By carefully choosing words designed to mislead, we work our sleigh-of-hand with those. Frederic Dannay and Manfred B. Lee, writing under the pen name Ellery Queen (also their detective's name) were particularly adept at presenting the "dying" words of a victim that appeared to mean one thing when actually they meant something entirely different.

Mysteries flourish in other media. Many of our most popular films and TV shows are mysteries thanks to the British who seem to love mysteries as much as they love shows about pricing antiques and cooking competitions. I agree on the mysteries. They can have the other two. Some of my recent favorites include *Broadchurch*, *Shetland*, and *Vera*. All three balance their mysteries with compelling characters and drama. A recent mystery movie that pokes fun at the genre is *Knives Out*. Action and mystery go well together when they are in balance. Understanding the craft of mystery writing is a necessary step to writing games whose mysteries satisfy as much as their action.

HORROR

We find horror intermixed with other genres just like mystery. *Alien* is a horror tale set in a science-fiction universe. The *Resident Evil* games as I mentioned are similar. The genre is inhabited by monsters. There's a wide range of monsters to choose from, human monsters like *Hannibal*, or the prehistoric reptiles from the *Jurassic Park* series. The scariest seem not to be the mindless killers of dead teenager movies that must rely solely on effects

FIGURE 16.7   *Oxenfree* Spooky teenage mystery/horror/sci-fi. It's not *Stranger Things*, but pretty good even though it has teenagers in it.

like shock and gore, even if they play on our standard fears of isolation and vulnerability (Figure 16.7).

Often, the most effective monsters are human, or at least anthropomorphic. The biggest monster in the first *Jurassic Park* is the T-Rex. But it is the raptors with that unsettling glint of intelligence in their eyes that are saved for the spine-tingling climax. Universal Studios owes its success in the 1930s and 1940s to its monsters, and the most popular were *Dracula*, *Frankenstein's* creation, *The Wolfman*, and *The Mummy*. Hammer Studios replicated their success in the 1950s and 1960s. Zombies have been with us just as long (*White Zombie* in 1932, 1943's *I Walked with a Zombie*, and others) but came into their own in the 1960s, first with Hammer's *Plague of the Zombies* in 1966 and more spectacularly with George Romero's *Night of the Living Dead* in 1968. It appears they may never die no matter how many times they're killed, or even change their behavior much, witness the pile of movies and video games that turn up every year.

It is the fact that there is a horrible caricature of humanity in all of these creatures that makes them resonate longer with us than nonhuman monsters and keeps them coming back to scare us time and again.

We're not going to linger on gore, but it is one of the elements of horror we address as writers. Again, it hits the player harder when humans become rotting corpses or begin to mutate than when unrecognizable tentacled blobs attack. The stories of horror writer H.P. Lovecraft have been a favorite source of material for movies and games. Very few low-budget horror film writers can resist the temptation to drop a reference to Arkham, Massachusetts, or place a Miskatonic University sweatshirt on a character.

The most effective of Lovecraft's writing comes when he describes the alterations in humans after their brushes with his mythical beings called the Old Ones. Whenever the Old Ones themselves shamble in for an appearance, he relies on suggestions and warnings that the descriptions are too horrible to imagine—not something that translates well into literal mediums like video games and movies.

Three other elements worth mentioning here show up in other genres. But horror is particularly dependent on them. We've discussed them: suspense, surprise, and shock. The key to their use is a word I've used many times: balance. Shocks and surprises are only effective if they are not overused, and if we take care to adjust their rhythms. An endless string of shock after shock after shock deadens the player. We want to vary when the shock occurs in our game and where the box is that Jack is going to jump out at us from.

We want to vary their intensity, all the while trying to avoid escalating things too far too soon. It's the same problem as player-characters becoming too powerful. If we rely solely on shock and surprise, each instance must cap the previous one.

Far easier, and in the long run far more effective, is to string the shocks together with suspense. Lengthen the time between the setup (a first dead body?) and the appearance of the thing that did the deed. Create a red herring surprise. Cause some laughter in the player and then choke it off with a blood-soaked claw.

In shooters, we send armies of drooling, bloodthirsty mobs after the player to keep the action intense. The arsenal that gameplay stealth and secrecy give us can be far more rewarding than simply bigger guns to splatter bigger monsters.

ROMANCE

This genre has struggled to find a comfortable home in games. Infocom's *Plundered Hearts* was an attempt at a text adventure version of "bodice-ripper" romance novels. It was not a commercial success. And it's not because the player-character was female. This fact didn't stop Roberta Williams' *King's Quest* series from being successful, or *Lara Croft: Tomb Raider*, or *Resident Evil*. Gender is not the difficulty. It's the idea of romance. And romance is about emotion. There is no denying that. But romance can show up in the unlikeliest of places (Figure 16.8).

Over the past few years, I've been approached several times about a multiplayer world of romance. But it looks like romance has found its way on to our computers on its own.

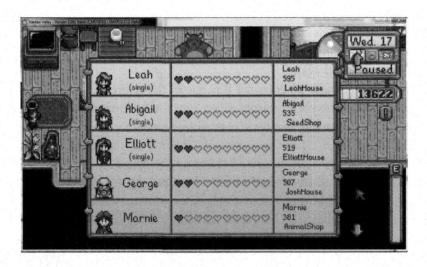

FIGURE 16.8 *Stardew Valley* includes a surprisingly flexible "relationship" element.

Romance is already online in a big way in MMOs, chat rooms, and dating services. And it's real. These are the romance equivalent of PvP. And they bring all the nuances human opponents bring to those games that AI can't provide. There are two sticky points the developer of a romance multiplayer game must get past. That's the first one. Romance arrived without our help. We may have missed our chance.

The second is that other very interesting element to romance: sex. Again, the Internet is already there, and we've seen the results both good and bad. The sensational stories make the headlines: online relationships that break up marriages, serial killers and pedophiles on the prowl for new prey. For every one of those, I expect there are quite a few healthy relationships that develop, as they can among singles anyplace.

But this is a book on writing, not sociology. And my writing answer to this dilemma is one word: *Titanic*. I was in Beijing when it was first released there. It was the number one movie by a wide margin for weeks.

Romance in movies does not only occur in romance movies. Even romance novels are comprised of other genres. *Edge of Night* was the mystery soap. In *Titanic*, there is an almost perfect balance of elements that appeal to a huge proportion of the mass market: the mystique of the subject matter; the suspense; spectacle; action; and yes, romance. It didn't even matter that the screenplay was nothing to write home about. It was the elements chosen and how they were balanced that made *Titanic* a phenomenal hit that appealed to just about every demographic in every country on the planet.

We will eventually see games that are romances at their heart. *Gone Home*, ostensibly a mystery game, is actually a love story. Most interesting is how the romance in the story is revealed. Dating sims proliferate but are obviously simulations. Unfortunately, romance in many games is delivered like a choice from a limited menu. If rom coms can do it on TV, why can't we?

WESTERN

Westerns have long been considered a wonderful genre for storytelling. What was the first narrative film? Can you remember that far back in this book? *The Great Train Robbery*. After falling out of favor in the 1970s due to saturation and the changing sensibilities of a post-Vietnam country, we have seen a quiet resurgence in them over the past few years in other media.

What about games? There have been western games since The Oregon Trail in 1971 (Dysentery anyone?). For a long while after that game they were not met with much success. In Chapter 6, I mentioned *Wild Wild West: The Steel Assassin*, a 1999 game I wrote and co-designed in conjunction with the movie Will Smith described as "just a thorn in my side." And I used it in Chapter 12 to illustrate how to adjust a game when you must cut a big chunk of it. It was a western and involved riding horses and shooting bad guys. Like the TV show it was modeled on, the game had very little else on its mind.

Westerns remained an under-used genre. When I wrote the first edition of this book in 2004 there was only one lone rider on the horizon: Rockstar's *Red Dead Revolver*, released to mixed reviews, featured yet again the same old revenge premise, "...a young man's innocence was lost when he witnessed the brutal murder of his family..." Sigh. Cliché meet cliché. It's okay. It's only a game.

FIGURE 16.9   *Red Dead Redemption 2*: an expansive western prequel.

Rockstar followed in 2010 with a spiritual successor to *Red Dead Revolver* called *Red Dead Redemption*, which did far better critically, earning a 95 on Metacritic, and featuring—despite some excruciatingly long cut scenes—some good storytelling as well as some novel twists on stories with similar themes. First off, instead of the bad guys, player-character John Marston's former outlaw gang, killing or kidnapping his family, it is the U.S. government who takes Marston's family hostage so that he will go after the gang's members.

The game's morality and honor systems are also effective: granting points that affect how NPCs view Marston, although he does have a typical western disguise: a bandana that allows him to cross ethical lines without taking hits to his honor and fame. All and all, the game was indeed redemption after their first attempt at a western. Both use spaghetti western tropes, style, and music. All plusses in my book!

2011 brought us the Kinect game, *The Gunstringer* that was a western, but cleverly had the player waving arms to manipulate the strings of its marionette player-character: the "puppet with no name."

Today westerns are a genre that is finally getting some serious notice, more in games than in movies and TV. Why? Rockstar's latest, *Red Dead Redemption 2*, was released in 2018 (Figure 16.9). The game set several records including a huge budget, huge sales, huge ratings, and a huge world to explore. (Don't forget huge amounts of dialogue!)

Its success has not been lost on other developers and several other western games are now out there. So, it's worth looking at some things to consider when writing a western game.

- **Clear themes** like the true nature of courage (*Shane*); family relationships (*Red River*); friendship (*Gunfight at the O.K. Corral*); the soul-crushing results of violence (*The Gunfighter*); responsibility (*High Noon*); and yes, even revenge (*The Unforgiven*). These films were often morality plays firmly grounded in melodrama, and happy to be there, thanks.

- **Expansive maps.** Just as we create huge worlds for fantasy games, we can do the same for westerns. Remember, your characters are going to ride horses. The time it takes to travel great distances expands your map. But don't leave a lot of space between destinations where nothing happens. Need faster travel? Teleporters in westerns are called trains.

- **Interesting travel options.** Horses, stagecoaches, riverboats, wagon trains, rafts, canoes, period locomotives.

- **Natural environments.** Mountains, deserts, forests, raging rivers, blizzards, all can present the player with unique challenges befitting the era in which the game is set.

- **Civilization and its cost can be measured.** Growing towns, forts, stagecoach stops, ranches, cabins, land disputes, hunting grounds, gold mines.

- **Characters both strong and weak.** All races, all ages, pioneers and city folk, and relationships and conflicts can be more intense when there are few neighbors, and cooperation is necessary to survival. Friends and heroes can come in all shapes and sizes. Have a look at the film *Old Henry* (2021) for inspiration, and yes, it is a mystery as well as a western.

- **Enemies both strong and weak.** They come in all shapes and sizes, too: bank robbers, gunslingers, cattle rustlers, land grabbing ranchers, corrupt politicians, hired killers.

- **History.** It's important that we face head on the darker side of history, and westerns can be an ideal place to start. They can give us a new lens with which to study who we are as human beings. Yes, science fiction and fantasy can provide a stage for us to explore many issues, too. But there's something fresh and new and closer to home about the stories westerns can tell. Remember, just as in any storytelling, if you want to make a statement the trick is to avoid preaching and instead get your message across thematically in westerns, removed in time.

CHAPTER 17

Storytelling in Virtual Worlds

MANY OF THE CONCEPTS covered in this book are just as valid for multiplayer games as for single player. However, we will now look at some topics that are chiefly the concern of multiplayer games. While on the surface they remind us very much of their single-player cousins and especially the multiplayer variations on those games, they can be very different. We'll begin with some caveats then some historical context from someone who knows what he's talking about.

I am not including *Pokémon Go* here. It's a cell phone game featuring an augmented reality overlay on our own massive world complete with player vs player (PvP) battles. That makes it an MMO, but storytelling is not what it is known for. *Sea of Thieves* is another game that is close to being an MMO, but it is missing some standards of true MMOs such as player progression. *The Elder Scrolls*: *Blades* is simply a hack and slash action game set in the world of *Skyrim* but not true multiplayer—there's a PvP arena and you can visit your "guild," but that's about it. I played it for months hoping it might grow into an MMO, but no such luck. And there is precious little story.

We'll also skip multiplayer versions of single-player games. Any real storytelling of the original single-player game is stripped away. Players are left with the game's world for context, its weapons, skills, and mobs. Game states and player statistics can be saved to be resumed at a later play session in these games, but the planets stop spinning; all the NPCs head home to dinner; and the mobs go into hibernation.

Now for a historical perspective, I'm going to hand the virtual micropone to Raph Koster. Raph is the CEO of Playable Worlds, a game studio devoted to virtual worlds. In previous lives, he led the design of *Ultima Online* and *Star Wars Galaxies*.

"Ever since the launch of *Minecraft* in 2009, virtual worlds have evolved away from the familiar

> DikuMUD: A text-based Multi-User Dungeon game format from 1990/91 that was the basis for many popular multi-user dungeons that grew into the type of Massively Multiplayer Online (MMO) games like *Everquest* and *World of Warcraft* (WoW).

DOI: 10.1201/9780429284991-22

model of classes, levels, and killing monsters derived from the DikuMUD heritage and today best exemplified by *World of Warcraft* (2004).

WoW's big innovation was to use narrative to lead players through the leveling process, a choice that subsequent games like *Star Wars: The Old Republic* (2011) and *Final Fantasy XIV: A Realm Reborn* (2013) doubled down on. The latter very successfully leveraged the long history of JRPG storytelling to tell epic stories with lengthy cinematics and compelling themes; this of course meant that every player went through the exact same narrative beats, very much as if they were playing a single-player game.

A similar emphasis on single-player controlled experiences led to the birth of the "looter-shooter" genre on consoles, exemplified by titles like *Destiny* (2014), which reduced the classic DikuMUD model to instanced encounters and a small massively multiplayer lobby. This allowed the encounters to be designed in ways very similar to classic single-player games, including traditional storytelling techniques. Ongoing content releases advanced the larger-scale storyline.

The path laid out by *Minecraft* was quite the opposite, and the result was a return to older styles of "sandbox" MMO play.

The survival game genre exemplified by games like *Rust* (2013), *DayZ* (2018), and *Valheim* (2021), though light on narrative, saw huge success by embracing crafting and open player vs player combat in a multiplayer setting holding up to a couple hundred players. These sorts of games proved to

> Sandbox: An open world that gives the user much more control of what they can do in it, including tell stories, and the ability for players in games like *Minecraft* to shape the world much as they would like.

be excellent generators of user-created narratives, like their sandbox predecessors. Other recent games such as *Sea of Thieves* (2018) embrace aspects of survival games by providing a shared open world with high risk of player killing, while focusing strongly on a small player party experience much like the old Diku model.

> Today we see a resurgence of interest in sandbox play of all sorts, with many studios working towards massively multiplayer community-driven experiences inspired by *Animal Crossing*, projects that hark back to the heyday of MMO sandboxes like *Ultima Online*, *Star Wars Galaxies*, and *Eve*. Even the multiplayer brawler genre known as battle royale is migrating in the direction of sandbox MMO gameplay, as shown by *Fortnite*'s gradual addition of play modes which encourage building structures and roleplaying. The result is the revived dream of a "metaverse," perhaps best exemplified today by *Roblox* (2006), which is a virtual world platform allowing anyone to build their own virtual worlds and add them to a hyperlinked network."

Okay, all set? Here are some issues to consider when writing for MMOs. The first is *persistence.*

Story in all games is not just written; it must be designed as well. The design dictates whether the game is linear or modular, something in between,

> Persistence: An MMO is said to be persistent because time passes, and events occur exclusive of whether players are present.

or a mixture of multiple structures. The design explains the story's relationship to the other parts of the game.

COMPUTER AS GAME MASTER

If a story in a virtual world is meant to help replace what is called the human DM or GM in tabletop role-playing games that do not need a computer, it must be worth the effort.

> DM: stands for the Dungeon Master, overseer and manipulator of a live role-playing adventure often involving exploration of a dungeon.
> GM: Game Master, a more general title found in all live role-playing games, including those not involving dungeon crawls.

Backstory is no trouble. Even static worlds have a backstory. It is easy to segregate it to make sure it doesn't get in the way or ignore it entirely. It's even easy to balance gameplay with the story by revealing it in quests or through the characters of NPCs. The challenge comes when both the world and the story move into the future together. GMs must keep on their toes to adjust to player input. Good GMs are like good bards who can improvise their songs without missing a beat. What reacts instead to the unexpected choices players make? The computer. And the computer is not as good at being human as it is at arithmetic.

What to do? Some MMO designers would say "nothing." As Raph points out, there remains a large portion who believe the story in the world is not the most attractive part of the MMO experience. So they are content to repeat tropes of the past, believing the larger selling point is the stories players write and tell themselves. And this is certainly a part of it, but even these stories must be seeded.

Why bother? If you believe that players can entertain themselves sufficiently, it certainly takes some pressure off. You can concentrate on providing enough sand and plastic shovels without worrying too much about narrative. Kids make up their own stories after all in real sandboxes.

Single-player games were in a very similar state as MMOs for many years. Developers overwhelmingly chose gameplay over story. Eventually, some designers began to realize a balance between the two might create a synergy out of which a richer entertainment experience might grow. We will explore how this can happen when computers stand-in for humans.

First, we will acknowledge that little stories can justify their telling because even if only a few players at a time experience them, hopefully many players can experience them over the weeks and months and years that follow. Epic stories should invite participation by many gamers all at once. That is the challenge we will now tackle.

THOUSANDS OF HEROES

In virtual worlds that want to tell stories, it is important that mechanisms be in place to allow the story to reach the greatest number of players. It shouldn't be forced on them. A lot of different types of players play massive persistent worlds, and not all will be interested, no matter how much we may want them to be, in story. But it should be offered to all. And that can mean thousands of players, all of them wanting to be heroes. We can't write individual stories tailored for each player the way we could in tabletop. If the only stories we have in the game are repetitive errands so players can be legends in their own minds, but no one else will notice, they'll feel cheated. Real heroes get noticed! How can we possibly tell stories that they can drive and make them think their deeds matter? The challenge becomes this: if all those protagonists don't get to launch major stories, who does?

In Chapter 4, "Character Roles," we examined some of the important roles NPCs can play in our game stories. They are particularly useful in virtual worlds because the few elements supporting authorial story are so often shoved aside. One of those roles is as pivotal characters. Several well-known characters from the *Lord of the Rings Trilogy* showed up in *Lord of the Rings Online* to offer quests and set events in motion. Being a hero can't mean always taking center stage in a virtual world but being a part of the events initiated by these major figures gives all players who participate a chance to share in the excitement. Tragic NPCs can add weight and meaning to the story. Players may not want to play such characters but interacting with them can be very powerful.

ONGOING STORY

In this section, I'll suggest a possible template to use for the release of the ongoing story and its new content. Don't mistake these for hard and fast rules that guarantee success. Adapt them to your own needs. First, let's look at the trap of episodic structure.

> Episodic structure: As in weekly network television shows or Netflix streaming limited series that are divided into episodes like chapters in a book.

Several potential challenges quickly become apparent. Every major story event we add to the world should have components that can be experienced by any player in the world simultaneously. Both high-level players and low-level players should face challenges that match their levels.

The often-used method is to continue an ongoing narrative in episodic chunks. However, episodic content dumps at regularly scheduled times can give players the chance to exit too easily. When new content only attracts the critical mass of players necessary to enjoy it in a short period of time once a month, players who can't participate during that small window of opportunity can find themselves left out in the cold. There will be fewer and fewer online in the troughs between the swells. A rigid episodic schedule works against the very social interaction designers want to encourage. Overlapping content increases the chances players will stay put because the story doesn't end. (Revisit this concept in Chapter 9, Arcs.) Surprise players with staggered updates and they won't want to miss the new material.

Yet another problem is our old friend immersion. All TV shows take place in universes that can be revealed as needed. It doesn't matter if that universe is a small town in Ohio or the neutral zone between Federation and Romulan space. Want to set a couple of scenes someplace we've never been, like a Romulan bowling alley? Do it. Want to introduce that wacky Klingon next-door neighbor? No problem.

In a virtual world players can explore every square inch. Every NPC can be found and interacted with. Players know there's no bowling alley yet, and if new NPCs are needed, their arrival will be noticed. Bundling up all our new content in one neat episodic package tells the players they are playing a game. The world isn't real. "Here's new stuff you didn't have before!" Every time we deliver new content like this, we just push the fourth wall aside and stuff the content into the world.

In soap operas with their multiplayer storylines, when their writers introduce new characters, they have two choices: the big splash and the slow build. The big splash is not as subtle. The character no one has ever seen before marches into the nearest crossover set and confronts the saintliest regular on the show with their love child. The slow build introduces the character in an almost offhand way and gradually either works them into an ongoing story or begins to reveal their own story. Or both. This builds suspense. Why is this character here, and what are they up to, the audience wonders?

In *The Gryphon Tapestry*, there were wolves in the forests to the southwest of the small village of Thornhollow. Most were mobs that players could kill. Occasionally, a local NPC farmer may have placed a bounty on them if his livestock were being attacked, increasing the benefit of hunting them. There was also an old gray wolf that had been in the forest, no one knew how long. He did not kill livestock, was only occasionally glimpsed, and he didn't act at all like the other wolves. There was an aura of mystery about him. He was there from the first moment players entered the world, even figuring in a quest or two. Months later, he would be revealed to be a shape shifter, a local beggar already established as a separate character, and much, much later as a powerful mage.

Another character was a kindly, but somewhat befuddled cleric at a local church, much loved in his community, and of great help and comfort to players. We were going to kill him off about three months into the game.

The first thing to do is prepare the way. Establish the foundations of upcoming story. The next step is to *mix the scale and length of narrative pieces* in a single story, or of stories themselves. Hang stories of all sizes and shapes on the overall arc. Connect them to each other by interesting and surprising means. Make some simple matrix quests, some one-offs, and still others that change the world in ways that support the narrative.

Before I get into detail, there's a very important concept from episodic television we need to be familiar with: *lead time.*

> Lead time: the time between the scripting, preproduction, and production of an episodic television show and its air date.

If a network TV show's premiere is scheduled for September 1, preparations for that and subsequent episodes begin in April or May. By the time September rolls around, shows want to have several episodes to choose from "in the can" (shot and ready to air), and scripts for as many more as possible in shootable form. Shows from streaming services that only run 6–10 episodes will often have every show in the can (completed). For longer network series by the end of the season, the lead time will have been chewed up and production companies will often be scrambling to stay two or three weeks ahead. Sound familiar? Virtual worlds aren't the only medium plagued by army ants.

And because our assets can take longer to create than television, we need even more lead time. In the suggestions that follow, you may be surprised by how far apart the writing and introduction of content must be to stay ahead. The thing to keep in mind is that because the material is written in stages, there are several chances to be flexible even with such extended lead times.

One other note: this plan may seem a lot more at home in waterfall development than agile development. I've used it in both environments, particularly since waterfall is almost nonexistent in game development these days. However, agile development should never be an excuse for a lack of preproduction. And it might interest you to know that while most of *Star Wars: The Old Republic* was built along standard agile/scrum lines and while the massive writing task was managed in the beginning within agile development cycles, Executive Producer Richard Vogel told me that they returned to waterfall for the writing because "It just worked better that way."

Okay, start by thinking of these stories in several layers. Begin with the ongoing story arc of the world that hopefully will never end. Next lay out content that will last a significant length of time, say three years. Now triple the amount of that content since the army ants always chew faster than you expect. Next, outline a handful of major storylines of three to six months' duration. And finally, toss in a varied selection of smaller stories that can be completed before the next new content is released. Make sure to overlap them all as they climb those stairs from Chapter 9.

Write your quests to support the stories. Plan to stagger and vary the introductions of NPCs who will launch the stories or figure prominently in them. Create new items, thematically consistent with the stories that introduce them. How do we keep track of all of this?

It doesn't matter if you use Word, HTML, Excel, a Wiki, Google Docs, or any of the other popular formats for creating design documents, but I would suggest first writing everything as if it were a continuing narrative. Want to build your stories modularly? Bravo! The first pass at this can be as simple as describing each module in a separate paragraph. Just remember that if you don't use some kind of hypertext-style environment like HTML or Excel or even bookmarks and hyperlinks in Word, make sure that your paragraphs do not directly reference one another. The references lie in floating variables that will attach themselves to the appropriate modules, depending upon any individual player's choices of where to go and what to do next.

Write four story documents so the task doesn't seem so overwhelming. Start with the overarching, never-ending story for the game. This is as much a vision statement as it is a story and is probably only a few pages at most. Have a pretty good idea where you want to be a few years down the road but know that this will almost certainly change based on the development of the game and the actions of your players. The key to all of this is having the flexibility to respond to your production's and players' needs without compromising your overall vision.

Next write a macro story document that describes your three-year story arc. This could be about sixty pages long and includes the major storylines that take several weeks to several months to complete, and as many shorter stories as possible. You just hit the major events and connecting tissue. The storyline should be dynamic. The players should be able to affect it. But you don't want your players in such control that you have no idea what your world will look like in three years.

The major characters of all of these should be present. And the story commencement and completion dates should, of course, overlap. Production management software can be used to track the dates you plan to release and complete stories. Know that here, too, the players will have a major effect on your plans and prepare to improvise if necessary.

When I was writing *Edge of Night,* I planned out the beginnings and endings of stories down to the day. Yet real life constantly intruded. Actresses became pregnant; cast members became ill or fidgety about their contracts; sets were not quite ready in time. Anything could happen. Sometimes I would write dialogue minutes before a scene was shot.

The audience could even affect us. One story I was very proud of was based on a news item I'd read about a Native American burial ground that real estate developers wanted to move to make way for a subdivision. I used that as the basis of a story of the clash of cultures, tradition, greed, even mysticism. I planned to run it for three months. The audience didn't like it. One woman from Iowa wrote in that "Indians are always trying to take our land." ABC asked us to shorten the story. Sadly, I had to finish it up in six weeks. And then I had to come up with something entirely new to take its place. I moved up the beginning of another story even as I prematurely wrapped up the first story.

If I had not been ready with the next story, I still had a fallback position. Many of us squirrel away a couple gallons of water, a few cans of food, and extra flashlight batteries in case of a natural disaster. I keep files of stories, ideas, characters from my imagination, news clippings, and moments from other stories that struck me. More than once emergencies arose, and these scattered bits and pieces, separate or combined, became stories I could use.

The next step is to write individual long-term story documents for each of your major storylines. The length will vary with the lengths of your major stories, but not every detail needs to be in place yet. Then write story breakdowns (outlines) that indicate most of the beats of any story and exactly how they are going to be revealed to the players. Is an NPC going to tell players a crucial piece of exposition if a quest is completed for them? Is a beat going to be announced on the news? Found on a scrap of parchment? Blurted out by a cocky NPC right before he's unexpectedly killed? These will probably run about fifteen to twenty pages.

Finally, write "scripts" that include *all* the details needed for the content, including NPC dialogue, step-by-step quests, new items, mobs, and so forth.

The first two macro documents (vision and three-year story arc) should be written early in preproduction. To give the team enough lead time, the long-term story documents for the first year or so should be completed well before alpha. Six months of the story breakdowns and scripts should be ready when the first testers arrive to begin playing. These detailed content scripts should be written with approximately two to three months' lead time. This time frame gives you a chance to adjust to players' actions, but still stay ahead of them. I could be only two weeks ahead on *Edge* because the physical production only took one day.

Remember, these stories will be staggered and overlapped so the three months of material will not begin or end simultaneously. Some stories will end before the three months are up. Others will extend long past that time.

Three months is a reasonable compromise between staying ahead of the army ants and remaining flexible to their changing appetites. Any longer than that, and your ability to respond to short-term player trends drops. Any shorter than that, and you risk ant bites on your ankles.

This schedule may feel relentless and unforgiving, but it is no more so than weekly episodic television or soap opera where content is added daily. If you don't take the time to properly prepare and do it as early in the production process as possible, the authorial storytelling in your virtual world will suffer. And naysayers will have one more "proof" it can't work at all. There is something else we need to consider when discussing the release of new content: the trap of episodic structure.

THE TRAP OF EPISODIC STRUCTURE

Asheron's Call was the first MMO to institute regular episodic updates to content. They based their delivery mechanism on television episodes. Every month, the servers were brought down, and new quests, NPCs, and items were added. Geography was changed. Towns could be permanently wiped from the map. Unlike *Horizons,* which came four years later, these changes occurred and then players reacted to them. *Earth & Beyond* followed this release pattern of monthly updates. *Star Wars Galaxies* was attempting to do the same in those first few months when I played it, but without much success. As I've mentioned, in those days *Horizons* was tackling the daunting task of releasing new content on a *weekly* basis.

This seems like a perfectly logical application of episodic structure to MMO storytelling. How is it a trap? In the hot summer months when air conditioners are draining the power grid, utility companies will institute what they call "rolling brownouts" to prevent a total blackout. Blackouts still happen. Remember Texas' power grid collapse in 2021? But by lessening the load, more can be prevented from occurring by spreading the load out over time and geography.

We face a similar situation in MMOs that rely on episodic structure, and several potential problems quickly become clear. When a new event was launched in *Asheron's Call,* everybody on a server would flood the location where it occurred. To prevent them from crashing the server, a unique form of involuntary teleportation was awkwardly worked into the game fiction to explain why players found themselves booted out of the area.

Here, the dilemma was that they wanted as many players as possible to participate in a major event like the release of new content, but their servers couldn't handle the load. One solution was to spread the effects of the content over more than one location. This fits in with the concept of providing things to do for players of all levels in each content release. Delivering that spread of activity will create only the occasional brownout of lag and not force a server reboot.

When story is provided in episodes, there is also the legitimate concern that players will complete one story episode and then stop playing. In network television, every act between commercials is not the same length. With staggered breaks and overlapping content, the channels hope to grab and retain their audience. Most network TV shows, as opposed to streaming services, are stuck in regular schedules that begin and end on the hour or half hour. Episodic content release in game production was copied from network television exactly, even if the analogy between the two mediums wasn't as explicit as it seemed on the surface.

Unfortunately, episodic content dumps at regularly scheduled times give players the chance to exit cleanly. If developers broke the rhythm of regular updates that players expected, and surprised them with staggered updates, impatient players wouldn't have been given time to think about giving up and going elsewhere.

Another problem with episodic structure is that players often only log on when new content is released. A world would suddenly have a population spike, like a resort town on the weekend, the day new content was released. This is a given of episodic television, and not a problem. Every week, regular as clockwork, viewers tune in. It doesn't translate to MMOs at all well. An interesting trend in streaming services today is to return to individual weekly updates rather than make all episodes immediately available. Recently Netflix announced it is losing hundreds of thousands of viewers. Experimenting with the decades-old network television model by several services indicates that they are concerned about subscriber retention.

Designers of MMOs work hard to encourage players to play with each other. One solution I hate is to provide higher levels of content (always involving the defeat of powerful mobs) that solo players cannot enjoy by themselves. The idea is that once a player has played enough to advance that far, they will have made enough friends to team up and defeat the bigger mobs. In actual practice, however, friends come and go, guilds dissolve, and people live in different time zones. Players may be ready for such an experience yet unable to have it for reasons that have nothing to do with their sociability.

When new content only attracts the critical mass of players necessary to enjoy it in a short period of time once a month, players who can't participate during that small window of opportunity can find themselves left out in the cold. There will be fewer and fewer online in the troughs between the swells. A rigid episodic schedule works against the very social interaction designers want to encourage.

Yet another problem is our old friend immersion. Bundling up all our new content in one neat episodic package tells the players they are playing a game. The world isn't real. "Here's new stuff you didn't have before!" Every time we deliver new content, we just push the fourth wall aside and stuff the content into the world.

Instead of plunking down a new set of static characters the moment you need them, all primed with exposition or a quest, introduce them over time *before* the story's point of attack is reached. One week a new merchant replaces a familiar face behind the counter and says they're new to town. The merchant may not become involved in the story for quite a while. We don't have to create new characters. Move an NPC that players know from one town to another. Give them a reason for the change of scenery. Whether the reason they give is true or not remains to be discovered by the players.

If we stagger the content delivery, we support the feeling that the virtual world is real and continuing. Characters come and go, their entrances and exits overlap. Stories may begin subtly or with a bang, and they too overlap just like in soap operas. We need to plan far enough ahead so that we don't have to slow down the release of relevant content when the population is ready for it. If the new content is tied to an ongoing story where players can't wait to find out what is going to happen next to themselves and their world, we can create pleasurable suspense like a good horror film. The shark in *Jaws* did not attack every afternoon at three o'clock.

REVEALING STORY

The delivery mechanisms at the writer/designer's disposal in a single-player game can be restricted by choices made as the game is designed. MMOs, because they have the potential of allowing us the entire range of methods to reveal the story, are far more flexible. Let's remind ourselves of some of the ways that stories can be revealed in a game.

- **Level restrictions.** Players can be forced to follow a linear path with level or item restrictions used as a sort of combination lock. The player must be a certain level and/ or carry a specific item to gain access to new content.

- **We can use town criers, bartenders, journalists, and other similar NPCs to dispense exposition, or to direct players to where it can be found.** This includes the backstory and current events. Providing ways to share the story draws interested players in and keeps them involved even if they arrived late to the game or missed some major story event.

- **NPCs that are not the usual information sources can be mined for gossip and rumors.** (See Chapter 4 for more detail.) Other NPCs may have windows on the future: magic spells, scientific devices, or simple intuition and deduction to foreshadow upcoming events like Cassandra running fruitlessly around Troy telling its citizens not to let that giant horse inside the gates.

- **Some NPCs may be fixated on certain plot points.** Others, like gossips, can be regularly updated with new exposition. Quest givers can change the quests they assign based on current events. Nowhere is it written that they must be static. Their interests can change as the story progresses.

- **Inanimate objects like books, journals, message boards, signposts, video screens, and so on can be used in obvious ways.** Keep the text succinct by supplementing it in other ways. Ruins may have plaques like historical buildings do: "On this site eleven months ago stood a flourishing city...." We could then salt the surroundings with NPCs who are witnesses, or who are present to study and rebuild. They can provide details in bits and pieces.

- **In all the above, story points do not have to be accurate or correspond to points from other sources.** We can establish reliable story sources and less reliable story sources, as we discussed in Chapter 4. These are not only NPCs. Books can lie. Everything you read on Wikipedia is not necessarily true.

Players don't need to start at the beginning of a story to become actively involved, if we provide entry points like flashbacks. "The story up till now" is a part of the world's history and should be readily available to newcomers in a variety of ways like chatty NPCs, expository quests, news archives, and more.

World-changing, ongoing story is easy to write. It retains its mysteries just like the ongoing story in other media. Players do not know what is coming until it is revealed at the designer's pleasure. Smaller stories and repeatable stories found in NPC encounters or quests are not so straightforward. For these smaller storylines, there is a trap in writing them the way you would a mystery. There are no secrets in MMOs. It's much better to embrace that fact and encourage players to spread the lore. There are other ways to provide surprise, the cheapest of which, of course, are random story elements, a gameplay solution.

A subtle variation is to keep those random elements within the context of the story. Use the reliability of witnesses, gossips, and commentators as random story elements. A pathological liar is about as random as you can get. Keep them in character, and you have a story solution as well.

Quests and missions are excellent mechanisms for the delivery of story; but in virtual worlds they are too many times constructed the same way they are in tabletop and single-player games, one of those patches in our design quilt that doesn't match. Let's look at how to build quests that better fit our multiplayer worlds.

TRUE MULTIPLAYER QUESTS

What do I mean by this? A single-player quest in a multiplayer game is one that resets its conditions for every player who undertakes it. If one player kills a creature named Randy the Rancorous Raccoon and is rewarded by the grateful Quest Giver, the next player in line will receive the same assignment, and Randy becomes Randy the Resurrected Rancorous Raccoon, ready to die again.

Why bother with true multiplayer quests? Everybody accepts the convention of solo quests, don't they? We accept conventions if there is no alternative, but when there is a plain alternative that supports story and immersion, there is no reason at all not to pursue it. If we don't do that, the verisimilitude of the world is broken, and the player's success is diminished because a thousand other players managed to do exactly the same thing. The quest story details are trivial compared to the gameplay mechanisms they serve. They are there simply as another way for players to receive experience or loot as rewards.

We already have respawning mobs and magically replenished resources in MMOs as a game convention, so that players will never be able to kill everything; and lumberjacks don't have to wait for new growth in forests to mature. Alternatives have not fared well. But if one were to come along that made sense, these fiction-breaking conventions could be done away with as well.

Just as developers want content that renews itself automatically to lessen the amount of new content we must create; it would seem to follow that respawning quests could work the same way. Replayability in single-player games is a feature. In MMOs, it is a necessity. We welcome it wherever and whenever we find it.

Replayability is not a concern when designing epic quests that advance the story, but in all other cases it must be confronted, or it chops away at the fourth wall, immersion, and players' willing suspension of disbelief. Even epic one-off quests to advance individual characters must feel like true multiplayer quests. This may sound like a paradox, but it isn't. There are two types of replayability:

- **One player can do some quests repeatedly.** The matrix FedEx quests fall into this category. When written simply, as in "Creature X is a nuisance, kill as many as you can," they are repeatable, and truly multiplayer. The repeatability can be timed, e.g., the quest is only available every twenty-four hours.

- **One player can only do a quest a single time, but the quest remains available for all other players, or at least those who match whatever requirements might be imposed.**

FIGURE 17.1   Hasten pauses long enough for a photo op.

Most of this kind of repeatable one-off quests falls into the category of single-player quests masquerading unsuccessfully as multiplayer such as the Journeyman Boots quest from *Everquest* where the quest for the boots resets for every player who catches Hasten (Figure 17.1), or Connla's Fever from *Dark Age of Camelot* where the ingredients for a plague cure are delivered by one player, but when the next player in line clicks on the same NPC seconds later the plague is back like an instantaneous variant of COVID.

Writing true multiplayer quests is about perspective as much as anything else. Matrix quest structure can make it easy. Even one-offs like the two ancient examples above can be reshaped once we stop blindly following the old paradigm of shoving single-player quests into our worlds and calling them multiplayer simply because more than one player-character can experience them. Almost any quest can be written as single-player or true multiplayer. The choice is ours. All that is required is the will to do it.

CROWD CONTROL

Instancing is an important concept that gives us more control over the environments we place our content in.

Instancing is usually done to remove the necessity for rival groups to compete for the same mob camps or loot. If players choose to enter a dungeon,

> Instancing: Creating a private but identical section of a virtual world, such as a dungeon, to limit the number of players who experience it at any one time.

a private dungeon (Dungeon 1A) is created at that moment. If a second group of adventurers want to enter the same dungeon, they find themselves in Dungeon 1B. When we used a form of this in *The Gryphon Tapestry* in 1999, we did it to support the storytelling since the camping of mobs was not a major part of the gameplay. It evolved like this:

One of my favorite zones in *Everquest,* which I was heavily involved in as a player at the time, was Castle Mistmoore, a sinister castle where high-level undead walked. The spooky atmosphere was painstakingly created. But then something happened. Lots of players wanted to play there. The atmosphere was destroyed by rooms and graveyards crowded with hordes of players lining up to attack helpless mobs. The graveyard was alternately funny and annoying, as players lined the walls ready to be the first to pounce on poor skeletons and zombies as soon as they appeared.

I wanted to avoid this in *TGT* so we could maintain control over the atmosphere in some of the crucial sequences in our stories. We created what we called story locations. One was a graveyard. When a player or a single group of players chose a story that took place partly in the graveyard, a version of the graveyard was created especially for them. When they found themselves there at night, they would be alone. Or rather there would at least be no other *players* with them... Any company they had belonged there. The spooky atmosphere was preserved, and a ghost story could be told without disruption from other players. If another group reached the same point in the story, they would find themselves alone in their own graveyard.

Londontown began life in 2007 as an MMO built by my students and colleagues and based on design work I'd been doing on my own since 1999. In *Londontown,* I extended this story location metaphor. Not only were there story locations that were instanced the way dungeons were beginning to be instanced, but I also instanced *hiring scenes,* certain forms of transportation, and of course, housing.

> Hiring Scene: initial contact with a quest giver where a player is offered the quest.

In a hiring scene, players can choose to accept or refuse the quest. (Some MMOs force players to accept quests before they've heard all the details. This is quest giver as used car salesman and should be avoided.) There are a number of very famous characters in *Londontown* that players would be familiar with. In none of the stories featuring these characters were their homes or places of business crammed from floor to ceiling with players begging for work.

Most developers approach the problem from the point of view of gameplay only. If fifteen people are all asking for quests simultaneously, and all that text, including NPC dialogue, is streaming past, too much can be lost in the process. So, we suppress the text display. The same holds true if the NPC granting the quest is voiced. In both cases, it's mandatory that a player only sees the text, or hears only the conversation of their encounter.

But still there may be dozens of other players standing nearby when the super-secret mission is granted to a player. This crowd ruins the illusion. The player is no longer special, with their own relationship to the quest giver; they are just one of many faceless adventurers lined up in a homeless shelter waiting for their soup bowl to be filled.

Just as graveyards are instanced, these meetings with quest givers, where appropriate, should be instanced too. Just because we are creating games is no reason to subject our players to each other twenty-four hours out of every day. Just as in real life, and certainly as in real drama, sometimes private moments are important.

Star Wars: The Old Republic adapted a similar model: story areas that only the player, or the player's group could enter to receive quests and rewards. These instances were separated from the rest of the world by colored force fields. Green meant you could enter. Red meant this area was not for you. Yes, it is a gameplay solution, not a narrative or immersive solution, but the instinct is a good one.

In *Londontown*, I wanted to emphasize a rigid class structure. I therefore allowed those of wealth and position to travel by private means, while only public transportation was available to the lower classes. While they were traveling, they could not be disturbed by other players, only scripted story events. Rest assured that there were attractions for all classes in this system. There are a lot of reasons players might want to forego private transportation for some other benefit.

Finally, housing was instanced. The geography of the game was urban, and therefore, its boundaries were limited to a certain extent. You can't add housing to an urban environment the way you could the vast expanses of countryside in *Star Wars Galaxies*. So private homes were instanced in two ways: there could be many wealthy addresses on certain streets, reached by private transportation, and many rooms in less affluent "apartment buildings."

Although instancing may have been initially designed to solve a gameplay problem, it is now another tool in our storytelling arsenal.

VARIETY

We've discussed varying story lengths to keep them from falling into ruts. We've talked about varying the length of lines in speeches to prevent their rhythms from falling into predictable, boring patterns. We can vary types of stories, too. Just because your world is high fantasy doesn't mean you can't tell stories drawn from life back here in the mundane world. Just because your themes are about greed and destruction doesn't mean you can't leaven them with laughter. Some stories can be funny, some sad; some thoughtful, some bawdy. Look at Chaucer's *The Canterbury Tales*. There is a rich spectrum of life on display, and the tales are better for it.

Trying to keep stories thematically consistent is good, but you don't have to illuminate the theme with the same color lights. Make people cry over it, make jokes about it. In the film *Seabiscuit,* the narrator, biographer, and historian David McCullough is heard in voice-over putting in perspective photographs from the Great Depression: "They called them forgotten men, but it was really a misnomer. They were wanderers. Men who left a shattered life in search of something new.... Men who left something new, desperately in search of something old...." As Charles Howard, Jeff Bridges' character in *Seabiscuit* proclaims: "Our horse is too small...our jockey's too big...our trainer's too old...and I'm too stupid to know the difference!"

Both lines nail the theme. There is worth in everyone if you dig down deep enough and give them a chance. The first is solemn and sad, the second boisterous and optimistic. Our themes deserve all the ways we can possibly find to illuminate them.

We can take recognizable characters from our own world and place them in any setting. As long as we're true to them in that new setting, they can provide a recognizable anchor for our audience. If we avoid anachronisms or parody, they keep us grounded in the humanity of our stories. They are recognizable because their human traits are universal.

Variety can and should be pursued when writing any game, but it is especially important in virtual worlds. We know we're going to find every opportunity to be repetitive to win the content race with players. We need to hide that repetition in any way possible. If two quests are basically FedEx of about the same length, difficulty, and with the same rewards, but one is heart-wrenching and the other hilarious, the player won't complain.

One of our smaller stories may concern a former hero's lost honor, another might be about farmer's rights, and still another the forbidden love between teenagers from rival clans. It is the diversity of our stories that adds to the breadth of our worlds as much as their acres of geography.

HIDING THE NUMBERS

In 2004, I wrote that after only eight years of massively multiplayer worlds, their paradigm was already showing its age. Players complained constantly about the level and loot *treadmill*. Yet now nearly twenty years later, that paradigm remains virtually intact.

> Treadmill: A term that describes the repetitious nature of killing or crafting to achieve the advancement of characters in games.

Music and sound effects are used routinely in other media to offer hints to how audiences are meant to feel and to foreshadow danger or delight. Our audience is trained to recognize them already. So why not use a technique of presenting information that does not break immersion?

Remember, in *Londontown,* we did not want NPCs with quests to grant to have markers floating in the air over their heads. Thanks to Norbert Herber's generative music, *Londontown* composed each individual player's soundtrack in real time. NPCs were identified by music cues. Players would not only be able to recognize which NPC currently had a quest to bestow, but also the type of quest: mysterious, dangerous, fun, and so on featuring appropriate individual musical themes. And the music would then track their progress. This idea of a personal soundtrack for storytelling and character development remains an unrequited dream.

Character development in virtual worlds normally follows patterns long established by tabletop and RPGs. Characters are mostly defined by their skills, attributes, race, and profession. Simply through utensil selection, we dictate to players how to play our games. If the only choices are either weapons or tools, then it is obvious to players they are meant to either kill or build. The names of professions like warrior or blacksmith also guide players. It is left up to the players to add distinct personalities.

This is not a bad thing. We can assign numerical values to all those character elements. That allows us to use the power of the computer to track a player's progress through the world. And tracking such advancement is important. Progress suggests forward momentum. It allows us to simulate progression in even the most static of virtual worlds. The world may not change, but the player can change within it.

The problem arises when these numbers are shared with players. If stats like hit points and health points, damage inflicted and taken, and so on are explicitly served up to players with numbers floating off the tops of characters' heads or health bars, it shouldn't be a surprise if players seize on those numbers as important. Certainly, in *Advanced Dungeons & Dragons,* the numbers are right there on the die that determines the outcome of battle and in the value of weapons that have their power indicated by a number. A short sword +2 hits harder than a short sword +1. Levels are tracked from one to twenty and are important for the additional power and skills a new level can add to a player-character.

But because a GM is in charge, the story of the game can absorb the personal choices of players and move forward. There is no time for repetitive behavior like camping or making the same weapon over and over again for experience. In a massively multiplayer game, however, if a player notices that a certain kind of mob is easier for his profession to kill than others, and that it provides reasonable amounts of experience every time one is killed, they are more likely to camp it. There is no GM to nudge them and say, "While you are hunting the Minor Clerks, you come upon a group of Middle Managers by the water cooler." Oops, no more camping. It's clear a larger battle is about to take place.

So again, we have a convention, share the numbers with the players, copied only because that's the way it's been done in the past. Some players will tell you they like the numbers. They will keep track of every experience point total needed for every level; which weapons hit for the most damage; and which armor protects best. These players are already here, making up a large portion of our market. They may be fickle and move from game to game as the next "generation" of multiplayer games is announced, or they can dip their toes in new games before returning to *Counterstrike: Global Offensive* or *Apex Legends,* but they've bought into those metaphors currently offered. We're still on the first generation of multiplayer worlds, folks, sorry.

For *Londontown,* I concentrated on players living in the virtual world and experiencing its ongoing story. The numbers were still there tracking player progress, but they were not shoved into players' faces. Since players could enjoy their lives in the virtual world without trying to become immensely powerful, there was no pressure to level or acquire loot. There are definite markers of progress players see, but the hierarchy is more flexible. Instead of advancing up a ladder-like career-obsessed corporate executives, players are allowed to find their own niches in the world and expand. Take a look at Figures 17.2 and 17.3.

The first figure is a typical chart of linear advancement for a character wanting to improve themselves while remaining within the ranks of the Church of England. Yes, you read that correctly. The ladder mimics the typical progression of characters in MMOs. Gain a level, gain more power, new skills, and so forth.

Figure 17.3 is an illustration of how a player-character might progress as a crime fighter without needing to climb a ladder. Here the player has experienced two linear

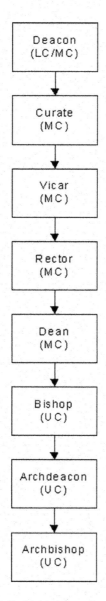

FIGURE 17.2 The typical MMO leveling ladder with ranks to gain found within a given profession instead of numbers.

progressions from professions within a police force and in private law enforcement. The resident started life as a private Watchman, moved to the police force where they chose to stay a bit longer as a Constable, breezed through Sergeant, spent a bit more time as an Inspector, solved a good number of cases as a Detective Inspector, and then headed back to the private sector and settled on life as a Private Inquiry Agent where their reputation continued to grow and grow.

Imagine within each box there is a list of cases (quests) this resident has solved. As a Watchman they may have solved only a handful before they decided to join the police force. As an Inspector, they needed to solve more cases to be promoted. They enjoyed life

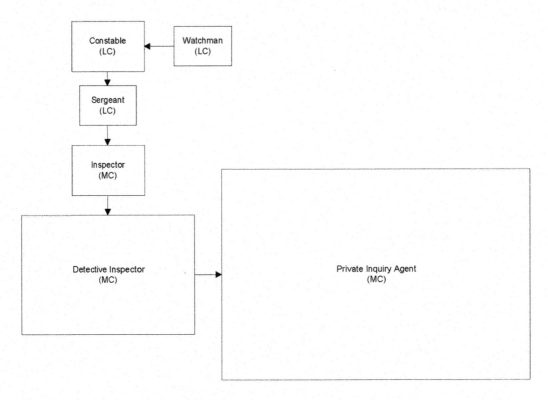

FIGURE 17.3   Players were able to settle down instead of climbing the ladder.

as a Detective Inspector quite a bit, so they had far more cases to their credit. And that reputation made it easy for them to gain clients once they decided to leave the force and take up detection on their own.

There is also no need to limit players to a single profession. Our detective friend in Figure 17.3 may, of course, change their mind and decide to become a surgeon. A noble calling, but a reputation for dissecting crimes will not serve in a hospital. They will have to begin again on the ground floor.

The bottom line is this: the player-character should be able to choose not to advance or at least not in the traditional sense of MMOs; yet always be assured of being a viable and productive part of the virtual community, offered new challenges, stories, recognition, and opportunities to affect the world. Once other paradigms for achievement are explored, the need for numbers diminishes.

I'm not the only writer/designer talking about hiding explicit numbers from the players. My reasons are simple, focused entirely on increasing immersion, protecting the fourth wall, and of foremost importance, supporting story. I'm advocating removing all those visible numerical equivalents of tabletop die rolls, not just for combat or leveling, but everything.

Any die roll result or check for balance the game makes can be expressed in a standardized way that players will recognize. You can even provide a chart in the documentation, if you wish, just don't have those numbers flashing past in the middle of a fight. You didn't see them when Stone took on twenty ninjas in an episode of *The Librarians*.

Sure, a TV show isn't interactive, but it would also destroy the fourth wall, and therefore harm your willing suspension of disbelief. (Check out another episode of *The Librarians* where they are trapped in a video game that resets at the beginning of a level each time they "die.".)

What makes us think the same isn't true in our worlds? They are commonly referred to as games, and they contain gameplay, but they are not only games. They are far more.

We've seen how we can escalate suspense and track the player-character's progress in the world by attaching a database to the character. In this way, the game engine can know which modules the PC has visited, and in what order, and can adjust the experiences in the remaining modules before the PC reaches them. We can create the illusion of a dynamic world that is altered by the actions of the player within it, a world where events pile on top of one another with purpose. Since the PC may alter the world in any number of nonstory ways as well, it provides a consistency of experience. We don't stop world-affecting gameplay for an insular story. The story affects the world, too. Maybe not in the same exact way. But it will feel appropriate, and that is what we are striving for.

So, we use NPCs who are not simply props or functions; we set up *a standardized* description of action so the player can quickly spot trends, success or failure, and specific text messages (again *standardized,* but not necessarily entirely repetitive) to report the outcome of encounters. If you're dying to use numbers, feel free to allow the merchants to count out change.

It is our duty as writers and designers of story-based genre games to do everything we can to guarantee the player a rewarding, fun experience. Therefore, we cannot totally abdicate authorship. We only need to keep it as integrated as possible through vivid characters who have lives of their own; gameplay that is consistent with world fiction and that supports ongoing story; and social systems that encourage emergent storytelling.

EMPOWERING EMERGENT STORYTELLING

We have concentrated on authorial storytelling in this chapter for two reasons. The first is, um, this book is about authorial storytelling. The second is that there are so many people developing games today who believe the players should be telling the story, and they don't need any additional support from an author. In this section, they're going to get it whether they like it or not. Even though many don't see room for authorial narrative when they promote players telling a story, I see a perfectly valid reason for encouraging player stories, even as we tell our own. We call this phenomenon emergent storytelling because it emerges from the world; we don't place it there.

Where did this idea of community storytelling come from? I see its origins in a couple of places. The first is the same as role-playing: children's games. The second is the phenomenon of the fan. I've had my share of delightful fan letters over the years, as well as some a lot less friendly.

Most fans are regular people who keep their fondness for a game or show or star or sports figure or team in perspective. At the far end of the spectrum are people who tangle up the object of their interest in their own lives. These are fans who *seem* to know the distinction between fact and fiction but can confuse the two.

When I was writing for *Quincy,* there were two prominent celebrity deaths within a short period of time in Hollywood: Natalie Wood and William Holden. Jack Klugman, the actor who played Quincy, a forensic pathologist, got more than one letter from fans asking him to investigate these "suspicious" deaths. An actress on *Edge of Night,* Sandy Faison, played a psychologist named Beth Correll. She showed me a fan letter whose author complimented her on her acting performance, and then proceeded to go into great detail about the fan's marital problems, asking for Sandy's advice. Get the idea?

For *Edge of Night,* I wrote a particularly intricate mystery centered on a murder in a hotel. As the story unfolded over several months, suspicion fell at least once on every single cast member, regular or guest-starring. When the story was at its peak fan mail poured in. I remember one letter in particular. It was several pages long, frantically handwritten. Since I was the head writer of the show, the letter writer had concluded that I was the best person to communicate with police chief Derek Mallory and detective Chris Egan (characters on the show played by Dennis Parker and Jennifer Taylor) and inform them that the letter writer had discovered the identity of the killer. The letter went on to explain in detail the author's solution to the crime.

I've responded to a few fan letters over the years. That was not one of them, nor was the invitation to join a coven in San Diego I received (complete with provocative Polaroids) when I was writing for *Tucker's Witch.* For the record, even though I wrote an episode of *Charlie's Angels* about the supernatural and was on staff on *Tucker's Witch* and *Blacke's Magic,* I am not now, nor have I ever been, actively involved in promoting the "old religion" in my work. Please don't reach for the wax and the pins. I'm not judging, only clarifying!

Fan fiction, something I believe the writer of the *Edge of Night* letter was engaged in even if they didn't know it at the time, occurs when nonprofessional writers become so enamored of the world created by the original authors that they want to add their own stories to it. It can be a very positive thing. Some write better stories than the writers of the original material. The important thing to realize is that content is not created in a vacuum. Oh, he was 100% wrong by the way.

Fan fiction attached to our worlds lies outside the game, usually online due to copyright and liability issues. In-game we can guide players, but we need ways to enforce rules. How do we go about empowering emergent storytelling? We stimulate the players' desire to tell stories. We can do this in several ways:

- **Construct a game world that players will want to inhabit, which sparks their imaginations.** Basically, take everything suggested in this chapter, and then add a hundred more things of your own that make your world immersive, exciting, and fun.

- **Set the stage for emergent storytelling with a detailed backstory, or lore, as it is sometimes called.** Unlike a single-player game that can get bogged down by backstory, the stronger the backstory in a virtual world, the more liable players are to seize on it, rather than having to create their own that may conflict with it now or in the future.

- **Compose with a single voice—not necessarily a single composer, but rather design and write with thematic and stylistic continuity, no matter how many**

developer-side authors are involved. Consistency in style and vision can help new storytellers find their voices. If you feel a crying need to have your dwarves speak like Scots, make sure they all do.

- **Provide platforms and tools for storytelling that are epic, like theaters for large performances and campfires that are more intimate.** Feature writeable books. Areas can be set aside in pubs for individual or small group performances. Overturned boxes placed on the corners of public gardens might encourage popular oratory and fiery debate like those in Hyde Park. Create a journalist class or profession that can submit material to newspapers or broadcasts. Allow for "amateur" submissions from non-journalists, too. Curate this material to retain editorial control. Players can't publish, but they can submit to NPCs, and then developers can make the decisions. The more avenues for expression the better, both formal and informal.

- **Create a filter so that the best stories can emerge.** Acknowledge their authors in rankings or grant them in-game awards.

All of these empower emergent storytelling that in no way interferes with the ongoing authorial storytelling writers and designers add. One kind of storytelling supports the other. Just like narrative and gameplay, they are not at odds with each other. To limit either is to limit a huge opportunity for the widest range of players to enjoy our worlds.

FOOTPRINTS IN THE SAND

In the future everyone will be famous for 15 minutes.

Andy Warhol

Well, fifteen minutes is not long enough in multiplayer virtual worlds. Players want to leave their tracks on our worlds, visible to all. Allowing players to have a real and lasting effect may sound like we're ceding too much control. But it isn't really, no more than allowing players to choose how they will experience modular stories removes authorial control. Yet it is one of the hardest challenges we wrestle with multiplayer games. Many developers would rather just avoid it.

When we looked at quests in Chapter 10, one aspect of the various levels of quests was how much they affected the world. We're now going to revisit quests for a short time; look at other ways players can affect the world; and see how this essential attribute of gameplay in turn affects storytelling.

In our hierarchy of quests, we found that even intimate quests can affect the world. If there is a robust news-gathering and dissemination system in place, other players can learn in-game of the achievements of their peers. Even minor incidents can be covered. Local happenings can be picked up by town criers or displayed on notice boards in town halls or pubs. These moments of glory can be as fleeting as an appearance or two on the nightly news; or become permanent additions to the world as souvenirs that can be discovered or citations and rewards that can be issued to individual players for display in their homes.

We can seed guilds and other political systems with NPCs, then allow players to gradually take them over. We can do the same with information systems. In *TGT*, we announced local events, like a limerick contest with prizes on a pub's message board, and then listed the best poets there. Explorers who discover new and interesting features like beautiful waterfalls or uncharted caves can be honored by the game naming those things on in-game maps. In *Anarchy Online*, launched in 2001, players and guilds could get powerful items named after them.

As in MUSHes, almost any system that allows change in a massively persistent world can be adapted for the use of players with the proper seeding and policing. There are obvious opportunities for abuse if you allow players the ability to type in public notices. "The developers suck!" is not the worst of these. But the potential for involving players and allowing them to affect their worlds makes the attempt a worthy one.

> MUSH: stands for multi-user habitat. These online communities emphasize the social aspects of virtual worlds.

Players can be allowed to affect our worlds in small ways, like winning a local beauty contest. Rewards may be even more tangible. I proposed personalized bricks like those you see outside museums which could be accumulated and used to build bridges to new islands in *Disney's Virtual Kingdom*.

In time, as more heroes emerge and more achievements have been recorded, chronicles of the world can be written for players to read. This may be authored by the world's team of writers. Part of these chronicles may also be fan fiction. The more story that is produced from either source, the more the world has a sense of history, a true passage of time, and the more that players feel a part of it. This gives players a huge stake in the world, yet another reason to keep playing, and to play the world as designed.

There is nothing more valuable to maintaining a community of players than allowing each one to leave their footprints in the sand.

CHAPTER 18

Storytelling in Small Games

I N 2004, I WROTE "Console games are the biggest part of the current gaming market." Not any longer. Today, millions more people play either standalone small games or social network games both falling under the heading of casual games.

Some, like *Candy Crush* and its various incarnations, are not interested in story at all. *Pokémon Go* allows players to play in an augmented reality version of the real world, but there is no real story beyond a setup for the gameplay. Others are story light and concentrate on gameplay like *Stardew Valley* or *Bistro Heroes*. And still others, such as *Gone Home, Episode: Choose Your Story,* or three smaller games I've written for that I'll cover in this chapter, did contain storytelling. Two of these games did not have a lot of room for story, but the third had plenty of room. While reading this chapter, please keep in mind the following quote from Nate Fox at Sucker Punch Productions, most recently Creative Director of *Ghost of Tsushima*:

> Make the story an integral part of the play experience and the synergy between [design and storytelling] will draw people's interest... both to the game play challenges and why they should care about overcoming those challenges.

STAR TREK: INFINITE SPACE

While I've written for what could be called casual applied games—sometimes called *serious* games—since the first year of this century (we'll get to these in Chapter 19), I began work on my first casual commercial game in 2010. I was the only professional writer beamed aboard Gameforge's casual MMO *Star Trek: Infinite Space* (see Figure 18.1). I was also design consultant along with Mike and Denise Okuda, a delightful couple who are the foremost Star Trek experts on the planet. If you want a definitive book on everything Star Trekkian, get one of theirs.

I am sorry this first game never launched. The team in Germany was excellent and we all learned how to do some very creative storytelling in very small bits. But sometimes

DOI: 10.1201/9780429284991-23

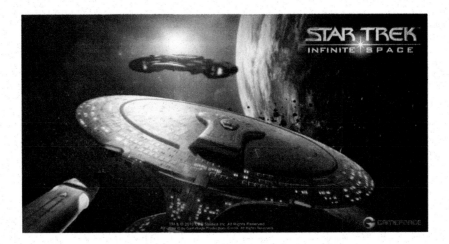

FIGURE 18.1 Today *Star Trek: Infinite Space* is currently taking up finite space on a shelf.

the planets refuse to align. In this case the issue was money, not the first nor the last time money or a lack of it kept a good game from releasing.

Two points I want to make here. First, I don't care how casual your MMO is, one writer is not going to be enough; and any writer who accepts a job like that should have their head examined. (That reminds me I still need to make an appointment for my examination.) Luckily, I was allowed to give a first writing job to several of my students.

The second point is that no matter how connected the writer and the company who hires them are, telecommuting is not easy. I've had more than my share of telecommuting. Game companies sprout in all sorts of far-off places. In 1999, I was living in Florida when I was lead writer and a designer on *The Gryphon Tapestry*. The development team was based in Maryland just outside of Washington, D.C. I slept on a cot in the producer's office every couple of weeks when I flew up for meetings. In 2001, I had my longest regular commute. Still living in Florida, I was lead writer on *URU: Ages beyond Myst* for Cyan, based in Spokane, Washington. Every couple of weeks I flew from one corner of the country to another. I remember how much I whined about the traffic when I was commuting on the freeways across Los Angeles and the San Fernando Valley when I wrote and produced TV. Florida to Washington State though? Yikes!

But let's make this commute back to 2010. Gameforge is a German company located in Karlsruhe, a short train ride south of Frankfurt. Keen Games, the developer of the game, was in Frankfurt itself. Very convenient, except for the fact that CBS, the network who owned the rights to the portion of the Star Trek universe we would be exploring, was in Los Angeles along with Mike and Denise, while I was living in Indiana.

Forget health benefits and pension plans, writers are often contractors, even when they can come to the office every day. They are contractors so developers won't have to pay their health benefits or add them to the stock option list. Here's the real problem: no matter how hard the developer tries to make you one of the team—some do, some don't—you are still an outsider. You cannot go to every daily standup or sprint review. You may show up and find somebody else sitting at your desk, or your car being towed. (I'm going to protect the guilty in this case.)

And because you are not there in a cubicle every day, even with email, text-messaging, access to the developer's intranet and Skype or Zoom, you will not be as up on changes that can occur within minutes to the design; you cannot rewrite on the spot unless you're present; you cannot be an immediate advocate for character and story. The game I'm currently writing is for a company in France. Regular Skype meetings, lots of emails, and a shared Google Drive are working pretty well, but they're still no substitute for being in the same building.

So, if you cannot be in the studio physically, it becomes part of your job to use every communication tool at your disposal to keep up to date with new builds and to maintain a continuing dialogue about your assignments and progress. Casual internet games are no easier to write for than the most expensive console games.

A big game like *Red Dead Redemption* 2 can luxuriate in dialogue scenes longer than the spaghetti westerns it emulates. There is no such indulgence in casual games. The primary craft is to reduce entire stories to a few lines of dialogue. For *Star Trek: Infinite Space*, I wrote mostly standard branching, occasionally web, dialogue trees as shown in "Land of the Blind" below.

Because the player communicates with away teams from the bridge of the ship, the entire story is told through small snippets of dialogue with NPCs on the main screen, brief opinions voiced by the player's NPC crew, and player dialogue choices. The player is allowed to repeat the story until a satisfactory conclusion is reached.

That's it: the entire story, a Star Trek episode in miniature. Even within such strict parameters, a meaningful story, one that would not feel out of place in a *Star Trek* film or TV episode, could be told without long-winded speeches. The longest section of text for all the stories we told was the mission briefing: a transmission from an NPC, an SOS, a message chiseled in stone, whatever, granting the quest. This quest was a one-off. Quests that advanced the continuing story were handled in the same way.

It is a seductive trap to try and answer as many questions as possible in a single speech or scene. But, in fact, withholding story or character revelation, doling them both out in hard-won snippets, is a primary tool in all good storytelling to maintain suspense and launch surprising twists. In casual games, the very nature of the beast requires the writer to do just that.

One-Off quest: A quest that is complete on its own, disconnected from other quests or story beats in the game.

Interesting stories can be told with very few of the tools available to us when we create games. If you cannot tell the story with the engine you have, let that be your guide on how you must change the story to match your capabilities. An example of one of these stories is shown in the box below.

LAND OF THE BLIND

==Author(s)==
Lee Sheldon

==Date==
7/9/2010

==Type==
Combo

==Faction==
Federation

==Overall Synopsis==
Asked to make a routine check on Talen 2, a planet of humanoids who are all blind from birth, the player's away team discovers the people are extremely fearful about an event they try to keep secret. The away team discovers that a single child has been born with sight, and the Talen are trying to decide whether to raise her as she is, destroy her, exile her, or blind her to maintain their culture. The player must make an ethical decision that will affect the future of an entire race, and its place within the Federation.

==Repeatable==
No

==Number of Players==
1 only

==Connections==
None

==Locations==
Bridge of Player's ship

==NPCs==
Player's NPCs if needed

==Assets==
Portraits of inhabitants: Human, but eyeless
Bekka, female human, age 6

Backgrounds for away team reports
Note: These can be used again in other missions.

==Purpose==
This mission presents a moral dilemma worthy of Solomon.

==Player Goals==
The player needs to:

   1) Determine the nature of the Talen's distress
   2) Determine the cause of the genetic shift
   3) Prevent the death of at least two children

==Rewards==
Varying degrees of Prestige Points based on player decisions. See Outline for suggested PP allocation.

==**Lore**==
There is no prerequisite for this mission.

==**Outline**==

BRIEFING

1) Starfleet orders the player to make a routine visit to Talen 2, to assure the inhabitants of the Federation's commitment to their sector. Talen is a staunch ally of the Federation whose entire population is eyeless, but who are not only self-sufficient, but who develop some of the highest technology in the Federation. Their nature is extremely hospitable, quite seductive in fact, and while other humanoid races can become smitten with Talens, no intermarriage has ever occurred. Starfleet says there is no real need for extra security precautions.

Player Choices:
  a) Accept mission
  b) Decline mission (END)

Result:
The player warps to the planet's coordinates alone. The player's ship comes out of warp and enters orbit around the planet. (NOTE: From this point on player can find info on Talen 2 in the ship's computer.) An away is assembled and beamed to the planet's capital city.

STORY ENCOUNTER - PLANET AWAY TEAM

The away team reports that the Talen hospitality delegation assigned to them seem more reticent, even secretive than usual. And the capital city is in something of an uproar preparing for a meeting of the T6, an assembly composed of the leaders of the major nations.

2) Player choices:
  a) Remind the away team to observe, but not to interfere in Talen's lawful governance.
  b) Order the away team to learn what it can about the T6 meeting.
  c) Search Starfleet records for information on the Talen culture.

Results:
  a) Away team reports that some team members appear to be becoming emotionally involved with members of the Talen hospitality delegation assigned to look after them. (reappears if c chosen)
  b) Away team reports that the T6 meeting is not a regularly-scheduled one, but hastily-called to deal with some internal Talen matter. No one will speak of the reason the meeting was called, but whatever it is, it is the source of the current anxiety in the population. (reappears if c chosen) (+1 PP)
  c) Player can learn about the seductive qualities of the Talens, and their Hospitality Delegations, which have been compared to Earth geishas, but include members of both sexes. (reappears if a or b chosen)

STORY ENCOUNTER - PLAYER'S SHIP

As soon as the player has chosen either results a+c or b+c sensors report a small, un-scheduled Talen shuttle craft has launched from the planet and is approaching the player's ship.

3) Player choices:
   a)   Hail the shuttle craft.
   b)   Order battle stations.
   c)   Probe the shuttle craft.

Results:
   a) Con reports no response. (+1 PP)
   b) Tactical and Security both go on alert.
   c) The shuttle craft is on an automatic course to intercept the player's ship. A single lifeform is reported aboard. Its characteristics suggest a small Talen, possibly a child. (+2 PP)

STORY ENCOUNTER - PLANET AWAY TEAM

Away team reports that the Hospitality Delegation are taking them into custody with no explanation.

4) Player choices:
   a)   Beam the away team back aboard.
   b)   Order away team to defend themselves.

Results:
   a) Engineering reports that sensors have been jammed. There's no way to get a lock on the away team. (b reappears)
   b) Away team refuses. They have become too emotionally attached to the Hospitality Delegation! (a reappears)

STORY ENCOUNTER - PLAYER'S SHIP

5) Player's ship is hailed from the shuttle craft. When the hail is put on the viewscreen, we see it is a human-seeming six-year-old child with eyes. She says her name is Bekka and her parents sent her to the player's ship to save her life. She confirms that she is Talen, not human. She says she doesn't know how to land the shuttle craft.

Her transmission is interrupted by a transmission from the T6. Bekka's parents have been arrested. The player is ordered to not let her board.

Player choices:
   a) Refuse to allow her to board. That will solve the Talen's problem without them needing to make such a soul-wrenching decision.
   b) Use tractor beam to bring shuttle craft aboard.

Results:
   a) Bekka says goodbye. Ops says that her craft will impact the surface of player's ship with minimal damage to the starship in X minutes.
   b) Bekka's shuttle craft is safely landed in the player's ship's shuttle bay. (+3 PP)

6) The T6 demands a trade: the away team for the child. They explain that she is Talen and her fate is their decision. Bekka is a genetic mutant. Talen will decide whether she is to be exiled, blinded or destroyed. They claim one of her parents must be a human, masquerading as a Talen. They will run tests to determine who the counterfeit Talen may be. If the player does not comply, the away team, along with the parent, will be put on trial as illegal aliens. Penalty for illegal aliens is death.

Ops reports that Talen warships have launched and are moving to surround the player's ship.

Player choices:
   a) Demand the release of the away team.
   b) Ask for more time to assess the situation.

Results:
   a) It's too late to use a tractor beam on the shuttle craft. Bekka must be beamed aboard immediately, if she is to survive.
   b) The Talen T6 grant the request. Bekka's shuttlecraft will hit the player's ship in X seconds.

   7) Player choices:
      a)   Beam her aboard!
      b)   Ask for more time.

Results:
   a) Sickbay reports Bekka is in good health. Her DNA suggests she is a full-blooded Talen, not a hybrid. This is a Talen genetic mutation, not the result of inter-species breeding. (+2 PP)
   b) Bekka's shuttlecraft impacts against the player's ship. Nothing is left.

   8) Player choices:
      a)   Beam her aboard!
      b)   Report to the T6 that Bekka is dead.

Results:
   a) Sickbay reports Bekka is in good health. Her DNA suggests she is a full-blooded Talen, not a hybrid. This is a Talen genetic mutation, not the result of inter-species breeding. (+1 PP)
   b) The T6 report that two other sighted children have been born. They have also learned that both of Bekka's parents are full-blooded Talen as well. It appears that something in the Talen DNA has altered. They will have to reassess their earlier position. Their culture will have to learn to live with this small minority, and possibly learn to adapt if more such children are born. They mourn Bekka's death and hold the player at least partly responsible. The away team will be returned immediately.

   9) Player choices:
      a)   Report the medical findings to the T6.
      b)   Report to Starfleet.

  10) Results:
      a)   The T6 report that two other sighted children have been born. It appears that something in the Talen DNA has altered. They will have to reassess their earlier position. Their culture will have to find a way to live with this small minority, and possibly learn to adapt if more such children are born. They thank the player for his courage in helping Bekka, and helping them to learn they were about to make a grave mistake. The player warps for home. (END, +3 PP)
      b)   The player is ordered to return to Starfleet to face an inquiry into the child's death due to the player's inability to save her. The player warps for home. (END, -X PP depending upon how many PP the player gained earlier in the mission. The net result is the player earns 0 PP)

INDIANA JONES ADVENTURE WORLD

In 2011, I wrote for the Facebook game *Indiana Jones Adventure World*. There are two topics to illustrate here. First is design and storytelling. Then we'll tackle taking mundane characters and giving them lives of their own.

In 2011, social network games seemed to be all the rage on Facebook and other social network platforms. Many companies were attempting to emulate the Zynga model of game mechanics featuring roadblocks that must be waited out or paid to disappear. But in 2011, Zynga's business model (feed the "whales," ignore the rest) began to stumble badly.

This was the cusp of the company's upcoming collapse in 2013. Regardless of the mechanics, just as in casual games, a social network game can force storytellers to focus on basics and find new ways of delivering stories. This is not a bad thing.

Whales: players who pay in cash to advance faster than most players in a game.

The above *Star Trek: Infinite Space* story, told in a single dialogue tree, was expansive compared to storytelling in the game that came to be called *Indiana Jones Adventure World*.

I was brought in as a senior writer two months before the game, first simply called *Adventureville*, then *Adventure World*, was to go live on Facebook (Figure 18.2). I set about creating a detailed long-term story. There was no consistent voice in the quests or characters. NPCs were simply there to dispense quests.

Dialogue was limited to a set number of characters and spaces in a file shorter than most tweets. Exchanges were never more than a handful of single tweets from NPCs who didn't

FIGURE 18.2 *Adventure World* at launch.

expect any response from players. There were no dialogue trees at all, and encounters were entirely canned speeches.

I created or re-created characters and backstories and added a number of hooks into a larger ongoing story. Most of these were scrapped when a partial license for Indiana Jones dropped like a rock into the pond of the game a few weeks after launch. One thing did not change. I worked on how all stories were told, structuring them as if they were a succession of fortune cookies opened every few hours or days by players (Figure 18.3).

Here's an example of a quest that started out being presented to the player by an unidentified Meso-American indigenous girl who just happened to be standing in a dangerous cavern inches from nasty critters. She was unconcerned about her danger. What she wanted was a love potion. The reason why was not addressed. When you collected the three bizarre ingredients for that potion, the quest was over. End of story.

I removed the indigenous girl, assigning the quest to an NPC named Emily Balderdash who already could be found at the expedition's basecamp (Figure 18.4).

We had so few NPCs to work with, it seemed appropriate to develop our regular NPCs instead of simply creating random characters as needed. Here is the story I wrote for Emily told in one-liners, launched by clicking on her, another NPC, and a couple of lines of quest text. First, mixed in with other idle text over several visits to the player's home base, were references to her love life.

FIGURE 18.3 *Indiana Jones Adventure World* after surgery.

FIGURE 18.4   Emily Balderdash is in love with a librarian.

(EMILY IDLE) My beau back in the states is a librarian. Every time I smell an old book, I think of him.

(EMILY IDLE) Oh, {playername}, my beau doesn't think jungles and romance mix! Hasn't he heard of Tarzan and Jane???

(EMILY IDLE) Long distance relationships are not easy

> Idle text: similar in function to idle animations, which are simple animations to avoid an NPC standing there like a stature, idle text is text that usually fulfills no other function than to give the NPC something to say when they have no current use in gameplay or story development.

In the first three idles we can already see an unhappy shift in her relationship. Another NPC has observed the same thing:

(KEN IDLE) I think Emily's having some trouble with her beau. She'd be better off with an army man than a librarian. Yessir!

Again, these are simply one of several possible idles that are updated when the player completes a section of the game. The next idle is foreshadowing:

(EMILY IDLE) {playername}, if you're heading back into the jungle, I may have a personal favor to ask…

And sure enough, soon after sending the player on several mission-related quests, Emily makes an appeal for the player to take an active part in her predicament:

(QUEST BESTOW) My beau back home is growing aloof. But I've found the recipe for an ancient love potion!

When the quest is completed successfully:

(QUEST REWARD) Oh, thank you, {playername}! This should make Jim's heart grow fonder! I am in your debt!

Later, now that the player has at least a small stake in her story:

(EMILY IDLE) {playername}, thank you for the love potion! I sent it to my beau in a box of candy!

But all is not roses:

> (EMILY IDLE) I really don't want to talk right now, {playername}. The love potion gave my beau Montezuma's Revenge!

It lies with the second NPC to apply the coda to the story:

> (KEN IDLE) One thing I've learned from Emily's love life: if she offers you candy, turn it down!

Okay, admittedly it's not love poetry worthy of Byron, but it's an acceptable little story with a beginning, middle, and end, a modicum of humor and heart, and that establishes a reason for gameplay. All within a series of ten tweets experienced by players over hours, possibly days of play time.

The key for the writer is being able to identify the necessary beats in the story, pare them down to the bare bone, and then find les seul mots juste to restore some character and interest to the dialogue, all skills that game writers, just as writers in other media before us, must develop. The media may change. The delivery systems may change. But if the desire is there, meaningful stories can still be told.

Story can directly enhance gameplay. It can raise the stakes. Higher stakes in the outcome of the action grabs the emotions. The gameplay fits more solidly into game fiction. There is more depth to the gameplay.

As we have seen, a number of games give players ethical decisions, and not only to choose the light or dark side of the force. Many shades of gray confront players. These choices don't overwhelm the entertainment. The designers don't stop the action and try to hammer home the theme. But by carefully finding moments where player choices have resonance, an entire game gains depth.

In casual and social network games, whatever the platform you're writing and designing for, make your characters vivid sketches instead of intricate portraits, minutely examined. This is not the same as writing stereotypes. It's replacing the soul-searching of a Russian novel with the sharp-edged conciseness of a *New Yorker* cartoon. With both gameplay supporting story and story supporting gameplay, the entertainment factor increases exponentially. Remember the word Nate Fox used at the beginning of this chapter: synergy. It's a beautiful thing.

THE LION'S SONG

I worked on *The Lion's Song* (Figure 18.5) from March 2016 to June 2017. The game was released in episodes on Steam as follows:

Episode 1 – Silence (July 7, 2016)

Episode 2 – Anthology (November 21, 2016)

Episode 3 – Derivation (March 16, 2017)

Episode 4 – Closure (July 3, 2017)

Ludum Dare: a prestigious international game jam where twice a year games are made from scratch over one weekend.

Game Jam: an event where games are made by individuals or teams in a *very* short period of time.

I worked in close consultation with Stefan Srb and Tobias Mayr, one of the best collaborations I've ever had. The game was Stefen's original idea. The first

FIGURE 18.5 *The Lion's Song* is all about storytelling.

episode of it began life as a Ludum Dare entry of his that placed first in the category of Graphics and Mood.

Stefan was Game Designer. Tobe was Producer. I was Lead Writer and Story Consultant. I reworked that first episode here and there, then wrote the last three episodes in collaboration with Stefan and Tobe.

The Lion's Song is set in Austria near the beginning of the 20th century. It features charming retro sepia graphics and is all about storytelling with a few key puzzles here and there. The player follows the lives of a female composer, a male painter, a female mathematician (who, in order to be accepted by her male peers, dresses as a man), and a male writer. Most "puzzles" concerned how these four characters could find the inspiration that gave each of them the ability to achieve their true creative potential. Players made many choices and the game adapted to them. Even though each episode had a beginning, middle, and end of its own, the game adjusted to player decisions and characters might cross paths with each other by chance in episodes featuring the others. In episode 4 the writer has a chance encounter on a train with three men on a journey to an unknown destination (Figure 18.6), each of whom discovers that he knows one of the other three main characters. That last episode is the coda that brings all the stories to an emotional conclusion.

We started out each working on his own episode. But Stefan's design duties and Tobe's parental leave made a major change in plans necessary. Using notes from our meetings I would write first drafts of each episode, then after discussion would rewrite until we were satisfied. I also checked and corrected localization Excel files to make sure my English was properly translated to German.

I'm going to share three scenes here. Track how I handled player choices. I hope the different paths possible due to player choices are all represented! In the second episode of the game the player-character is Franz Markert, a painter who can visualize "layers" in the subjects of the portraits he paints, allowing him to reveal their true natures. But he cannot see inside himself. He is a cipher, suffering with self-doubt. In these first two scenes he takes some advice to visit a local doctor (Figure 18.7) who may be able to help him.

FIGURE 18.6   A fateful journey.

FIGURE 18.7   Sigmund Freud psychoanalyzes a troubled painter.

Freud's Office

[Franz is stretched out on a divan much like in Franz's workshop. Freud sits behind him.

1. FRANZ: I don't know what you want me to say! (GO TO 2)

2. FREUD: Many of my patients find it hard to talk about themselves. (GO TO 3)

3. FRANZ: What do you do? (GO TO 4)

4. FREUD: I kick the furniture after they leave. (GO TO 5)

5. FRANZ (laughs): Does that help? (GO TO 6)

6. FREUD: No, it hurts like hell. But it's better than me kicking *them*! If they won't talk, how can I help? (GO TO 7)

7. FRANZ: I've had blackouts. (GO TO 8)

8. FREUD: Wonderful! (writes it down) (GO TO 9)

9. FRANZ: No, they aren't! (GO TO 10)

10. FREUD: Wonderful that you're talking. Not the blackouts. What typically happens on days when you lose time?
    PLAYER CHOICE 4
    4_0. My model arrives. (GO TO 11)
    4_1. I paint my portraits. (GO TO 11)
    4_2. My model leaves. Sometimes happy. Sometimes not. (GO TO 14)

11. FREUD: Do you talk to your models? Ask about their lives? (GO TO 12)

12. FRANZ: Yes, it helps reveal the layers. (GO TO 13)

13. FREUD: Naturally! You're psychoanalyzing them!
    Close conversation

14. FREUD: Exactly like my patients. Sometimes happy. Sometimes glaring at me with murder in their eyes. (writes it down)

Close Conversation
FADE OUT/FADE IN
Time has passed.

[Franz and Freud are as before.]

1. FREUD: Let's pick up where we left off in the last session. You paint your portraits. What happens after your patients leave? (GO TO PLAYER CHOICE 5)
   PLAYER CHOICE 5
   1_0. I... I don't know exactly... (GO TO 2)
   1_1. I guess I blackout. (GO TO 2)
   1_2. There's something else... but I can't see it... (GO TO 2)

2. FREUD: I spoke with Madame Thernhardt. (GO TO PLAYER CHOICE 6)
   PLAYER CHOICE 6
   6_0. She told me she was a patient of yours. (GO TO 3) [**Franz's empathy layer flickers irregularly.**]
   6_1. What did she say? [**Franz's empathy layer flickers irregularly.**] (GO TO 3)
   6_2. You talked to people who know me? (GO TO 3) [**Franz's private layer flickers irregularly.**]

3. FREUD: She mentioned—(GO TO 4)

4. FRANZ: Wait! Wait! Something just happened! (GO TO 5)

5. FREUD: Please share it. I want to be excited, too. (GO TO 6)

6. FRANZ: I saw a layer! My layer! (GO TO 7)

7. FREUD: Reflected in my glasses! Me symbolically seeing into your soul! (GO TO PLAYER CHOICE 7)
   PLAYER CHOICE 7
   > 7_0. No, not at all. (GO TO 8)
   > 7_1. Your glasses? I'm not even looking at you. (GO TO 8)
   > 7_2. No, you weren't seeing into my soul. (GO TO 8)

8. FREUD: Oh. Well, that's disappointing. Where did you see it? (GO TO 9)

9. FRANZ: In my mind's eye, Horatio. (GO TO 10)

10. FREUD: Aha! Shakespeare! Although Hamlet didn't turn out very well in the end. Oedipal naturally. Narcissistic. Thought all of Denmark revolved around him... (GO TO 11)

11. FRANZ: My own layer! That's the first time!
    Close Conversation
    > In the following scene an aging actress, Madame Thernhardt is modeling for Markert.
    FADE OUT/FADE IN
    > Time has passed.

1. THERNHARDT: Act Two. The young painter looks haggard. His model looks as fresh as a tulip bud. (GO TO PLAYER CHOICE 4)
   PLAYER CHOICE 4
   > 1_0. Why did you become an actress? (GO TO 12)
   > 1_1. What is your favorite roll? (GO TO 15)
   > 1_2. What is your principal vice? (GO TO 16)
   > 1_3. Were you and granddad in love? (GO TO 21)

12. THERNHARDT: So that handsome young men would fall in love with me. (GO TO 13)

13. FRANZ: Tell the truth now! (GO TO 14)

14: THERNHARDT: That WAS the truth! Of course, after a time I realized I could take the audience by the hand, open their eyes, and lead them into a new world. There was power in that. And love. [**Her joy of acting glow remains.**]

15. THERNHARDT: Nora in Ibsen's *A Doll House*. A strong woman ahead of her time! Henrik told me he wrote *Hedda Gabler* for me. But she was a milksop. I would much rather make my exit with a door slam instead of a pistol shot. Also, I was a bit too old for the part by then... [**Her joy of acting glow remains.**]

16. THERNHARDT: Schnuckel, really! What kind of question is that to ask a lady! Oh, never mind. I'm an actress, not a lady! (GO TO PLAYER CHOICE 5)
   PLAYER CHOICE 5
      1_0. Is it sex? (GO TO 16)
      1_1. Is it alcohol? (GO TO 17)
      1_2. Is it gambling? (GO TO 18)

16. THERNHARDT: Sex is delightful. But it's not a vice. It's a necessity! Like breathing or eating or good reviews. [**Her flirtatious glow remains.**] (GO TO 19)

17. THERNHARDT: Drink can be a convivial companion of the moment, but it will never be a friend. (GO TO 19)

18. THERNHARDT: I've only gambled on love, Schnuckel. Once I thought I'd won, but it wasn't to be. (GO TO 19)

19. FRANZ: What is it then? (GO TO 20)

20. THERNHARDT: Why, gluttony of course. I'm surprised you can paint me and still need to ask. [**Her gluttony glow remains.**]

21. THERNHARDT: That's not a question I'm prepared to answer, Schnuckel.

CLOSE CONVERSATION

There cannot be many video games that feature Sigmund Freud and Gustav Klimt and include a Shakespeare reference and a comparison of the merits between Ibsen's *Hedda Gabler* and *A Doll's House*. It was a fruitful and fun collaboration and I'm very proud of the result. I'm also amused by the fact that it received praise for its localization into English from German. The game was, as I said, written in English. Whether you are faced with only a few beats to tell an entire story as in *Star Trek: Infinite Space* or are lucky enough to be writing a game that is all about storytelling like *The Lion's Song*, or somewhere in between, there are challenges in smaller games you will face and joys you will discover.

The key is being able to identify the necessary beats in the story, massage them to fit your game, and then find les seul mots juste to create some character and interest in the dialogue, all skills that game writers, just as writers in other media before us, must develop. The media may change. The delivery systems may change. The size of the stories may change. But it is possible to deliver story in the most cramped of packages.

A restriction becomes a learning experience, and even with the leanest of opportunities your game may offer, you can achieve a satisfying result. I started this chapter with a quote. I'll end it with another. Here is the famous "shortest story ever written" (attributed to Ernest Hemingway): "For Sale, baby shoes, never worn." In six words there is clarity, surprise, and real emotion. All are qualities worth striving for.

CHAPTER 19

Storytelling in Applied Games

In [Egypt] arithmetical games have been invented for the use of mere children, which they learn as a pleasure and amusement.

Plato (360 BCE)

There may be dice and play-things, with the letters on them to teach children the alphabet by playing; and twenty other ways may be found, suitable to their particular tempers, to make this kind of learning a sport to them.

John Locke (1692)

It's time to briefly enter the world of applied games, the idea of which, as you can see, has been around a lot longer than video games. These are also referred to elsewhere as serious or educational games, neither word that I like very much. Who wants to play a serious or educational game unless they are forced to? For greater detail on how my classes and four of my applied games were alternate reality games designed to be played in the real world in real time, please have a look at *The Multiplayer Classroom: Designing Coursework as a Game* (CRC Press, 2020) and *The Multiplayer Classroom: Game Plans* (CRC Press, 2021). One of the games, *Skeleton Chase 2*, covered in detail in *Game Plans*, is referred to in this chapter.

In what follows we will briefly touch on some storytelling challenges I faced in video games and virtual worlds that I've selected from 2000 to 2015. Some were successes, some not so much, but each is a game that sought to do more than just entertain.

To be a successful writer of games requires more than the craft we consider in this book or innate talent. You must be able to sell your ideas to others: publishers, the executives at the studio that employs you, and most importantly your team. You need to be a team member—someone who recognizes the collaborative nature of games. If you want to become a team leader, diplomacy and management skills are also crucial. And you must overcome the delusional, harmful idea that while programming and art require professionals, anyone can write.

DOI: 10.1201/9780429284991-24

When writing for applied games, you must add to all these the fact that now you're not simply telling a story that fits a game, but that game is being applied to education, training, intervention, healing, advocacy, and many other possible goals with important real-world consequences.

To accomplish these goals, you will partner with professionals in other fields: educators, doctors, sociologists, soldiers, businesspeople, entrepreneurs, politicians, law enforcement, and any number of professions. Few of those you'll collaborate with know how to make games. But as so many people think anyone can write, many believe they are qualified to design games, even if they've never done it before in their lives. In fact, some will declare proudly that they don't play games. Each will have their own ideas as to how to answer a need they suspect can be addressed with a game. It is your job to help them to the best of your ability.

What if they are so far off track, it's obvious that the problem they're addressing, and the usual ways for solving it, are not going to work? What if they're missing some fundamental concept like engagement or immersion? Before you even begin, you are faced with a decision. You must try and explain to them what they're missing, and if they don't understand or refuse to follow your advice, you can walk away, or you can remind yourself that you're a professional, suck it up, and give them the best game you can under the circumstances. At least you tried.

Believe me, this happens more often than you can imagine. It's why so many applied games deserve to be known by that other word: serious. What we know as writers of games is that the *intent* may be serious, but the *experience* must be as engaging and surprising and exciting as the best commercial games with nothing on their minds except fun.

ABSTRACTION

My first experience with applied games was a project led by Darion Rapoza at Duke University in 2000–2001. Funded by a grant from the National Institute on Drug Abuse, the narrative was set in outer space, and the drugs used were fictional, but closely mirrored the effects of real illegal drugs of today. Before I arrived, Darion had realized that a level of abstraction was needed to seduce players into a game, the object of which was to realize that while some drugs may enhance performance or perception in the short term, the consequences—dependency, physical deterioration, loss of income, and others—were grave.

So, he already knew that to make a drug intervention that was preachy and OTN (on the nose) might appeal to those treating addiction, no amount of finger wagging could replace *The Truth*, the working title of the game.

In the scenarios I created, the drugs acted as buffs do in a commercial game.

But when the effect of the buff wore off, the player found vital stats reduced. If the player continued to rely on a drug, the short-term benefits decreased, and the consequences increased. In that way, players could learn without the game preaching exactly what they were doing to their bodies.

> Buff: A performance enhancing spell, item or substance that allows the player-character or their companions to perform beyond their usual abilities or skill sets.

We set the game in outer space with an *X-Files*-like conspiracy, making up names and sources for drugs, and providing physical challenges and mental puzzles similar to commercial games. In this way we were able to abstract the issues involved in a much subtler, more effective, and yes, entertaining way, than placing our story in a halfway house for addicts, or even an affluent high school where peers admired overachievers.

Too many games fall out of balance by being too literal. Of course, some applied games swing too far the other way, as well, becoming entertaining at the cost of the message getting lost in all the excitement. Abstraction is an important tool in all games that seek to replicate a small portion of the world and make it seem real. It's even more important in applied games where simulation (already abstracted) is emphasized. A number of things can go wrong:

- **The lesson becomes too obvious.** Players are willing to suspend their disbelief only so far. Hammer home the thinly disguised real purpose of the game and they switch into neutral, playing it in class because they must (and it's far preferable to listening to somebody lecture at them for an hour), but skeptically keeping what the game wants them to learn at arm's length.

- **The game becomes too complex.** Trying to mirror real life too closely can overwhelm players with complexities, and the lesson is buried somewhere underneath.

- **The game becomes too mechanical.** Game mechanics are front and center, repetitive and dull. We risk the players getting lulled into the sort of twilight state that monotonous classroom exercises can induce.

- **The lesson is lost as soon as the computer is turned off, or the inevitable classroom discussion is ended.** Without stickiness to the message, the message becomes transient.

Appropriate abstraction, something I emphasize upfront to all my colleagues and clients, is a critical first step to a successful applied game.

STORY STRUCTURE

The 4th Street project at the University of California Berkeley's Graduate School of Journalism was an interesting consultation in 2005. The project's goal was to build a small, multiplayer world, consisting of a few blocks in downtown Oakland, California. Today 4th Street lies at the junction of State Highways 880 and 980. However, in its heyday in the 1940s and 1950s, the street was a mecca for jazz musicians from all over the world. Unfortunately, the clubs and the history all have disappeared, buried beneath concrete pylons and rushing traffic.

Most of the issues that the team building the virtual world faced were familiar: creating characters and building quests, but one major problem refused to go away. They wanted to capture the joy, the vibrant life, and the sometimes edgy lifestyle of 4th Avenue in its jazz days. But they were faced with an unhappy ending: No matter what they did, players would be left with the ghosts of characters moving to the syncopated beat of the street, fading to an image of lifeless concrete in all directions.

We couldn't invent a happy ending. But we who create worlds are the masters of time. I suggested reversing the story's timeline. What if they started with the interchange, rushing cars and rumbling trucks, then let it all fade away to reveal the past, not entirely golden, but alive? Every play experience would end with the music, the musicians, the dancers, and the life that was 4th Street in full swing.

The lesson here is simple: never let your story fall into the trap of chronology. As Quentin Tarantino showed us in *Pulp Fiction*, chronology is often best disposed of entirely, trampled beneath drama. In this case a simple U-turn in the structure of the story they wanted to tell would turn a dead end into a vibrant memory.

You want your players leaving every play session with a feeling of accomplishment, even triumph, not frustration at an obstacle they could not overcome. Because they will carry that feeling of triumph or dejection with them stronger than anything that went before. Research has shown us audiences first remember the climax of a movie, then the beginning, and then everything else. Who said, "Always leave them laughing?" One of the greatest British comedians of all time: Tommy Cooper. You may remember the quote, if not the speaker. Always leave your players with something that makes them want to come back for more: laughter, tears, an image, or a song. Choose life over concrete.

BALANCE

The times I've been most successful creating applied games is when the building of the game was an equal partnership. Just as I said earlier in this book that gameplay and story should be built simultaneously and balanced, with ideas flying in both directions, so too must gameplay and story now be built simultaneously and balanced with this new third element: application.

The times when I was expected to take dictation from nonwriters and game designers, no matter how accomplished in their chosen fields, have not been as fruitful. In fact, they often do not get off the ground. Here's an example of such a project.

I was only seven years old when I was given an opportunity to play one of the victims of a commercial passenger jet crash at Cleveland Hopkins Airport to help train emergency teams. I had makeup applied to my leg. I'd suffered a break so bad that the bone was sticking out of a somewhat realistic puncture wound. The seriousness of the exercise is obvious. The fun for a seven-year-old kid moaning and yelling on a major airport's runway was indescribable.

Imagine my delight when in 2009 I was contacted by a professor at a major eastern university to create a game for a government grant application. The topic was: disaster preparedness!

Only a few months before, US Airways Flight 1549 had made an emergency landing in the Hudson River in New York City. So, I was all ready to help crash a plane, cause an earthquake (players had averted an earthquake that was threatening to strike Bloomington in *Skeleton Chase 2*), or any other mayhem that would create the backdrop for a compelling scenario designed to engage and immerse participants to where learning what to do in such a catastrophe became second nature.

No. What the professor wanted to do was teach people to store up water and canned goods. He wanted the players to use their own money to buy these. That was it. Both could have been handled in a compelling game, but that chance had been stripped away. The grant application was rejected. Potential squandered. In this case from a total lack of balance.

I can contrast that with the many applied games projects where I partnered successfully with subject matter experts. I adjusted to meet their pedagogical goals; they adjusted to keep the games compelling. In contrast to a few misfires, I've managed to work on multiple projects with people who did their jobs and let me do mine. And yes, those games were invariably the most successful.

Sustained Narrative

Still cited as a "new" approach to teaching, Task-Based Learning (TBL) or Task-Based Instruction (TBI) has been around for a long time. Often connected specifically to learning language, it can be found everywhere from corporate training to art instruction. In essence, it strives to entice students to focus on a task to learn certain skills, rather than focusing on the skills themselves.

This is certainly a step in the right direction. We know from boss raids in MMOs like *World of Warcraft* that players, focused on bringing down an especially difficult mob, learn strategy and tactics without being taught them explicitly. The result in their eyes is victory. All the learning that goes into that victory is a collateral benefit.

What is often missing from the TBL approach are all those benefits writers and designers and filmmakers enjoy when there is a solid sustained narrative in place; in games sharing equal importance with gameplay. With a goal of immersing a player or student in an experience, so that the learning flows from that experience, a sustained narrative gives us everything TBL can and more.

If we had created the first two *Skeleton Chase* games as a series of tasks built around the subject matter of health and fitness, it would have been easy. The first game in the sequence was actually played by students who were already enrolled in a class called Lifestyle Physical Activity that each week covered topics such as stress, disease and life expectancy, nutrition, and substance abuse. And each of the game's episodes used these as its theme.

One section of the class was a control group working out in a gym. Students in our class section played *The Skeleton Chase* (2008). For the students playing the game, I could have written focused levels. The level on stress could have dealt with helping a student who was getting behind in coursework, and was too stressed to catch up, certainly pertinent to the players' own experience. The level on disease and life expectancy could have focused on a reunion with an aging relative and recognizing the life changes they had gone through, eliciting an emotional response from players that would have drawn them into the experience more than a simple lecture. These are typical of a thoughtful TBL approach.

But look at what we would have lost:

• A continuing story with cliffhangers that could draw players in and make them want to continue playing to find out what happens next.

- Reappearing NPCs with whom players can establish relationships.

- Linking of topics by something other than a single common learning target such as becoming physically fitter or mastering a foreign language.

- A ratcheting up of the stakes.

- Opportunities for collateral learning are increased exponentially. Each episodic situation becomes more layered by where it fits in the overall narrative.

- Creating narrative-driven reasons for acquiring knowledge or skills that become useful in later episodes. In TBL this layering of knowledge or skill is dependent upon learning progress alone. In a sustained narrative, it is reinforced by the continuity of the story.

The art of a good story is in drawing us deeper and deeper into its spell. We've just spent an entire book together exploring how all the techniques from old and new media can collaborate in creating compelling characters and stories. Why restrict these opportunities to small pieces of an overall structure that is already in place thanks to the desired learning outcomes.

In the end, the sustained narrative of the first two *Skeleton Chase* games helped players become fitter and healthier without explicitly teaching them anything about health and fitness. That is at the heart of why I use as much abstraction as possible and create sustained narratives. Players learn as they learn in a video game, focused on tasks and the context, not the lessons being learned.

Footprints on the Page

In 2009–2010, my last academic year at Indiana University, I was a consultant on a literacy system being developed by Edutainment Systems LLC that was planned to eventually include many adventure games. I designed the first game for *Captain Heartless* before turning it over to a former graduate student, Phoebe Elefante, to do the writing. I had started my commercial career with a children's adventure game, *Once Upon a Forest*, and I enjoyed returning to those roots.

At the heart of the Edutainment Systems approach was a desire to allow a child to not only experience an adventure game but also to respond to it in a very direct way, thereby teaching the child through doing. To this end players were provided with books in which to write their own stories. All my experiences with applied games have convinced me of the importance of actively involving the player in the fictional experience. In this case, the fictional experience, the world of the game, encouraged children to become more than players in a very direct way with a wonderful overall reward. The books could be printed out at the conclusion of the game for the kids to keep. Sadly, I could not find any mention of this game online, so I have no idea how the story ends.

DEALING WITH TEXTBOOKS

In 2012, long before the United States was submerged beneath an epidemic of OxyContin addiction, I consulted on a game designed to teach an online course in statistics funded by a grant at a prestigious university in New England. The sustained narrative placed the student at a statistics company that did contract work for a pharmaceutical company that was about to release a major new drug. But students would discover discrepancies in the initial research that had to be tracked by learning a semester's worth of statistics. Were these just errors or a deliberate attempt by the pharmaceutical company to mask issues with the new drug?

A demo, the beginning of the game, was built in Unity, and appeared quite professional. I looked forward to testing it. My player-character arrived at the statistics company for a job interview and met the character who would be my boss. My first assignment? Checking the data? Investigating the pharmaceutical company? No, I was playing the game to learn statistics. I was sent to a virtual library to find a textbook on statistics that had been simply digitized in the game and… begin reading it… The plan was that as the player progressed in their investigation, they would first read relevant chapters. Note: the textbook was not needed. Everything in it could have been teachable in the action of the game. The game did not get its second round of funding.

I ran into a similar situation that same year, but there was a happier outcome. As all too often happens, quite a bit of work had been done on the gane before I arrived. I was hired by Advanced Training and Learning Technologies in Virginia as "lead writer," on a math game called *The Lost Function*, but was soon also helping to design the game. Why? A nice-sized 3D world had been developed of a small town hidden somewhere in farm country. But two issues were quickly apparent.

First, there were no clear stakes for the player to care about. A magical orb had disappeared from the town square, and with it the ability of the townsfolk to do math was also gone. This was going to make having a successful corn festival really hard. But that was about it. There was no real story to hook players and get them to care about the town's predicament. That could be fixed with deepening the characters, giving them relationships between one another, giving the player a personal quest to find a friend who had disappeared, and rescuing some major characters from a Ferris wheel on fire (Figure 19.1), all while helping with math to see that the corn festival could still go on.

FIGURE 19.1 Think *Brigadoon* with lots of corn, some danger, but no singing.

The second issue was whenever a math problem was presented to the player it looked like a page in a textbook. Happily, this was a far more successful collaboration than the statistics "game." While the "textbook" feel was never entirely eradicated, it was surrounded by adventure. The small team was talented and very willing to build a video game that was designed for entertainment but was also able to teach. I had a great time working on this game. We achieved our goal with the game and mapped out a sequel to teach a higher level of math. While *The Lost Function* was never the major hit it could have been, it received some great reviews and tested extremely well. No sequel was made, but the game is still available online at https://www.atltgames.com/lostfunction/. Have a look!

The Sky's the Limit

We're almost ready to conclude our discussion of applied games. Before I close this chapter, I want to briefly mention a video game that was a class project for my last class taught at Worchester Polytechnic Institute. The second half of the class was the final term in spring of 2020. COVID-19 had struck, but luckily, with some students already out of town, it was planned to be an online-only class already. During that term we completed a game begun in the previous term that ended in December. It was an applied game called *The Earth Was a Garden*. Its topic was the reality of climate change. There are any number of games out there aimed at children that already address the threat to our planet, often with explicit lessons on how to try and reverse it. We took a different approach. From an early student-written design document:

> We want the player to experience the beauty of nature at its peak and see it change through time. An important goal is to have the player enjoy their time playing so they will not notice that it is a game on climate change. We want the player to come to the realization of the dangers of climate change on their own.

Sometimes being too literal can make a game feel more like learning or work, not a game at all, even if it is set in a fantasy world with cute graphics where players still must Recycle with a capital R. Sometimes sneaking up on players is more dramatic, like when the solution to a mystery is suddenly revealed and all the clues fall into place. The realization of a theme that the player discovers on their own can make the message equally powerful. *The Earth Was a Garden* consisted of several apparently benign mini games: fishing, bird watching, butterfly catching, and gardening.

As the player moved through the levels however there were fewer fish and butterflies caught, birds to watch and fewer plants to be grown. But the game continued to reward the player for completing each activity as if this was okay, clearing each level faster and faster than the one before. The final level however when the ocean level had risen and no fish were left to catch, when there were no more crops to grow, and the sky was empty of birds and butterflies, the game cut to a final, simple screen featuring Gaia (Mother Earth) and the title of the game: *The Earth Was a Garden* which now had a new meaning for one word: "was."

The game was rough around the edges given the time to build it, the small number of students (only four in the second term), and the skill sets of the students, but it demonstrated the power of storytelling over the literal translation of facts to make a game.

Many of my students came to the schools where I taught determined to work for the developer of their favorite AAA commercial game. If they left four years later with only one piece of knowledge beyond their skills, talents, and portfolios, it's this: there is a much bigger world of opportunity out there. I have yet to find a real-world issue, whether it is a pandemic or a war or a warming planet, that cannot be successfully addressed by applied games. When I wrote this chapter in the previous edition of this book, teacher Mary Kelly Friedman was about to embark on a multiplayer classroom to teach the Holocaust at a Jesuit High School in Colorado. I know in my heart it went well.

There is no reason that applied games can't be every bit as engaging and immersive as commercial titles. All we need are the vision and the will to make them.

PART V

Reflections

CHAPTER 20—POSTLUDE: ENDGAME

SELECT doors.

The vast doors, wood, black with age and studded with rusting iron, swing open. The Player can choose to return to the cliff above the now impassible chasm or move into the lair.

INT. WIZARD'S LAIR

A vast space filled with unfathomably complex devices and magical implements. The Wand of Yearning floats on end, slightly angled above a pedestal to one side. It isn't glowing. Incongruously, there is what looks like a playpen on the other side of the room, but as the PC and however many of the group have survived enter, it's impossible to see what it may be inside. The Wizard stands waiting. He is huge, no frail magician, but a well-muscled giant standing at least 15 feet tall. In his headband, the Tormentor's Jewel blazes with a potent green light.

WIZARD

You've come at last, I see, but not with heads respectfully bowed. Very well. May your valor prove worthy of your choice.
The Wizard begins hurtling Flame Bolts at the party.

1.IF the Player chooses to ATTACK the Wizard, the weapons and spells of the party will do one tenth of the usual damage. The Wizard has over one million hit points.

DOI: 10.1201/9780429284991-25

WIZARD

Where are all your dreams now, mortal? I will eat them as you die.
Eventually, the Wizard will kill the entire group.

2.IF the Player tries to TAKE the Wand of Yearning, it can be picked up and equipped, but it remains cold and lifeless. ATTACK the WIZARD with wand:

WIZARD

The wand is useless against my strength!
Eventually the Wizard will kill the entire group.

3.IF the PC moves to the playpen, the player-character can see inside where a baby squirms about, gurgling softly, a greenish glow encasing it. Its eyes are fixed on a small green jewel that floats in the air above it. The jewel is exactly like the one the Wizard wears. It's the PC's baby, alive after all, but in some way a part of all the disasters that have torn the PC's homeland apart.

4.If the Player tries to ATTACK the baby with weapons or spells, it is unharmed.

WIZARD

You would kill your own child? Your lack of parental affection surprises me. But no matter. It is invulnerable while under my protection!
Eventually the Wizard will kill the entire group.

5.IF the Player tries to ATTACK the floating jewel with weapons or spells, it is unharmed.
Eventually the Wizard will kill the entire group.

6.IF the Player tries to ATTACK the floating jewel with the wand, the wand begins to glow brighter and brighter. The Wizard screams.

WIZARD

Noooooooo!!!
Jagged bands of green energy are discharged from the jewel to the one in the Wizard's headband. Green energy encases his body as he shakes uncontrollably. The jewel in the crib shatters, and a moment later, the Wizard disintegrates in an earthshaking explosion of green light.
Pieces of the jewels and the Wizard vanish. The baby is unharmed. The protecting green glow is gone. The baby is looking directly at the PC, waiting.

The Player has two choices:

1.Comfort the baby.

2.Kill the baby.

Postlude: Endgame

Our revels are now ended. These our actors
As I foretold you, were all spirits and
Are melted into air, into thin air;
And, like the baseless fabric of this vision,
The cloud-capped tow'rs, the gorgeous palaces,
The solemn temples, the great globe itself,
Yea, all of which it inherit, shall dissolve,
And, like this insubstantial pageant faded,
Is rounded with a sleep.

William Shakespeare, The Tempest

We've come to the end of the quest. I hope you've found a reward or two along the way. Don't take a word I've said, or anyone else quoted in this book living or dead, as law. Feel free to disagree and go your own way. At least you will be choosing and not making it up as you go along. Ah, one of my themes! Listen to the echoes of the past. Surprise, surprise. My favorite theme is memory, after all. Learn the work others have already accomplished before you begin. Learn from other media. Build on those games that have gone before, don't just copy them. Know a rule before you break it.

Have respect for your characters. Give them lives and purpose. Avoid stereotypes. Respect your stories. Give them a weight equal to your gameplay. Avoid clichés. Balance is important in all things from gameplay to characters in opposition to real life. Construct gameplay and story together, allowing them to support one another. Synergy. Be consistent in the worlds you construct.

Have respect for your players. If they have been kind enough to buy your game, and the word "story" is on the box, give it to them with all the craft and professionalism used to deliver stunning 3D graphics and exciting gameplay. Design the story as part of the entire experience, don't segregate it.

I'm sure I've forgotten something, but before we're through, Mr. Laing would like me to take a moment to put all of this into some perspective. There are three topics worth

DOI: 10.1201/9780429284991-26

addressing, I think. Remember Art with the capital "A"? That's one. Next, I think we should remind ourselves of some of those questions from the first chapter: questions like "Why make games?" "What kind of games do we want to make?" "Should they have meaning?"

I'm going to start with a third (why be linear?). There is one other thing that is worthy of respect: writing. I remember...

A long time ago I was invited by a friend of mine, Christine Foster, to speak to an extension class she was giving at USC. Christine was an executive at Columbia Pictures then, and her class covered a lot of aspects of script development for movie and TV production. One of the students asked me a question about breaking into TV and the movies as a writer, which I will never forget: "How little do I have to write?"

I admit I just stared at him for a moment in disbelief. I don't remember what my answer was. I'm sure I talked about the length of treatments or how detailed story pitches should be or something. But that question shocked and offended me, and I know what I wanted to say: "Get up. Walk out the door. Go away. You will never be a writer. Stop wasting your time and ours."

Writing is not just a craft you can learn. For most writers, it is a vocation. I know I would write whether or not anybody was willing to pay me. I have no choice. Writing defines who I am. I don't know what age I was when I began making up stories and poems and songs. I know I started writing them down as soon as I could write. I have been very lucky. Except for a few months as a clerk in the Samuel French office (the play publishers) in Hollywood (when I would often come home and write all night), I've made my living as a writer my entire adult life. I intend to write until the day I die.

While I hope you have found some suggestions in this book that may help you, I haven't attempted to dictate surefire techniques to writing successful games. I cannot magically turn you from a tyro to a professional. That happens inside. Rather, I've tried to share with you a lot of thinking, much of it by writers far wiser than I, about what it takes to create characters and write stories—thinking that spans centuries and media.

We do not need to reinvent the wheel. To try is hubris. One book can do little more than scratch the surface of all that's out there that can assist us to grow as writers. There is an entire world of culture and history, drama, film, literature, all waiting to inform and inspire you, as it has me.

Throughout the years I've been in this industry, there has been a lot of hand wringing over why games are dismissed by critics. I'm not talking about the reviewers online or in our print publications. Occasionally, criticism can be found there, but we need to understand the difference between a *reviewer* and a *critic*.

Here comes my last two definitions, I promise. Be warned: Many people see these two words as synonyms.

Both review. Both offer opinions. One places these in a broader context that affects us as human beings. Critics are not going to take our industry seriously unless we stake out some of that cultural and historical territory for our own.

Reviewer: A writer who summarizes in retrospect the important points of a creative work and offers an opinion on how others will respond to it.

Critic: A writer who reviews creative works with an eye toward their place in culture and history.

Of course, we can't just sit down one day and decide to turn out Art. It's hard enough to create popular entertainment. Rembrandt didn't try to create Art. He painted portraits to survive. Shakespeare wrote poetry and plays and acted in them. Mozart composed music. They were most concerned with doing the best job they could. Nobody likes to get pelted with vegetables, after all. They created Art almost in spite of themselves.

What each did do was try to find their own voice and use it to communicate. They knew what had already been done and tried to build on it. Creativity is instinctive, though, not intellectual—wrong side of the brain and all that. Salieri tried. Mozart tried and succeeded beyond all possible expectations. There are no guarantees. But remember the ultimate quest from Chapter 10, "Games: Charting New Territory"? Sometimes the search is enough. Remember Don Quixote de la Mancha? He succeeded without realizing it. Like Rembrandt and Shakespeare and Mozart.

If we're lucky, we might make something more; a game that endures; something fine that we had a part in creating that will touch the hearts and minds of generations unborn. Anything is possible. The important thing is to have the will to try.

I've had it said to me by more than one game company executive that it doesn't matter what the rest of the planet thinks of us. Our industry makes billions of dollars in profits. They can think that way. Making money is their vocation. But I've heard the same words from writers and designers, too. And we can't afford to be that cavalier.

My advice to you is just that: do the best you can. Worry about entertaining, by all means. That's what they pay us for. Be subversive, of course. Sneak some meaning in there between the explosions. Try something special. Take something that is important to you, that *speaks* to you, and share it with others. Art will take care of itself.

There is power in the ability to create. Don't you feel it when you write? Feel the moment when the awareness of the act of writing fades; when the doors between the conscious and unconscious minds are thrown open; and your soul pours out on to the page. That is raw power.

The pen is indeed mightier than the sword. And like the sword, it should be wielded with some responsibility. Writing is a gift. We should find a meaningful way to say thank you for being blessed with it.

I think we have a responsibility to recognize what it is we do, and how it affects other human beings. And all the technology in the world cannot take that responsibility away from us. A friend wrote to me not long ago. It was a letter sent through the mail. Remember those? He has been a writer for a long, long time. The tone of the letter was sad and bitter, and can be summed up in his final sentence: "Now that the whole culture is one vast comic book, who gives a f**k, really?"

We should, though. Earlier I mentioned studies that indicate attention spans are getting shorter. (I remind you here in case you've forgotten.) If the attention spans of our children *are* getting shorter due to television and computer games, do we just adjust to it and perpetuate it, or should we see if we could be part of the remedy instead of part of the cause? An editor friend suggests that "Maybe our attention spans just adjust to our environment, whatever it happens to be at the time, and can therefore readjust when the situation changes again." She could be right. None of us have to agree on the answer to the question. But we'd better at least recognize the implications and examine how we feel about it.

In Chapter 1, "Myths and Equations," I asked, "Why make games?" There will be as many different responses to that question as there are people who try to answer it. Each one will be shaped by who we are, what we believe, and what we want to accomplish in our lives. I do it for several reasons, I think. It's a form of entertainment I enjoy. And I want to share that joy. I love stories. I love experiencing them. I love writing them. This is a medium where storytelling is often misunderstood, neglected, or abused. It has become a personal challenge for me to try and change that.

And that leads me to our next question: What kind of games do we want to make? Should we decide just to make games that are cool, and let meaningful stories remain the province of other media? We can fall back on all sorts of excuses like "Stories and games are different." But that's all they are: excuses.

"Should games have meaning?"

Not all of them. But some should. For every hundred clones of last year's bestselling action game, a few games that strive for more are welcomed. We need balance, not saturation.

Here are a few more questions to ask ourselves as we create our games. Some are simple to answer, some not so simple.

"Is the game fun?"

One of our primary concerns, as it should be. We are part of an entertainment medium, not professors (er, okay, some are...) or theologians (possible!). If our games aren't fun, it won't matter if we had any other lofty aspirations for them.

"Does the game move me?"

I wrote an episode of *Quincy*—a show that occasionally stepped over the line from entertainment into the lecture hall—based on a true case about a father accused of electrocuting his severely handicapped son. The boy had a particularly gruesome degenerative condition that was calcifying his brain, literally turning it to stone. As I wrote some of the scenes, tears rolled down my cheeks. I knew what had to be said, as difficult as it was to say it. We are masochists at times, I guess. But it was my responsibility to convey that emotion to my audience. I hope I succeeded.

We can't write true emotion into our games if we shy away from it, just as an actor will never move an audience unless they can find the necessary emotions within them. We need a balance between craft, talent, and our own sensibilities. Otherwise, the performance will stay mechanical and uninvolving; the words will remain ink on a page.

"Does the game make the world a better place for its having existed?"

If all we create is a shadow, glimpsed briefly, then gone, what purpose have we served? If we squander this power—this gift—granted to us, we are diminished.

Not all of us would like to make, or are capable of making, a game that will endure or touch those hearts and minds. But some of us must try. Imagery without meaning is empty and artless. We owe it to ourselves and the future to strive for more.

There are no universal answers to these questions. But a failure to address them is a lost opportunity to communicate with the player, our audience. It is a failure to communicate with ourselves.

Index

Note: **Bold** page numbers refer to tables; *italic* page numbers refer to figures.